Wicked Flesh

EARLY AMERICAN STUDIES

Series editors:
Daniel K. Richter, Kathleen M. Brown,
Max Cavitch, and David Waldstreicher

Exploring neglected aspects of our colonial,
revolutionary, and early national history and culture,
Early American Studies reinterprets familiar themes and
events in fresh ways. Interdisciplinary in character, and
with a special emphasis on the period from about 1600
to 1850, the series is published in partnership with the
McNeil Center for Early American Studies.

A complete list of books in the series
is available from the publisher.

Wicked Flesh

Black Women,
Intimacy, and Freedom
in the Atlantic World

Jessica Marie Johnson

PENN

UNIVERSITY OF PENNSYLVANIA PRESS

PHILADELPHIA

Published by
University of Pennsylvania Press
Philadelphia, Pennsylvania 19104-4112
www.upenn.edu/pennpress

Printed in the United States of America on acid-free paper
1 3 5 7 9 10 8 6 4 2

Library of Congress Cataloging-in-Publication Data
ISBN 978-0-8122-5238-5

To Aliette "Cuqui" Nuñez Medina

To Mae Frances Johnson

To Clyde A. Woods, James E. McLeod, and Stephanie M. H. Camp

To Ira Berlin

To New Orleans, *before the Storm*

Contents

~

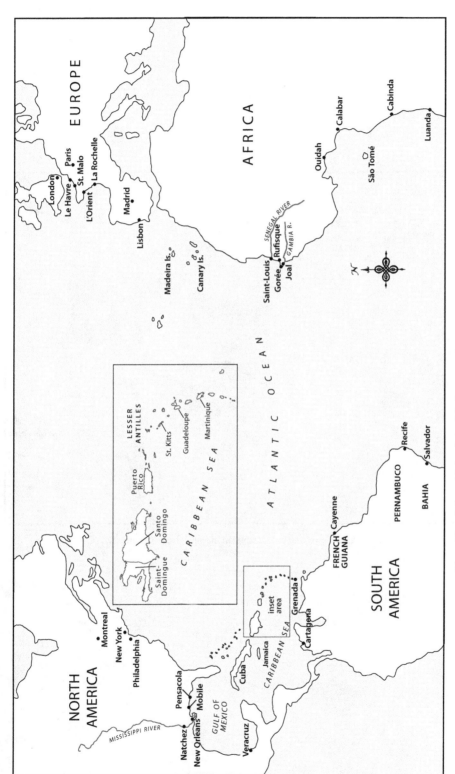

Map 1. New Orleans' Atlantic world, circa 1685–1810.

Map 2. The Gulf Coast and the Caribbean in the eighteenth century.

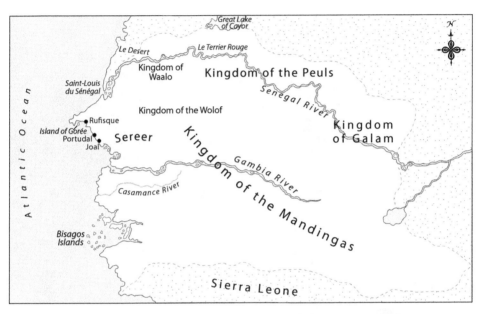

Map 3. Senegambia. Adapted from Guillaume Delisle, "Carte de la Barbarie, de la Nigritie, et de la Guinée," 1718. Original map available at the Geography and Map Division, Library of Congress, https://lccn.loc.gov/2005625339 (accessed January 21, 2020).

Introduction

⌒⅄⌒

The Women in the Water

Be the woman in the water.

—Rae Paris, *The Forgetting Tree*, 2004

Wicked Flesh: Black Women, Intimacy, and Freedom in the Atlantic World examines how African women and women of African descent used intimacy and kinship to construct and enact freedom in the Atlantic world.[1] Over the course of the eighteenth century, women of African descent who were not enslaved acquired property and social status in Africa and the Americas. In a unique position to claim their own labor, free African women and women of African descent negotiated, challenged, and appropriated categories of difference. They engaged in and were forced to engage in intimate relations across gender and race, with individuals enslaved and free. They established families beyond biological kin, and across race and status. They accumulated property and distributed legacies across generations. Intimacy and kinship became key strategies in their bids for freedom and were central to how and what freedom looked like on a quotidian basis. Using the history of black women in New Orleans as a lens for exploring black women's experiences across the Atlantic world—from coastal Senegal to French Saint-Domingue, from Spanish Cuba to the swampy outposts of the U.S. Gulf Coast—*Wicked Flesh* argues that African women and women of African descent endowed free status with meaning through an active, aggressive, and sometimes unsuccessful intimate and kinship practice. Their stories, both in their successes and failures, outline a practice of freedom that would shape the city that emerged on the shores of the Mississippi and laid the groundwork for the emancipation struggles and tensions of the nineteenth century.[2]

The legal, social, and political codification of racial slavery created the status of "free person of African descent."[3] Although freedom would emerge as the quintessential struggle of the nineteenth century, free status in the eighteenth century remained a new and unfamiliar state of being. Free status gained its texture from struggles between slaveowners, slave traders, imperial authorities, and Africans and people of African descent resisting imperial demands and the institutionalization of chattel slavery. As Africans and people of African descent escaped bondage by securing manumission or formal release from bondage in diverse and inventive ways, free people of African descent became the remainder of an unresolvable equation created by the mathematics of transforming human beings into chattel property.[4]

Free status did not define freedom. Like the rise of chattel slavery itself, the nature of free status under slavery relied on constructions of gender and sexuality rooted in the circum-Atlantic exchange of black bodies and plantation commodities. Intimate acts mated with edicts, codes, and imperial jurisprudence to produce bodies of law like the 1685 Code Noir, the first comprehensive slave code written for the Americas.[5] The Code Noir and edicts like it established partus sequitur ventrem, meaning that the slave or free status of the child would follow that of the womb, harnessing reproducing bodies to the expansion of slavery. Slaveowners and imperial authorities reinforced slave codes with martial force, using shackles, whips, and arms forged and wielded by white and black laborers at the command of imperial officials to maintain and reproduce slave status. Free status also required the wombs and labor of black women, and would be no less intimate or violent. Free status manifested in the interstices of manumission laws preoccupied with sex between European men and African women. It lingered in the machinations of slaveowners who declared African women lecherous, wicked, and monstrous even as those same slaveowners navigated colonial masculinities and imperial desire for black flesh.[6] Free status, manumission, and legalistic escapes from bondage did not free black women from these representations or protect them from the predations of men (and women) who wielded them.[7]

Freedom gained definition when and as African women and women of African descent pushed back against their own enslavement and subject position. These women, when encountering Atlantic slavery, whether along the African coast or in the Americas, did not limit their understanding of freedom to legal or official status, no matter how triumphant the manumission battle that was won. They could not. First, slaveowners, traders, and colonial officials themselves resisted honoring distinctions between slave and free or illuminating a definitive path from bondage to freedom. Second, at every step of the way, as slaveowners, traders, and colonial officials attempted to harness black women's bodies, labor, and lives to the industry of slaving, African women and women of African descent challenged them in return with their own understandings of what, where, and how their bodies should be used, their labor expended, and their lives lived. African women and women of African descent who survived the horrific crossing continued to turn to what was available (intimate and kinship ties), practicing freedom even when they could not call themselves free. Exceeding the boundaries of the manumission act, African women and women of African descent demanded freedom as a project of ecstatic black humanity in the face of abject subjection and against slavery as social death.[8]

Understanding the role intimacy and kinship played in black women's lives highlights black women's everyday understanding of freedom as centered around safety and security for themselves and their progeny. Safety, particularly safety from intimate violence, and security lay at the heart of decisions to secure or reject patrons, partners, lovers, and other kin. Black women's intimacy with individuals ranged along the spectrum of coerced to strategic, from fraternal to sexual. Determined to build community and make generations, imagining futures that were, if not beyond bondage, at least buttressed against harm, they cultivated, protected, and defended kinship networks. They engaged in a range of practices meant to safeguard their bodies and their legacies. At times this included legitimating kinship ties through formal sacred institutions like the Catholic Church. Practicing freedom did not necessarily mean seeking a freedom removed from other social relations in society. At other times, women participated in or created new institutions and less formal criteria for choosing kin. Slaveholding societies were violent, brutal places. Black women were not immune from this, and some of their actions enfolded with existing relations of exploitation and domination. Creating and protecting kinship networks sometimes meant denying access to their chosen community, even despite biological ties. Safety and security for some women included exploiting enslaved labor, particularly the labor of enslaved women, with all of its attendant violence. The freedom that black women practiced was murky, messy, and contingent. It also adapted as times and circumstances changed. *Wicked Flesh* embraces the contradictions as exemplifying how high the stakes were and how precarious the search for safe space could be in a world of slaves.

Slavery's rise in the Americas was institutional, carnal, and reproductive. The intimacy of bondage provided slaveowners, traders, and colonial officials with fantasies of plantation increase and riches overseas that trickled into every social relation—husband and wife, sovereign and subject, master and laborer. The story of freedom and all of its ambiguities began in intimate acts steeped in power, shaped by the particular oppressions faced by African women and women of African descent, as well as the self-conscious choices they made to secure control over their bodies and selves, their loved ones, and their futures. Intimacy—corporeal, carnal, quotidian encounters of flesh and fluid—tied free and enslaved women of African descent to slaveowners, colonial employees, and imperial officials. These encounters also tied African women and women of African descent to the African men, children, and others around them in "tense and tender" ways.[9] This book is about the nature of those intimate and kinship ties, their ebb and flow, their power and their violence, and the role African women played in making freedom free for all people of African descent.

Guided by Rae Paris's call to "be the woman in the water," *Wicked Flesh* positions black women as swimming at the crossroads between empires and oceans, diasporas and archipelagos. By engaging them in the overlapping diasporas they traversed, this study argues, a fuller history of freedom, black humanity, and resistance to empire begins to be revealed.[10] *Wicked Flesh* explores this contested, radical, and deeply human meaning of freedom through the experiences of free African women and women of African descent living, traveling, and laboring in New Orleans, one stop along a congested eighteenth-century Afro-Atlantic circuit. This story begins in Africa, attuned to the importance of centering the African continent in studies of the African diaspora. It follows African women and women of African descent through the Caribbean archipelago as they are enslaved and transported to New Orleans. It is framed by the current of people, goods, and ideas that flowed to the Gulf Coast over the course of the eighteenth century, while also responsive to the way shifts in imperial administration could reset colonial societies, disrupting linear narratives of development or progress. To navigate these waters, *Wicked Flesh* follows individual women and girls, identifying where they appear in the current between Senegambia and the Americas, and relinquishing their stories where they disappear from the record. This book is neither a biography nor a microhistory. It is a history practicing the same murky, contingent, and fluid freedom the women under study experienced in their everyday lives in an effort to circumvent an archive of disappearing bodies, limited detail, and excessive violence.

To center New Orleans as the quintessential site for investigating black women's practices of freedom in the Atlantic world, *Wicked Flesh* necessarily drew from archival documents written in multiple languages, scattered in institutions across Louisiana and the world.[11] Any history of women of African descent during the period of slavery must build a narrative using fragments of sources and disparate materials. *Wicked Flesh* is no exception. The sources used often contain incomplete information, were official documents written largely from the perspective of colonial officials and slaveowning men, or exhibit racialized biases against all people of African descent, as well as heterosexist biases against women across race. In other words, searching slavery's archive for enslaved and free black lives and knowledge requires additional labor from historians. Marisa Fuentes has eloquently theorized the ethical and corrective stakes of this process as reading along the bias grain, like "cutting fabric on the bias to create more elasticity," to show enslaved women as a "spectral influence" on white and black men and women.[12] *Wicked Flesh* joins Fuentes—and others—in calling for an accountable historical practice that challenges the known and unknowable, particularly when attending to the lives of black women and girls.[13] Although it is critical to respect the limits of each document, by bringing material together in careful and creative ways, snippets of black women's lives begin to unfold.

Wicked Flesh from Senegal to New Orleans

In Senegambia, where this story begins, succession conflicts, intermittent civil war, and resistance to state power occupied the Wolof rulers of Kajoor, Waalo, and Bawol, as well as rulers and societies in nearby Futa Tooro and Galam. Bracketed by the Senegal and Gambia rivers, an array of polities lived, labored, and jockeyed for power. The Wolof states that emerged from the disintegration of the Jollof empire was deeply influenced by Muslim polities to the north and Mande to the east. In 1695, Latsukaabe Faal united the Wolof kingdoms of Kajoor and Bawol under himself, a dynasty that ruled into the nineteenth century.[14] Wolof kingdoms were hierarchical and polygynous, with landed aristocracies and royal dynasties. Caste and slavery organized social relations.

Imperial expansion within and among the Wolof, which included absorbing
and attempting to absorb and enslave other groups like the Sereer and Pulaar,
did not begin with European contact. Wolof royals and aristocrats took advantage of trade with Europeans to gain power and prestige as part of centuries-
older struggles between kingdoms and dynasties. Europeans did not introduce
slavery or imperial conflict into West Africa—but when and as it benefited
them, they did exacerbate it.

In households and villages, Wolof, Lebu, Fulbe, and Bamana women, children, and men attempted to manage the transformations, predations, and
opportunities beget by these internal conflicts, conflicts only exacerbated by
European trade. Eighteenth-century encounters with Europeans along Senegal's Atlantic coast had their origins in Portuguese-Dutch-Wolof trade alliances, raids, and struggle for dominance in the late seventeenth century. By
1659, French soldiers and traders drove the Dutch from the mouth of the Senegal
River and founded the *comptoir* (administrative outpost) of Saint-Louis. In
1677, the French repeated this action at Gorée, expelling Dutch and muscling
aside British traders to establish a second *comptoir*. Saint-Louis and Gorée
occupied two Atlantic islands—the former on the island of N'dar at the mouth
of the Senegal River and the second on the island of Ber off the Cap Vert Peninsula, the westernmost tip of the African continent.[15] The islands themselves
lacked fresh water and arable land, but for French traders preoccupied with
Atlantic trade, they provided other amenities. From Saint-Louis and Gorée,
French traders accessed the gold, gum, ivory, and slave trades of the Senegal
River. European trading companies and European and African merchants
used Saint-Louis as a base, sailing inland along the river as far as Fort St. Joseph
at Galam, where they met North African caravans of goods and slaves on their
way east across the Sahara. Gorée offered overseas ships a refueling point before
travel south to the coastal *escales* (trading posts) of Rufisque, Portudal, and
Joal, as well as Albreda on the Gambia River. Saint-Louis and Gorée also served
as military bases, fortifying the French against rival African and European
raids and attacks.

African women at the *comptoirs* of Saint-Louis and Gorée were part of the
network of residents, traders, and commercial agents that extended from the
Atlantic coast into the African countryside. They became stewards of hospitality, cultivating a culture of taste and aesthetic pleasure that facilitated trade
between Europeans and Africans. They married European men but eschewed
Catholic marriage, seeking some measure of control and familiarity in their

unions. Instead, residents at the *comptoirs* created *mariage à la mode du pays* ("marriage in the manner of the country"), an alternative conjugal institution that modeled Wolof and Lebu custom. *Mariage à la mode du pays* gave African women at the *comptoirs* access to European goods and offered European men access to trade networks operated by traders in the countryside. These intimate partnerships also came with risks. As the wives of European and African men in patriarchal societies or mothers of children born between French and Wolof patrimony, African women navigated competing claims on legacies of property and trade they developed over their lifetimes. Meanwhile, slave trading and the existence of enslaved African women at the *comptoirs* demonstrated the limits of African women's opportunities in the wake of Atlantic slaving. All African women lived in the shadow of transatlantic trade, but only some held enslaved women as *captives de case*, the designation given to slaves belonging to residents at the *comptoirs*. Enslaved labor facilitated free African women's social position, supporting their hospitality and trade labors while easing the drudgery of everyday household duties.

As free status and enslaved labor became more and more relevant for African women at the Senegambian *comptoirs*, a harder boundary between free and slave emerged across the Atlantic as enslaved Africans began to arrive in the French Antilles. In 1625, Pierre Belain, Sieur d'Esnambuc, a buccaneer and privateer, sailed to St. Christophe (St. Kitts) with a royal patent to establish a French colony, initiating France's Caribbean venture.[16] In no time at all, French interlopers spread from St. Christophe to Guadeloupe, Martinique, the western half of Hispaniola, and the nearby island of Tortuga. These islands, especially Tortuga and French Saint-Domingue, became bases for contraband trade in cattle, hides, precious metals, and slaves, as well as serving as experiments in commercial agriculture. After tobacco failed as an agricultural crop, indigo, coffee, and, above all, sugar came to dominate production in the French Caribbean, especially on the island of Saint-Domingue. Sugar production required massive amounts of labor, labor that plantation owners greedily compelled from enslaved African women, children, and men.[17] By 1674, after mismanagement led the Compagnie des Indes Occidentales (Company of the West Indies) to go bankrupt, the French Antilles (Saint-Domingue, Martinique, and Guadeloupe) united under Crown jurisdiction. Imposition of Crown rule signaled a renewed commitment to asserting control over white and black populations and a fresh determination to make a profit overseas.

Asserting Crown authority included formalizing and standardizing slave law (including the fact that status follows the mother), supporting slave trade to the Caribbean, and boosting settlement.[18] The appeal of commercial agriculture drew the attention of eager landowners. With Crown support, French migration to the Caribbean increased, especially to Saint-Domingue. In the fertile plains of Saint-Domingue's Northern Province, colonists established sugar plantations and mills for processing cane. In the Western and Southern Provinces, sugar plantations and mills appeared alongside coffee and indigo plantations. As a result of the buccaneer generation's clandestine maritime commerce at Tortuga, and with the northern coast's proximity to favorable trade winds and ocean currents, Cap Français (or Le Cap) became a favorite destination for ships arriving from Africa and Europe.[19] Port-au-Prince, in the center of the colony, emerged as the second busiest port and the island's administration center. At the southernmost end, freebooters traded with Jamaica and the British Caribbean from ports like Les Cayes. These coastal enclaves received goods and slaves, supported plantation production occurring in the interior, and became hubs connecting Atlantic societies throughout the Caribbean and along its littoral—including a tiny post on the Gulf Coast named New Orleans.

When African women and women of African descent found themselves funneled into *la traversée* (the journey across the Atlantic to the Caribbean and the Gulf Coast), they entered a world where understandings of sex, gender, race, and power honed on the African continent no longer applied. The Middle Passage enacted a special terror that ungendered the captives who were sucked into it, reducing women and girls and boys and men to units of measured "flesh," as scholar Hortense Spillers has described it.[20] On slave ships journeying to the ports of the Americas, African women and women of African descent experienced the terror of captivity and the violence of commodification as a gendered violence against their bodies, minds, and senses of themselves. Experiencing *la traversée* impressed on those who survived it that life in the Americas would never be the same as it was on the African continent. The tragedy of *la traversée*, however, did not erase personal histories and epistemologies from across the ocean. Although forcibly transported as enslaved laborers, African women and women of African descent entered the maritime, military-colonial, and plantation societies of the Atlantic world as lovers, wives, daughters, and mothers with their own ideas about where and how to shape the new world they found themselves in.

Arriving along the Gulf Coast from West Africa as early as 1719, African women and women of African descent experienced a world in the throes of this racialized, imperial Atlantic project. Established on a crescent strip of land near the mouth of the Mississippi River, New Orleans began as a swampy outpost populated primarily by French colonial officials, soldiers, and traders.[21] Just as at Saint-Louis and Gorée, the French chose to establish themselves at the location for strategic purposes. Just as in the Antilles, France's first priority was securing the Gulf Coast against European rivals and creating commercial ties with colonies elsewhere—in this case, New France (Canada) and French colonies in the Caribbean.[22] Despite the similarities, Africans who arrived along the Gulf Coast entered a unique world. In Louisiana, an indigenous population dominated, ranging from large, hierarchical states to *petites nations,* as French called the smaller, Native nations.[23] When it came to plantation agriculture, Louisiana also faltered behind its Caribbean neighbors. In fact, initial forays in tobacco farming met with early and violent resistance from the Natchez Indians. In 1729, the Natchez Revolt and multiple African slave conspiracies ended Crown interest in the region. The Gulf Coast also experienced a major imperial shift in the middle of the century. After the Seven Years' War, France relinquished Louisiana west of the Mississippi to Spain in the Treaty of Fountainbleau (1762), a major administrative change that introduced new laws and institutions into the colony.[24]

Structural oppressions generated by slaving and empire elicited parallel responses and practices of freedom on both sides of the Atlantic. In Senegambia, in their careful navigation of intimate geopolitics and kinship demands, free African women refused to be bound by French imperial limits on their rights to their bodies, their property, or their social mobility. In New Orleans, mutable and dexterous black women did what they could to disrupt the new demands that use and possession placed on their bodies. Their strategies centered intimate and kinship practices influenced by West African precedent and by the unique hardships experienced by enslaved and free along the Gulf Coast and the Caribbean archipelago. Practices of freedom ranged. Women and girls sought new arrangements of kin in the wake of loss and mourning. They learned to interpret European slave codes, pursued formal manumission, and returned again and again to officials when their freedom became contested. They created intimate and kinship ties that generated means and subsistence for themselves and their kin. They showed up in defense of themselves and each other. They sought joy and pleasure, gave birth, mothered spaces of care and celebration, and cultivated expressive and embodied aesthetic practices to heal from the everyday toil of their laboring lives.

In their actions and refusals, black women on both sides of the Atlantic ascribed meaning to freedom that spiraled beyond European definitions. In Senegambia, these practices emerged as practices of patronage that incorporated marriage and baptism, as well as aesthetics of hospitality, pleasure, and taste. In the Americas, these refusals and transgressions deepened in the face of Europeans' monopoly of power and expanding slave law. In *Wicked Flesh*, black femme freedom describes practices of freedom that emerged across the Atlantic and that not only transgressed but also refused to abide by colonial ideas of freedom as manumission. Black femme freedom gestated in the Americas, where African women and girls recently arrived and those of African descent born on foreign soil were forced to create new raced and gendered selves from flesh lacerated by the Middle Passage. Doing so required them to navigate ideas of gender that congealed against ideas of blood and race, licentiousness and sexual access, commodification and labor. These practices flowed within and along changing meanings of blackness and African descent, femininity and womanhood. Black femme freedom resided in enslaved and free African women and girls' capacity to belong to themselves and each other. It demanded a promiscuous accounting of blackness not as bondage and subjection, but as future possibility. It rejected discourses of black women as lascivious or wicked, and transmuted them into practices of defiance and pleasure for themselves. Black femme freedom enacted a radical opposition to bondage, reinterpreting wickedness as freedom, intimacy as fugitive, and blackness as diasporic and archipelagic.

Telling Black Diasporic Women's History

Wicked Flesh is a history of black women who experienced the contours of bondage and freedom as slavery and the slave trade began to unfold. It describes their everyday fight for some sense of humanity. This study owes much to scholarship and scholars telling black diasporic women's history as a history of freedom.[25] The nature of this work is unique. In Brenda Marie Osbey's poem "Madhouses," a woman named Felicity describes the bawdy behavior of a cohort of irreverent and defiant New Orleans black women.

Dancing and daring their way through New Orleans, Felicity warns that these "madhouses" have many secrets but "i am telling only / as much as you can bear."[26] Scholars of black women's lives have engaged in similar dances of irreverence and defiance, revealing the known and reveling in the unknown, pushing the boundaries of narrative and the archive.[27] Wicked Flesh would be impossible without this rich research on women in slaveholding West and West Central Africa, the United States, and the Caribbean. Such scholarship began the difficult task of placing labor, lives, and discourse about black women at the center of plantation production and the post-emancipation society.[28] This book continues in this tradition, centering African women and women of African descent as complicated, carnal, and flawed subjects whose lives, nonetheless, mattered.

Wicked Flesh draws inspiration from Gwendolyn Midlo Hall's groundbreaking study on the African presence in Louisiana. In Africans in Colonial Louisiana, Hall rewrote the history of the Gulf Coast as a history of Africans from Senegambia and other parts of West Africa forced into labor far from home, whose influence appeared in slave resistance, music, dance, foodways, the economy, and systems of belief.[29] In the years since Hall's publication, work on Gulf Coast's black diasporic heritage expanded tremendously. Wicked Flesh joins work by Hall, Ibrahima Seck, Emily Clark, Ibrahima Thioub, and Cécile Vidal that has argued that the provenance of Senegambia in the French slave trade to Louisiana and the presence of Senegambians in the region were central to shaping black life and culture as it developed.[30] This study also expands on scholarship by Cécile Vidal on the Caribbean roots of New Orleans society; and Jennifer Spear, Sophie White, and Kimberly Hanger, particularly their focus on the material, intimate, and community activities of enslaved and free people of color in French and Spanish Louisiana. Their research demonstrated the importance of Africans and people of African descent to sustaining faltering Gulf Coast outposts, their complex relationships with indigenous laborers, and the many strategies they used to secure manumission for themselves and others.[31] Wicked Flesh builds on this oeuvre by arguing parallel intimate and kinship practices existed between Senegambia and the French colonies in the Americas, despite differences in imperial context. These practices reveal themselves when employing a gendered racial framework that centers African women and women of African descent but are obscured by an empirical or colonial analysis that brackets empires into discrete, disconnected regions.

Making connections across empires allows a new history of freedom to be written.[32]

As a study of intimacy and kinship, *Wicked Flesh* attends to the intimate violence that enslavement brought into the lives of black women and girls. Joseph Miller, in his discussion of domestic slavery in Africa, described the global premium placed on women and girls purchased or traded as slaves, "domiciled and dominated," for their forced physical, reproductive, and sexual labor.[33] Jennifer Morgan's reproductive history of enslaved women in West Africa, Barbados, and South Carolina linked European writers' prejudicial portrayal of African women's bodies and fertility to British slaveholders' assumptions about African women's potential as workers in the New World.[34] Arlette Gautier, Bernard Moitt, and Dominique Rogers likewise describe similar dynamics for black women in the French Caribbean, offering critical examinations of intimacy, kinship, and the relationship of both to labor demands, opportunities for manumission, and family formation.[35] *Wicked Flesh* surfaces stories of everyday terror that characterized life in slaveholding societies for black women and girls. By connecting this violence as it appeared in the lives of women and girls from Senegambia to the Gulf Coast, *Wicked Flesh* identifies intimate violence as a central link between Africa and its diaspora, critical to how colonial officials, slaveowners, ship captains, and even husbands sought power over black women as units of property and labor.

However, telling a history of black women and intimacy during slavery means more than confronting violence.[36] *Wicked Flesh* explores ways black women sought out profane, pleasurable, and erotic entanglements as practices of freedom. Embodiment (the intersection of the material and the metaphorical) and aesthetics (an expressive culture of selfhood) informed African women and women of African descent's practices of freedom. From the cultures of taste they managed and profited from at the Senegal *comptoirs*, to the feasts, dances, and material expression they forged in the Antilles and on the Gulf Coast, the women in *Wicked Flesh* took embodiment and aesthetics seriously. They risked their lives to create hospitable and pleasurable spaces, managed entrance into them deliberately, and circumvented authorities who declared them wicked and tried to stamp out their efforts. As LaMonda Horton-Stallings notes, "What is profane changes over time depending on when and where it originates."[37] To explore those changes, especially over time and space, the microhistorical and quotidian take center stage, implicating homes and bedrooms, hospitals and workshops, biases and bodies as sites of ongoing struggles to define black humanity.

Wicked Flesh is told through the eyes of the women themselves, in an overlapping structure that mirrors the overlapping diasporas they existed in and created. Chapters 1 and 2 explore life at the Senegambian *comptoirs* of Saint-Louis and Gorée from the perspective of free African women like Seignora Catti, Anne Gusban, and Marie Baude, each of whom navigated the terrain of slavery and freedom in differing ways. Marriage and baptism, cultures of pleasure and taste, and hospitality labor engaged in by free African women at the *comptoirs* is the special focus of the women seeking safety and security in these chapters. Chapters 2 and 3 explore how these practices impacted three groups of people: free African women who had ties to European and African men, *captifs du case* at the *comptoirs*, and Africans forced onto slave ships headed to the Americas. For enslaved people en route to the Gulf Coast, the upheaval caused by the Natchez Indians' confrontation with French settlers, especially the Natchez's acquisition of slaves as spoils of war, extended the predations, disruptions, and commodification of the slave trade well beyond disembarkation. Reflecting this, Chapter 3 narrates black women's and girls' experiences of *la traversée* as a long Middle Passage that ends with their being largely invisible at the intersection of two Gulf Coast institutions—the free black militia composed of formerly enslaved men who fought against the Natchez, and the Ursuline convent complex, built up to assist white female refugees of Natchez-French violence. Mirroring the overlapping diasporas the women moved through, Chapter 4 moves backward in time to when African women and women of African descent first begin to inhabit the diasporic and archipelagic terrain of the Gulf Coast, exploring how their lives and labors become beholden to the Antilles in colonial structure and yet reminiscent of the Senegambian coast in population.

Chapters 4 and 5 narrate black women's experiences as French colonial officials attempted to tie black womanhood to the use, possession, and labor that could be forced from black female bodies. Chapter 4 explores the embodied experience of these discourses through the eyes of women like Suzanne, the wife of Louis Congo, a New Orleans "negro executioner," and introduces the concept of the null value as a mechanism for naming archival silences even when reading along the bias grain. Chapter 5 delves deeper into these women's challenge to French colonial power, following girls like Charlotte, the daughter of a French colonial officer, as they demanded manumission for themselves.

This chapter introduces the concept of black femme freedom as a way to characterize practices of intimacy and kinship that exceeded and superseded the manumission act. For black women, these practices also occupied the realm of the profane, the corporeal, and the erotic as they created spaces for pleasure, spirit, and celebration. This practice of freedom drew censure from French and, later, Spanish officials who retaliated with bans on enslaved and free black people's behaviors, such as hosting night markets and wearing headwraps. Chapter 6 continues by exploring the impact of imperial change on practices of freedom, drawing on the perspectives of women like Magdalena, María Teresa, and Perine Dauphine. With a new colonial administration came new institutions and privileges, including the opportunity to register last wills and testaments. Free women of African descent used these legacies to proactively choose kin, a practice of freedom that could be quite fraught when debates over who could be claimed as kin intersected uneasily with racial ideologies, property, and social hierarchies. *Wicked Flesh* concludes with a look into the Haitian Revolution's refugee diaspora to New Orleans, and it foreshadows changes that awaited people of African descent as New Orleans entered the American nineteenth century.

"Concede nothing," New Orleans writer, artist, and activist Jeri Hilt wrote on the ten-year anniversary of Hurricane Katrina, "You alone are the reckoning."[38] After Hurricane Katrina, public reckoning with the African diasporic influence on the Gulf Coast, and New Orleans in particular, slid from public view. In the years since, scholars, artists, and activists refused to concede to a history of New Orleans that ignored the ways black women, children, and men shaped the city. In 2009, Leslie Harris and Connie Moon Sehat founded the New Orleans Research Collaborative, to bring together individuals pursuing a historical and critical evaluation of New Orleans. In 2011 and 2012, Emily Clark, Ibrahima Thioub, and Cécile Vidal, with the support of l'École des Hautes Études en Sciences Sociales in Paris, organized two international colloquia to explore connections and comparisons between Saint-Louis and New Orleans. Post-Katrina book-length studies by Lawrence Powell and Ned Sublette positioned New Orleans as an American city—and American cities as beholden to black diasporic labor and culture.[39] Commemorative campaigns—including the opening of the Whitney Plantation and Slave Museum in Monroe, Louisiana; museum exhibits such as *Purchased Lives*, curated by Erin Greenwald at the Historic New Orleans Collection in 2015; and the activist group Take 'Em Down NOLA's successful campaign to have four Confederate monuments removed from the tourist landscape—have linked black New Orleans history to West Africa, the Caribbean, and the United States.[40]

The late Clyde Woods described Hurricane Katrina as a "blues moment," an unnatural disaster that "disrupted the molecular structure of a wide array of carefully constructed social relations and narratives on race, class, progress, competency, and humanity."[41] New Orleans history is layered with such blues moments, events and processes that fracture supposedly well-understood narratives of race and gender, class and color, slave and free. In the way of those moments, the work of remaking, remixing, and remembering black life has always been black intellectual work. *Wicked Flesh* explores what that work looked like in the hands of the African women and women of African descent who founded the city. This book is dedicated to Clyde Woods and others gone before their time. It is shaped by life in the wake of that storm. It is a love letter to this memory—of a deep Black New Orleans.[42]

Chapter 1

⌒⋎⌒

Tastemakers:
Intimacy, Slavery, and Power in Senegambia

> Regarding the wives of the Bambaras, they are free, so I am unable to force
> them to follow their husbands, I will engage them [here] however possible.
> —Julien Dubellay, Company director, Saint-Louis du Sénégal, 1724

Sometime in the 1680s, at her home near Rufisque, "Seignora Catti" welcomed
Wolof dignitaries and their companions to a lavish dinner. Seignora Catti was
the African widow of a Portuguese trader. A wealthy merchant in her own
right, Catti had leveraged her status as the wife of a European against her commercial savvy and the opportunities and experience of living in the middle
ground between the Atlantic Ocean to the west and Wolof sovereigns in the
east for her own benefit. Seignora Catti had secured property, insider commercial knowledge, and political power. She became an *alcaide* (commercial
agent) for Latsukaabe Faal, the *damel* (ruler) of the Wolof state of Kajoor.
Catti also enjoyed considerable conspicuous wealth, at one point presenting
the *damel* with a horse worth fourteen slaves.[1] Catti owned land near the capital
city, slaves she employed in slaving and commodity trades, and a compound
she opened to visitors from around the region and the world, including European merchants, ship captains, and commercial agents, as well as their servants
or slaves.

Among her visitors that day was a Frenchman named Jean Barbot. Born near
La Rochelle, Barbot arrived in Senegal as a commercial agent for Compagnie
du Sénégal (Senegal Company) slavers. Barbot described Catti as a gracious
host, "a black lady of a good presence and a very jovial temper," comfortable
with receiving visitors, especially foreigners unfamiliar with Wolof customs.[2]

At dinner, she directed him to sit cross-legged on a mat on the floor with herself and the other guests.[3] A slave passed around a large bowl with water, which guests used to clean their hands. As the only stranger, Barbot received a china dish for his meal, while the rest of the company ate couscous and boiled meat in communal fashion from large plates. As dinner began, Catti took a moment to show Barbot how to eat his meal. She "caught my hand to invite me to fol- low her example" as "she used both hands to seize one of the pieces of boiled beef and tore it into scraps by sticking her thumbs in it."[4] Catti then used her fingers to press couscous and meat together into balls small enough to eat before making "signs to me [Barbot] with her head and her hand that I should start eating."

Seignora Catti was not the first or last woman along the Atlantic African coast to secure a position of "high standing" at the intersection of European encounter and African ambition.[5] Over the course of the Atlantic slave trade, African women descended from trade and kinship relations between European and African traders established homes and compounds at trading forts and posts up and down the West African coast. On the Gold Coast, in a practice that came to be known as *cassare*, Osu women formed households with Danish men who arrived to trade for slaves and goods with Ga-speaking groups at and adjacent to Fort Christiansborg. In Lagos, during the latter part of the nine- teenth century, Christian marriage developed into a mechanism for maintain- ing status among the African elite, particularly repatriated freed slaves from Sierra Leone. Farther south, in West Central Africa, Luandan women in inti- mate and commercial partnerships with Portuguese men maneuvered to gain wealth and prestige from their circumstances.[6] In the case of Saint-Louis and Gorée, the Portuguese and Dutch preceded the French, and the descendants of these long-established Afro-European families peddled their knowledge of the terrain and commercial contacts to the influx of French and other European traders arriving for transatlantic exchange after the mid-seventeenth century.

Offering hospitality, comfort, security, pleasurable company, and gastro- nomic largesse in a practice of hosting and accommodating guests was an important part of commercial life in eighteenth-century Senegal.[7] In this, Catti excelled. Catti's hosting prowess emerged despite Barbot's impression of the dinner, which has been described as "perhaps the most uncompliment- ary and ungracious of many contemporary accounts by Europeans of meals with Africans."[8] Although it would have been common to eat with one's hands in Europe during this time period, Barbot registers his disgust with Catti's hands on the food, the contents of the meal itself, and the "tepid" water he and his fellow travelers were encouraged to drink. Despite his reluctance, Barbot participated in the dinner, and he described doing so out of geopolitical vulnerability. Barbot could not afford to ignore or insult Catti or any of the traders he encountered because of the impact that social infractions could have on future French commerce. Barbot entered into trade arrangements with and through Catti's carefully catered ministry, an Atlantic African culture of taste that came to characterize relations between Senegambian women and European men for the next century.[9] In return, some African women were able to enter into commercial exchanges that secured access to European goods, intimate exchanges that tied them to European husbands *à la mode du pays*, as they acquired homes, dependents, and slaves for their own use. On the ground, trading-company employees, sailors, traders, and others arriving at the *comptoirs* demanded food, clothing, intimate companionship, and labor from African women. African women played a central role in providing the same, consensually and otherwise, by trading, laboring of their own accord, or hiring out their slaves.

Seignora Catti's and Jean Barbot's differing dining experiences reveal developing terms of engagement between Africans and Europeans in the eighteenth century. Certain rituals would attend to increasing interaction and trade relations. Food would be exchanged, living spaces would be shared, and entertainment would be offered. New tastes would emerge. Europeans' taste for goods and slaves would beget circumstances, policies, structures, and mandates in reaction to African women's own industry and agency. Women on the Senegambian coast, from diverse circumstances and steeped in an African context already familiar with regional forms of slavery and increasingly familiar with Europeans, responded to changing social, political, and commercial relations by making their own demands. Their taste for goods and slaves changed as Atlantic ideas of race, slavery, and gender began to intercede on their lives. Along with trade relationships and military control of the coast, what was at stake for African women, French interlocutors, and Wolof intermediaries were the contours of an ideological debate just beginning to emerge in the French Atlantic over the boundaries of bondage and the meaning of freedom. Barbot's veiled contempt and Catti's pedagogical assistance presaged conflicting worldviews on a collision course with each other, and the Senegal *comptoirs* set the stage for what was to come.

REINE DU WALO, WOLOFFE.

Figure 1. Ndeté-Yalla, lingeer of Waalo. Elite women's aesthetics are well represented in this image: layers of cotton *pagnes*, the *mouchoir de tête* or headwrap, jewelry on full display, and the leisure activity (smoking during the day near a stream). Painted by Abbé David Boilat. Boilat, *Esquisses sénégalaises: Physionomie du pays, peuplades, commerce, religions, passé et avenir, récits et légendes* (Paris: P. Bertrand, 1853), plate 5. Courtesy of the Bibliothèque national de France, Paris.

Women at the Senegal *Comptoirs*

During the 1680s, women like Catti, or Lucia, an Afro-European woman who dealt in the gold trade and whose consort, a French official named La Coste, operated out of Albreda, became active participants in Atlantic commerce and trade with visiting Europeans.[10] For African women, part of the exchange often involved hospitality and favors of the domestic and intimate variety. Visitors like Barbot, European men ignorant of even the basics of how to eat dinner properly, must have crossed Catti's doorway on more than one occasion. Her practiced tutorial suggested the ease with which she and women like her would have been trained to cater to guests and the importance of their training for brokering commercial exchange between foreign entities. Viewing the work Catti does in this context reorganizes European travelers' hypersexualization of African women in their narratives to reveal African women's labor and bodies of knowledge as entangled with the economies of intimacy and power that facilitated both Atlantic exchange and the exchange of goods itself. It likewise provides a useful thread connecting Catti as a wealthy female trader (a predecessor of the nineteenth-century *signare*) to the labor of women domestics—enslaved and otherwise—entering and exiting the compound at the same moment.

For free and propertied African women, their work included creating appealing and pleasurable spaces for African and European visitors who hoped to trade. Around 1685, a *marabout* (Muslim cleric) living in a village along the trade route between Saint-Louis du Sénégal and the interior of the Wolof kingdom of Waalo, entertained the director of the Compagnie du Sénégal, Michel Jajolet de la Courbe, with stories and tales. While he spoke, the young women of the village, "adorned magnificently," joined the young men in a dance, moving to the sound of drums. La Courbe and his entourage watched the show, an entertainment that the *marabout* and leaders of the village had arranged for guests. When La Courbe finally prepared to retire, a young woman appeared at the door of his cabin to whisk the mosquitos from his room. La Courbe fell asleep guarded by *gris-gris* (protective talismans or amulets made of animal and inanimate material) and awakened to the daybreak hum of the Muslim call to prayer.[11] La Courbe's relation of this visit did not, however, recognize or even much acknowledge the women around them or their labors. La Courbe took for granted the industry of hospitality as well as its intimacy. However, in bodies undulating before strangers, removing pests from closed and private quarters, and presenting in public an "adorned" and aesthetically pleasing appearance, African women labored for La Courbe in a range of capacities, many of them intimate and corporeal, all in a deliberate effort to make their guests' visits more pleasurable.

Women like Catti took advantage of Atlantic trade, but from and through a distinctly Senegambian context where kinship and patronage structured social relations. Although striking to La Courbe, Wolof society offered models of elite women, savvy in politics and commerce. Aristocratic women, as one historian described them, ranged from wives and mothers of large property owners, to the queen (*lingeer*) herself. The *lingeer*, for example, "usually the king's mother, sister, or aunt," received her own revenue from provinces under the king's purview, but also had charge of a retinue of royal slaves she might employ as domestics or as field laborers.[12] Wolof society was patrilineal and hierarchical, but elite women could operate lucrative commercial ventures within the limits of their sometimes vast households. In addition, maternal lineages owned or could claim property, including slaves and cattle belonging to the households of men who married well, giving mothers of sons access to another form of property acquisition through intimacy and kinship.[13] Wolof, Pulaar, and Lebu societies were also polygynous. It was customary for multiple wives to operate as managers and producers of their own households, although often not without tension between wives and the children of wives.[14]

Men like La Courbe found themselves embedded in a world in which African women's intimate labor, consumptive and productive, shaped trade relations. Sor, the village where the *marabout* entertained him, was more than a stop en route to Waalo. It lay within a cluster of islands, forts, and compounds at the mouth of the Senegal River, habitations increasingly integrated into an Atlantic and trans-Saharan market of gold, cotton, and slaves. Sor was separated from the island of Saint-Louis by a narrow waterway, and the families who resided there were familiar with foreign visitors, especially European ones. Women fanned mosquitos from La Courbe and his men as they ate dinner and conversed with their hosts. Young women danced with young men of the village to the sound of drums. La Courbe's titillated portrayal of the women he encountered may have emphasized the exotic and illicit, but it also revealed ways rituals of diplomacy on the coast relied on pleasure and comfort economies created through African women's labor. Europeans seeking to trade along the coast encountered rich, diverse polities with women in an array of social roles: from royal wives and mothers, to "Portuguese" *ñhara* traders and enslaved concubines, to traders and heads of households, to market women and girls navigating pirogues along the rivers or meeting ships at sea.

At the *comptoirs,* and on farms and in homesteads surrounding them, women encountered French visitors and experienced the rise of new trade relations in unique ways. Their relationship to slaving and empire shifted in time to their intimate proximity to and kinship with Europeans, African men, and each other. A small cohort of African women navigated complex networks of kinship and sexual liaisons with European Company men. Some of the women descended from households formed by the wives and daughters of Portuguese and Dutch visitors of the past, men who died or disappeared as the French displaced them. However, not all women who arrived or resided at the *comptoirs* claimed ties to these *ancien* intimate partnerships. Some migrated to the coast, attracted to opportunities for trade or labor in the *comptoirs;* some came as kin; and some were enslaved to African employees of the trading companies. Diverse cultural engagements with European traders offered African women at the *comptoirs* the opportunity to accumulate social capital and property in homes, goods, and slaves. Atlantic trade at Saint-Louis and Gorée provided access to new forms of social status that women on the coast often secured by embodying certain coveted, if gendered, statuses—wife, free or *libre, négresse* or *mulâtresse,* Catholic or *mahometante* (Muslim), *habitant* (a resident) or unpropertied. As wives, as *négresses* and *mulâtresses,* as *libres* and not enslaved, as property owners, African women navigated gender roles created at the intersection of race, bondage, and the rise of an Atlantic African trading system.

The French did not colonize Saint-Louis or Gorée in the eighteenth century. They entered a complex web of social and commercial relations created by Africans themselves. Three African states—the Wolof kingdoms of Kajoor, Bawol, and Waalo—claimed jurisdiction over the islands and posts along the coast. The *damels* blocked French merchants from trading beyond the coast; taxed trading companies for their use of the islands; sold French supplies like food, water, and timber at a cost; and charged traders duties on items exchanged.[15] Within but not subordinate to Wolof authority, Lebu fishermen traded with the French as well, providing provisions for the growing communities at Saint-Louis and Gorée and ferrying goods between the islands and the coast.[16] The *damels* had grown familiar with European traders as early as the fifteenth century when Portuguese and Afro-European traders inserted themselves into trading networks connecting trans-Saharan commerce from

Mauritania to European ships arriving along the coast. By the seventeenth century, Kajoor established its authority over trade relations with Europeans on Senegal's Atlantic coast, drawing them into an existing network of taxes, tribute payments, and political theater in which hospitality and kinship played a central role.[17] On the ground, Africans continued to manage trade relations and work for European traders and Company entities, and with each other.

African women participated fully in these interactions. In 1445, Portuguese explorers attempted to land at Gorée but failed to secure a place on the island.[18] By the 1440s, Portuguese *lançados* and *tangomãos* explored the Atlantic islands of Madeira, São Tomé, the Azores, and the Cape Verde archipelago; conscripted the Guanches, the indigenous group of those islands, into labor; and began trading for gold and slaves with coastal Africans from the Senegal River down to Sierra Leone. Dutch and British traders followed.[19] The Portuguese traders' Afro-European descendants, described at different times and by different European groups as Crioulos, Portugaise, and Portingalls, created trading enterprises throughout the West African coast, living and working in communities created around the mouths of the Senegal and Gambia rivers and in Sierra Leone.[20] Afro-European and African middlewomen and commercial agents living and working along the coast used these networks for their own ends. By the time the French arrived, they entered as renters and leasees to Senegambian landlords, beholden to an African world created by coastal residents' relationship to Atlantic trade and rooted in the coast's political and economic ties to sovereignties like the Wolof in the countryside. African women existed on the coast as the descendants of these earlier interactions, but opportunities to trade with a new cadre of Europeans also attracted women and men to the coast. As French trading-company officials and employees settled into life at Saint-Louis and Gorée, African women and men were among the first to join them as permanent residents, engaging in trade with and provisioning the company in exchange for transatlantic merchandise.[21]

The geography of the *comptoirs* facilitated networks of trade and intimacy. The French built Fort Saint-Louis on an island the Wolof called N'Dar, a long and narrow sandbar at the mouth of the Senegal River, nestled between Langue de Barbarie and Sor.[22] As early as the 1680s, La Courbe expressed open concern about the presence of African women coming from the villages at Sor to trade on the island. Returning from a journey away from the fort, he found "several women from Bieurt and other neighboring villages, who had brought hides, millet, *pagnes* or cotton cloths, because they are the ones who control almost all the trade of Senegal." Women used their own slaves to perform this labor, purchasing hides from farther inland and having them shipped to the coast. "They buy them cheaply," La Courbe complained, brought them to the coast on their heads or on donkeys, then transported them to the fort in pirogues. For La Courbe, these trips threatened illicit commerce and intimate liaisons. He complained that some of the women arrived under pretense and really intended to "débauche the whites to secure some goods" since "these women never make love without self-interest."[23] Company directors could not afford to anger their neighbors. Navigating the deadly choppy waters between the sandbars required skilled navigators, forcing officials to employ sailors from the coast to shuttle them between the islands and ships at sea.[24]

Gorée, in contrast, became a preferred refueling site for French ships engaging in coastal trade, but the French relied on Lebu fishing villages on the coast to supply them with water and subsistence items. Despite the arid land, by 1723, at least one map of Gorée outlined the population of African descent, segregating slaves marked for transit and others by category: *habitants, gourmettes chrestiens* (Christian laborers), and Bambaras.[25] Deep within Fort Saint-François, in the shadow of military officials, the *captiverie* held slaves marked for Atlantic transit, detained until departure. Outside and beside the barracks stood the homes of the *habitants*, primarily free people of African descent. From the entrance of Fort Saint-François, a road wound past a cemetery and a slaughterhouse toward the *village des gourmettes chrestiens* where Africans employed by the company lived. Farthest from the main fort sat the *village des Bambaras*, or, to the French, the village of slaves who did not live with their owners but were still employed on the island.[26] The neatly segregated population plotted on the 1723 map hinted at the social fissures developing on the island as a result of French administration, Wolof hegemony, and Atlantic African commercial enterprise during the first decades of the eighteenth century. The French linked religious affiliation with status and labor: free laborers were Christian while Bambaras were either Muslim or enslaved or both. On the map, each group lived in "villages" located at progressively greater distances from the main fort, parodying real or imagined social boundaries.

These maps, however, remained French fantasies.[27] Flouting regulation, Company employees and soldiers eschewed lodging in the humid, drafty fort to live with African women in much cooler straw cabins around the island. Men arriving via maritime labor streams from French coastal towns, which were quickly becoming Atlantic hubs during the late seventeenth and

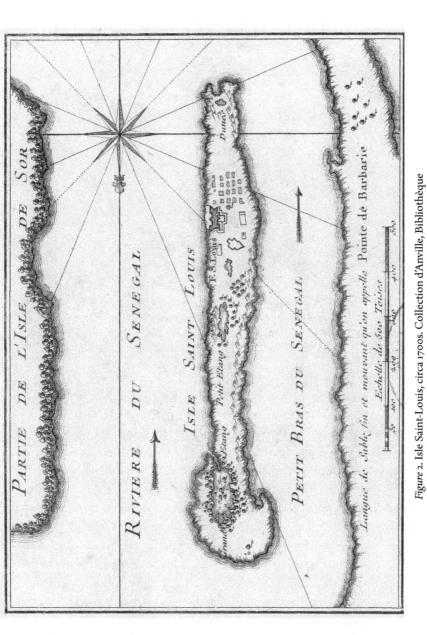

Figure 2. Isle Saint-Louis, circa 1700s. Collection d'Anville, Bibliothèque national de France. Courtesy of the Bibliothèque national de France, Paris.

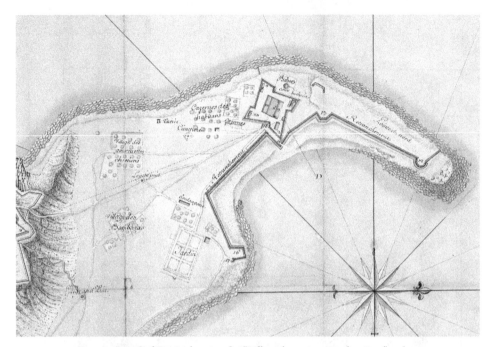

Figure 3. Detail of Gorée showing the "*Village des gourmettes chrestiens*" and "*Village des Bambaras.*" Profile de l'Isle de Gorée pris sur la ligne ABCD— Gorée mars 1723. By M. Wallons, Dépôt des fortifications des colonies. Courtesy Archives nationales d'outre-mer de France, Aix-en-Provence.

early eighteenth centuries, did not lightly reject African women's labor or hospitality.[28] Clear physical boundaries between white employees and the African women surrounding the employees offering hospitality, labor, or trade goods could not be maintained.[29] At Saint-Louis and Gorée, African women played a critical role facilitating trade between the French, villages on the coast, and larger imperial entities like the Wolof even farther inland. Women provided labor that ranged from provisioning Company employees and slaves, to securing slaves awaiting transit to the Americas, to maintaining fortifications and sailing vessels. Their children supported a residential population on the islands as it grew by cleaning, cooking, washing, chopping wood, drawing water, and performing other grueling domestic labor.

The everyday reality of life at Saint-Louis and Gorée was marked less by clear and segregated boundaries between populations and more by the rise

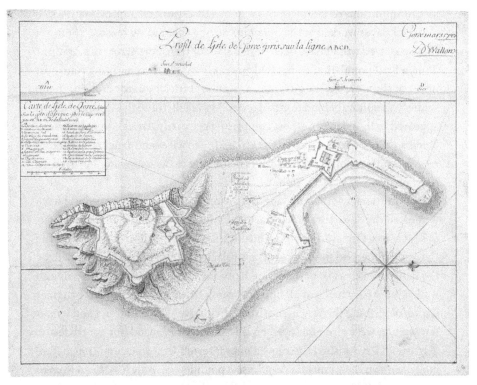

Figure 4. Isle de Gorée, 1723. Profile de l'Isle de Gorée pris sur la ligne ABCD—
Gorée mars 1723. By M. Wallons, Dépôt des fortifications des colonies.
Courtesy Archives nationales d'outre-mer de France, Aix-en-Provence.

and fall of ocean tides or the ebb and flow of the Senegal River. "If water routes
were the earliest form of travel," historian John Thornton has noted, "then the
streams of the ocean must be joined to land streams if we are to see the full
dimensions of the Atlantic world."[30] High-water season defined the timing and
placement of trade between the Upper and Lower Senegal River, between
Saint-Louis, Gorée, and the constellation of *escales* (trading posts). Trade, in
goods and slaves, likewise structured much of social and political life at the
comptoirs. In February, the trading season commenced at Saint-Louis. Many
of the adult men, European and African, left to trade upriver and south, toward
Gorée and the *escales* of Joal, Portudal, and Rufisque.[31] The trading season also
brought African slaves to Saint-Louis and Gorée as laborers as well as for trade.
It brought French ships en route to the Americas to Gorée, which functioned

as a resupply and refueling outpost. Officials estimated approximately two hundred slaves worked at the *comptoirs* during the trading season.[32] Some of these enslaved would have been designated for transport across the Atlantic. Thus, a final population comprised any *captifs* at the forts awaiting transport on slave ships across the Atlantic, as well as African guards and European soldiers remaining behind to guard them. As a result, through May, Saint-Louis appeared to be a sleepy outpost comprising primarily African women house-holders, their slaves and servants, the free African wives and daughters of absent traders, and sixty or so African slaves belonging to the Company and used for labor or awaiting embarkation.

As mothers, wives, and daughters, women at the *comptoirs* would have witnessed the departure of the maritime migrant labor force on their danger-ous journeys. Drownings, raids, and mutinies were a reality for those working the trade route, and their "woeful farewell" to their loved ones acknowledged the dangers even as it marked time between seasons. Those setting sail also wailed "as if they had lost all hope of seeing them again," François Saugnier wrote, describing the way men wished their wives and children good-bye. A few women were also employed on the ships that engaged in river trade and also would have wished their loved ones farewell with some emotion, before embarking on their journey. As *pileuses* (pounders of millet), African women cooked and did laundry for the crews.[33] Trade caravans remained away from the *comptoirs* for months, stopping at other *comptoirs* or smaller coastal towns or *escales* for trade or provisions. The trade did more than French prejudice or policy to separate families living on the island from those on the mainland, laborers from kinfolk, and slaveowners from enslaved for months at a time. The trade also united and reunited families all along the water route, linked from the *escales* along the coast to Galam upriver.

The return of the trading ships to Saint-Louis and Gorée was cause for celebration. Those who survived reunited with families left to wait at the *comp-toirs*. Return also meant an infusion of resources as the Company paid in kind or in gold those who returned alive. Grain and other subsistence goods also arrived with the trading caravans, refilling Company stores with items for purchase. By the mid-nineteenth century, celebratory feasts accompanied the return, complete with drumming, dancing, and griots' songs.[34] It also meant the arrival of enslaved Africans for purchase and transport. The combination of pleasure, play, and reunions with kin on the one hand and the brutal evidence of trade in human cargo on the other was characteristic of life on the coast for the duration of the slaving era. Social capital, status, and pleasure could never be uncomplicated or uncomfortably separated from enslavement, the quotidian brutalities of slave trading, and the growing economy of chattel bondage of Africans and people of African descent. This was especially true for African women and women of African descent who inhabited the Atlantic zone at the edges of both slavery and freedom.

Laboring as employees of the Company may also have appealed to women making their way to the *comptoirs*. As Wolof, Pulaar, Sereer, Soninke, Mande, Bamana, or Lebu women from the countryside made their way to the coast, officials incorporated them into the mix of work and exchange. As traders, women supported trade between the garrison and the coast by furnishing officers, soldiers, and traders with provisions from the hinterland. Suffering a shortage of European laborers, African women and girls also found work as cooks, domestics, and laundresses. Some African women and girls who labored for the Company were slaves hired out to the French by their African or European owners. As a residential population on the islands grew, tasks like cleaning, cooking, washing, chopping wood, and drawing water became daily responsibilities taken up by and falling to African women.[35] The Company also employed African men and boys, many Wolof and Muslim, including the African sons of Company employees, as sailors, guides, and translators; as soldiers and security guarding slaves awaiting transit to the Americas; and as laborers who maintained fortifications and sailing vessels.

European goods and access to them came to mark free African women's status, defining elite African womanhood on the coast. The cotton *pagnes*, madras cloth transported from India, became symbols of distinction as women used them to create elaborate *mouchoirs de tête* (headwraps).[36] These conical formations, derived from traditions of adornment already in circulation in the Senegal delta, became the distinguishing feature of the late eighteenth-century and nineteenth-century *signare*. Women also draped multiple *pagnes* around their bodies in displays of wealth and conspicuous consumption, and as acts of beautification. In a practice called *këfelu*, one scholar has noted, Senegambian women draped *pagnes* strategically and specifically to augment their hips and buttocks.[37] Building homes *en dur* using European brick or tile also distinguished residents with property and wealth from others. Although these homes did not weather heat or storms at Saint-Louis and Gorée very well, their use expanded as access to these materials (and the social meaning behind them) increased.[38] The culture of taste being created along the coast extended to more than *pagnes*. African women also received glass beads, gold jewelry, and European clothing in the form of dresses or shoes. African men received items as well, including *eau de vie* (alcohol), firearms, gunflints, and iron tools. Archaeological excavations at Gorée uncovered European ceramics, glass, and building materials like bricks, tiles, and nails dating from this period of European trade. At both Saint-Louis and Gorée, as women engaged with the French as a result of these trading flows, they began cultivating and indulging in a taste for transatlantic merchandise.

Free African women managed taste and defined standards of hospitality at the *comptoirs* through these performances of wealth, prestige, and decadence. Public dances called *folgars* became spaces for women to display themselves and their retinues, as well as their grand hospitality. Louis Chambonneau described these gatherings as opportunities for griots to sing praise songs to those in attendance, to women as well as men, European and African.[39] Michel Adanson, a naturalist and traveler who journeyed to Senegal's coast between 1749 and 1753, described the *folgars* in detail. Led by the young people of the *comptoir*, attendees formed a square around boys and girls, who gathered at opposite ends and prepared to dance. To the music of drums, performers would sing with spectators in call and response. As they sang, "a dancer stepping forth from each line advanced towards the opposite person that pleased him most, to the distance of two or three feet, and presently drew back in cadence, till the sound of the tabor served as a signal for them to come close, and to strike their thighs against each other." These dances lasted much of the night as attendees drank "strong beer made of millet," *eau de vie*, and palm wine, and ate their fill. *Folgars* may have also operated to attract European suitors to the unmarried daughters of different families.[40] Women cultivated more private celebrations, like the *mbootay* or *botaye*, with each other, sharing resources for support and community. With the *mbootay*, women or women and their families gathered in one or another's home in order to pool whatever resources they had available for food, drink, and other refreshments in a feast of mutual celebration. Griots as well as drummers attended these closed events. Over time, the *mbootay* developed into a ritual used to mark significant life events such as marriages, births, and deaths.[41]

Women like Catti did not distance themselves from their West African context. Indeed, their political and cultural agility—first with the Portuguese and Dutch and then with French and British traders—was already at work within the region itself, in a crucible of constant exchange, plasticity, and even violent tension between ethnicities and polities in the region itself. The disintegration of the Jollof empire and the battle between regional societies like the Sereer and Pulaar for autonomy and selfhood against Wolof hegemony required Senegambian men and women to shift identities, religions, even locations readily. This fluidity required men and women to cultivate skills of adaptation and co-optation that had African roots to become cultural brokers for complex continental African societies. African women built lives amid tensions between empires in the region and centuries of intimate contact with European traders traveling up and down the coast.

Intimacy, Kinship, and Slavery on the Coast

Mariage à la mode du pays developed as a mechanism for forming intimate and kinship ties across Wolof, Pulaar, or Lebu and European lines. Rather than formalize marriage unions before Catholic priests or missionaries, African women entered formal liaisons with European men "in the manner of the country." According to Jones, the process of forming a *mariage à la mode du pays* followed coastal marriage customs derived from Wolof and Lebu society. It was the male suitor's responsibility to approach the family of his potential wife and secure permission. This conversation included a negotiation and an exchange of goods—slaves and other gifts—which would confirm the intention to marry. Typical arrangements included a house, secured by the husband for his new bride and necessary to establish a propertied livelihood at the *comptoirs*. This property, by matrilineal customs shared by the Wolof, Pulaar, and Lebu, was to be retained by the wife and passed on to her kin and other dependents. In addition, all parties agreed that the union ended after the husband's death or disappearance from Senegal. The marriage celebration itself included the talents of the griots and a feast thrown by the husband. *Mariage à la mode du pays* accompanied other traditions. Some of the children of such unions took their fathers' last names. Some of the wives may have changed their first names to French names.[42] For African women and their families, these marriages involved carefully arranged and orchestrated negotiations meant to secure property and facilitate commercial ties that would benefit kin in the interior.

As a practice of kinship and patronage, women along the coast may have used *mariage à la mode du pays* to acquire property and patrons in an unpredictable world. Death consumed European lives at the *comptoirs*. The names of French and British sailors who lost their lives to disease, drowning, or violence along the coast suffused civil registers. African women married *à la mode du pays* had to contend with the likelihood of losing their husbands and marrying again, multiple times, as the sea and the river took men's lives. These deaths would have been tragic, but they also would have left the widows in possession of property and wealth accrued during their husbands' time on the coast. Some women may have found *mariage à la mode du pays* to Europeans lucrative for this reason. Women from the polygynous intimate worlds of the Wolof may have preferred the monogamy that *mariage à la mode du pays* offered. As African wives to white men, women did not split control of property, households, or attention from European husbands with other wives.[43] Marriage to European men presented an alternative to marriages consecrated in Wolof and other Senegambian societies, where husbands retained the right to marry multiple wives at once, and each wife managed her negotiated property and dependents as she saw fit.[44] In some cases, the women entering marriage arrangements may have been enslaved and faced little choice in the matter.[45] By the mid-eighteenth century, the proximity of death and coastal matrimonial practice transformed *mariage à la mode du pays* into a unique institution more common than Catholic marriage. It remained that way for over a century; not until after 1850 did marriages formalized in the Catholic Church by sacramental authorities become more common at Saint-Louis.[46]

A list of employees compiled in 1720 provides the earliest dated reference to a woman of African descent on Senegal's coast being described as a *signare*. In a ledger that listed the money owed inhabitants employed at Saint-Louis by the Compagnie des Indies (Company of the Indies), French official Saint-Robert wrote "SIGNRE" next to the name "Paula de Rufisk." Paula, the widow of S. Charles Cavillier, lived at Gorée.[47] "Rufisque," a French-African reformulation of the Portuguese "Rio Fresco," had a European presence as early as the 1630s, when Capuchin missionaries arrived to convert and baptize local residents. Rufisque became a principal Wolof-French *escale*. As a widow, and with no other occupation listed, it is probable that Paula inherited the livres listed as part of a debt owed Cavillier. However, Paula also may have had her own credit with the Company, a phenomenon that would have distinguished her as one of a handful of African women listed in such ledgers. Whatever the terms the Company debt to her may have been, Paula's entry as a signare in a list dominated by African and French men was remarkable, particularly as distinguishing signares in official documentation was not common until the mid-eighteenth century.

By the eighteenth century, the term *signare* described women whose wealth, property, and status placed them among the social elite of women along Senegambia's coast. A reformulation of the Portuguese *senhora*, the honorific *signare* did not apply to all African women or even all women with intimate or commercial ties to European men. By the mid-eighteenth century, to be a *signare* required a matrix of social markers, including property ownership, slaveownership (often of female slaves), and *mariage à la mode du pays* with European or Afro-European men.[48] Conspicuous consumption and circulating European goods, including gold jewelry, fabric, and, by the nineteenth century, homes built in "Portuguese" style, have all been attributed to *signares*. *Signares* were situated socially in the upper echelon of Saint-Louis society between traders and *gourmettes* (free African laborers hired by the Company). "Grumetes and free African and Muslim residents shared equally in forming the cultural environment of the towns," Jones notes, "but signares produced métis children who could also rely on their kinship with European men to act as cross-cultural brokers." As the eighteenth century proceeded and daughters followed in their mothers' footsteps, a new generation of mixed-race traders and commercial agents sprang up along the West African coast.

Kinship and intimate ties connected communities of African descent growing at Saint-Louis to those forming at Gorée. Like the water routes bringing European and African traders back and forth from Saint-Louis to Galam, Gorée, Portudal, Joal, Rufisque, and beyond, African women at Saint-Louis and Gorée, propelled by trade, opportunity, and desire, moved with ties of kin beyond any boundaries that French or other European officials could put in place. In 1720, Marie Thereze Yecam Semaine resided among men and women working for the Company at Saint-Louis. She was the *négresse* widow of Joseph de Gorée. Michel de Gorée, her son with Joseph, lived and worked at Saint-Louis. The Company, perhaps resigned to their presence, began to add African women and men to trading-company employee rolls. In 1720, the Compagnie des Indes paid François Aubin, a mulatto carpenter, 150 livres for work completed.[49] In 1724, Antoine Le Bilan, *nègre libre*, worked for the company as a caulker while Malietal and Le Fleur, both *nègre libres*, were employed as translators. Young boys like Andre, a *rapace*, also worked for the Company.[50] Employees, African and European, built families who resided at the *comptoirs*. Men like Michel de Gorée and Dominique, *nègres chrestiens,* even traveled back and forth to France, following routes created by Atlantic trade networks.[51] Sometimes, however, claiming intimate ties also meant refusing mobility and demanding the right to stay in place. In 1724, Julien Dubellay, then the governor of Saint-Louis, sent a detachment of Bambara soldiers to Galam. He could do nothing, however, about their wives, who, he noted, "are free, so I am unable to force them to follow their husbands." In their refusal, the wives of the soldiers defined freedom for Dubellay as a right to mobility on their terms and no one else's—not even their husbands'.[52]

Forming unions with European officials, soldiers, and traders, African women brought networks of kinship across and beyond the coast into contact. Michelle Bertin, *mulâtresse,* was the wife of Pierre LeLuc, a shipmaster at Saint-Louis. Michelle's *mulâtresse* sister, Anne Bertin, was the wife of a company clerk named Nicolas Robert. These liaisons between free African women and French men created a new generation of female *habitants* with direct links to France. In 1736, Anne Bertin followed her husband to France. The Bertin sisters joined women like Angelique Bottement as part of a generation of women building their lives at Saint-Louis. Bottement, a native of Paris who may have been one of the few white women at Saint-Louis, engaged in a liaison with Jean Boutilly dit Le Rouge, a white soldier employed by the Compagnie du Sénégal. Jean may have met Angelique in France, where she had been born, or in Senegal, and the formal nature of their relationship remains unknown. After Jean's death in 1730, Angelique claimed to be Jean's widow.[53] In June 1731, Angelique remarried in Saint-Louis to the carpenter Pierre Anger, another white employee. While African women and French men entered into a range of partnerships, most remained unrecognized by Catholic officials until the nineteenth century. The marriage between Angelique Bottement and Pierre Anger was only one of a handful of official Catholic marriages listed in the civil registers.

While some women like Anne Bertin faced the Atlantic, following their husbands to new lands, most widows and wives of *mariage à la mode du pays* did not. Early eighteenth-century population counts for Saint-Louis and Gorée were uneven and inconsistent, but by the 1750s censuses document a resident population of African descent. In 1755, a partial census of Saint-Louis counted over 750 African men, most enslaved, and over 1,500 enslaved and free women in an island population of about 2,500.[54] In 1776, over 1,500 "mulattoes" and "free blacks" lived at Saint-Louis and some 900 of them were women. In 1785, only seven hundred Europeans were counted at Saint-Louis, mainly soldiers, in contrast to over three thousand Africans and people of mixed race.[55] At Gorée, from an estimated sixty-six free Africans in 1749, the number of people of African descent increased to over three hundred in 1767.[56] By the second half of the eighteenth century, these widows and wives had taken up the mantle left by the Portuguese *ñharas* to become the Afro-French-inflected *signares*.

At Saint-Louis and Gorée, free African women who married *à la mode du pays* endeavored to marry several times as their husbands left the coast, returned to Europe, or passed away. The households created could be extensive, making marriage, inheritance, and strategic and insistent claims on property a key practice against the precarity of being left alone or abandoned. However, *mariage à la mode du pays* also occurred between residents of African descent. As with Charles Thevenot and his wife, Marie-Isabelle Baude, marriages between those born on the coast were also welcomed, particularly as a cohort of free African residents grew. Thevenot, described as a sailor of African descent and as *mulâtre* in the register, would later become the mayor of Saint-Louis, and the Thevenots were a leading *habitant* family at Saint-Louis in the late eighteenth and early nineteenth centuries. Marie-Isabelle was also of African descent. Others continued to marry Company employees and officials. In 1767, a roll of residents at Gorée listed a *signare* by the name of Catherine Baudet. Baudet had married three times, each time to a Company official and employee—S. Porquet, S. Pépin, and S. Franciéro. Her children included Jean and Nicholas Pépin, Marie-Anne Porquet,[57] Pierre and André Franciéro, and Anne Pépin, a *signare* who would later on be described in UNESCO documents as the owner of the "House of Slaves" of Gorée.[58]

The *métis* community that emerged from unions between *signares* and European merchants would come to occupy key positions of social and political power in French colonial Senegal in the nineteenth century. However, it would be wrong to treat this later fact as a foregone conclusion of the earlier period. All Wolof, Sereer, Lebu, and Pulaar women, in their sexual encounters with European and African men as Company officials, Wolof agents, Afro-European traders, sailors, and more, did not have indiscriminate access to wealth or opportunity as a result of their unions. As the dinner at Catti's abode demonstrates, some women encountered Europeans from already-subject positions that skirted the edges of servitude and threat and intimacy and sexual labor. These encounters rode the spectrum of coercion and what passed for consent in a slaveholding society. French colonial officials and, later, French writers and artists created a fantasy of the seductive *signare* that tangled and confounded questions of violence, rape, and bondage. After French rule ended, the *signare* became a symbol of Senegal identity as routed through *métissage, métis* political status, and social distinction.[59] Upholding and managing this identity has been important and even empowering to the descendants of the *signares* who continue to create *mouchoirs de tête* and engage in elaborate pageantry at festivals like the *Fanal* (lantern festival) at Saint-Louis.[60] Scholar Lisa Ze Winters has placed the image of the *signare* against the fraught history of the slave trade from Gorée, emphasizing the coast's history of slave trading across the Atlantic. Noting the juxtaposition of the "opulent signare" and "the slave" in tourist documents and historical recollection, Winters argues that the *signare* has been forced to stand in "for all of the parties responsible for the tremendous wealth acquired through the theft and enslavement of captive Africans" while "a history of theft, rape, captivity, and torture" is rewritten as decadence.[61] Attuned to domestic slavery of a different kind, scholars like Martin Klein, Ibrahima Thiaw, Ibrahima Thioub, and Hilary Jones have noted that slavery was indigenous to the African continent before the arrival of Europeans, and was quite alive and well along Senegal's coast. The existence of enslaved women who labored to maintain the culture of taste that free African women managed carried profound implications for society as it emerged at the *comptoirs*.

Enslaved women at Saint-Louis and Gorée navigated multiple layers of intimacy, kinship, and power that converged on the *comptoirs* from the countryside. In Wolof society, slaves existed as part of an elaborate hierarchy that included aristocratic elites, *marabouts*, griots, and a variety of occupational castes, peasants, and slaves.[62] Slaves and their descendants could appear at all levels of this hierarchy, but slaves did not have the protection of kinship groups or lineages. Individuals could be enslaved for refusing to convert to Islam, as prisoners of war, as criminals, or some version of all three as non-Muslim polities like the Bambara or Sereer discovered. Among the Fulbe, farther inland from the *comptoirs*, slaves functioned as kinless outsiders, subject to redistribution, concubinage, forced labor, or pawnship.[63] Because of their social fungibility, that is, their ability to be used, exchanged, and dispersed without protection and in multiple ways, slaves were employed in a variety of ways within their masters' households and fields. Slavery in West Africa did not always mean agricultural labor. Enslaved men labored in administrative positions or could be drafted into the *ceddo* (royal slave warrior caste).[64] Enslaved women served as wives and concubines, domestics, *pileuses*, and other household-related laborers. By the 1720s, slaves were also used to harvest gum and grain and to manage livestock like cattle and horses as part of the spreading influence of Atlantic trading in the region.[65]

Slave status in Wolof society followed generational lines, but the tie between perpetual bondage and maternity or paternity was ambivalent. This did not mean reproduction could be uncoupled from bonded status. African women, as slaves, did not control sexual or reproductive access to their bodies or their lineages. They could not determine their own intimate ties and their children, and any property they produced belonged to their owners. Slavery was not racial in the nineteenth-century definition of race as biological, inherited, and legislated. However, slavery did mark *difference* and subjection. In West Africa, slavery served to distinguish between individuals who could accrue the privileges and protections of social, political, and economic ties to kin (free) and those who could not (slaves).[66] In Wolof society, non-Muslims could be subjected to enslavement, regardless of conversion to Islam.[67] For women, their intimate and kinship labor distinguished them from their male counterparts even when free; as slaves, this labor distinguished them further as subjects without protection and without recourse. Enforcement of status, even status following the mother, would have strained the resources of slaveowning elites.[68] Despite that, particularly in places like the *comptoirs* and *escales*, where domestic slavery requiring household, hospitality, and sexual and reproductive labor dominated, "the capture and retention of women, not the slaughter of their men, was the point of slaving."[69]

In Wolof society, over the course of their lifetimes, slaves could gain and lose social status in ways similar to free persons. Slaves could secure leadership roles and grow more independent. Slaves could also be re-sold, pawned, or captured by rival polities. Highly valued slaves served as managers within the agricultural complexes of the elites. Slaves serving in the *ceddo* could advance up its ranks.[70] Islamic precedents influenced institutions of slavery and slave trading in Senegal. The enslavement of prisoners of war and non-Muslims, as well as the sale of enslaved women to traders for sale along trans-Saharan slave trade routes, was common.[71] Masters acquired slaves by purchase, rather than by reproduction. War, trade, and pawnship were the most common ways of obtaining slaves.

Differences between purchased slaves and slaves born within households were important. *Jaam-juddu,* or *captifs de case,* were slaves who worked within households and on agricultural complexes. Even among *jaam-juddu,* those born within households or complexes received more privileges, such as land ownership and opportunities to buy their labor, than newly purchased slaves could receive.[72] In Wolof society, it was taboo for masters to sell slaves born within households, which may have provided enslaved women, children, and men a sense of security and space to gain wealth of their own.[73] *Jaami-buur*, or *captifs de la couronne*, were royal slaves. Many royal slaves became part of the *ceddo*.[74] Some nonroyal elites also owned thousands of slaves who formed and occupied entire villages of their own. Whether as part of the *ceddo*, in villages, or within households, slaves held by Wolof masters were able to build autonomous, prosperous lives that belied their status. Nevertheless, slaves did not own their labor and remained kinless subjects incorporated into someone else's household, unable to create or draw on their own kinship lineages for protection.[75] When slaves died, any wealth they accumulated during their lifetimes passed to their owners.[76]

As the number of African women and men residing at Saint-Louis and Gorée grew, residents obtained slaves of their own, hiring them out to trading companies and employing them within their households. Many of the slaves were identified as or identified themselves to officials in the parish registers as *mahometantes*, or Muslims. Others were identified as or identified themselves as Bambaras and may have been non-Muslim Africans or ethnic Bamanas from beyond the coast. The term "Bambara" was used by the French to describe a particular cohort of slaves employed by the Company, generally as slave soldiers.[77] However, especially after 1712, during the expansion of Segu Bambara, ethnic Bamana may have found their way to Saint-Louis and Gorée after being sold or captured.[78] Even among so-called Bamana, identity was elastic. Bamana integrated and adopted members into their society, especially women, children, and men captured during raids and war. In the parish registers, officials listing *mahometant* or *mahometante* slaves did not provide additional ethnic information, except at times to describe the registrant as a *mahometant(e)* "de Senegal." Alongside enslaved soldiers, enslaved hired out to the trading company and other *captifs du case*, or slaves belonging to residents of the *comptoirs* and not available for trade across the Atlantic, another category of bondsperson resided at the *comptoirs*. Arriving in waves along the trade routes came *captifs* to be sold to the Americas. Awaiting transport aboard slave ships, these African women, children, and men had been sold to the Company or individual traders, and, once transport was available, they would be loaded for sale to slaveowners waiting across the Atlantic.

The French at Saint-Louis and Gorée, for their part, recognized captive Africans as property and trade items, even awarding slaves to traders for work completed. In October of 1722, Pierre Charpentier, a Company director at Galam, paid an Afro-European merchant, Etienne La Rue, one slave for work completed.[79] By the 1720s, Company directors in France also connected slavery at the *comptoirs*, particular enslaved labor and issues of slave control, to their dreams of establishing lucrative export trade in enslaved persons to points across the Atlantic—including the relatively new colonial venture of Louisiana. A revolt against the French at Arguin, a *comptoir* upriver from Saint-Louis, resulted in Company directors in France ordering trading-company officials in Senegal to enslave any *mahometants* who had been taken prisoner and send them immediately to Louisiana.[80] However, the forced labor of these prisoners of war and revolt had meaning and use to officials at the *comptoir* that the directors in France had not calculated on. St. Robert, then a director at Saint-Louis, did not send the prisoners ahead. Instead, to supplement deserters, some fifty Bambaras were kept at Saint-Louis and Arguin to cut wood and make salt. St. Robert then hired a man named Boualy as an interpreter to work alongside them.[81] Company officials in Senegal did what they could to avoid hiring able bodies from free African residents.

The autonomy that enslaved Africans at the *comptoirs* exhibited made free status difficult for French officials to discern, much less regulate. Blackness could not be equated with bondage and the French assigned labels of "slave" and "free" to individuals based on a contradictory and complicated mixture of characteristics. These characteristics included race (*nègre* or *négresse, mulâtre* or *mulâtresse*), ethnicity (Bambara or "de Senegal"), occupation, religion (*mahometant[e]* or Catholic), and local reputation. The French presumed *laptots* to be *noirs libres* who worked only during the trading season, while *gourmettes* were free laborers stationed on the islands and working for the Company.[82] But *laptots* and *gourmettes* may also have been slaves of *habitants* hired out to the trading company or, as Adanson noted, were the mixed-race children of French men by enslaved or free African women.[83] Officials also assumed those labeled as Bambaras were slaves, but Bambaras were also employed as soldiers and trusted to defend French interests as far as Ouidah in the Bight of Benin.[84] The French presumed *nègres chrestiens* to be free people of color and, perhaps, somewhat assimilated and amenable to French interests. Catholic or not, however, some of these men and women may have been slaves. In 1686, two *nègres chrestiens*, Sala and Jasmin, warned La Courbe, future commandant of

Saint-Louis, about an attack from the *damel* of Waalo. As La Courbe scrambled to fortify the island, he relied on two other *nègres chrestiens* to lead patrols and investigate the threat.[85] On the ground, the clearest distinctions that could be made by the French existed between slaves owned by residents of the *comptoirs* or living near the coast, and slaves purchased specifically for the Atlantic trade, waiting in the *captiveries* for departure.

Enslaved women, children, and men played a significant role in shaping life at the *comptoirs*. By the mid-eighteenth century, as contemporary travelogues as well as Company officials reported, a majority of those living and working at Saint-Louis and Gorée were enslaved. The rise of this resident population of enslaved Africans developed within a generation of the consolidation of the French presence at Saint-Louis and Gorée. This emergence of a captive majority also coincided with the most aggressive slave-trading years at Saint-Louis, Gorée, Portudal, Joal, Galam, and related ports and *escales*. Between 1726 and 1775, over 45,000 enslaved Africans would depart from these ports for plantations and captivity across the Atlantic—the most the region would see depart from its shores over the entire period of slave trading in Senegambia.[86] These two linked phenomena—the rise in the slave population at the *comptoirs* and the peak of the Atlantic trade—reflected the impact that Atlantic slave trading had on the presence and provenance of enslaved populations and the growth of slaveholding societies along West Africa's coast.

Patterns of slaveholding that emerged at Saint-Louis and Gorée among French employees and free African households did not look like plantation slavery in the Americas or even in West Africa. Instead, slaveholding practices at the *comptoirs* developed from Wolof precedent, but were adjusted to the new seasonal labor demands, domestic priorities, oceanic marketplace, and geography of terror that accompanied the rise of Atlantic trade at the outset of the eighteenth century. To have an impact, terror in this instance did not require slaves to be traded extensively or regularly from the coast. The number of slaves traded from either Saint-Louis or Gorée across the Atlantic comprised a minority of the transatlantic slave trade as a whole. Atlantic slave trading, however, exacerbated already-existing subjections and elaborated on new terrains of difference and possible loss of kin by the everyday fact and presence of slave ships, slave revolts at the *comptoirs*, the arrival of merchants ready and willing to purchase enslaved Africans, the fear and precarity of *captifs de case* and free Africans who might be mistaken as being for sale for the Atlantic trade, and the creation of ordinances to protect those who were free. Enslaved and free

Africans at the *comptoirs* watched, waited, and heard rumors of enslaved people dying at the *comptoirs* when multiple droughts destroyed supplies of grain. They would have seen firsthand what St. Robert, writing in response to trading-company demands for slaves, described as the plight of slaves who died in irons, who died from illness due to close quarters, and who ran away to escape the toxic conditions.[87] As Marisa Fuentes has noted, for enslaved and free blacks at the port town of Bridgetown in Barbados, the very geography of Atlantic port towns lent itself to controlling and punishing those in proximity to the dead, diseased, and dying.[88]

Africans described the shadow that Atlantic slaving left on those who remained behind. Working along the Senegambian coast in the 1720s, one British factor stated: "The discerning Natives account it their greatest Unhappiness, that they were ever visited by the Europeans. They say, that we Christians introduc'd the Traffick of Slaves, and that before our Coming they liv'd in Peace; but, say they, it is observable, that whereever Christianity comes, there come with it a Sword, a Gun, Powder and Ball."[89] In the 1770s, a French traveler related a song sung at Gorée that described the impact of Atlantic slaving, particularly enslaving African women, on intimate and kinship ties:

> The Damel has pillaged the village of Yéné
> He has taken my woman captive
> I have so much sadness since then
> That I do not want to drink palm wine or eat couscous
> My woman will sail to the islands
> I will ask to become a captive with her
> I would rather be a captive than free without her.[90]

The development of slaveholding at Saint-Louis and Gorée mirrored the growth of slaveholding in port towns like Elmina, Ouidah, Luanda, and Cape Town. Analyzing slaveholding in Atlantic African port towns situates the continent as central to Atlantic history and adds a level of complexity to the history of ports and towns throughout the Atlantic world. A necessary preoccupation with analyzing and historicizing plantation slavery in the Americas positioned ports, towns, and cities like New Orleans as extensions of the plantation complex, even if as spaces of opposition where the plantation's immense and physical brutality might be eased. Such a perspective collapses the peculiarities of ports as geographies with their own creative and unique violence against enslaved people, black politics of resistance and survival, and histories of racialization. The focus on port towns as extensions of plantation slavery likewise shifts the geography of the Atlantic world from Africa (where plantations did not develop until the nineteenth century) to ports and towns of slaveholding societies in the Americas. Slavery at ports and towns like Saint-Louis and Gorée did not so much mirror bondage on plantations or ports in the Americas as they refracted the past and present in slaveholding in West Africa while serving as prophetic projects where officials, free African and white slaveowners, and enslaved Africans themselves struggled over the meaning of African lives held in bondage.

Femmes de Mauvaise Vie at Saint-Louis and Gorée

At Saint-Louis and Gorée, eighteenth-century Atlantic commerce spearheaded by French trading companies, including commerce in slaves, opened space for African practices of intimacy, slavery, and power to crash against elements of racial hierarchy emanating from plantation societies across the Atlantic. Always exploitative, slavery existed as one status among many that African women experienced, degrees of alienation that did not equate neatly to boundaries between "slave" and "free." In this world, practicing freedom for free African women at the *comptoirs* meant navigating carefully around multiple terrains of bondage—including the gendered racial hierarchy of Atlantic slavery. Slaves at the *comptoirs* enjoyed some freedom of movement and autonomy. They resided in the households of their owners, in the households to which they were hired, or in separate "villages" distributed throughout the island.[91] Bambara slaves were stationed as soldiers at trading posts throughout the region, accompanied, at times, by their enslaved and free wives.[92] Opportunities for enslaved people to acquire property existed, but primarily for enslaved men employed in commerce. Enslaved women most often found more limited opportunities among the ranks of household slaves and domestic laborers in homes and compounds, as well as on the farming areas on the mainland beyond the *comptoirs*. These positions were less conducive to individual accumulation of property or elevation of social status than those available to men. In practice, enslaved women's everyday labor mirrored the gendered labor that free African women without slaves were expected to do for their families in their households and compounds. Across status, African women, those in bondage and those who were not, juggled roles as mothers, wives, and daughters that placed them in uneasy tension with European and African husbands, fathers, and sons.

In the Antilles, the French had already begun experimenting with a series of edicts that remanded the children of enslaved mothers in the Antilles to perpetual slavery with limited access to manumission. In 1685, King Louis XIV signed an "edict concerning the enforcement of order in the Islands of the Americas." This was described in later years as a *Code Noir* (Black Code).[93] A collection of legal proscriptions, the *Code Noir* was the Crown's first comprehensive attempt to regulate slavery in the French Atlantic and the first imperial slave code written by a European monarch specifically for its colonies in the Americas. The *Code Noir* defined slaves as property and declared that their status would match the status of their mothers. Slaveowners in the French colonies of the Americas joined their British counterparts in harnessing the forced reproductive labor of African women's wombs to furnish bodies for plantations and colonial societies throughout the Americas. *Partus sequitur ventrem* (or "status follows the womb") gave birth to a new world order. It promised generations of captivity, perpetual bondage, and the specter of forced sexual contact.[94] The *Code Noir* also clarified how slaveowners could manumit or formally free their slaves from bondage. After 1685, slaveowners of at least twenty years of age could free their bondspeople without cause and without paying a tax. Freedom was also bestowed on enslaved people "declared sole legatees," "named executors of their wills," or the guardians of the slaveowner's children. The code even gave unmarried men in concubinage with enslaved women an opportunity to free them through marriage.[95] The 1685 *Code Noir* structured black freedom in the New World as subject to slaveowner whimsy, accessible in response to specific acts of service, but otherwise beyond the grasp of the majority of those who were enslaved. As a whole, African descent signified perpetual enslavement.[96]

Back at Saint-Louis and Gorée, the 1685 *Code Noir* did not apply, and trading-company officials instituted neither a slave code nor a manumission policy until the nineteenth century.[97] In 1688, Louis Chambonneau, a trading-company director at Saint-Louis, believed it would be possible to send French men and women to Senegal "to settle and be given plots as it was done in the Americas in order to plant tobacco, indigo, cotton, and sugar cane."[98] However, he cautioned against exploiting the labor of *"nègres captifs* . . . for fear that in this country they will kill all the whites." It was trade, he stated, not plantation agriculture, that would secure French prospects in Senegambia. Regardless of imperial designs in Africa, the French were minorities living on small islands in the shadow of powerful African states. As the *Code Noir* created formal categories of slave (*esclave*) and free (*libre*) or freed (*affranchi[e]*) across the Atlantic, trading-company officials on Senegal's coast lacked the monopoly of power needed to formalize similar boundaries between slave and free among African residents.[99] Quelling rebellious employees, maintaining good diplomatic relations with African traders, and defending against rival European entities preoccupied them.

Company officials who sought to avoid conflict with Wolof landlords passed measures protecting African traders and allies from accidental enslavement and forced deportation to the Americas. Company directors discouraged employees from involving themselves in contests over enslaved property. In 1721, the Compagnie du Sénégal directors in France issued regulations outlining proper employee conduct in the *comptoirs*. Company officials were forbidden from freeing slaves without the consent of Company directors in France. Soldiers were prohibited from assaulting or otherwise mistreating *nègre libres*. Employees could not send *captifs du case, nègres chrestiens,* or *gourmettes* to the Americas.[100] The same protections were extended to "*nègres* of the [Wolof] Kings" and "*nègres* of the country" who came to Saint-Louis and Gorée to trade. These rules were directed at employees themselves and passed to protect the mercantile interests of the trading company by promoting good diplomatic relations between the garrison and its local allies.[101] Soldiers were also prohibited from assaulting or otherwise mistreating the *captifs* of free Africans at the *comptoirs*.[102] This protection extended to slaves belonging to free blacks, Christianized blacks, *gourmettes*, and other employees of the Company, as well as Wolof emissaries and other Africans from the countryside who came to Saint-Louis and Gorée to trade.

At the same time, Company officials on both sides of the Atlantic shared an antipathy to intimate relations between African women and their European employees. In the Antilles, before the *Code Noir*, the children of these unions had some access to free status, if haphazardly. In 1664, the children of enslaved women by French men in Martinique and Guadeloupe served their mothers' masters until they were twenty years of age, but were free thereafter. In 1672, mixed-race slaves were declared free at age twenty-four.[103] In 1673, M. du Ruau Palu, an agent-general of the Compagnie des Indies, declared that slave status should follow the mother. He argued that the previous custom of freeing mixed-race children encouraged enslaved women to purposely have children with

French men so their children would one day be free. By 1680, the Superior Council of Guadeloupe declared that status would follow the mother, complaining of the "wickedness of the *négresses*" who "debauch themselves to free men without considering the horrible sin they commit in the hopes of having free children."[104] However, into 1681, in Martinique, female and male mixed-race slaves were freed at ages fifteen and twenty, respectively. Also, in Martinique at the same time, white men who fathered mixed-race children were still fined 1,000 livres and required to pay another 1,000 if they wished to purchase the child from his or her owner.[105] In sexual liaisons between African women and European men, slavery, property, and lineage entangled. And French officials, traders, and sailors increasingly shared a discourse of reprobation and punishment that blamed African women for sex occurring across the color line.

Whereas colonial officials in the Antilles resorted to fines to prevent carnal relations, colonial officials along Senegal's coast failed to intercede in employees' intimate activities for diplomatic reasons. By the 1680s, La Courbe was in Senegal being ordered by Company directors in France to stop unions between African women and French employees. The Company's stance was clear. Directors described the women on Senegal's coast as *femmes de mauvaise vie*, a euphemism for women engaged in sex work.[106] When La Courbe arrived at Saint-Louis, he expressed shock at the corruption of employees and priests, who "each had a wife" of African descent and "each had his share to eat," living in part off of rations distributed by the Company. La Courbe's description of European men "living as liberally and overtly with the *négresses* as if they are their legitimate wives" reflected prejudicial views of partnerships, which may have ranged from sexual labor of enslaved women to long-term partnerships with residents. La Courbe's account delegitimized intimate ties between European men and African women, regardless of *mariage à la mode du pays*, in part to supplement his primary interest—French control over commerce along the coast. La Courbe worried that "scandalous pleasure" encouraged Company employees to satisfy African women with "the most beautiful and the most precious merchandise of the Company."[107] Instead of a culture of taste and hospitality created by African women, La Courbe viewed the intimate encounters African women and employees engaged in as an illicit consumption of Company goods. Despite expressing distrust of local women as well as insurgent employees, his power to control such interactions remained limited. When he confiscated the women's property and expelled them from the *comptoir*, he faced a small mutiny from Company employees and African residents who demanded their return. The incident reflected Company officials' own vulnerability and subservience to the demands of their own employees.[108] Labor and hospitality provided by African women was such an important part of military life, soldiers mutinied when Company officials attempted to expel African wives and domestics from the island or enforce the Company ban on cohabitation.

If the French described African women, in general, as hypersexual or parasitic, the children of European-African unions were viewed as a further barrier to consolidating French authority in the region. In 1688, Chambonneau warned that if the French wished to establish themselves in Senegal, they must "rigorously prohibit" interracial unions. He asked Company directors in France to send French women to Senegal in order to prevent employees from forming unions with African women. Otherwise, the Company would "risk repeating the experience of the Portuguese at Gambia," whose children "have made the country even more black."[109] Chambonneau expressed his bias against blackness as a matter of power. Along with lineage, he defined racial difference using phenotype, culture, and religion. He noted, for example, some of the "Mores [Moors]" were "as white as we are" and "the Europeans in the Company of *Négresses*" have "*blans mestis*," or white-looking mixed-race children, but he expressed approval of "the *moresses* who were Christian."[110] Controlling resources, however, meant controlling proximity to blackness—which required controlling intimacy between Europeans and Africans. Company-issued regulations for its *comptoirs* in January 1688 included prohibitions against living with *négresses*, going to *négresses*' homes, letting *négresses* enter employees' homes, and going to *négresses*' villages for internal trading.[111]

Chambonneau did not reference the *Code Noir*, but its discourse around the monstrous libidos of African women suffused his and other French officials' interpretations of intimate practices on the Senegambian coast. The 1685 *Code Noir* gestured toward African women's untamed libidos as initiating interracial sex and offered a legal fiction of manumission meant to channel those libidos into productivity. Laws and edicts preceding the promulgation of the *Code Noir* grappled with how to regulate the inevitable sex acts inherent to slaveholding societies. These official proscriptions defined what, how, and with whom sexual acts could occur and still be of benefit to the reproduction of bondage and empire. European officials, slaveowners, travel writers, and missionaries also imagined, deliberated upon, and adjudicated black women's sexuality to create one that served the needs of slaveholding and colonial control. On one side of the Atlantic, in the "wickedness of *negresses*," as in the 1680 Guadeloupe edict, enslaved women became raced and gendered into categories of womanhood through their forced physical and reproductive labor and their presumed exorbitant heterosexual lust (for white men), a lust capable of producing both the spectacle of mixed-race offspring and an illicit desire for freedom. On the Senegambian side of the Atlantic, where commercial connections took primacy over plantation labor and enslaved property, Company officials could not use hereditary bondage, restrictions on manumission, or racial slavery to consolidate power. However, African women's culture of taste and intimate practices continued to be viewed as threatening to French commercial interests, and officials did their best to police all social boundaries between African and European.

By the 1720s, Company directors in France stepped in even further to prevent white employees from having inevitable social and intimate relations with the Africans around them. In 1721, Company regulations issued from France discouraged white and black residents from cross-gender socializing. Officials forbade commerce and intimate relations between African women and Company directors, prohibiting them from public concubinage, from "enjoying them" or "permitting any others to enjoy nor to debauch the women," lest they set a bad example for Company employees. Employees were prohibited from living with Africans or living away from a *comptoir*.[112] African men as well as women were barred from attending gatherings with white employees. Directors also forbade "cohabitating" with "the negresses," selling resident Africans across the Atlantic, or interracial socializing (drinking together, dancing).[113] These regulations failed in part because attempts to enforce them led to revolts among employees. Only a few years later, in 1724, and perhaps viewing such prohibitions as futile, Julien Dubellay, a commandant at Saint-Louis, suggested providing relief to employees. Of marriageable women at the *comptoirs*, he noted there were only "five young mulâtresses, twelve to fifteen years of age." Like Chambonneau, he asked Company directors in Paris to send young French women "not just for the captains of the ships and sailors but also for the workers and others." This, Dubellay argued, "would prevent young men from returning to France faster and get the good will of the sailors especially, who are needed for the trade."[114] Directors in France refused.

French officials' failure to stem *mariage à la mode du pays* as a practice increasingly became entangled with their perception of African women as libidinous and illicit. Into the 1730s, Company officials in France continued to suggest that preventing intimate relations between European men and African women would stop the contraband trade or "the particular commerce which the husbands will do much easier with the help of their wives and the contacts [their wives] have." By 1737, members of the Superior Council at Saint-Louis suggested lifting the prohibition on European and African intermarriages in part to allow the council to better legislate such commerce.[115] Lifting the ban would also promote Christian ideals of chastity and charity. For African women, "many women and girls would retire from the crime" of living in sin, and African men "would cease living off of the goodwill of the whites."[116] Council members added that lifting the ban would encourage good workers to settle down and remain in Senegal. The council finished by reassuring directors in France that they would "use all necessary discretion" when allowing marriages to proceed, to avoid allowing "bad subjects" to enjoy the privilege. The Company does not appear to have responded, but formal Catholic unions between whites and blacks appear to have been prohibited into the 1750s. Adanson commented that French men continued to be prevented from marrying the *négresses* or from bringing wives from France.[117]

For French officials, the culture of taste and hospitality African women maintained at the *comptoirs* was fraudulent and dangerous. African women cultivated and participated in a life at the *comptoirs* that was threatening because it exceeded official French control. That does not mean there was anything egalitarian or altruistic about this world. Free African women owned and relied on enslaved laborers, especially women, to maintain their standard of living. They remained subject to their husbands, fathers, and male heads of households. Enslaved women labored in excruciating ways with little recourse or relief. Social life at the *comptoirs* also owed much to the Atlantic slave trade, which attracted European traders to the coast with an array of goods for purchase. To the extent that a practice of freedom operated at the *comptoirs* in the first decades of French engagement, it did not manifest in manumission policies for those enslaved, which the French could not conceive of implementing. In a world where practices of patronage and kinship structured broad swaths of women's lives at all levels of society, freedom glimmered in their determination to define the terms of what intimacy and kinship could mean. In Senegambia, French officials confronted women who, to return to the wives of the Bambara soldiers, were free and were not going anywhere. Draped in madras cloth, African women continued to refuse formal Catholic marriage for another century, preferring rituals of partnership and households more attuned to their needs and aligned with those practiced in the country beyond the *comptoir.*

* * *

Over the course of the eighteenth century, at precisely the same moment the Atlantic trade began to speed forward, a woman-identified, water-based deity awoke. Named Maam Kumba Bang at Saint-Louis and Maam Kumba Castel at Gorée, these *rab* (or spirits) protected the coastal towns.[118] *Rab,* when manifested through spirit possession, were capable of pouring into their adherents an otherworldly womanhood so potent that men could become women when taken over by them.[119] By building *rab* altars, holding processions, and offering libations, residents could solicit supernatural favors on their behalf. Maam Kumba Bang and Maam Kumba Castel joined a coterie of spirits that came into existence at the crossroads of African and European interaction, in a moment when the protection of *gris-gris,* crosses, and *salaams* stopped being enough. It was no coincidence that these spirits of the Atlantic African zone were said to hold sway over the river and the ocean, the primary routes by which disruption and opportunity increasingly arrived at Saint-Louis and Gorée.

The forces that assailed the Atlantic African coast were so disruptive, confusing, titillating, and provocative, that residents of the coastal towns developed new spiritual powers to assist them in managing it. Atlantic trade at Saint-Louis and Gorée provided access to new forms of social capital. Women along the coast accessed this capital on terms familiar to their Senegambian context. At the same time, Atlantic commerce unleashed a spectrum of violence linked to enslaved status and European empire. At Saint-Louis and Gorée, African women, free and enslaved, found themselves drawn into complex webs of kinship that restrained and expanded. In the same decade that Catti modeled proper eating habits for Europeans, the king of France promulgated the 1685 *Code Noir,* creating formal categories of slave and free that would structure black life in parts of the Americas for generations to come. The French failed to consolidate colonial power at Saint-Louis and Gorée, but, in attempting to do so, French officials generated a discourse of anxieties as well as new methods for policing African women's intimate and kinship practices. These anxieties and methods would make their way across the ocean and reappear in locales far from Senegal's coast, in both the Caribbean and Gulf Coast Louisiana.

For women like Catti, the trader-hostess with whom this chapter began, freedom did not hold the same meanings it would for enslaved and free women of African descent in the Americas. But the practice of freedom engaged in by African women and women of African descent in the slaveholding societies of the Atlantic world began in exchanges like these on the Atlantic African coast. Women in coastal Senegambia engaged in practices of patronage and alliance with Europeans, but with a distinctly West African understanding of the meanings behind kinship, hospitality, marriage, property, and labor. In contrast, French officials, in France and in Senegambia, linked intimate and kinship relations between European men and African women directly to French colonial projects and the labor of managing empire. The French demographic minority limited official ability to shape a manumission policy or control the enslaved African population at Saint-Louis or Gorée. Slavery already existed along the coast and in the countryside, in a different form. Atlantic trade, however, still created a complex population at the *comptoirs* and along the coastline. As the eighteenth century proceeded, Africans along the coast would increasingly suffer gendered racial violence that looked more and more Atlantic than African in nature. In the years to come, living at the *comptoirs* meant contending with the intimate violence that Atlantic slaving and French imperial desires for conquest had unleashed.

Chapter 2

ↀ

Born of This Place:
Kinship, Violence, and the Pinets'
Overlapping Diasporas

Deposition de Marie Baude, femme du dit Pinet.
—"Affaire criminelle," mémoire, Saint-Louis, Senegal, 1724.

One June day in 1724, a Senegambian woman named Marie Baude stood before a court clerk, the former and current Company directors, and the governor of Fort Saint-Louis du Sénégal. It was an afternoon and these venerable French men called her before them to answer questions about a murder that had occurred the night before. According to several witnesses, her husband, Jean Pinet, a gunsmith for the Company stationed at Saint-Louis, killed a *mulâtre* sailor named Pierre LeGrain in their home.[1] It made sense that Marie Baude, as Jean Pinet's wife and a resident of the home where the murder occurred, would be asked to testify. Marie's testimony, however, offered few details of the night in question. She avoided incriminating her husband. Instead, she emphasized that she had been asleep when the entire affair occurred and therefore could not be of much aid. Her opaque witnessing occurred in the face of testimony suggesting Pierre LeGrain threatened or joked with Pinet that he would rape his wife, Marie. This threat led to his murder.

Marie Baude was part of a cohort of African women born of overlapping European and African Atlantics. As the eighteenth century dawned, women along the coast navigated multiple levels of power and threat in search of safety and security for themselves. Already a Senegal native, the daughter of a French man, and the wife of a white Company employee, Marie was also the potential victim of intimate violence and a reluctant participant in the inquest against her husband. She epitomized ways African women's practice of patronage and kinship indigenous to the continent confronted gendered racial violence generated at the epicenters of slave-trading outposts. African women at the *comptoirs* accessed a lucrative but dangerous world, one where kinship ties they forged existed alongside both the tumult of a coastal society still in the making and the intimate violences of the Atlantic world. As children, enslaved and free, male and female, began to be born at the *comptoirs*, a new generation emerged that had to navigate African practices of patronage and kinship in porous and tense ways.

Slaveowning and otherwise propertied women like Marie Baude accrued wealth and prestige, but the reality of life at the *comptoirs* remained patriarchal and hierarchical. Some women, as new mothers, godmothers, and witnesses, turned to Catholic baptism as a mechanism for creating and cementing kinship ties between each other. Others made claims of property and birthplace that affirmed their right to the fruits of African and European society, and their lives at the intersection of both. Still, even for women with property, the space they created for themselves sat at the intersection of French and Wolof patriarchal and hierarchical spheres of influence. Where sons born at the *comptoirs* might secure employment with the Company or in the river and coastal trades, options for African girls remained limited. Whether through Company officials, Wolof agents, or African or European husbands or brothers, control of resources continued to skew toward European and African men.

Slavery and the labor provided by slaves played a crucial role in African women's everyday experiences at Saint-Louis and Gorée. The labor engaged in by enslaved people, often women, shaped the livelihoods of slaveowning women on the coast by making their daily existence easier, increasing their wealth, and providing evidence of their status. Enslaved to residents of the *comptoirs*, women, children, and men were shielded from sale to the Americas. But slaveholding societies were inherently violent in myriad ways, and slaveowning African women at the *comptoirs* also enacted violence and extracted labor through violence against the slaves they owned. In the shadow of overlapping European and African Atlantics, enslaved and slaveowning women also overlapped and clashed in numerous quotidian ways—as the daughters and wives of African and European men, as property owners and heads of households, as unpropertied residents, as enslaved laborers, as *négresses* and *mulâtresses* (when described by French residents), and even as Catholics and *mahometantes* (Muslims). African feminist scholars, including Fatou Sow,

Ayesha Imam, and Aminata Diaw-Cisse, have noted that age, sex, status, ethnicity, religion, and position in society construct sex and gender, all shaping women's experiences in African societies.[2] In eighteenth-century Saint-Louis and Gorée, slavery, ethnicity, religion, gender, and even racial designation shaped women's everyday experiences, influencing how they would seek safety and security, who could be protected, and whose lives would be forfeited to the violence of the trade.

Anne of the River: Baptism in Senegal

At Saint-Louis and Gorée, African women and women of African descent left a documentary trail of their intimate and kinship networks as they submitted to and accessed civil registers. At times leaving their mark but more often allowing the officiant to serve as proxy when unable to sign or mark themselves, African women attested to the relationships they were part of. They recorded their names, race, ethnic designations, and religious affiliations. They marked or were marked as having free or enslaved status. As residents at the *comptoirs*, women appeared as mothers and godmothers, as wives, and as witnesses celebrating births or mourning deaths. The infrequency of formal Catholic unions and the prevalence of death among European men become clear as the entries marking deaths from sickness and drowning overcrowded marital unions. Like the presence of Catholic religious authority, the registers themselves were neither comprehensive nor consistent. This did not prevent them from exposing social interactions across gender, race, and status as they had salience to the women themselves.[3] Saint-Louis and Gorée parish registers illustrated webs of filial and intimate ties through marriage and godparentage that stretched across time and place.

Company officials attempted to institutionalize racial and sexual differences, passing ordinances and regulations they hoped would manage intimate and kinship practices across race, gender, status, and nation. They aimed for social control and economic expediency on their terms. They failed. By 1730 at Saint-Louis (1777 at Gorée), residents began documenting the extent of that failure in the *registres paroissiaux* (parish registers).[4] Alexis Périer de Salvert, commandant at Arguin and brother to Etienne Périer, the future governor of Louisiana, ordered parish registers created in 1721. The parish registers tracked births, deaths, and marriages among inhabitants at Saint-Louis and (later)

Gorée. The registers were to be sent back to Paris as part of official correspondence between the coast and the metropole.[5] In France, a representative of the Catholic Church, usually the *curé* (parish priest), would have compiled the registers, and registration would have accompanied rites of baptism.[6] However, no *curé* resided permanently at either Saint-Louis or Gorée until 1779. Religious authority was provided by itinerant missionaries, *cures* and *aumôniers* (chaplains) attached to the garrisons, and *curés* and *aumôniers* assigned to merchant vessels stopping to trade seasonally at the port.[7] When no religious authority was present, Company directors stepped in to register life events.

The majority of extant registrants received baptism at Saint-Louis, the seat of trading-company power along the coast for much of the eighteenth century. Between October 1730 and September 1735, sixty-three residents were baptized at Saint-Louis, fairly evenly distributed between those identified as female and those identified as male.[8] The vast majority of those baptized were born at or in close proximity to Saint-Louis. Three were listed as explicitly from Saint-Louis. Most registrants, especially those less than a day old when they were baptized at the "Church of Senegal," were listed as simply "born of this place" or "native to this place."[9] Some of the baptized were described as born or native "of Senegal," an identifier that encompassed Saint-Louis and Gorée, but might also have indicated birthplaces as far inland as Galam.

"Born of this place" marked a new category of inhabitant—a child indigenous to the *comptoirs* who would grow up in overlapping worlds. F. F. Carlton, as the chaplain at Saint-Louis, baptized Marie Jeanne, "native de Senegal," when she was twenty days old.[10] In April of 1732, Dominique Joseph Courbe, *aumônier*, baptized a fourteen-year-old boy from Galam "belonging to" M. Bergeron. A man named Benoitt stood as his godfather. A woman named Louison, described as a *mulâtresse*, stood as his godmother.[11] In at least one case, "born in Senegal" did not mean being of either black or African descent. Michel[le] Pierette, the daughter of Etienne le Prince, *garde magasin* for the company, and his wife, Marguerite Morel, a native of Paris, was baptized a week after her birth.[12] Of those baptized and listed without a birthplace or "native of" specified, two-thirds were slaves of or "belonged to" other residents.[13] Loss of kinship was one of the constituent elements of bondage in West Africa as well as in the Americas. This loss surfaced as missing and unmarked birthplaces and natal kin in the registers of the *comptoirs*.

Of those whose ages were recorded, the majority were infants and baptized when they were less than a year old, often at less than a month old. When Fr.

Dominique Courbe baptized Marie Anne, the "legitimate daughter" of Nicolas Grobert, *commis*, and his wife Anne Grobert, *"mulâtresse* and native de Senegal," she was only seven days old. Michelle, the natural daughter of Marie Bertiche, a *négresse chrestien* belonging to Mathurin La Place, a surgeon, was also only a month old when she was baptized. An elder Madame Michelle Bertine stood as godmother. Jeanne, the daughter of Catin Magdeline, a *mulâtresse chrestien* and "native de Senegal," belonging to Pierre Aubry, *garde magasin*, also received baptism in the month of her birth. Like Michelle and Jeanne, more than half of those baptized as infants less than a month old were also slaves or the children of slaves. Some of those baptized were identified as having either a mother or father described as *mahometant(e)*. The baptism record for Pierre, the slave of Charles Thevenot, listed him as the child of an unnamed black Muslim man and woman (*nègre and négresse mahometants*). Young adults were also baptized, but few adults or elders. One of the oldest was Anne, about seventeen years old, and the daughter of Mousée, a *nègre mahometant*. Anne Combaquerel, a *négresse chrestien*, was also baptized. Anne Cornier, the *mulâtresse* spouse of S. Jacques Arnaud, master of ships, and Monsieur Antoine LaMugre [*sic*], master of ships, stood as godmother and godfather.[14]

The men, women, and children receiving baptism at Saint-Louis and Gorée were not the first Catholics to reside at the *comptoirs* or along Senegal's coast. A century before, Alexis de Saint-Lo, a Capuchin priest, journeyed to "Cap-Verd" and baptized several dozen African-descended "Portugaise" men, women, and children at Rufisque.[15] Upon sailing within view of Rufisque, Saint-Lo described being welcomed by men and women in pirogues and leading them in Mass for the first time in eight years. The enthusiasm for Saint-Lo's visit, including receiving him with "great affection" and "kissing their robes," was led by two African women, Dame Philippa and Signoura Pascha. Philippa's home served as a makeshift chapel where the priest performed baptisms, including four godchildren sponsored by Philippa herself. In spaces like Rufisque, in the network of kinship, commerce, and community formed by Gorée, Joal, and Portudal, baptism would have been a familiar rite to experience, just as it would have been familiar to see an African woman in charge of organizing access to it, rallying community members, and sponsoring baptisms of her own.

The prevalence of baptism in the registers contrasts markedly from the absence of formal Catholic marriage as sanctioned and recorded at the *comptoirs*. From 1730 to 1819, thirty-one Catholic marriages were registered at Saint-Louis,

and from 1777 to 1824, there were only nineteen at Gorée.[16] Only two instances
of registered Catholic marriage appear in the first five years of Saint-Louis's
État Civil. One was the marriage of two white French residents. In June of 1731,
French carpenter Pierre Anger married Angelique Botteman, a French woman.
Angelique was the widow of Jean Boutilly, a soldier working for the Company
who died in Senegal. The second marriage joined the mason Louis Mambeau,
nègre chrestien, residing at Galam, with Louise Barthelemy, "native de Senegal."
Both marriages were remarkable in their own way. While no official barriers
existed barring French residents from marrying each other at the *comptoirs*,
the absence of European women along the coast made these rare. The second
marriage, while a marriage between two people of African descent, likewise
marks a remarkable union. In a world where many Africans continued to profess
if not practice variations of Islam, and where *mariage à la mode du pays* allowed
residents to create hybrid households of multiple faiths, it was unusual for
couples like Louis and Louise to choose to formalize a union with sacraments
and in the register.[17] Meanwhile, formal marriages across race continued to be
frowned upon.

Baptism and godparentage drew the few European and African women
into dense webs of kinship among each other, across the divides of culture,
race, ethnicity, and status. Pierre and Angelique's marriage may have been
unique in the register, but they too integrated themselves into existing kinship
networks. Five months after her first husband's death, Angelique had given
birth to a son. Friar F. Baston, then priest at Saint-Louis, baptized the boy as
Jacques Sebastien Boutilly.[18] Standing as godfather and godmother were
Jacques Collé, native of France, and Michelle Bertin, *mulâtresse*. This is the
same Michelle who sponsored the daughter of Marie Bertiche, the *négresse
chrestien* "belonging to" Mathurin La Place, *maître de barque* (Bertiche's daughter died only a few days later). In sponsoring Jacques, Michelle added the boy
to her filial responsibilities, the same obligations she extended to her other
godchildren. In choosing Michelle as godmother, Angelique requested Michelle
expend some of her patronage, labor, and resources on her son, Jacques, a
responsibility Michelle accepted.

Unlike West Central Africa, the Senegambian coast continued to be largely
Wolof and Muslim, identities that bled into the records of baptisms themselves.
Saint-Louis godmothers described or were described as *mulâtresse* and *négresse*,
at times with the qualifier *chrestien*, in the registers. Many had European first
names like Anne, Catherine, Marie, and Michelle. However, several of the

godmothers bearing witness also declared Senegambian second or third names. Magdelaine Hyacinthe Monbau, described as a *négresse* "native du Sénégal," sponsored multiple children: Françoise Madeleine, Magdeline, and Louise, a fifteen-year-old girl. Françoise Madeleine was the daughter of François Aubert, a Bambara Catholic, and Combagenne, a *négresse* of Senegal. Magdeline, the daughter of Guette, a *"mahometante"* belonging to André, a *nègre*, was the youngest, having been born less than a month before her baptism. Louise, the eldest, described as a *"fille libre,"* was the daughter of Amar Bingue and Siriag. Her godfather was Jacques François Aubert, a bookkeeper at Galam. Anne Monbouë, a *négresse chrestien* and the wife of the ship captain François Yaraso, agreed to be the godmother for Pierre. Pierre's mother and father were unnamed but described as *mahometants*.[19] It also appears that registrants, their parents, or their owners, if enslaved, were primarily choosing women of African descent as godmothers and white Company employees as godfathers. This pattern mirrors baptisms across the Atlantic in places like New Orleans where, during the second half of the eighteenth century, the goal may have been to "find godparents of equal or preferably higher status for their children and thereby gain privileges for those children."[20]

Despite the absence of Catholic marriage or *mariage à la mode du pays* across race in the registers, French authorities often recognized African women as spouses of French men. In 1733, Marie Thomas Larue (a surname that translated in English meant "the street") passed away. Born in Senegal, Marie Thomas Larue was the spouse of S. Larue, an *ancien capitaine* for years employed by the trading company on the coast. Well after Marie Thomas's death, the Larues continued to operate ships and manage trade across the *comptoirs* and *escales* of the region, even sending ships across the Atlantic as far as Louisiana and Saint-Domingue. If Friar Domingue Joseph Courbe balked at listing her as such, such reluctance was not reflected in the registry. Quite explicit instead was Marie Thomas's status as the wife either by sacrament or *à la mode du pays* of a well-known employee of the Company, the first *mulâtresse* to appear in the Saint-Louis death register interred with sacraments at Saint-Louis. Two years later, when Anne Larue, possibly either the daughter or sister of Marie Thomas, passed away at Saint-Louis, she too was interred with sacraments. Despite the lack of formal marriage records, officiants also recognized marriages by entering them into the registers as *fille legitimes*. Distinguished from *fille naturelle*, the designation of *fille legitime* acknowledged the marriages of the parents who produced the child at the baptismal font. Between only 1730 and 1735, officials recorded eleven children as *fille legitimes*, marking them as the children "born of this place" as well as the product of formal Catholic marriages or *mariages à la mode du pays*.[21]

Women with property and status used baptisms to broaden their kinship networks; witnessing and sponsoring baptisms was part of a growing free African community. Anne Larue not only sponsored godchildren of her own, but also appeared as a witness before multiple baptisms of enslaved girls and boys of multiple ages. According to the records that have survived, she was the most active participant in baptisms in 1730s Saint-Louis. Anne Larue signed her name as a witness at eleven baptisms, and she sponsored, as godmother, four others, before she passed away in 1735. Sponsoring multiple children was not uncommon for African godmothers at Saint-Louis during the eighteenth century and may have accompanied communal and kinship responsibilities to those baptized, as well as signaled increased wealth in people and dependents.[22] However, how exactly godparents and their godchildren socialized remains obscured by the imperial archive. If godparentage and baptism practices mirrored those in eighteenth-century Catholic societies in the Americas, sponsorship placed a heady responsibility on godparents. In the French Antilles, godparents played a role in protecting and supporting godchildren, making baptism a point of contention for slaveowners who worried that it might facilitate manumission.[23] Along the Gulf Coast, baptism and godparentage created similar fictive kinships between white and free woman of color sponsors and enslaved or free children of color.[24] Even as baptism created a cohort of sponsors with distinct responsibilities, it did not entail a wholesale adoption of Catholicism by residents of the *comptoirs*, particularly at Saint-Louis. As late as the 1780s, African women and men at Saint-Louis baptized children and adults, and even went to Mass, but continued to marry *à la mode du pays*, practice Islam, and carry *gris-gris* and otherwise combined systems of belief as they saw fit.[25]

Practices of patronage and kinship, as well as precarity along the coast, may have encouraged women like Anne Larue to view godparentage as a useful supernatural and social tool for claiming kin. Anne Larue, like Marie Thomas, joined the small cohort of women who sponsored baptisms in early eighteenth-century Saint Louis. Anne Bertin sponsored three children over the course of one year; Michelle Bertin sponsored five. Magdelaine Hyacinthe Monbau sponsored three along with Marie Baude and Marie Marguerite Morel, the wife of M. le Prince, *garde magasin*. Catin Magdeline and Marie Bartheleme each sponsored two children. Other women stood as godmothers only once. Whether once or multiple times, it is important to understand Catholic baptism at Saint-Louis and Gorée during these years as an unusual practice. Saint-Louis and Gorée remained heavily Muslim, a phenomenon that revealed itself even in the baptism registers as Senegambian *chrestiens* sponsored *mahometant* baptisms. The incidence of baptism and salience of Catholic identity would change by the end of the century particularly among male and female *habitants* or householders, and emerge as a strategy for endogamous community formation.[26] During these first decades of the eighteenth century, to cement and create a variety of kinship ties, this small cohort of African women stood before an itinerant chaplain and used baptism and godparentage in a context where such rituals were not commonplace. The kinships they created spanned gender, status, and religion, as well as race.

Drawn into this community of accountability and patronage were those listed as *mahometants*: African women, children, and men who espoused Islam. How willingly *mahometant* mothers and fathers resorted to baptizing their children remains unclear, but several selected godparents from among residents with Catholic and Islamic designations. Anne sponsored Jeanne, the daughter of Senegal *mulâtresse* Catin Magdeline; Hiarac, the ten-year-old son of Hiarac and Circa, *mahometants* of Senegal; and Olimpiate Radegonde, daughter of Catherine Andrieu and Jean Jacques Souttron, a Company medic.[27] Christine Barthelome, *négresse libre*, sponsored Anne Magdeline Christine, daughter of Samague and Cafsou. Her father, Cafsou, declared he was a *mahometant*.[28] The children themselves exhibited the increasing racial and cultural fusion occurring at the *comptoirs*. Anne Cornier, *mulâtresse* and wife of a shipmaster named Jacques Arnaud, sponsored Anne, the daughter of Mousée, a *nègre mahometant*, and Anne Combaquerel, a *négresse chrestien*.[29] Marie Bartheleme was the godmother of Barbe, daughter of Mathilde who was a *négresse mahometante* and a slave belonging to Louison Marcher.[30]

Whether by choice or coercion, enslaved children and adults also experienced baptism. Pierre, for instance, a slave when he was baptized, was the child of Muslim parents. He was sponsored by Anne Mamboué, a Catholic *négresse*, and Charles Thevenot, a *mulâtre* sailor. Thevenot, his godfather, would become one of the leaders of the *habitant* community on the island, going on to marry Marie-Isabelle Baude, a *mulâtresse*.[31] By 1779, they would stand as witnesses at the marriage of their son, Jean-Jacques Thevenot, to Marie Madeleine Estoupan de St. Jean, the daughter of Blaise Estoupan de St. Jean, the former governor of Gorée, and Louison Kiaka, his spouse *à la mode du pays*. As influential as this household became, Pierre's status in it and in relation to the Thevenots' as a slave and godchild disappears from the written record. Pierre's disappearance and silence speak to the relevance baptism may have had at the *comptoirs*. Catholic baptism may have been wielded by owners as a performance or practice of faith they intended to extend to their slaves. It also may have been less a ritual of faith and more an act of power they imposed upon some or all of their dependents—captives, servants, or domestics. Some may have been targeted because of their identification with Islam. It even may have been requested by those enslaved as a way to create a powerful link to an influential family. Whatever the reason, infants and children from an array of backgrounds were brought by their mothers, fathers, owners, and guardians to the chapel at Saint-Louis. An intentional decision, baptism created new patrons and kin indigenous to the overlapping Atlantics the *comptoirs* resided in. Although a small group, the ramifications of belonging and not belonging to these networks would emerge decades later in the ascendance of *signares*, *habitants*, and *métis* as stakeholders in the region.

Residents also chose to baptize their slaves, although not every resident or every slave.[32] At the *comptoirs*, compulsory baptism did not exist for those enslaved as it did in the Americas. Sacred authorities made baptism accessible to everyone, free or enslaved. Some African residents, primarily women, may have used baptism to enhance their status and assert their power as heads of households and managers of dependents. Mothers and fathers without property, as well as mothers and fathers of enslaved children, appeared before officials to have their newborns baptized. Baptism did not ameliorate the experience of slavery on the African coast. But as the *comptoirs* became a crossroads for African women, men, and children of different origins, propertied and unpropertied, for enslaved and free, for those allied with Europeans, and for those with stronger ties to the countryside, baptism offered residents a way to organize kinship from within the overlapping Atlantics. In other words, some may have chosen baptism as a protective metaphysical device and mechanism for claiming patrons or kin at the *comptoirs* itself.

Baptism did not create egalitarian ties between residents. It could not, for instance, compensate for fissures between African women who had disparate social statuses as Atlantic African society formed at Saint-Louis and Gorée. Anne, for instance, sponsored multiple children, but she did not or was not asked to sponsor the children of her own slaves, Alquemon and Bassé.

Alquemon became pregnant while hired to Charles Thevenot, and Catin Magdeline, a *mulâtresse,* sponsored her daughter Angelique.[33] Bassé, who became
pregnant in the service of M. Aubrey, a *garde magasin,* had Marie-Isabelle Baude
godmother her son Louis.[34] Through the 1730s, African women used Catholic
ritual to cement intimacies and create new kinships, but these ties also occurred
and were invoked within the bounds of slavery.

Born of This Place: Property and Kinship in Atlantic Africa

While baptism offered one mechanism for staking kinship claims to the people
and places of the coast, property and inheritance offered another. Anne Bertin's
mother owned enough slaves to concern the Superior Council. As a *négresse,*
"quite advanced in age," Anne owned or was in possession of several slaves left
in her possession by her daughters, Anne and Michelle. Michelle lived at Saint-
Louis. She was the widow of Pierre Le Luc and godmother to several of the
island's children: two slaves named Charles and Louis, and Michelle, the
daughter of the Catholic *négresse* Marie Bertiche. Anne, second only to her
sister in numbers of godchildren, had moved to France to live with her husband,
Nicolas Grobert. Anne Bertin, their mother, lived at Gorée with the slaves
under dispute. According to Michelle and Anne, the slaves laboring for their
mother belonged to them. They reported that "some of the slaves were given"
to one daughter as part of her marriage contract, and "others were acquired
later." The council, however, could not determine who owned which slaves and
when the property came into their possession. Unable to establish provenance,
they refused to confirm that all of Anne Bertin's property could pass on to her
daughters.[35] Instead, the council wrote to France, expressing its confusion
about how to divide the property and whether it could confiscate any enslaved
property at all. In addition to the Bertin-Groberts, the council reported that
"there are a number of other women here with bastard children and it has
been the practice of the Company to let them inherit the property of their
mothers."[36]

African widows of deceased Company employees built significant legacies
out of retaining the property of their husbands, and they did so in the face of
Company resistance. Initially, trading-company officials accepted that women
would inherit husbands' property, even providing back wages to widows. After
Pierre Charron, a sailor working for the Company at Saint-Louis, passed away,

his daughter, Marie Charron, *mulâtresse*, received his wages. Marie Thereze Yecam Semaine, *négresse*, received back wages after her husband, Joseph de Gorée, a *maître de barque*, passed away.[37] In 1734, as part of a new set of regulations, officials declared that persons who died while employed by the Company must "give up their effects that are not declared."[38] Two years later, the Superior Council at Saint-Louis asked Company directors in France to confirm the rules on inheritance, stating that it was customary for the wives and lovers of employees and their children to inherit any of the employees' effects. Company directors in France did not agree. The Company refused to allow the illegitimate children of employees to inherit property, stating that the effects of men who died in Senegal should go to their closest living relatives, not to their "bastards." After 1736, directors encouraged Company officials at Gorée and Saint-Louis to confiscate the goods of those who died, including any slaves, and credit the heirs with items of equal value. However, holding African women to Company standards on the ground remained a struggle.[39]

As women at the *comptoirs* defied French patriarchal definitions of inheritance and descent, they resisted Company attempts to bar them from claiming their property. Married *à la mode du pays*, women entered into alliances and exchanges of property defined by Wolof and Lebu custom between husbands-to-be and their fathers.[40] Although negotiated by men, property proceeded by matrilineal descent; in other words, property and goods brought into the marriage by the wife, and any accrued during the marriage, passed on to her kin, not to her husband's family.[41] As European fathers of African daughters passed away or departed the coast, just as the role of head of household fell to wives left behind, the role of negotiator and defender of property fell to mothers left to lead their homes.

For women like Anne Gusban, property and its legacy played a crucial role in how they defined their womanhood at the *comptoirs* as well as how they survived as heads of households on a patriarchal coast.[42] In 1737, Anne Gusban, a Gorée *négresse*, petitioned Company officials to reinstate her daughter Anne's inheritance. The Compagnie des Indes (Company of the Indies) employed Anne's father, Gusban, a *mulâtre anglois* sailor, on trade and travel along the Gambia River.[43] Gusban named ten-year-old Anne as his beneficiary. Among Gusban's effects was a seventeen-year-old girl, an older woman, and a young boy, all slaves. The Council of Gorée confiscated the slaves and compensated the Gusbans with glass jewelry, but Anne declared these substitutions "*marchandises basses*," worthless compared to the slaves themselves. Anne asked the

Company to return her daughter's slaves or replace the confiscated slaves with ones of equal value. Anne also accused the Company of preferential treatment, arguing that officials allowed white employees to pass property to their mixed-race children without dispute. "Under what pretext," she admonished, "would you take the slaves of my daughter for the company[?]"[44]

Anne Gusban justified her request by stating that Gusban's legacy was her daughter's birthright—both as his daughter and as a resident of Gorée. "My daughter," she wrote, "is born of this place; it is not the same with the whites who come to serve the company and who are not forbidden from keeping their slaves[?]; her father gave you good service, Messieurs."[45] Anne Gusban identified her daughter and her deceased partner as productive members of Gorée society. Free African women were also aware of the important role that residents of color played in trade and defense at the *comptoirs*. In a subtle warning, Anne Gusban suggested it would be best if the company respected African property and inheritance rights or "we will be unable to tell the countryside that the company is not just like the Roy Damel [the king of the Wolof] who is in favor of pillaging." In other words, Gusban mounted her petition against the Company by positioning herself as a strategic countervailing force on behalf of the Company and against Wolof interests, a client who could claim that her patron—the Company—did not pillage, steal, or betray its subjects. Gusban demanded redress through the strategic position she and others like her had cultivated along the coast as intermediaries between the Europeans and Wolof, as "born of this place," a space of overlapping Atlantics. Its nativist and assertive tone directly challenged any myths the Company or Company directors held about the stability of their own authority over the coast.

At the same time, inherited property and wealth also deepened divisions among residents at Saint-Louis and Gorée. Contests over property ownership and succession demonstrated how vulnerable slaves and free Africans without property could be. In 1736, an unnamed slaveowning *négresse chrestien* died at Saint-Louis. She did not have any known heirs but she left behind seven slaves and at least one dependent, an unnamed *négresse affranchie* (freed woman of color). The Company did not consider this unnamed free woman of color her next of kin, but they did not disinherit her completely. Company officials confiscated five of the deceased's slaves and sold them into the Atlantic trade. Two of the slaves, described by officials as "defective," were left in the hands of the *négresse affranchie* and the matter appeared to be settled. (It is unclear what became of the deceased woman's home.) A year later, however, this

Saint-Louis *négresse* risked losing her property when Antoine Grenier, the deceased woman's grandson and a *mulâtre* living in Nantes, wrote to the director-general to claim his inheritance.[46] Unlike Anne Gusban, this *négresse affranchie* did not lose her slaves. The Company credited Grenier 1,560 livres for the five slaves it confiscated and sold, and it made no mention of the slaves left with the *négresse affranchie*. The Company also noted that it was compensating Grenier "per the custom on this coast." The *négresse affranchie* remained at Saint-Louis. With the death of the *négresse chrestien*, she may have found herself without a patron and, as a result, without any means of support. The Company allowed the unnamed *négresse affranchie* to keep the two least healthy slaves, but if she lacked other kin or a community to return to, life would have been difficult for her. Without enslaved labor, servants, or other dependents, free Africans could not claim elite status and would likely have to labor for themselves.

Slaveownership distinguished propertied women from unpropertied women of African descent in critical ways. Slaveownership played a critical role in free African women's ability to manage Saint-Louis's and Gorée's households. At Saint-Louis and Gorée, African women played a critical role facilitating trade between Europeans and the Wolof kingdoms of Waalo, Kajoor, and Bawol on the mainland, but their role required hard labor. The work engaged in by women ranged from provisioning Company employees and slaves, to securing slaves awaiting transit to the Americas, to maintaining fortifications and sailing vessels. As the residential population on the islands grew, cleaning, cooking, washing, chopping wood, and drawing water became daily concerns.[47] While African and Afro-European women with slaves became known for the culture of taste and displays of hospitality shaping life at the *comptoirs*, those without slaves, servants, or households labored alongside enslaved women as bakers, cooks, gardeners, laundresses, nurses, seamstresses, and general domestics.[48] The most grueling labor—grinding millet, laundering, or cooking—were the primary occupations of enslaved African women and other women unable to defer such labor to their female slaves.[49]

Bertin, Gusban, and unnamed slaveowning women like the *négresse affranchie* pressured Company officials, case by case and example by example, to adhere to *comptoir* custom over metropolitan policy. Precariously balanced between Wolof and French systems of legacy and partnership, between propertied and unpropertied livelihoods, African women at the *comptoirs* would have witnessed a system that could work for them as readily as it could work

1. *Negresse esclave*.   3. *Marabou ou Prêtre du Pays*.
2. *Signare de l'Isle St Louis*.   4. *Negre armé en Guerre*.

Figure 5. Published in 1789, Dominique Lamiral's narrative of his time on the Senegambian coast included depictions of the types of Africans he encountered: (1) A *négresse esclave* (black female slave), (2) a *signare* of Saint-Louis, (3) a *marabout* or "priest of the country," and (4) an African man armed for war. Lamiral, *L'Affrique et le peuple affriquain* (Paris: chez Dessene, 1789). According to scholar George Brooks, this is the earliest known representation of a *signare*. Courtesy of the Schomburg Center for Research in Black Culture, Manuscripts, Archives and Rare Books Division, New York Public Library.

against their favor. Company officials honored specific inheritance requests while creating policy meant to divest African women at Saint-Louis and Gorée of inherited property, evidencing the limits of French imperial power in an African context. Wolof ties to the *comptoir* operated, in part, through female heads of households and traders, but their marriages to European men may have made it difficult for them to remarry into their home communities if they lost their wealth.[50] More important, with Company employment available to their sons, mothers required property to forge new marriages of property and opportunity for their daughters. These contradictions reveal some of the precarity of African women's power as heads of households, wives, and mothers. African women used and relied on intimate and kinship ties to build wealth in commercial ties and in links to other residents, husbands, communities farther from the coast, and dependents and laborers. This wealth offered real protection against the uncertainties of the Atlantic world, but retaining one's position required creativity, determination, and persistence. The Company's attempts to take property, particularly enslaved property, threatened to leave women at the mercy of wealthier residents, Company employee predations, and, possibly, the Atlantic slave trade itself.

For enslaved women, these complicated dynamics of kinship and bondage within households at Saint-Louis and Gorée meant the Company's decision to sell residents' slaves across the Atlantic impacted the women directly. Ranging from forty years of age to only five, the slaves belonging to the original *négresse chrestien* represented property lost as well as the dissolution of a kinship unit. In 1758, Michel Adanson provided a snapshot of the complicated households at the *comptoirs*. He observed that African boys hired out to the Company as sailors and laborers were treated as free, regardless of whether their mothers were slaves. As long as their fathers were French, he remarked, they were considered "masters."[51] He also described the households of thirteen of the wealthiest free African residents of Gorée.[52] In these compounds, free African women managed women, men, and children of all statuses.

The household of Gracia, a thirty-five-year-old *négresse*, was the only one explicitly *sans enfants*. At least one of the thirteen householders supported elders as well. Penda Kassano, a forty-five-year-old *mulâtresse*, lived in a brick house with her mother and her grandmother, a *négresse* about seventy-five years old. Charlotte Mulâtresse's household included her daughter Angelique and her son-in-law Louis Kabass, a skipper. Few men appeared in Adanson's estimation. At least one of the men, Fatiman Nègre, had two wives. These

Figure 6. Interior of a home at Gorée, 1859. Sketched by E. de Bérard for "Voyages et Expéditions au Sénégal et dans les contrées voisines," *Tour du Monde*, 1859, p. 33. Courtesy of the Bibliothèque nationale de France, Paris.

households employed between six to twenty slaves, often with more than one owner between them. The slaves in Maria Teresa's household were split between herself, Isabel Morin, and Terese Duma. Finally, Adanson also counted about thirty "interloper or refugee" women, children, and men residing among the householders, seeking protection from a range of ills.[53] As heads of households or *habitants*, free African women understood retaining property as the key to wealth accumulation, but it was also the root of family security.

Of the households noted by Adanson, ten were headed by women, three by men. Only six lived with their own sons or daughters, but almost all of Gorée's prominent female householders supported either their own or someone else's children. The women running these households would have relied on enslaved and other dependent labor. When Jacques Doumet de Siblas described the black population of Gorée as having "hardly any masters or heads of households," save "the women [*maîtresses*] who are called by the Portuguese name *Signara*," he was describing expansive, multigenerational households like these.[54] In 1779, four of the five largest slaveowners on the island were African women: Louison Kiaka, Marie Yasin Sade, Marie Gonefall, and Suzanne d'Etegueye. Each owned twenty or more slaves, except Louison Kiaka, who owned forty-six. The fifth, "the habitants Pellegrin," was likely the Pellegrin family.[55] An image of a Gorée household created a century later and accompanying a French travel journal captured both the urbanization that would occur on the island over time and the continued use of enslaved and dependent labor by free African woman householders (see Figure 6). The *comptoirs*, as Mark Hinchman noted, were lands of women and "the fact that she [the *signare*] is not working indicates her status," selling, at the same time, a fantasy of decadence to European readers.[56]

Marie Baude, la Femme Pinet

When Marie Baude's husband killed a man of color, he placed her safety and security, her household and her property, at risk. Testimony about the event varied but the broad outline of the evening was clear. While at the house drinking with a couple of sailors, Jean was joined by Pierre LeGrain, a *mulâtre* sailor. One witness claimed he had "half a bottle of eau de vie" (the alcohol of the coast) in his hand. The group of men engaged in drinking and the expected frivolity of a playful evening. At some point, tempers ran high and conversation between Jean and Pierre grew heated. The conflict culminated in Pierre making a sexual boast or threat against Marie Baude and her sister, still living at Gorée. André, a twelve-year-old "nègre Chrestien et Portugais" and Jean Pinet's slave, offered the most colorful testimony. André testified that Pierre LeGrain "told Pinet, in the presence of two other sailors, he intends to f—— his wife and f—— his sister-in-law at Gorée."[57] The missing verb is *foutre*, a slang term for sexual intercourse and apparently inappropriate enough to discourage the clerk from writing it out in full. The verb used by the clerks in André's testimony was *vouloir*, which makes it difficult to read the level of aggression of LeGrain's words. If translated as "intends to," it could also be read as a "wish," a "desire," or as a "will," each reading changing the level of the threat. However, none of these nuances change the fact that LeGrain made a sexually threatening remark directed at Jean Pinet's wife and sister-in-law, a remark meant to be understood as at the expense of and threatening the manhood of Jean Pinet himself. Likewise, the potential for violence on Marie Baude suffuses LeGrain's remark.

Pierre and Jean fought. Jean eventually gained the upper hand. He kicked Pierre several times before taking up one of the swords lying around the forge and striking the sailor down. He left Pierre for dead "in the doorway of his forge" while he relocated with his guests to the hospital "to continue drinking." When asked if Pinet knew before he left that Pierre LeGrain was dead or dying, André stated, "He heard Pierre LeGrain cry out, 'Mon Dieu, je suis mort,'" at the same time Pinet left the house for the hospital with the two sailors. LeGrain said it once more and then stopped responding. Another witness, who came across the body, when he went to visit the house later that night, rushed to find Jean at the hospital. He informed him that "there is a dead person sprawled in [the] door of his forge." According to this witness, Jean responded with a curt, "It is just a *mulâtre*, I'm not very bothered by it."[58]

Unlike other witnesses, Marie Baude offered few clarifying details. Her most revealing answers were included in her biography. For the record, Marie stated her full name, that she was *la femme de dit Pinet*, twenty-three years old, and from Joal, an *escale* south along the coast from Gorée. As soon as officials began their questioning, Marie Baude stated she had gone to bed before the murder occurred and slept through most of the night's events. She repeated this claim throughout the interrogation. She offered no clear information about the timing of events and the nature of the violence that had occurred.[59] She claimed not to know that her husband had killed anyone or anything about any injuries he incurred. She also claimed to know nothing about the individuals involved. She was aware an insult had been offered, but she described the comment made against both her and her sister as "a matter of little consequence." André's testimony, in contrast, suggested Marie Baude was in fact awake. When asked if Marie Baude wished to oppose her husband, André stated she did wish to but Jean paid her no mind (*le mary n'enossa sa femme*). Historians of Atlantic slavery have described how women of African descent used silence and dissemblance to avoid being forced to testify before slaveowners and representatives of the state.[60] Although at different times and places, such parallels may speak to the critical role silence played in encounters between women of African descent, colonial officials, and imperial authorities.

Jean Pinet hailed from Rochefort, France, one of several French towns that became active Atlantic hubs during the late seventeenth and early eighteenth centuries. Rochefort was one of several coastal towns involved in the Atlantic trade, among them La Rochelle, Rouen, Dieppe, Nantes, and Bordeaux. Rochefort, however, was unique. In the 1670s, Rochefort joined Brest as one of two naval centers established specifically for the purpose of supporting France's military interests at sea. His service with the Company brought him to the islands of Saint-Louis and Gorée on the Senegal coast.[61] Jean, arriving from Rochefort, first found work at Gorée, where his training as an artisan earned him a modest income and some small distinction within the island's labor hierarchy.[62] Jean was the only gunsmith employed at Gorée, a lucrative position that may have played a role in the connection he made with a young woman named Marie Baude, described only as "the daughter of S. Baude."[63] By 1721, thirty-two-year-old Jean was married to then eighteen-year-old Marie in a ceremony at Gorée.[64] While details about S. Baude remain to be uncovered, Marie's father was wealthy enough to give the officiant a fourteen-year-old slave named Gabriel Manuel "in recognition of the celebration of the marriage of his daughter with le. Sr. Jean Pinet, gunsmith."[65]

Over the next few years, Jean Pinet and Marie Baude moved from Gorée to Saint-Louis, at the mouth of the Senegal River, where Jean continued to serve as gunsmith. The Wolof kingdoms of Kajoor, Bawol, and Waalo claimed jurisdiction over Saint-Louis and other trading points along rivers and the coast.[66] The *damels* controlled trade in the region and blocked French traders from extending their influence beyond the coast and rivers. Wolof officials rented the islands of Saint-Louis and Gorée to trading companies, and they charged at all of the trading posts for provisions like millet, water, and firewood. Intermediaries exacted annual tribute and duties on individual goods, including slaves.[67] Gorée too fell under Wolof administration. From Gorée, merchants traded with the coastal *escales* or unfortified posts at Rufisque, Portudal, and Marie's native Joal. The *escales* bordered the states of Kajoor, Bawol, and Siin, primarily, all Wolof principalities, all connected through economic and social ties to administrators, traders, and residents at the other *comptoirs* and *escales*. Meanwhile, French officials attempted, with meager regiments of two or three dozen soldiers and other employees like Jean Pinet, to occupy Saint-Louis and Gorée.

As *comptoirs* at the intersection of African and European imperial rivalries, the threat of raids or outright warfare loomed constantly, with a special impact on women. In 1729, the governor at Gorée raided Joal "to avenge the constant insults that the blacks of that district carried out against the French." When

Table 1. Troop Population at Gorée, 1692–1776

Year	Regiment	Officers
1692	35	—
1723	10 to 40	—
1725	25	1
1734	40	—
1736	39	—
1741	112	—
1755	40	—
1758	210	7
1763	126	6
1767	100	—
1774	100	—
1776	100	3

Source: Adapted from Marie-Hélène Knight-Baylac, "La vie à Gorée de 1677 à 1789,"
Revue française d'histoire d'Outre-Mer 57, no. 4 (1970): 388.
Note: A dash indicates that data did not exist or were unavailable.

the Gorée contingent arrived, the French burned all of the houses. As they
retreated in apparent success, the French were ambushed in a Joal counterattack that killed several, including the governor himself. French survivors captured were ransomed to the Company of the Indies for, among other things,
the equivalent of the powder and balls the French had used and stolen in their
raid.[68] The defense of Joal would be a success, but the loss of homes, the threat
of future retaliations, and the terror of the attack would linger. Women, as
managers of households, dependents, and slaves, would bear the brunt of the
everyday labor of reconstituting homes and family in the face of raids such as
this one.

Marie Baude joined a networked community increasingly "born in this
place," united by *mariage à la mode du pays* and baptism, and spread across race
as well as status.[69] Despite French officials' attempts to regulate and segregate,
Company employees hired women from the mainland to work as domestics,
cooks, laundresses, and millet pounders. Women appeared on census rolls as
bakers, gardeners, cooks, and healers.[70] The Company purchased some provisions from the *damels* and received meager supplies from France, but African
women formed impromptu markets near the main fort and in villages around
the island.[71] Interracial socializing also continued to occur. Men like Jean Pinet

and Pierre LeGrain interacted across cultural, ethnic, and even language differences, united by *eau de vie* and the monotony of military life in a Company
town. Whether Marie's relationship with Jean enriched her with property and
status or vice versa remains unclear. But by 1724, Jean and Marie lived in a
house with a forge where Jean could do his work, and they owned at least two
slaves—a twelve-year-old boy named André, described as a *Portuguais nègre*
Christian, and a twenty-two-year-old slave named Basil, described as from
"Gambia."[72] By the 1730s, a second Marie Baude, born at Gorée and possibly
the *mulâtresse* sister of Jean Pinet's wife referenced by Pierre LeGrain, was also
living at Saint-Louis. She sponsored multiple godchildren, including Catherine,
the child of André Stuard Calfat, *nègre libre*, and Guette, a *mahometante*. She
also stood as godmother for Marie, the daughter of Fatimah, a *mahometante*
slave, and Charles, a slave belonging to Sebastien Devaulx, a Company director
at Saint-Louis.[73]

Even in these networks, African women at the *comptoirs* remained subject
to fathers, husbands, and local officials. For Marie Baude and others, their
status as wives, daughters, heads of households, or laborers existed in uneasy
tension with patriarchal domestic arrangements. In 1722, Samba Bambara, a
former interpreter working for the Compagnie des Indes at Galam, asked Pierre
Charpentier, the Company director there, to "prevent the marriage of his wife
Yeram-Galé with the *marabout* of Grande-Terre." If Yeram-Galé, who resided
at Saint-Louis, was "absolutely set on it," Samba Bambara asked Charpentier
to "cast her from the island, along with a half blind slave woman who belongs
solely to her." The rest of her possessions, Samba Bambara claimed, "should
remain because they belong to him."[74] Samba Bambara was a longtime employee
of the Company, and Charpentier agreed to do what he could. As a result, both
Yeram-Galé, who may have been free, and her female slave faced expulsion.
Free African women, less likely to hold social or political positions in relation
to the Company that might make them indispensable in the ways men like
Samba Bambara had made themselves, lived precarious lives as well. At the
same time, the half-blind, enslaved woman owned by Yeram-Galé, as a result
of her bonded status, found herself subject to her owner's misfortune, her
existence as property leaving her vulnerable and with little to no recourse.

Yeram-Galé found the options available to her remained limited. The labor
her husband engaged in for the Company made him a resource. The claims of
a former employee and intermediary like Samba Bambara meant more to the
Company than a wife in her position. She simply did not have as much value

to the Company as Samba Bambara. Intimate labor, free African women like Yeram-Galé found, resided on a spectrum of coercion and volition that still left them with fewer options than the men around them. As Anne Gusban and other women discovered, despite the fluidity of *mariage à la mode*, which allowed women to marry serially as employees, soldiers, and traders died or departed, their husbands' disappearance and reassignment to other parts of the empire disrupted their lives, threatened their property, and, in doing so, complicated the security of their status as wives and as free. Company officials also exercised the power to evict African women from their homes, destroy their markets, and expel them from the island, acts that may have been part of what Anne Gusban had at stake when she formed her defiant petition.[75] They could be "put in irons" if they displeased Company officials, a fate that befell the "wife of Portail" who "had some differences" with a *négresse mahometante* and "one other creature who were in good graces" of the Company director.[76] These desertions, deportations, and detentions perpetuated the vulnerability of women and their households.

In addition, African women's ownership of domestic slaves, whom they baptized, hired out, and used in their own households, expressed its own character of dominance and violence. Slavery played a significant role in women's everyday life on the island. For enslaved women and women without slaves of their own, the everyday labor of cooking, cleaning, and maintaining households at the *comptoirs* subsumed their daily lives. Women's lives at Saint-Louis, Gorée, and *escales* along the coast were grueling. Owning slaves allowed women of African descent to release themselves from household labor. Slaveowning African women earned income by hiring their slaves to the trading companies and to Company employees for domestic labor. Slaves also served as conspicuous markers of wealth and status, as Seignora Catti demonstrated in her performance of hospitality with Barbot, and they distinguished slaveowning women as property owners and women of distinction. The possibility and economies of sexual labor could not be separated from domestic labor as employers demanded companionship and physical work from those they hired out. Women like Catti appropriated women's sexual labor for service, and the performance of pleasure necessary to hosting and accommodating strangers.

When free Africans hired enslaved African women out as slaves to other households on the island, those who were hired faced threats and expectations of sexual engagement. Abla, a *mahometante* and slave of Marie Harnagey, was hired out to Charles Thevenot, *mulâtre*, a sailor and Company employee. At some point during her time with him, Thevenot and Abla's relationship became intimate. Abla eventually conceived a daughter by him. She named her Anne.[77] She had at least one other daughter by him. Both were recognized by their father and baptized. Abla did not become a spouse of Thevenot and does not appear to have been freed. Whether in acts of violence, coercion, or volition, if constrained, on Abla's part, enslaved women engaged in sex as part of the daily reality of forced labor. To add to the complexity, the ritual of baptism created a kinship tie of a different kind between Abla, her child, and the child's father, Thevenot.

Enslaved women faced coercion and violence of all kinds, including the kind of intimate violence implied in Jean Pinet's criminal case. A year after LeGrain was killed, a soldier named La Vigne raped and beat a young *négresse* slave belonging to the *mulâtresse* wife of one of the shipmasters. La Vigne was thrown into irons and sentenced to *passer par les baquettes*, a kind of military gauntlet, "as an example for all others."[78] That he was brought to justice may have been the result of her owner's appeal and her marital ties to one of the shipmasters. Enslaved women's everyday experiences served as a stark reminder of the multifarious meanings underlying slave and free on the island. For some, but not all, African wives, their status may have afforded them certain protections. In 1685, while touring the Gambia, Michel Jajolet de la Courbe recorded the tale of an Englishman, Captain Hodges, who killed the child of a woman he was living with. According to La Courbe, Hodges was jealous that the baby his wife gave birth to was black. Enraged, he crushed it in a mortar and fed it to dogs. The violent captain would not leave her, however, "because she had brought much wealth [to the marriage] and, moreover, she was his wife *á la mode du pays*."[79] Whether this account turned out to be true in part or in full, Jean's own act of murder and his dismissive regard of LeGrain's dead body on the grounds that it was "just a mulâtre," suggests its own deeply problematic, racialized, and hierarchical claim on Marie Baude. Jean's violent intent would have been symptomatic of broader trends at the *comptoir* and along the coast.

In the aftermath of the investigation, Jean was found culpable for LeGrain's death. He expressed some protest over the proceedings by refusing to sign his testimony, but, signature or not, Jean was deported from Saint-Louis on *L'Esperance*. He was consigned to prison in Nantes. In official documentation, the Company director at Saint-Louis expressed regret for his role in the affair.

Claiming Jean would not have resorted to such violence outside of the insult given his wife and sister-in law, the interrogators recommended a king's pardon on Jean's behalf.[80] Signing their names, they sent their request ahead to Nantes. Jean's action and his exile ultimately charted Marie Baude's path to Louisiana.

* * *

Women at the *comptoirs* lived in the midst of moments like La Vigne's act of rape, Hodges's infanticide, LeGrain's sexually harassing threat, and Pinet's murderous outburst. In reaction to a violent claim on Marie Baude's sexual personhood, Jean himself made a violent claim that exemplified the spectrum of intimate violence in relations between men and women on the coast, within households and beyond. It is possible Marie's testimony accurately reported the night in question—asleep and in bed, she perhaps did not realize an altercation had occurred until the next morning. But the ambiguity of Jean Pinet's act of violence, with his casual reference to the dead body of a *mulâtre*, and the precarity of Marie's status as *la femme* in an Atlantic African society of kinship bonds and boundaries (itself ominously connected to Atlantic slaving and American bondage) all may have forced the narration of an impossible event. Marie Baude, for her own safety and security, perhaps could not have reported events differently, even as her very silence, as witness and wife, articulated slavery, race, sex, and the intimacy of empire.[81]

There would be no one act or action that could free women from the inequalities inherent to the Atlantic African societies in which they lived. Neither free nor marital status shielded African women from the ramifications of slavery, slave trading, the growing French presence, and Wolof imperial rivalries along the coast. Patronage and filial networks formed by baptism, godparentage, and marriage (whether formalized as Catholic or *à la mode du pays*), intimate unions with well-placed Company employees, and even the intimacy of dissemblance became practices that offered some protection, suggested resistive and political possibilities yet unavailable, and cultivated the formation of new kinds of community. These practices did not come outside the bounds of the terror of Atlantic slaving. In fact, free African women as slaveowners themselves would be implicated in enacting violences of bondage in the ways that appropriated enslaved women's domestic and sexual labor for their own ends. For African women enslaved at the *comptoirs* and *escales*, life was hard, precarious, and dangerous. African women who owned slaves, cultivated partnerships with

Company employees, and managed households of dependents did not hesitate to participate in these same acts of violence *and* were subject to threats of violence themselves.

As African women and women of African descent living in a world of slaves secured baptisms for their dependents, entered *mariages à la mode du pays*, and demanded their property rights and claimed legacies, they carved a measure of safety and security for themselves. This practice also required them to create new gendered and racialized identities for themselves as Catholics, as wives, or as people "born of this place," that is, born of overlapping Atlantic and African worlds. By 1789, Dominique Lamiral claimed to observe these fusions in the spiritual practices of an elder *mulâtresse* who "waited like the *Mahomé-tannes*" for the new moon to appear before prostrating herself while making the sign of the cross "in thanksgiving."[82] For African women at the comptoirs, intimacy and kinship defined membership in a coastal community in formation. For some, life at the *comptoirs* led to political ascendancy, as the families of property owners came to dominate Atlantic African society at Saint-Louis and Gorée, embracing identities as *signares, habitants,* and, finally, in the nineteenth century, as *métis.* In that sense, these practices occasioned the survival and security of women at the crossroads of imperial unrest. For others, these practices supported the inherent violence of the *comptoirs* as slaveholding societies, gesturing to the murky meaning of freedom in the Atlantic world more broadly. For a third group, slaves bound for sale across the Atlantic, that murky meaning would begin to crystallize as the boundary between slave and free grew sharper.

Chapter 3

⌒⁓

La Traversée:
Gender, Commodification,
and the Long Middle Passage

Boarded one mulâtresse pasagere [bound] for Missisipi.
—Cdt. Préville-Quinet, "Journaux du bord de *La Galathée*," 1728

In 1728, Marie Baude left the *comptoir* of Saint-Louis off the coast of Senegambia and embarked for a muddy outpost named New Orleans, near the mouth of the Mississippi River. Like so many passengers crossing the Atlantic during the first decades of the eighteenth century, she traveled aboard a French *négrier* (slave ship) and in the company of hundreds of shackled men, women, and children.[1] However, and unlike the majority of Africans making the same voyage from West Africa to New Orleans, she did not embark as a slave. As a free African woman, Marie Baude traveled of her own volition. Jean Pinet, a Compagnie des Indes Occidentales (Company of the West Indies) employee sent to France for the murder of the *mulâtre* sailor Pierre LeGrain, had been deported to Louisiana. Marie Baude traveled to meet him, her enslaved property in tow. Unfortunately, if she imagined her property or free status would protect her from the everyday uncertainties of the early Atlantic world, Marie Baude, "la femme Pinet," was mistaken. Alongside sailors and slaves, she endured a grueling journey many did not survive. When she arrived on the Gulf Coast, trading-company agents detained her, claiming she owed the Company duties on her slaves for transporting them from Gorée.[2] Marie Baude's husband appealed on her behalf, but the slaves were sold with others arriving on the same ship. Without property and an ocean away from home,

Marie Baude's freedom, marital status, and racial designation took on a different meaning.

In the great map of transatlantic slave voyages, both Saint-Louis and Gorée played minor roles, furnishing small percentages of enslaved labor to the Americas in comparison to ports farther south at the Bight of Benin or West Central Africa.[3] In regional networks of commerce and exchange, trade in slaves for sale to the Americas never eclipsed other goods, such as gum or palm oil. In the local geography of the everyday, however, Africans bound as slaves for sale were a ubiquitous part of the landscape. The most vulnerable at the *comptoirs* were those designated for sale to the Americas. As tastemakers, property owners, and laborers, African women played a critical role in shaping an Atlantic African culture of taste at Saint-Louis and Gorée. Families like the Baudes, the Larues, and the Thevenots; itinerant laborers like the *pileuses* and market women; and *captives de case* cooking, cleaning, and otherwise supporting their owners' households all built a complicated and unique world. A final category of women passed through the *comptoirs*, their lives reshaped by the logic of the Atlantic slave trade. The same trading season that brought access and power to some women at the *comptoirs* subjected others to an unmaking process of horrific intensity by transforming them into commodities.[4] African women at the *comptoirs* lived in the shadow of the *captiverie* (the slave hold), but only some experienced *la traversée*—the fateful and fatal Middle Passage crossing to the Americas.[5]

African women, men, and children forced into, as Stephanie Smallwood has described it, "the slave ship's one-way route of terror" did not follow a straight path from the African continent to the port of New Orleans.[6] Centering black women and viewing Atlantic slaving through the lens of intimacy and kinship, *la traversée* emerges as a predatory network of exchanges, forced migrations, and acts of resistance rooted in war and conquest. For enslaved women and girls bound for the Gulf Coast, the Atlantic passage threw them into a world of repeated attempts to dismantle their womanhood, girlhood, and humanity, as slave traders, trading-company officials, and would-be slaveowners struggled to make a profit from their flesh. Shuttled between the Wolof, other African polities, and a French minority in Senegambia, women who landed in Louisiana found little respite. Instead, viewed as property by Native American and European alike, enslaved Africans were swept into networks of property and exchange being built between slaveholding Natchez, Choctaw, and Chickasaw polities and Gulf Coast Louisiana's French minority. When these networks disintegrated and French violations sparked the Natchez Revolt, African women, children, and men were captured, sold, traded, and deported across the Gulf South and to the Caribbean by European and Native alike.[7] This extended journey marked the route to the Gulf Coast as a long Middle Passage, a crossing that devastated everything it touched. Even a free African woman like Marie Baude found herself severed from kin, patrons and protectors, community, and customary intimate practices. For women and girls pushed into *la traversée*, forging kinship ties and protecting the most intimate parts of their lives became perilous, desperate, and, for many, ended only in death.

Women and Children in the Slave Trade to Louisiana

In 1696, at Gorée, a slave ship confiscated by a French squadron commanded by the Comte de Gennes found itself stuck on the coast. Although redirected to Saint-Domingue, it remained "cloaked in the same place a few leagues from the land, though the wind had always been very good." When captives began to expire from lack of food and water, those still alive directed the ship's captain to one of the *négresses*. Skilled in the "diabolical sciences," she was "the cause of their dead." When beaten by the surgeon and told to confess to the curse she had placed on the ship, the *négresse* responded that "since he [the surgeon] was mistreating her without reason, and without having the right to do so, she would eat his heart." The surgeon died two days later. Afraid and confronted with dwindling supplies, the captain returned to the *négresse*, "resolved to treat her gently" and "made her the most beautiful promises in the world" if she would remove the hex on the ship. After some negotiation, she agreed. The negotiation included returning her "with some others of her company" to the shore.[8]

Women like the skilled *négresse* taken on board Gennes's ship mobilized an array of tools against the rise of Atlantic slaving in the eighteenth century. By the 1690s, French investors, trading companies, ship captains, and sailors committed to the slave trade. In 1644, the first documented French slave ship to reach the French Caribbean from the African continent—an unnamed ship with enslaved cargo purchased along the Rio Grande in Senegambia—landed at least one slave on St. Christophe. By that time, the enslaved demographic of the Caribbean comprised a polyglot population of Africans kidnapped and trans-shipped from slave ships and plantations; laborers conscripted from the

Carib, Arawak, and Taino Indians of the Caribbean; and Native nations like the Yamassee who had been traded or deported from the mainland for resisting European encroachment.[9] In the decades that followed, Dutch, French, and British soldiers, sailors, and buccaneers crossed the Atlantic west, creating a world of banditry, ribaldry, and contraband trading in defiance of imperial attempts to enforce or secure trade monopolies. In 1674, after mismanagement led the Compagnie des Indes Occidentales to go bankrupt, the French Crown united the colonies under its royal administration, including the island colonies of Martinique and Guadeloupe. In 1697, the western half of the island of Hispaniola, Saint-Domingue, joined them. Imposition of Crown rule signaled France's renewed commitment to asserting control over white and black populations overseas, to make the colonial enterprise profitable. The promise of plantation production captivated imperial officials, metropolitan investors, and would-be slaveowners. In occupying Saint-Louis and Gorée, and displacing the Dutch and English, the French hoped to use the Senegambian coast as a base of operations, shipping enslaved Africans from Saint-Louis and Gorée and preventing traders under other flags from doing the same. Corsairs even patrolled the coast, confiscating ships sailed by European rivals, including any Africans on board.

Enslaved women and girls forced into the slave trade confronted traders and middlemen, ship captains, and company officials determined to reduce them from *captives* to *pièces d'Inde*. In 1728, Jean-Baptiste Labat described the *pièce d'Inde*, the primary measure of commercial exchange on the West African coast. A "measure of potential labor," the *pièce d'Inde* derived from the *pieza de India*, which entered circulation during the first centuries of slave trading under the Spanish and Portuguese. From 1595 to 1773, Spain outsourced its slave-trading enterprise to foreign entities, drafting lucrative contracts called *asientos*. These contracts required a unit of measure for the new (human) cargo being transported across the Atlantic. To better consume them, Spanish turned enslaved Africans into *piezas de India*, literally pieces or parts of the Indies.[10] Like all currency, the meaning and worth of the *pieza de India* fluctuated. By the eighteenth century, for French traders, a *pièce d'Inde*, according to Labat, was a male slave, between eight and thirty years old, with all of his digits and limbs, as well as "eyes, ears, teeth," and was not "hunchbacked or lame." Differences in age, gender, or faculties became the basis for further negotiation between slave-trading factors, company officials, or ship captains desperate to make ends meet. Slave traders exchanged or recalculated captives' worth by using size, shape, or sex to achieve fractions of a *pièce d'Inde*.

In moving from captive to *pièce d'Inde*, gender or, to put it another way, Africans' understanding of themselves as women or girls, men or boys, held little value to slave traders. The early trading-company charters made this clear. In 1628, the Compagnie de Saint-Domingue (Saint Domingue Company) charter did not distinguish between male and female slaves or by age. Any African could be chattel and transported to the colonies.[11] By the eighteenth century, slave traders operating on the West African coast considered age a determiner of size and strength, not childhood or maturity. They measured the reproductive capacity of captives, regardless of sex, by weighing breasts, measuring penises, and inspecting vaginas. Slave traders studied enslaved Africans to predict fertility, health, productivity, and fitness for Atlantic passage, and while seeming to affirm gender, these invasive evaluations actually rejected the human metrics that gender required—intimacy, kinship, rites of passage, community, and sociality. Slave trading was a business bent on reducing humans with an array of complicated genders to the base biological metrics of relevance to plantation production. In this manner, for slave traders, African women, children, and men became finite and arbitrary arrangements of body parts to be negotiated and subdued. Two children, as Labat noted, because of their size, might approximate one *pièce d'Inde*. A female adult, somewhat larger and with reproductive potential, might approximate three-quarters of the same.[12]

This experience of commodification was then confirmed in the array of material goods exchanged. On the same coast where some African women draped themselves in necklaces, cotton *pagnes*, and other luxuries circulated by the slave trade as markers of their gendered selves, others struggled to maintain a sense of their womanhood in the face of the violent ungendering of the slave trade. Ship captains and slave traders fed a taste for luxury goods and implements of convenience, arriving ready to trade iron farming tools, cornets or horns, whistles, cotton *pagnes*, ankle bracelets, beaded necklaces, alcohol, and arms for slaves. The system of exchange was elaborate and specific. One *pièce d'Inde* might purchase a shoulder sack with a chain or strap or one hundred pints of *eau de vie*. And as Africans crossed the Atlantic world, so did the *pièce d'Inde*, an efficient and modern currency responsive to changing situations. In 1721, trading-company officials in France set the exchange rate of

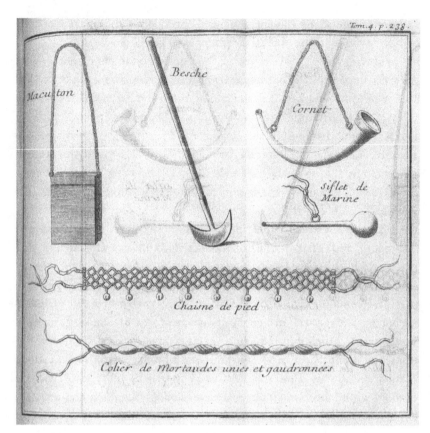

Figure 7. Commodities and commodification: necklaces, tools, and other items exchanged for slaves on the African coast. Jean-Baptiste Labat, *Nouvelle relation de l'Afrique Occidentale* (Paris: Pierre-François Giffart, 1722). Courtesy of the Library Company of Philadelphia.

pièce d'Inde for Louisiana colonists. According to investors an ocean away, a single *pièce d'Inde* equaled 660 livres, paid back over the course of three years in tobacco or rice.[13] Transmuting humans into quantifiable, exchangeable property required an imperial investment in disaggregating enslaved productive, reproductive, and sexual labor. It required lacerating gender and "reduced people to the sum of their biological parts, thereby scaling life down to an arithmetical equation and finding the lowest common denominator."[14]

Although slave traders needed to reduce Africans to biological components to turn them into trade goods, in one of the devastating and perplexing logics of Atlantic history, merchants, slave traders, and sailors still targeted African women and girls for particular and peculiar *gendered* violence.[15] Over and over, imperial desire for black and female flesh caught enslaved women and girls in its crosshairs. For enslaved women, the terror of sexual predation began well before their arrival on the coast or embarking on a slave ship. In 1725, Guiabé, head of Tamboucane, a key trading village near Galam, complained to company officials of *laptots* who raped one of his female *captives de case* and disappeared with her. Guiabé claimed she was not the only one missing. Two of the women of the village were also gone, kidnapped by *laptots* employed on *La Fidélé*. At each step in the trade, strangers subjected captive women and girls, as well as men and boys, to intrusive physical examinations, evaluating them based on perceptions of beauty, as well as physical, sexual, and reproductive capacity.[16] African women and girls were valued as more than trade goods. They were valued as receptacles of licentious misuse. In 1715, a ship captain sailing for the Compagnie du Sénégal (Senegal Company) purchased, from the *damel* of Kajoor, "une négresse" for his own lecherous abuse. He bought her for this purpose and paid in two or three bars of iron and some brandy.[17] Until the practice was outlawed, on arrival in the Antilles, trading-company officials chose a handful of *"nègres de choix"* from the "most handsome Blacks in the cargo" to be their own.[18] Slavery, as Walter Johnson noted, did not dehumanize the enslaved. The reality was worse. As humans, enslaved Africans "could be manipulated: their desires could make them pliable. They could be terrorized: their fears could make them controllable."[19] Slave traders required the human-ity of their slaves so that the atrocities they visited upon them would matter.

If the history of slaving is one of women, in the words of Joseph Miller, "domiciled and dominated," the Atlantic slave trade inculcated in slave traders a taste for violating African women and girls.[20] To turn humans into commodi-ties, slave traders were forced to do more than create race. They also needed to dismantle the gender of their cargo. At the same time, slave traders, investors, merchants, and officials also imagined and created genders out of the fraction-alized mess left behind—abused *négresses*, kidnapped *captives de case*, and even *mulâtresse* passengers. If, as C. Riley Snorton argues, gender is a "racial arrange-ment," then a series of genders were born in the crucible of Atlantic slaving where abuse, theft, and purchase defined the gendered precarity of both African women and women of African descent in the slave trade.[21] To put it another way, in *la traversée* sexual access intersected with property to make black women and girls trade objects of desire and acquisition. These racial arrangements had real implications. Of those awaiting sale to the Americas in Senegambia's *comptoirs*, a significant minority was female. From 1701 to 1807, women and girls composed a third of all slaves embarking from Senegambia to the Caribbean while almost 20 percent of all slaves were children.[22] Overall, the trade moved more men, but women and girls did have a presence in it, including on ships to Louisiana.

African women and girls departing from Senegambia did not wholly succumb to enslavement. They played a role in creating what David Eltis and David Richardson described as the most resistive stream of the slave trade over its four centuries of existence.[23] Just as free African women used intimacy and kinship to shape a set of practices at the *comptoirs*, intimacies and kinships in the form of alliances, conspiracies, and organized resistance among women, children, and men allowed enslaved people bound for the Americas to act together against slave traffic, ship captains, and company officials. The *négresse* sorceress was not the first to band together with her troupe and fly in the face of those who would subdue her. In 1678, at Arguin, north of Saint-Louis, a French ship confiscated from the Dutch 120 *mahometant* slaves of both sexes, according to the *commis* of the Company, Josias Mathelot. Disagreements between the Dutch at Saint-Louis and the Trarza and Brackna traders had led to the enslavement of dozens of women, children, and men. En route to Saint-Domingue, these captives "provided themselves with pieces of iron and such weapons as they could," and took the ship. The captain and crew shut themselves in the cabin and turned their guns on those in revolt. When the insurgents realized their assault was failing, "forty of the most obstinate of them, men and women, leap'd into the sea together." As a group, "and holding their mouths quite open, they swallow'd down the sea-water, without moving arms and legs, till they were drown'd, to show their intrepidity and little concern for death."[24]

Free African women and their *captives de case* would have seen and heard about shipboard revolts off shore, as well as revolts by those held captive at the *comptoirs* themselves. Slaves marked for transit were employed as laborers at the *comptoirs* before they embarked, work that included cleaning ships and breaking rocks for roads and other projects.[25] This labor may have presented the enslaved an opportunity to organize their resistance. In October 1724, the fires on the ramparts burned, lighting up the sky above Gorée. Soldiers scrambled around Fort St. François, trying to restore order. The afternoon before, fifty-five captives bound for sale to the Americas rose up. In the heat of the afternoon, they broke out of the *captiverie*, killed S. Gaspard Boucher (the guard), and armed themselves with blocks of wood, axes, and anything else they could lay their hands on. Two slaves were killed and twelve were wounded. Soldiers shut the door of the fort before they could escape, containing the insurrection, and lit the fires along the fort walls as illumination and warning.[26]

The insurgents held their own through the night, but with no escape route out of the fort, in the morning, they surrendered. Guards led the captives out of the fort two by two and French officials at Gorée executed the three leaders, one by strapping them to blocks of wood and quartering them. Two others were killed by firing squad. All died to serve as "an example to all others." The revolt and the executions would have been witnessed or heard throughout the tiny island, especially by African and European *habitants* living near the fort itself. For those who did not see and hear the insurrection, the smell of smoke and gunpowder would have alerted them that something significant had occurred. "Everyone was there," officials declared in their deposition afterward. The fires that allowed company "to see everything that would happen" also illuminated the event for residents, enslaved and free alike. Geopolitical conflict between the Wolof *damels* and French Company officials laid the foundation for these and other intermittent skirmishes, political tensions that filled the *captiveries* or led to forced deportations from the coast.

By the mid-eighteenth century, just as officials at the *comptoirs* articulated their fears about relations between European employees and African women of the coast, Atlantic slave traders were articulating their own gendered assumptions about Africans of different ethnicities and their capacity for Atlantic bondage. Traders viewed Wolof men, for example, as recalcitrant and ill suited for slavery in the Americas, a plague on slave ships. Wolof women, however, came to be described by visitors like Pruneau de Pommegorge as "lovely and well shaped, with a singular intelligence" and acuity with French. Wolof women were "highly esteemed" by purchasers in the Americas who paid higher prices for them and employed them as domestics.[27] However much Wolof women may or may not have been desired by slaveowners across the Atlantic, women arrived in the *captiveries* of Saint-Louis and Gorée from across West Africa, boasting an array of polities, ethnicities, and linguistic traditions. In the region surrounding the *comptoirs*, Wolof, Bamana, Lebu, Sereer, Mandinka, Fulbe, and an array of smaller societies shared, negotiated, and battled for territory and resources. In the late seventeenth century, slavers transported captives from the Senegal and Gambia river valleys, the Futa Jallon highlands, and the kola forests of Sierra Leone. By the end of the eighteenth century, slaving had expanded into the areas north of Benin and Biafra. Many enslaved arrived on the coast from as far as the kingdoms Oyo and Asante, as well as the Niger River valley.[28]

A number of enslaved arrived on Senegambia's coast as prisoners of war between Islamic polities and their non-Islamic neighbors. Religious conflict was sparked in part by the predations of the slave trade; African women, children, and men captured as heretics by Wolof warriors or those caught in raids between rival households or villages all helped supply slaves for trading. It also shaped Africans' self-identification. The term "Bambara" emerged as a pejorative for individuals or communities enslaved or who practiced indigenous religions, regardless of origin. The Bamana, the ethnic group the term "Bambara" supposedly described, were a Malian people who did not practice Islam. They increasingly found themselves caught in regional skirmishes over land, slaves, or religion, leading to their reputation among French and Africans of being fierce soldiers and warriors. By the first half of the eighteenth century, war had become the economic and political driver of the state of Segu.[29] In another example, the Sereer-Safen also maintained their independence from the Wolof kingdom of Bawol, touting their ethnic difference and resisting demands by the Islamic polity for labor, tribute, and religious conversion.[30] These complex arrangements and rearrangements of identity emerged in the heat of the slave trade as well as in the geopolitics of the rise and fall of kingdoms in the region. European as well as African slave traders played a role in shaping and commodifying ethnicity (and with it gender), playing off of these changes as they occurred and reducing dense lifeways and social networks to their crudest elements.

Beginning in 1719, slave ships began to bring enslaved women, children, and men to Louisiana en masse, forcibly transported first by the Compagnie d'Occident (Company of the West) and then the Compagnie des Indes. Between 1719 and 1743, twenty-three French slave ships left the West and West Central Africa coasts. Each carried men, women, and children for sale and disembarked most or all of their enslaved cargo in Louisiana. Of those twenty-three ships, sixteen carried slaves purchased or loaded at either Gorée or Saint-Louis or both.[31] Another six arrived from Ouidah, one of the busiest slave-trading ports of the eighteenth century, in the Bight of Benin. A single ship arrived from Cabinda in West Central Africa. Twenty-two of the twenty-three ships arrived over the course of eleven years, creating an immediate, concentrated, and critical mass of enslaved labor direct from the continent. While the first wave of French slave ships arrived from Ouidah, the majority of the ships arriving after 1721 arrived from Senegambia, a population that described themselves or were described by traders and slaveowners by a range of ethnic denominations—Senegal, Wolof, Sereer, Pulaar, and Bambara from Senegambia; Mina from Benin; Congo from Cabinda; and more.

The year 1721 marked the first documented arrival in Louisiana of female slaves shipped from Africa. Over the course of the entire French slave trade to Louisiana, just over a quarter of the slaves sold were female.[32] Twelve of the twenty-three ships to make the crossing left behind enough data to confirm the gender composition of their human cargo. Of these, nine ships left behind enough data to calculate percentages of women on the ships. The lowest percentage, 10 percent female on *La Flore*, arrived in Louisiana in 1728. The highest percentage, 46 percent female on *La Mutine*, arrived in Louisiana in 1725. Across all nine voyages, the percentage ranged, never dropping below 10 percent and never higher than 46 percent.[33] Numbers, however, tell only one part of the story. African women and girls arriving in the colony during this time shaped the colony's development beyond the boundaries of the slave-ship register.[34] African women and girls shaped slave-ship captains' practices for optimizing, streamlining, and modernizing trading. As they landed in Louisiana, although quantitatively at the margins of trading-company ledgers, they remained central to slave trading as it occurred.

Investors, for instance, took for granted the culture of sexual exploitation that attended Atlantic slaving, permeated slave ships, and afflicted women and girls on the ships. In the instructions provided to *Le Duc du Maine* and *L'Aurore*, African women factored into Company officials' estimations of wealth and expected cargo. Along with detailed instructions admonishing captains to avoid lengthy voyages, disease, and unnecessary stops along the way, officials directed captains to "prevent the black women from being debauched by the nègres and the crew." As surveillance technologies, trading-company directives reflected a push to rationalize and control intimate violence as a natural and inevitable expense of the slaving enterprise. They acquiesced to white male fantasies, anxieties, and performances of power and mastery.[35] The slave trade generated a genre of instructional material like this, issued to traders who rushed to meet the demand of investors entering what would become John

Law's "Mississippi Bubble." The guidelines and directives were meant to ensure that captains and crews succeeded in transforming human beings into lucrative cargo. With these instructions in mind, *L'Aurore* became the first documented transatlantic slave ship to arrive in Louisiana, followed by *Le Duc du Maine*, both in 1719 and both from Ouidah.[36]

Although officials did not tally the gender of slaves on *Le Duc du Maine* and *L'Aurore*, African women certainly figured as part of the cargo of these ships. In the slave export data from Ouidah in those years, 1717–21, almost 40 percent of slaves leaving the port were female and a quarter of them were children.[37] If the ships leaving Ouidah followed this trend, a significant number of enslaved women and girls would have been among those transported to Louisiana on these ships. Africans sold from Benin, particularly Ouidah, found their way into bondage from many directions. Also described as the Slave Coast, the Atlantic slave trade in Benin thrived in ways it would not in Senegambia. The same year *L'Aurore* procured captives for its trip across the Atlantic, the king of Ouidah built a fortress, financed in part by profits from the slave trade.[38] The instructions provided to *Le Duc du Maine* included special requests for "several blacks who knew how to cultivate rice and three or four barrels of rice for seeding, which they were to give to the directors of the company upon their arrival in Louisiana."[39] It was loaded with *bouges* (cowries) for the purpose of making just such a trade when it arrived at Ouidah in late 1718. The same expectation likely accompanied *L'Aurore*, *Le Duc du Maine*'s companion ship. In those years, rice cultivation in areas like Benin was the domain of women.[40]

Between 1720 and 1721, traders offered somewhat more legible documentation on African women and girls arriving on slave ships to Louisiana. Two ships embarked from Senegambia en route to Louisiana. In July 1720, *Le Ruby* arrived from the Senegal concession, the first from Senegambia. At the time, the Company at Saint-Louis suffered from one of its periodic food shortages and could offer the captain supplies for only one hundred and thirty captives.[41] In quick succession, though certainly not quick enough for complaining would-be slaveowners waiting in New Orleans, four ships arrived in New Orleans. *L'Afriquain*, traveling from Ouidah, arrived in March with fifty-three women and thirty-five girls in a group of one hundred and eighty two enslaved Africans. *L'Afriquain* arrived alongside *Le Duc du Maine*, just returning on its second voyage from Ouidah to Louisiana. *Le Duc du Maine*, a much larger ship, carried nearly twice as many captives to the Gulf Coast. One hundred and twenty-one women and thirty-seven girls—nearly half of those enslaved—arrived in

Louisiana on *Le Duc du Maine*. Following close behind, *La Néréide* arrived at Biloxi from Cabinda (West Central Africa) in April with sixty-six women and twenty-six girls among two hundred and ninety four slaves who survived the journey.[42] At least one ship, *Le Charles*, never arrived in Louisiana. Embarking from Ouidah in October 1720, *Le Charles* "burned at sea within sixty miles of the coast."[43]

The year 1721 marked a definitive shift by the Compagnie des Indies from Ouidah to Senegal. With the rise of Saint-Domingue as a market for slaves, Company officials in France encouraged a return to Saint-Louis and Gorée where the French enjoyed preferential access to trade at the *comptoirs*. Attempts to drive traffic to Louisiana from Senegambia, however, largely failed. In 1721, only *Le Maréchal d'Estrées* arrived in Louisiana, after a tumultuous journey, with almost two hundred slaves to sell from the *captiveries* at Saint-Louis and Gorée.[44] The gender and age distribution of slaves disembarked was not specified. It would be another two years before ships with documented cargo of *négresses* and female *nigrittes* from the continent would reappear at the mouth of the Mississippi River. In 1723, *L'Expédition* and *Le Courrier de Bourbon* both departed from Gorée and arrived in the fall. *L'Expédition* carried twenty women, one boy, and three infants out of a total of one hundred captives. *Le Courrier de Bourbon* disembarked forty female slaves, women and girls, out of a total of one hundred slaves. The women and girls of these ships entered *la traversée* weakened by increasing scarcity on Senegal's coast. Too few slave ships were arriving at Saint-Louis and Gorée to meet the supply. More slaves also meant more mouths to feed at the *comptoirs*, and the Company lacked the resources to supply them all.[45] As enslaved Africans waited at Gorée, Galam, Joal, and Gambia, they wasted away in shackles, grew ill, and died, or escaped their holdings.

Although traders failed to consistently document the gender and age of captives, African women and girls appeared in the documents in other ways. Women and children were often among those slaves exchanged for food and water. On their first voyages to Louisiana, *L'Aurore* and *Le Duc du Maine* stopped in Grenada to resupply.[46] When they did, the lieutenant stationed there forced the captains to exchange healthy slaves for old and sick ones. Exchange slaves constituted a subset of a broad trans-shipment trade between slaveholding societies of the Americas. An evolution of the seventeenth-century policy about *nègres de choix* was occurring when officials at intermediary ports often forced captains to exchange Africans from the continent for local sick or disabled slaves before the ship could receive supplies or aid.[47] *L'Afriquain, Le Duc du Maine,* and *La Néréide,* all bound for New Orleans, made stops at Grenada to resupply, and all were forced to exchange healthy slaves for what the captains described as old slaves, sick slaves, or slaves who were "habitual maroons." Among those exchanged from these ships, at least one girl disembarked at Grenada, trading places with women, men, and children who may have been older or of limited ability. Those exchanged faced the pain of leaving behind kin, confronting the work of building new communities of support in an unfamiliar slaveholding society.

Ship captains lost human cargo to exchange and sale at ports of call throughout the slave trade. After 1727, the port of call used by ships arriving in Louisiana moved from Grenada to Martinique and Saint-Domingue. At Saint-Domingue, slave traders compelled captains to sell slaves outright. In February or March of 1727, *L'Annibal* arrived on the Gulf Coast after a harrowing twenty-three months at sea with only half of the women, children, and men it embarked with, because the other half succumbed to both illness and wealthy merchants after a stop at Saint-Domingue.[48] In the case of Martinique and Saint-Domingue, purchasers consistently preferred enslaved men, full *pièces d'Inde,* leaving women and girls to remain en route to the Gulf Coast.[49]

Women and girls also surface in the silences at the margins of the ships' logs. As a fraction of a *pièce d'Inde,* women and children did not constitute healthy trade items, a currency conversion that applied on both sides of the Atlantic.[50] After the captain of *La Néréide* refused to trade slaves for supplies at Grenada, the enslaved Africans who arrived at Biloxi disembarked sick and starving. Some twenty-eight slaves died after landing, and others remained sick for days or died afterward. And yet, on arrival, colonial governor Jean-Baptiste Le Moyne, Sieur de Bienville, described the selection of bondspeople delivered by *La Néréide* as "good and well sorted." Bienville did not so much describe the health as the gender distribution of those disembarked from *La Néréide*—nearly 70 percent of the ship's captives were male. In June, *Le Fortuné* arrived in Louisiana from Ouidah with sixty-four women and eleven girls of a much larger group of three hundred and three enslaved Africans. Some thirty-seven Africans had died en route. As with *L'Afriquain, Le Duc du Maine,* and *La Néréide,* some of the slaves were confiscated on behalf of the Company. Bienville again praised the captain for his "well sorted" selection, an enslaved "cargo" dominated by males—two hundred and five men alongside twenty-three boys—at nearly 75 percent.

No conception of African women and girls as a weaker sex or in need of special care or comfort existed. When *L'Afriquain, Le Duc du Maine,* and *La Néréide* arrived at Biloxi, Company officials confiscated some forty slaves to work on the river, bringing ships, goods, and passengers upriver to New Orleans, "to provide public works and for subsistence."[51] Adult men and women fitting this description would have undertaken such work. The rest were sent on to New Orleans to be sold to slaveowners managing concessions and tobacco plantations from Chapitoulas to Natchez. As women and girls landed, Company officials, ship captains, and river workers confiscated a handful for domestic, subsistence, and, more than likely, sexual labor at Biloxi. Historian Gwendolyn Midlo Hall noted that the enslaved women who arrived in Louisiana were fortunate because "Bienville and his friends were interested in seizing and displaying wealth, not in creating it."[52] To be certain, Africans arriving in Louisiana did not encounter the same deadly conditions as those funneled into the grueling plantation complex elsewhere in the Caribbean. However, a desire for conspicuous displays of wealth in a climate of men needing, wanting, or demanding labor and companionship of all kinds placed enslaved African women and girls at especially disadvantaged and vulnerable positions. Ill health did not stop Company officials from appropriating enslaved labor for public works, purchasing slaves for themselves, or exchanging older bondspeople for newer ones.

Even as colonists in Louisiana struggled to subsist for themselves in a foreign space, a taste for female captives as labor, power, and display reigned. When *L'Expédition* arrived in 1723, few supplies were available, a general famine reigned, and most colonists could not purchase slaves. Their bodies already under stress, African women, children, and men grew sicker waiting at Biloxi. Jacques Fazende, the Company official in charge of inspecting arriving ships, assigned fifty of those from *L'Expédition* to build fortifications and to create levees. Fazende did not specify gender, but enslaved people labored on public works, regardless of gender. Fazende sent another three described by the captain as "good sailors" to the river trade, another occupation that may have employed men as well as women, just as it had on the Senegal River. He then confiscated the unsold survivors on behalf of the Company. He sent some of the confiscated slaves to the plantations of the Compagnie des Indes to build cabins and to farm and otherwise labor there. However, officials still distributed enslaved Africans as political gifts to curry favor and power, or they exchanged recently arrived slaves with slaves of their own. Bienville, for instance, swapped a little girl for one of the twenty arriving adult women while two Superior Council officials confiscated adult men for themselves.[53]

In the hold of the ship, on the decks, in the labor of surviving the inexorable pressures of *la traversée*, African women, children, and men defied the logic of an economy that would diminish them to things and render them invisible. In 1723, the women and girls on *Le Courrier de Bourbon* witnessed the first slave conspiracy recorded in a captain's log for those ships embarking for Louisiana. *Le Courrier de Bourbon* departed Gorée two years after the revolt at Fort d'Arguin, a year after St. Robert expressed concerns about the lack of resources, the surge of deaths in *captiveries*, and the dearth of ships to transport crowded captives to the Americas, a year before slave revolts that devastated Galam and Gorée. *Le Courrier de Bourbon* disembarked from Gorée in July 1723 with forty slaves from the Gambia. The captain described them as either sick or debilitated (*fort exténuée*), so much so that he refused to take more and told the governor and *garde magasin* to distribute those left at Gorée to another ship. Within days of embarking, two slaves were caught in a suicide attempt: one tried to jump overboard and had encouraged a second to join. The one attempting to jump was punished by being tied to a cannon and whipped (*coups de garcette*). Scurvy struck the ship, attacking slaves and crew, and measles began to spread among the enslaved. Some fifteen slaves, men and women, according to the captain, contracted the disease, which would eventually kill twelve. *Le Courrier de Bourbon* made it to Grenada in September, where, per custom, the director forced the captain to exchange slaves for supplies. The captain sold one man and one woman and her infant for stores to continue to Louisiana, but decided to remain at Grenada to give all of the captives an opportunity to recover from so much illness.[54]

Le Courrier de Bourbon remained at Grenada for a few weeks. In early October, the day the ship was set to leave, a young captive attempted to get the crew's attention, gesturing toward the quarter-deck. Language barriers prevented the boy from speaking in detail, or doing more than expressing a sense of danger. The captain sent for two women, *négresses*, one of Saint-Louis and one of Gorée, to translate. Both women professed ignorance and innocence, stating they did not know what the boy was speaking of. The captain, heedless, exposed them both on the cannon to be whipped, but the two women continued to refuse to explain what the boy said.[55] Only after punishing several other slaves, implicated, presumably, by the same child, did one of the women, the *négresse* from Saint-Louis, admit that an older man, a *nègre* around forty-five years of age, was a sorcerer who had led a contingent of slaves in plotting a slave revolt intended to massacre all of the whites, and that the other woman, the *négresse* from Gorée, knew about the revolt just as she did. The woman from Gorée at first refused to admit the same. The captain proceeded to punish her until she too implicated the same man as the leader of a plot to "cut the throats of the whites."[56] The plot, though widespread, did not lead to the death of the entire contingent. The captain, concerned that illness and desertion had already run rampant and reduced the profit to be made, chose to make an example of the leader. The accused sorcerer was tied up, hoisted into the air, and shot dead. Assuming the two *négresses* and the young boy survived scurvy, measles, and the voyage itself, they would have landed at Balize on the Gulf Coast with about eighty-seven other slaves, bringing with them memories of death, insurgency, and magic forged during *la traversée*.

The geography of captivity aboard slave ships reassembled gender in crucial ways, also creating space for resistance. Captains and crew, following Company mandates for speed and efficiency, stowed Africans according to space, allocating less to women and children who were believed to be smaller. Shorter men, especially those with visible disabilities such as missing limbs, were also allocated less space. At the same time, it was not uncommon to leave women and children unshackled. Both women and children were assessed, according to European assumptions of gender and age, as less threatening and easier to subdue. This freedom made their role in shipboard revolts a crucial one. Along with the crew of *Le Courrier de Bourbon*, the captain and crew of *L'Annibal*, on its second voyage from Senegal to Louisiana, also discovered the folly of this. In 1729, after trading at Saint-Louis and Gorée, the ship was sent to the Gambia River, where captives had been waiting for months in the *captiveries*, dying as a result of crowded, destitute conditions. The crew secured some three hundred slaves, but before they could depart for the Americas, the enslaved revolted. Seizing what weapons they could, insurgents took the crew by surprise by launching an attack from, among other places, the women's compartment of the ship. Some forty-five black men escaped the ship while almost another fifty slaves were wounded in battle.

The crew subdued the ship and killed the leaders of the revolt, but resistance continued. After making its way across the Atlantic, *L'Annibal* stopped at Saint-Domingue in July. While there, "a troupe of the négresses" barged into the main sleeping quarters and assaulted M. Bart, the sous-lieutenant. Terrified, and perhaps with memories of the revolt on the Gambia River just a few months before, Bart jumped out of one of the windows. The crew managed to sound the alarm and subdue the women. When asked, the women explained that they attacked because they were frightened the whites had kept them on board only to eat them. Bart later claimed to have mistaken the women for men coming to kill him.[57] While the gendered math of slaving commodification may have positioned female slaves as less than or deficient in the Atlantic economy, enslaved Africans exploited this same math to expose and create gaps in the security of the regime. Intercoastal Afro-Atlantic resistance occurred because enslaved Africans organized it. In the revolt on the Gambia River, the gendered geography of the ship and the poorly constructed women's compartment provided spaces for insurgents to attack from. In the revolt at Saint-Domingue, gendered assumptions about women's lack of resistance and a consequent lack of security provided space for the women to attack the lieutenant. The gendered dynamics of slave revolt on ships could also work against women and girls. In the revolt on the Gambia, African men, for the most part, made their escape, while three women and two infants were killed. In the end, *L'Annibal* never made it to Louisiana. They sold the rest of their cargo at Saint Louis du Saint-Domingue because of the "continued mutiny of the negres." The remaining slaves—including the *négresses*—were sold in Saint-Domingue before the ship returned to France.[58]

Faced with impossible choices, African women, children, and men sometimes found other, more devastating ways to be accountable to and for each other. On board *La Venus*, which left Senegal in April 1729 with at least twenty-one women, girls, and boys, Africans organized a mass suicide en route to Louisiana. One afternoon, a month at sea, a contingent of captives, all Wolofs, began to throw themselves overboard. Five succeeded in doing so before the crew intervened and secured the rest. Despite attempts to recover the enslaved, as one crew member described it, "They all drowned, although we threw them several poles and other things. They did not at all wish to save themselves."[59] Sowande' Mustakeem described suicides of this nature as "slave ship runaways," or a practice of maroonage and escape from bondage that enslaved Africans viewed as a practice of freedom. Noting the dangers of viewing suicide through Western or European modes of life and death, Mustakeem notes that enslaved Africans "carried understandings of an active spirit realm comprised by deities, ancestors, and the spirits of loved ones already passed and collectively central in the lives of the living."[60] The archive does not disclose whether those who made the terrifying decision to take their own lives rather than proceed on the voyage prayed to Allah or Maam Kumba Castel, the water deity who emerged at Gorée during the era of the slave trade.[61] The choice, however, and the kinship that joined the enslaved together in the act of self-destruction, reveals practices that responded to and even defied the loss and dispossession of *la traversée*.

These flashes of resistance during the passage to the Americas bear witness to the presence of African women and girls as more than ungendered marks in the slave-ship log and as transgressing their role as commodities for exchange and profit. At the same time, death, exchange, and grueling labor haunted African women and girls aboard the slave ships even when officials did not document their presence. For instance, *La Mutine* and *L'Aurore* embarked from Senegambia in the same year. On *La Mutine*, which departed Senegal's coast in February 1726, thirteen women perished at sea compared to five men. On arrival in Grenada, four captives, including two women, were exchanged for supplies to continue to Louisiana. *La Mutine*, with about two hundred slaves for sale, arrived in Louisiana with seventy-nine women and at least one girl.[62] Upon arrival, in similar proprietary fashion, and because of a lack of colonists with means to pay, slaves from each ship were requisitioned to build levees, buildings, and other public works.[63] The captain of *L'Aurore*, which left the Senegal *comptoirs* a month after, did not note the gender and age breakdown of its human cargo, but when one reads along the bias grain, the experiences of unnamed women and girls surface.[64] Those enslaved on *L'Aurore* rode the same route to Louisiana but were also held at Saint-Louis and along the Gambia for two months.[65] Those days spent waiting in the hold of the ship took their toll. Over twenty slaves died after the ship left Senegal and before it reached Grenada. Another forty expired before it reached the Gulf Coast. *L'Aurore* embarked with a massive cargo of three hundred and fifty captives, among them sixty women, men, children, and possibly infants who never survived *la traversée*. In 1728, the captains of *La Diane* lost fifty women, children, and men after they embarked from Ouidah.[66] *Le Duc de Bourbon* arrived at Balize in 1729 after losing over sixty of its four hundred women, children, and men.

As the slave trade, particularly to Louisiana, grew more and more treacherous, African women and girls appeared in ships' logs solely in death. Death, illness, and disease struck captives in a range of ways. While their reproductive capacity may have been desired by traders, for captives of age to experience menstruation en route added to enslaved terror and discomfort. Menses also could have been misdiagnosed as a number of illnesses, including scurvy, dropsy, or dysentery, a bacterial disease spread through oral and fecal contact, which could manifest as bloody stools.[67] *Le Prince de Conti*, after stops at Martinique and Saint-Domingue, arrived in Louisiana from Senegal in September 1727. Forty Africans not distinguished by gender in the logs died and the survivors suffered from dysentery and a "bloody flux" that left them blind or close to it. The captain died of scurvy. For those young or experiencing menses for the first time, having their first cycles in the midst of the blood, death, and sickness that saturated these ships' passages would have been traumatizing. As their deaths, when acknowledged, became tallies in the margins of ships' logs and registers, they were accented with crosses to denote Catholic baptism, notations to signify pregnancy, and, if captains found it necessary, a few words on the cause of death.

After 1727, returning to France with anything less than the requisite and expected amount of goods equivalent to the *pièces d'Inde* required explanation. Captains and pilots offered these explanations in the tally of the dead as ships made the crossing, and these explanations were necessarily about age and gender as a result. In 1728, after dysentery and scurvy decimated the undocumented women and girls aboard *Le Duc de Noailles* as well, killing over seventy en route from Senegal to Louisiana, the only gender documentation from this voyage came from the dead—fourteen women, nine girls, and nine infants. Like *Le Duc de Noailles*, the genders and ages of those enslaved were not documented on *La Venus* except in death. En route from Gorée to Louisiana in 1728, seven slaves died, including five women, and another fourteen infants also expired. After doing battle on the African coast and off the coast of Cuba, *La Flore* arrived at Balize with some 350 slaves. Almost fifty died en route, including an unknown number of women of the forty who originally disembarked from Senegal. Officials on the other side of the Atlantic likewise discounted arriving children. When *L'Expédition* landed in New Orleans, Fazende did not count the total number of children dead or alive as they were "not mentioned on the bill."[68] In other words, children did not approximate enough *pièces d'Inde* to warrant notice even in death. Where they ended up or whether they even made it to New Orleans remained a mystery.

In 1730, *Le Saint Louis*, the final ship to document the gender of captives on its voyage, embarked from Senegal's coast and arrived in Louisiana. Its arrival marked the end of an era. *Le Saint Louis* embarked from Gorée in the midst of raids and petty warfare. Peace treaties broke down under European pressure to access the gum trade flowing from Mauritania. A mutiny among sailors occurred on board *La Néréide* while the crew waited on Senegal's coast for more captives. *Le Saint Louis* delayed its own departure as its crew attempted to help quell the violence on *La Néréide*. *La Néréide* and *Le Saint Louis* eventually left together, both en route to Louisiana. *Le Saint Louis* departed Senegal with seventy-one women. Along the way, a mysterious illness took hold of the crew of *La Néréide*. While slaves suffered the effects of scurvy, the crew members began to catch the fever, beginning with the captain, spreading to the chaplain, and eventually reaching the lieutenant. Death wreaked havoc among the sailors. By the time both ships stopped at Saint-Domingue to resupply, *La Néréide* was so overwhelmed by illness that *Le Saint Louis* was forced to take over its cargo and crew. By the time *Le Saint Louis* arrived in Louisiana, at least five of the women embarked on both ships and seven infants had died on the voyage. More than the final ship to document the gender of captives on its voyage, *Le Saint Louis* was also the last ship to arrive under the Compagnie des Indes. For another forty-seven years, with one exception, the mass arrival of African women, children, and men had ended.

To transmute people into things, *la traversée* tore at gender, intimacy, and kinship as they existed on the African continent. In instructions, ships' logs, and letters, agents of the Compagnie des Indes imagined, investors financed, and slaveowners or would-be slaveowners purchased fantasies of mastery that redefined African ethnicity, gender, and age in ways that reduced people to flesh. Colonial officials and slaveowners sought well-sorted cargos of adult, male *pièces d'Inde*, but these metrics tell only part of the story. Slave traders also operated under the assumption that African women's and girls' bodies existed to be used, exploited, and ultimately sold for profit.[69] And once beyond the coast, the monopoly of power lay in the hands of captains, sailors, and Company employees and officials in the Americas, leaving women and girls vulnerable to use of the most nefarious kinds. But for Africans, the *pièce d'Inde* never set the final terms on what they expected of their own existence. Black feminist theorist Hortense Spillers described the Middle Passage as a "dehumanizing, ungendering, and defacing project of African persons."[70] The Atlantic crossing from the African continent to the Gulf Coast subjected those caught in it to this project and all of its brutal caprice. Also, the resistance that slipped through the cracks— from the women who aided slave-ship resistance, from those who committed suicide, from the mobilization of spiritual power and healing knowledge against enslavement by sorcerers and their allies—laid the foundation for what would become practices of freedom in the New World.

Marie Baude's Marginalia: One *"Mulâtresse Pasagere"*

In 1728, Marie Baude boarded the slave ship *La Galathée* at Gorée. *La Galathée* embarked from L'Orient in May 1728, arriving at Saint-Louis near the end of June.[71] The frigate moored without incident and loaded approximately 131 *"negres, negresses,* and *negrillons"* before proceeding to Gorée. There, Marie Baude boarded with her enslaved property in tow. Her arrival caused the captain to write in the margins of his ship log, "Boarded one *mulâtresse pasagere* [bound] for Missisipi."[72] This short listing sketched the terrain this free African woman entered. It marked her as less than a wife and more than a slave, identifiable only through the gendered racial nomenclature of the Atlantic world. It placed her in uneasy proximity to the African women and girls on the ship, who entered as captives, and, like her, appeared mostly in the margins of ships' logs—often with black crosses marking their deaths. And yet Marie Baude's experience was not the same. Baude's journey on *La Galathée* to Louisiana reveals African women's shared precarity crossing the Atlantic world as well as the uneasy differences between black women's possibilities in Atlantic Africa and the Americas. Embarking on *la traversée*, Baude would be stripped of her own intimate and kinship ties because the alchemy of ungendering and commodification that governed slaving implicated all that the trade touched—even a married woman with free status traveling of her own free will. At the same time, for the enslaved women and girls around her, the stakes were much higher. Marie Baude could not have chosen a worse voyage to embark on. From the margins of the register, but in close physical proximity to the dehumanizing brutality of life aboard slave ships, Baude bore witness to the crush of transforming people of African descent into things.

After being deported to Nantes, Jean Pinet remained in prison for two years. Near the end of January 1726, he received a *brevet de remission* commuting his sentence but with conditions. These conditions seemed simple. Once again, he was to be employed as a gunsmith for the Company. This time, he was required to "serve the rest of his days at the garrison in Louisiana." Jean's agreement also required him to take an apprentice. For his service as gunsmith he would receive 300 livres a year (not a small sum). This nomination occurred at the request of Company officials in New Orleans, the colony's capital, where the garrison was in dire need of his skills.[73] The decision to send Jean to Louisiana could be considered an act of mercy as well as pragmatic. Jean's exile to Louisiana filled a vacancy left by the last gunsmith, "le nommé

Gamian." But that was only part of the story. The Crown commuted Jean's sentence during the nadir of French migration to Louisiana. Beginning in 1717, under the aegis of the Compagnie des Indes, through 1720, some seven thousand French colonists traveled to the colony.[74] This initial French migration resembled French migration to Saint-Louis and Gorée—these first arrivals were primarily white men either employed by the Company or *engagés*, indentured to the Company. It differed in the significant number of colonists sent to Louisiana by force. The *forçats*—prisoners, orphans, debtors, and the poor—were deported from cities across France to fulfill Company labor demands.[75] These deportations ended after 1720, but reports of the dismal conditions at New Orleans and along the Gulf Coast furnished by deportees' experiences helped discourage large-scale migration from France. By 1726, European settlers avoided "Missisipi." Meanwhile, in Louisiana, death, out-migration, poverty, and drudgery claimed lives or drove colonists back to France.[76]

Along with migration troubles, settlers quickly discovered that plantation production along the Gulf would be difficult. Saint-Domingue's success with sugar put Louisiana investors to shame. Sugar required land that Native nations occupied, financing to secure slaves and build mills for processing, and a growing season that Gulf Coast Louisiana could not provide. Winter frosts destroyed cane before it could be harvested, and seasonal hurricanes and floods ruined crops. After two years, the Compagnie d'Occident was absorbed into the Compagnie des Indes Occidentales. The Compagnie des Indes Occidentales, determined to make a profit, invested in transforming the Gulf Coast into a plantation society, one modeled after British tobacco plantations in the Chesapeake. It secured a monopoly on French slave trading from Senegambia and in 1719, the first ships bearing enslaved Africans arrived in Louisiana, cargo that was immediately purchased by landowners eager to produce agricultural staples in the region. In 1721, Bienville was appointed governor and formed a Superior Council. With this official step, the Company established a Superior Council to govern its rising population, support plantation management, and supervise laborers. The men who made up the Louisiana Superior Council, as slaveowners and concessionaires, were well aware of the profits to be made from plantations. They demanded enslaved African labor and the resources to make Louisiana a gem of the empire.[77]

In 1721, those Company's resources disappeared. French migration to Louisiana slowed to a trickle. Fewer than two thousand European colonists remained.[78] New Orleans was becoming a Gulf Coast *comptoir* of young, male migrants from France; French-Canadian *coureurs de bois* (fur traders) passing through on their way down the river from New France to barter and trade; Native men and women of various nations; and an increasing population of people of African descent.[79] Africans continued to arrive and when Bienville was replaced by Étienne de Périer as governor, Périer convinced investors in France and landowners in Louisiana that the future of production lay in tobacco—and at Natchez. At some point between 1726 and 1728, as the death tally rose in the slave trade from West Africa to Louisiana, Jean Pinet asked the Company for permission to bring Marie Baude and her slaves to Louisiana from Senegal. Company officials consented, but required the slaves to work for the Company to pay back the cost of the voyage. Jean Pinet agreed and waited for Marie Baude to arrive.

What Baude may have known about the Middle Passage before embarking is unclear. News of the 1724 slave revolt at Gorée would have been carried to Saint-Louis along the common wind of rumor and speculation.[80] Slaves and slave ships would also have been a common sight at both Senegal *comptoirs*, although by the 1730s, overall departures of slaves from Saint-Louis and Gorée had fallen and the number of slaves owned by free African residents at the *comptoirs* had increased. At least one Senegambian slave-trading family, the Larues, owned a ship and traded for slaves along the Senegal River. Etienne Larue, captain of *Le Fier*, did industrious work trading up and down the river, and, at times, across the Atlantic. Larue issued several receipts to the Company for payment. In 1735, his relation, Anne Larue, living at Saint-Louis, owned an enslaved woman named Antagaye. By 1749, free African women owned ten of thirteen households at Gorée. Another ten years later, free African women at Gorée managed expansive households of children, unpropertied free people of color, and as many as twenty or thirty slaves. By 1755, African residents at Saint-Louis owned more than five hundred slaves, while the Company held only ninety-eight of the island's slaves.[81] At Saint-Louis and Gorée, *mulâtresse* householders like Anne Larue, Marie Térèse, Charlotte, Cati Louette, and Penda Kassano distinguished themselves from unpropertied women—many of them described as *négresses*—by owning homes, goods, and slaves.[82]

Baude may have seen something of the slaving process. Company regulations protected the slaves of African residents from mistreatment and sale across the Atlantic. While not foolproof, most of those sent across the Atlantic arrived at Saint-Louis and Gorée from beyond the *comptoirs*. After being inspected by the Company director or another official, women, children, and men were stripped naked, assessed for their value, placed on canoes, and sent out to slave ships moored in deeper waters.[83] Slave ships were the connective tissue of the Atlantic world. Technological innovations of the early modern period, slave ships were peculiar creations, part "war machine, mobile prison, and factory," with complex racial-sexual landscapes.[84] Ships were also "cultural and political units," maritime territories ruled by captains, and populated by heterogeneous crews, occasional passengers, and enslaved Africans seized for sale across the Atlantic.[85] For the majority of Africans crossing the ocean in the eighteenth century, encountering the Atlantic world began on slave ships and along their itineraries. And on La Galathée, African bondage dominated. The captain described the lot of slaves being taken across the Atlantic as "naigres" or "naigresses," choosing not to differentiate between race or perceived racial mixture, ethnicity, or age.[86] The crew was heavily male, and while passengers were not uncommon aboard slave ships, the captain acknowledged only one female passenger on the voyage.

As a passenger, Baude's journey would have been difficult. For the captains, crews, and passengers, la traversée was violent and terrifying. Dangerous weather, sickness, and the possibility of slave revolt threatened the success of every voyage. But of the twenty-three slave ships to travel from Senegal to Louisiana during the French period, La Galathée's journey was especially fraught. By October 1728, when La Galathée embarked for Louisiana, one of the sailors had drowned and a male slave had already died of unspecified causes.[87] Two days into the journey, death began to stalk the ship. Scurvy and an unspecified, general illness killed several slaves and most of the crew. Along with illness, the ocean was a considerable threat. Drowning claimed the life of at least one négresse. Children succumbed to the terrors of the Middle Passage. At least two of the dead were suckling infants, a loss that would have had a deep impact on everyone on board, women especially. On average, a slave or crew member died for nearly every day of travel between Gorée and the first stop, Les Cayes on Saint-Domingue's southern coast. In total, thirty-three slaves died on that first leg and at least nine of them were female.[88]

Much of Baude's experience on La Galathée must be left to speculation. For example, if Baude or her slaves suffered any illness, there is no record of it. Although women as a whole were vulnerable to rape on Atlantic crossings, and African women and girls were especially vulnerable, there is no record of sexual violence on Baude's journey. If enslaved women or girls on La Galathée resisted, their participation in shipboard insurgency remains obscured by the archival record. At one point, the captain uncovered a raid on the ship's stores being planned by the captives. He had one of the enslaved organizers hung and administered *la calle* (keel hauling) to four others.[89] Given the practice of leaving women and children unshackled on ships, it is reasonable to imagine that at least one of the slaves who participated in the raid could have been female. Unfortunately, such acts of violence or resistance remain impossible to quantify and recover.

In December 1728, *La Galathée* stopped at Les Cayes so that its crew and human cargo could recover from the sickness and death. In the 1720s, Les Cayes became the center of commerce in southern Saint-Domingue. By the 1720s, Les Cayes comprised a fort, administrative buildings, churches, and a multiracial population.[90] It served as a way station for ships traveling between West Africa and Louisiana; it was a safe port of call where captains drew on Company resources to house, treat, and feed sick slaves and crew. Les Cayes, in Saint-Domingue's Southern Province, exemplified the wide chasm separating legal fiction from brutal reality. The Les Cayes outpost offered traders an opportunity to build illicit commercial networks with the British in Jamaica to the east and with the Spanish in southern Cuba to the north. Contraband sugar, slaves, cattle, and subsistence products circulated between the three colonies openly, and the clandestine exchange became crucial to the survival of residents on the southern coast.[91] Les Cayes and its satellite settlements of Jacmel and Saint-Louis de Saint-Domingue were isolated, and the ports received only sporadic supplies from France. In 1698, the king granted the Southern Province to the Compagnie de Saint-Domingue. Company officials hoped to capitalize on the trade with the English and Spanish and provide African slaves to the rest of the colony. By the late 1720s, ships en route to Louisiana picked Les Cayes as a refueling port, avoiding the demand of planters at Cap Français and the exchange economy at Grenada. *L'Annibal, La Néréide, Le Duc de Noailles,* and *Le Saint Louis* each made pit stops there.

Baude and her slaves may have disembarked, taking the opportunity to rest and interact with the community. The promise of the Compagnie de Saint-Domingue attracted settlers from France and around the Caribbean. By 1713, more than six hundred settlers migrated to the southern coast as soldiers, traders, and laborers. The population in and around Les Cayes included free people of color migrating from other parts of the Caribbean and portions of the Spanish mainland, as well as enslaved women and men who arrived via the

Atlantic and Caribbean slave trades. Four free people of color, including one woman, owned enough property to be counted in a Company census.[92] Fifteen years later, across the *quartier* (principality) of St. Louis, officials counted twenty-five free men of color old enough to bear arms.[93] By 1730, free people of color were building lives for themselves in the Southern Province. At least thirty-two marriages with people of color were contracted, along with ninety-seven recorded births. Additionally, some thirty free men of color and nearly as many children made Les Cayes their home.[94] At Les Cayes, the captain of *La Galathée* expressed concern that "all of the crew are ill and in the Company building with all of the sick blacks." *La Galathée* rested at Les Cayes for several days, hiring sailors and laborers from the fort as emergency crew.[95] In the end, forty-five slaves and seven of the crew remained in Saint-Domingue, too sick to continue.[96] The respite, however, was short. By mid-December, *La Galathée* was back at sea. By the time the ship arrived on the Gulf Coast, some ninety slaves had died, including several women.

In January 1729, *La Galathée* dropped anchor at Balize, a French fort. During the previous ten years, Balize and Dauphine Island had been processing stations for slaves entering the colony. Balize, a small outpost with a church and a Company building, marked the southernmost reach of French officials in Louisiana. The Mississippi River was too dense for ships to navigate to New Orleans. At Balize, inspectors like Fazende processed all merchandise brought for sale into the colony, including captive Africans, and secured it all for the journey upriver. Days could pass while captains, passengers, crews, and bondspeople suffered in the rain or sun, swarmed by mosquitoes and flies while they waited for trading-company officials to meet them by riverboat.[97] When officials finally arrived, concern for the health of the captives disembarked after *La Galathée*'s painful march across the ocean initially distracted them from the presence of one *mulâtresse* and her enslaved property.[98] When attention did turn Baude's way, confusion ensued. At first, she was detained. Officials levied a tariff of 120 livres on each of her slaves, then confiscated them, "leaving her with only a petite Negrite," about five or six years of age. Baude was then forwarded "hastily" to New Orleans.[99]

The Company's ease at stripping Baude, "*la mulâtresse pasagere*," of her enslaved property echoed with the same logic of ungendering and commodification that structured *la traversée*. Her experience after landing in Louisiana contrasted markedly from the Company's failed attempts to divest free African women of Saint-Louis and Gorée of their inherited and acquired property. At

Saint-Louis and Gorée, property belonging to Africans remained protected, and the Company was an ineffective and inefficient guarantor of estates. By crossing the Atlantic, a transformation occurred that targeted the four hundred women, children, and men embarked from Gorée, and it implicated everyone on the ship. Baude, *La Galathée*, and the captive women, children, and men around her exemplified the complicated links and fissures between slavery and freedom in Senegambia and Louisiana, the overlapping diasporas of gender, race, and power that crossed ocean currents from the Old World to the New. *La Galathée's* itinerary provided everyone on board a practicum in the ambiguities of transforming human beings into chattel. It provided no clear primer on the making and practice of freedom. And upon arrival in New Orleans, Baude transformed into the nameless (and kinless) *la femme Pinet*, the unpropertied wife of a Company employee. She became a distant version of the free African woman with property married to a successful, if murderous white artisan on Senegal's coast, living in a community of slaveowning women of similar wealth, race, or status. She left no testimony on the particulars of her experience of *la traversée*, the residue of her crossing only a note in the margin of the slave-ship register.

For the women and girls who accompanied her, enslaved and subject to cruelty from the moment they stepped onto the decks of the slave ship, their transformation into slaves in the Americas did not end at the outpost at Balize. Enslaved African women's journey to the Gulf Coast did not occur because of marriage, employment (dubious and duplicitous as indentured contracts may have been), or Catholic missionary fervor.[100] Political tensions between African and European empires charted these women's paths across the Atlantic. Slaving acts engaged in by ship captains, Company officials, and slaveowners, from instructions issued by investors to punishment delivered by captains and crew, transformed them from the women and girls they knew themselves to be in their home communities into Atlantic currency. As vulnerable as their womanhood and girlhood may have been before enslavement, whether as laborers, wives, or subordinate members of their family households, nothing compared to the physical, social, and emotional devastation wrought by *la traversée*. Women and girls in the slave trade entered a world of confused math, one where they did not add up even in their own commodification—they were but fragments of the *pièce d'Inde*. Upon arrival in New Orleans, their journey through and between slaveholding entities shifted from African and European to Native and European, each with their own logic about the value of enslaved women and girls.

Atlantic slaving created new genders. Out of the fragments left by *la traversée*, an African diaspora extended across the Atlantic to Louisiana. Hall accurately and rigorously located the "African roots of Louisiana's Afro-Creole
culture" in the African continent, identifying Senegambia and the concentra-
tion of women, children, and men arriving directly from the continent along
the Gulf Coast during the first decades of the eighteenth century as compos-
ing the heart of black life on the Gulf Coast.[101] Historian Ibrahima Seck located
the vestiges of Komo, a Mande secret society utilized by the Bamana and
Manding living west of present-day Senegal in southeast Mali and along the
Niger River. Bambara and other Mande speakers experienced raids, kidnapping, and enslavement across the Upper Guinea region, predation that accompanied sale to European traders farther west along the coast.[102] The enslaved
soldiers frustrating Saint-Louis and Gorée governors' attempts at control were
described as Bambara and likely part of these waves of capture and control.
For African women and children born into enslaved communities infused by
Senegambian–West African lifeways, who survived *la traversée* and the brutal
first decades of the trade, who remained in New Orleans and along the Gulf
Coast as enslaved, free, or fugitive and maroon laborers, the search for kin,
safety, and security continued with stunning vitality.

However, Baude did not arrive at a mini-Senegambia. For people of African
descent, the Senegal and Gulf Coast enclaves were not identical. At Saint-Louis
and Gorée, slavery existed as one captive experience among others, not limited
to those of African ancestry. Officials at Saint-Louis and Gorée did not and
could not systematize difference on the basis of African ancestry and slave
descent. The provenance of free Africans surrounding the slaveholding *comptoirs* and the proclivity of whites to revolt against enforcement prevented any
hardening of the boundary between slave and free until the nineteenth century.
In the Americas, this was not the case. Africans in New Orleans and the Gulf
Coast *comptoirs* overwhelmingly arrived to live and die as slaves.[103] In Louisiana, women of Native nations, not of African descent, played the role of hosts
and intermediaries, offering hospitality, comfort, security, and pleasurable
company to French guests. Although no longer an encouraged imperial policy,
mésalliance between French men and indigenous women continued to occur
as men sought alliances, laborers, and instructions on how to navigate a foreign
land.[104] By 1719, Gulf Coast Louisiana inherited an archipelagic, Antillean legal
culture that marked Africans as foreign and subordinate through black female
reproduction and sexuality—it presumed slavery to follow the mother, viewed

Figure 8. Desseins de Sauvages de Plusieurs Nations, Nue Orleans, 1735. Colored
pen and ink by Alexandre de Batz, 1735. Gift of the Estate of Belle J. Bushnell,
1941. Courtesy of the Peabody Museum of Archaeology and Ethnology,
Harvard University, PM41-72-10/20.

free Africans and free people of African descent as threatening the institution
of bondage, and punished intimate relations between white men and women
of color with the force of law. Over the next few years, African women and
women of African descent would be faced with crafting new genders and pushing the boundaries of bondage in a foreign land where the geopolitics of intimacy and kinship continued to intervene in their lives. It did not take long for
these tensions to explode.

The Natchez Revolt and the Long Middle Passage

The Natchez Revolt, and the conspiracies, dispersals, and especially the institutions that emerged in its wake, shaped the nature of freedom for African
women, children, and men for years to come. Occurring only a decade after

the first slave ships began to arrive, its devastation and trauma blended seamlessly with *la traversée*, in the process creating a long Middle Passage that endured well after captives' arrival in Louisiana. Africans entered *la traversée* as a result of imperial rivalries between African polities and Europeans invested in Atlantic markets. They were captured as victims of warfare, kidnapping, and social or political discontent and misfortune. The slave ship enclosed bondspeople in a devastating world of forced dislocation, commodification, physical deprivation, and violating precarity. Enslaved Africans landing in the Americas experienced *la traversée* as an assault on their bodies, minds, and senses of themselves. For those arriving in Louisiana, slaving did not end at disembarkation. French, British, Natchez, and Chickasaw purchased and traded African slaves in imperial rivalries with each other and with Atlantic markets in mind. As war with the Natchez broke out, Africans and people of African descent found themselves ransomed as captives of war, pursued, kidnapped, pawned, and once again torn from kinfolk—experiencing, in other words, the precarity of imperial warfare and the commodification of slaving in ways that refracted their recent Atlantic passages. The Natchez Revolt extended the embodied violence and trauma of their Middle Passage well past the point of disembarkation and deep into the Native country. It offered Africans and people of African descent a curriculum on the perpetual insecurity that would attend slavery, blackness, race, and resistance in the New World. In its wake, African, European, and Native alike would test the limits of slavery, freedom, and empire on the Gulf Coast.

With very few exceptions, Africans arrived on the Gulf Coast enslaved, and their numbers increased over time through the slave trade, not reproduction. From 1719 to 1723, just over two thousand slaves landed at Biloxi or Ship Island.[105] In 1721, two-thirds of households contained slaves, "the widest dispersal of slave ownership in the history of the town."[106] Beginning in earnest after 1721, the two largest concessions at Natchez, the White Earth (Terre Blanche) and St. Catherine plantations, also received Africans directly from arriving ships. Black communities formed on those plantations, on surrounding farms, and at the fort, as they harvested tobacco, built fortifications, and worked in the cypress swamps above and below the post.[107] Native nations of the Gulf South also engaged in a robust indigenous slave trade and incorporated enslaved Africans among slaves they owned or exchanged with Europeans and other indigenous nations.[108] By 1726, New Orleans remained predominantly white, but as a result of populations like the one at Natchez, Louisiana could be described as a "black majority colony."[109] By 1731, one year after *Le Saint Louis* disembarked its human cargo and two years after Baude arrived, New Orleans' African-descended population rose to about 20 percent, a considerable fraction of the town's African-European-Native milieu. Alexandre de Batz captured this nonwhite representation in a sketch, *Desseins de Sauvages de Plusieurs Nations, Nue Orleans, 1735*.[110]

The long Middle Passage dragged Africans already exhausted by the oceanic traumas of *la traversée* farther up the Mississippi River to the plantation outposts above New Orleans. Slaveowners, large and small, secured bondspeople on credit and, more rarely with specie, as ships landed at Balize, Dauphine Island, and the west bank of the Mississippi River across from New Orleans. Most travel to plantations upriver occurred by flatboat, sometimes piloted by enslaved men, with captive Africans once again following waterways to their destinations. The large plantations at White Earth and St. Catherine, or at Chapitoulas and the Compagnie des Indes plantation, employed the most enslaved black men, women, and children, largely from the continent or a generation removed.[111] In 1720, African slaves likely labored on the caravan sent upriver by Marc Hubert, St. Catherine's proprietor, which included eight boats "loaded with merchandise" and himself, his family, sixty laborers, and a domestic "he had brought with him from France." Enslaved laborers helped him to raise a water mill and harvest tobacco.[112] In 1728, Chépart, after being appointed commandant at Fort Rosalie, brought several Africans to the post from New Orleans with similar goals in mind.[113] By 1729, the two plantations at Fort Rosalie were home to some of the largest concentrations of black men, women, and children along the Gulf Coast. Two hundred and eighty black women, children, and men were enslaved at the post itself and, as at New Orleans, Africans traveled often between the fort and the enslaved communities on plantations in the area.[114]

Alongside indigenous slaves and European settlers, enslaved Africans constructed housing and levees, farmed, and carried out the subsistence duties of daily life by collecting firewood, drawing water, cooking, and laundering. Slaveowners set slaves to work clearing land, cutting down the cypress swamps to make way for buildings and plantations, making pitch and tar, or harvesting indigo, rice, and tobacco. Settlers with fewer resources—and fewer or no slaves—made their way by securing smaller land shares or squatting on the larger concessions, planting indigo and rice for sale, and corn for subsistence where they could.

Indigenous populations dominated the region Africans entered. From their Native Ground, an array of nations capitalized on opportunities to trade with the French, purchase slaves, and acquire goods.[115] Large nations did so from a position of power: the Natchez, Choctaw, and Chickasaw cultivated trade relationships with the French and defended their alliances with the British and Spanish. The Natchez, in particular, viewed the French not as guests and renters, but as strangers and trading partners to be cautiously incorporated into the broader hierarchy and on Natchez terms.[116] As the colonial population increased, tensions led to raids and skirmishes, instigated by Natchez warriors of the White Apple, Jenzenaqe, and Grigra villages. Enslaved Africans quickly found themselves caught in the crossfire. In 1722, White Apple warriors killed an enslaved black man named Bougou.[117] When Bienville and Stung Serpent, the Natchez war chief, calmed the waters, Bienville's demands included the head of a free black living at White Apple "where he had made himself chief of a party."[118] In 1725, after much political maneuvering by his rivals, Bienville was recalled to France.[119] The new governor, Étienne de Périer, arrived with a special mandate to aggressively develop the land around Fort Rosalie into tobacco plantations worked by African slaves.[120] For the French, Louisiana belonged to them by right of conquest. For the Natchez, the French had overstayed their welcome. For Africans on Natchez land, as recent arrivals and children beginning to be born on Louisiana soil, they had little control over who purchased them and where they labored. In 1728, when Chépart demanded the White Apple village relocate to make way for tobacco production, the Natchez revolted.[121]

On the morning of 28 November 1729, an estimated seven hundred or more Natchez warriors arrived at Fort Rosalie. While Baude and her slaves waited at Les Cayes for *La Galathée* to continue on its journey to New Orleans, African women and children at Fort Rosalie, many of them recent arrivals to the colony, struggled to survive an outpost in upheaval. Some three hundred women, children, and men waited and watched as Natchez warriors killed dozens of white colonists, then plundered the storehouses, buildings, and boats at the outpost. Within hours, they killed 145 French men, 36 French women, and over 50 French children.[122] With the fort under their control, Natchez warriors herded most of the Africans together, keeping them alive and captive alongside some fifty white women and children.[123] Able-bodied captives, white women laboring alongside African, helped to package confiscated goods, mend clothing, cook, secure firewood, pound corn, and otherwise attend to the new masters of the fort. Some enslaved people served as porters, transporting goods about the reclaimed settlement.[124] Those who did not work remained cloistered in two of the main buildings, supervised by the wife of the Great Sun, or chief. [125] When the looting finished, the Natchez burned the homes of the French inhabitants. Black women and girls may have watched but would undoubtedly have smelled the smoke as the buildings turned to ash. Any belongings that black women claimed as their own would have gone up in smoke alongside that of their owners as the Natchez celebrated their victory.

Back in New Orleans, African women, children, and men grappled with news of the revolt and a growing backlash from white settlers. African men faced a governor willing to use them as weapons against both white panic and further Native insurgency. When Fort Rosalie refugees arrived in New Orleans, word of the revolt brought residents running to the riverbank.[126] The survivors of the attack arrived naked or barely clothed, maimed and wounded. They reported that "everything was on fire and covered in blood at Natchez." The governor turned to the Choctaw as the next largest nation of allies and mobilized a military force to attack the Natchez, reclaim people and property (of which Africans were both), and subdue the region. Suddenly, across New Orleans, rumors spread that the African slaves were on the verge of rising up as well.[127] Panic gripped the town. White settler terror about a Natchez attack combined with long-existing suspicion, anxiety, and fear of a wholesale Native-African revolt. Without provocation, the governor sent a group of enslaved black men belonging to the Company on a mission to massacre a village of Chaouchas downriver from the town. Later, he justified his strategy to Company officials in France as one of divide and conquer. In contrast to the Natchez warriors' offer of incorporation, Périer used the Atlantic lexicon of use, possession, and commodification when he noted, "If I had been willing to use our negro volunteers I should have destroyed all these little nations which are of no use to us, and which might on the contrary cause our negroes to revolt as we see by the example of the Natchez."[128]

For black women, serving in French military campaigns would not have been an option. As women, they would not be enlisted as soldiers. African women did participate, but as enslaved labor, the property of soldiers, officers, and artisans engaged in war work. They likely would have helped dig the entrenchments Périer commissioned around the city, laborious work that fell to slaves, regardless of gender.[129] Meanwhile, the risks they faced included exposure to raids, physical capture and resale, and the gendered violence that accompanied warfare. At the same time, Périer sent or allowed French troops to brutalize New Orleans' black community. According to one report, Périer challenged black slaves to show their loyalty and enlist in the coming expedition against the Natchez.[130] After the first attack on the Chaouchas, Périer continued to use enslaved and possibly free black labor. A few days after, a detachment of twenty volunteers, including six black volunteers, traveled upriver to warn the Illinois settlements, pick up *coureurs de bois*, and distribute arms to colonists at the settlements. Périer did not formally offer manumission to those who fought, although an offer appeared later. But this meant the choices faced by enslaved black men did not amount to much. They included continued persecution, suspicion, and threat from white settlers and their own owners, who feared and imagined bloodshed or taking up arms in a war that black slaves played little role in sparking and might not return from. Of course, a third option remained available to all slaves in New Orleans, regardless of gender—allying with and absconding to those Native nations in revolt.

As currency, property, and pawns, black women, children, and men from Natchez to New Orleans continued to suffer the ungendering violence of *la traversée*.[131] Some may have endured the Atlantic crossing as recently as a month before.[132] The Natchez were a slaveowning polity and used black slaves to procure European goods, to leverage ransoms, and to broker alliances with other nations and also with the French or British in the region. In one account of the November attack, Natchez warriors slaughtered French cattle and fed it to Africans at Fort Rosalie, "intending to go and sell them later to the English of Carolina."[133] In another, after the attack, warriors celebrated their victory by seizing "brandy, flour, and the rest in dry goods, like shoes, hats, powder, [and] musket balls," from a supply shipment recently arrived from New Orleans, drinking and carousing into the night.[134] When attempting to secure the loyalty of the Choctaw against the French, the Great Sun offered one of the chiefs "a young Frenchman, a negro and a horse."[135] When three African slaves escaped from Natchez custody and made it to New Orleans a few days after the first attack, they claimed that warriors intended to sell the Africans "who were not of their party" to the British.[136] In the aftermath of the revolt, African women, children, and men at Natchez found themselves once again captured as both prisoners of war and property of value and forced away from newly formed kin and loved ones. *La traversée* had recommenced.

Africans' value as booty, bodies, and allies intersected with their gendered experience of war and revolt. In the tradition of *ceddo* warriors and Bambara soldiers, African men at Fort Rosalie may have seen the revolt as an opportunity and then absconded to the Natchez.[137] Natchez leaders cultivated strategic solidarity among Africans who might have similar reasons for outrage. Reportedly two black *commandeurs* (slave drivers) worked on behalf of the Natchez to procure support among enslaved Africans. The *commandeurs* secured the support of "several negroes" and, to convince others, promised that in the ensuing conflict all who rose up would get their freedom. Périer described the freedom offered Africans in the African-Natchez alliance as one where the Africans "remained with them; and that our [French] wives and our children would be their slaves."[138] While Périer was certainly giving in to the panic of the moment, as well as writing to paint his own actions in a favorable light, he also described the process of incorporation familiar in Natchez country. Natchez warriors did single out French women and children for enslavement and viewed them as leverage against the French and as possible recruits for incorporation into the Natchez nation. That the Natchez promised African warriors who fought alongside them freedom, incorporation into the nation, and access to the same spoils of war, should come as no surprise.

In contrast, enslaved African women and women of African descent may have had more complicated responses to the revolt. Some might have found that remaining with their French owners was attractive. Others could have seen allying with the Natchez as a better opportunity, a chance to choose a laboring life under new masters over death in a frontier war. These women may have been compelled by the leadership positions women in Natchez society held. As intermediaries and advisors, elite Natchez women were responsible for the politics of marriage and geopolitical alliance. Some Natchez women used that political awareness to save their own kinfolk. One woman, Tattooed-Arm, whose *mésalliance* with the missionary St. Cosme led to the birth of the Great Sun now leading the Natchez assault on the French, attempted on multiple occasions to sabotage the attack.[139] Reports of other women with intimate ties to French colonists informing on the attack abounded.[140] War also brought with it gendered violence as people were deemed the spoils of war. French accounts of rape during the conflict centered on white women captives abused by Natchez warriors or, in at least one instance, by black men allied with the Natchez.[141] African and indigenous women would have experienced rape and sexual predation as well as being reduced to property and prisoners of war. How enslaved women at Fort Rosalie responded to such threats, however, remained unclear.

At New Orleans, some Africans viewed the bedlam of war and panic as an opportunity to make alliances with each other. Drawing on kinships forged across *la traversée* and intimacies wrought by bondage, bands of slaves united to take their freedom from their owners. Two slave conspiracies, one during the summer of 1731 and a second near the end of the same year, evidenced African attempts at outright revolt. In both cases, officials claimed to be suspicious of rumors of revolt, but this did not stop them from torturing and executing suspected leaders. The first revolt, organized by Bamana slaves and set to occur in June of 1731, was revealed when an enslaved woman domestic told her friend that after the revolt she would rename herself "Madame Périer." Officials executed eight black men as leaders by breaking them on the wheel, and they executed a ninth leader, a woman, by hanging.[142] That December, a second conspiracy led to the arrest of a black driver. Le Page du Pratz, writing about the conspiracies many years later, would attribute the June revolt to an interpreter and slave driver named Samba from Senegambia who had also led revolts against the French at Fort Arguin and on the slave ship *L'Annibal*.[143] Possibly a fabrication in an already-embellished account, du Pratz may have been referring to the same Samba Bambara who demanded that the Company at Senegal expel his wife from Saint-Louis. If this Samba Bambara did find his way to New Orleans, he would presumably have lost his life in the panic over black revolt.[144]

Over the coming months, African, French, Choctaw, and other Native allies succeeded in dismantling Natchez hegemony on the Gulf Coast. Marie Baude arrived in New Orleans in January 1729 as the first French campaigns against the Natchez were deployed from New Orleans. With each new alarm, rumor, or military excursion, hysteria engulfed the town. Baude would have just missed the chaos caused by the sounding of alerts around the city on the nineteenth, a ruckus that drew residents out of their beds near midnight, some rushing to escape on ships, others running through the streets, wailing. The news from survivors still trickling in from other settlements and their terror added to the panic.[145] By the end of that January, the French attacked. At least fifteen black fighters joined a combined French-Choctaw force to meet the Natchez in battle, along with black men who were not armed and enslaved laborers. In the struggle, they found themselves fighting other black men—the Natchez's African allies. At least some of these allies helped facilitate the French loss and Natchez escape by defending the gunpowder reservoirs from the Choctaw and aiding the Natchez in entering the fort.[146]

African women and children struggled to stay alive, pulled in multiple directions as French, Choctaw, Natchez, and their respective black male allies attempted to retain or recapture them. By March, when an initial peace was declared, black male soldiers had helped the French and Choctaw recapture fifty to one hundred women, children, and men of African descent.[147] As precious as enslaved Africans might have been as *pièces d'Inde*, when identified with insurgency, revolt, and violence *against* French rule, that value became corrupted. For three recaptured slaves "who had been most unruly, and who had taken the most active part in behalf of the Natchez," Périer allowed the Choctaw to burn them alive "with a degree of cruelty which has inspired all the Negroes with a new horror of the Savages, but which will have a beneficial effect in securing the safety of the Colony."[148] In August 1730, reinforcements from France arrived, led by the same Périer de Salvert who once issued instructions for proper behavior at Saint-Louis du Sénégal. Salvert and Périer led another French-Choctaw-African expedition upriver, battering with cannons the Natchez who remained at forts along the Black River.[149] By February 1731, the Great Sun negotiated a peace that included the return of the rest of the French women, children, and Africans they held. For those Africans who sided with the Natchez, peace did not ensure their safety. Nineteen men and one woman of African descent returned to captivity among the French, along with fifty black slaves who sided with the Natchez against the French. The rest, the Natchez claimed, had been killed. French soldiers imprisoned the Great Sun, Tattooed-Arm, nobles, and about forty warriors. In all, about two hundred Natchez women, children, and men were sent to New Orleans, where they were placed on ships and sold for the profit of the Company in Saint-Domingue.[150]

Meanwhile, women, children, and men of African descent, as chattel property and general and domestic labor, remained scattered across Choctaw territory.[151] Choctaw, Tunicas, and allies among other Native nations expected to share in the spoils—French women, children, and Africans—as part of their promise to go to war. The Choctaw, in particular, proved especially intransigent about relinquishing the enslaved black people they captured. With the Natchez threat neutralized, Périer sent emissaries to Choctaw villages across the region to negotiate, cajole, and threaten chiefs into relinquishing captives. The tables turned on the French when Choctaw chiefs like Alibamon Mingo demanded large ransoms for each slave taken from the Natchez or they would be sold to the British.[152] The Choctaw used the conflict to reopen a broader set of negotiations, sending a delegation of chiefs to New Orleans to demand lower duties on European trade goods.[153] As with the Natchez, the Choctaw understood Africans as fungible, and became particular about what goods they demanded in exchange. The chief of the Cuchtushas refused to relinquish the black slaves he held unless paid in limborg cloth, refusing "jackets, guns and a kettle." Individual Choctaw named specific compensations of their own. A warrior named Poulain demanded a horse in exchange for his black slave.[154] As a whole, black women, children, and men once enslaved on tobacco plantations at White Earth, St. Catherine, and within or about Natchez found themselves in varying circumstances. Those who did not end up in Natchez, Choctaw, or British hands as the spoils of war were redistributed to anyone who could purchase them.

The Natchez Revolt changed the direction of slave trading, slaveownership, and plantation production in the region for decades to come. Natchez descendants themselves understood their dispersal not as a struggle over land and trade, but as a tragic story of incorporation gone wrong. According to one Natchez descendant, the Natchez were careless when they allowed the French to establish themselves in "the suburb below the town." They relied on French "blind devotion to love" toward their women to weaken them. After having destroyed the French at Fort Rosalie, they took advantage of the spoils, but "they had no idea that there were any Frenchman [*sic*] to avenge their horrid deed."[155] The French, however, also failed to destroy the Natchez. At least one contingent escaped capture, never declared peace, and hosted African allies among them. In 1731, at least one Bamana slave made his way among black communities at New Orleans to encourage them to join the rebellion as a way to secure their freedom.[156] Absorbed by the Chickasaw in 1731, the Natchez continued to harass French colonists from Chickasaw territory until 1735, when, fearing pressure would compel the Chickasaw to relinquish them, the remaining Natchez separated and joined the Creek and Cherokee.[157]

In the aftermath of the revolt and with tobacco production considered a failure, the trading company relinquished the colony of Louisiana to Crown rule. In 1733, royal officials appointed a royal governor, based at New Orleans, to oversee all of lower Louisiana, including its holdings along the Gulf Coast. The Crown then returned Bienville to this illustrious role and sent him back to Louisiana. But the loss of trading-company control over Louisiana confirmed that the center of gravity in the slaveholding French Atlantic had shifted south. French slave ships all but ceased to transport Africans from West and West

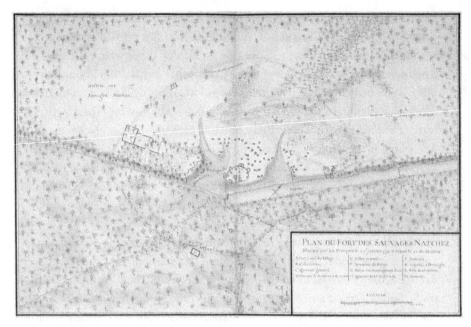

Figure 9. The Natchez surrendered to the French on 25 January 1731, although some accounts claimed bands of Natchez escaped into the woods, evading French capture. Fort of the Natchez blockaded by the French on 20 January 1731 and destroyed on 25 January. Courtesy of the Bibliothèque nationale de France, Paris.

Central Africa to the Gulf Coast, vying for Saint-Domingue, Martinique, or Guadeloupe instead. In 1734, Company directors in France circulated a *mémoire* to their officials managing trade off Senegal's coast. They explained that a reorganization had occurred and outlined a new set of best practices for trade to Saint-Domingue and Martinique. Perhaps inspired by the utter failure of diplomacy and exchange between Natives and French along the Gulf Coast, the new directives also included strategies for employing Africans at the *comptoirs*, wages that should be offered, and regulations for managing the concession.[158]

The Crown resumed administration over Louisiana, but according to the sugar-addicted geopolitics of the Atlantic world, New Orleans had moved to the edge of imperial interest and history. Indigo cultivation became the major plantation product of the region, an industry led by the Chauvin brothers, Claude-Joseph Villars DuBreuil, and Bienville, all concessionaires in the

Chapitoulas area nearer New Orleans. Without trading-company financing to encourage voyages, slave-ship captains diverted their attention to the Caribbean. DuBreuil would grow wealthy enough to privately fund one slave ship from West Africa to Louisiana, the 1743 voyage of the *Saint Ursin* direct from Gorée. Most of the captives who disembarked from that voyage would be integrated into the DuBreuil properties and contributed to his amassing the most wealth of any settler in the colony by 1746. DuBreuil, however, would be the exception, and Louisiana indigo did not become popular with planters or purchasers abroad. With plantation production diminished and few new imports of slaves from the continent, Louisiana shifted into becoming a society with slaves.[159]

The Natchez insurgency also led to the consolidation on the shores of the Gulf Coast of a new colonial institution for men of African descent. African men who fought for the French impressed them with their bravery and savagery, leading to the formation of the free black militia. Périer noted the fifteen men "who were permitted to take arms did deeds of surprising valor. If these soldiers had not been so expensive and so necessary to the colony it would have been safer to use them than ours who seem expressly made for Louisiana, they are so bad."[160] According to officials like François Fleuriau and Jacques de la Chaise, black soldiers who fought against the Natchez should be offered their freedom. Fleuriau suggested fifteen men in particular, including Trudy, Caesar, Crispin, and Legro [*sic*] for these special manumissions. Whether each of these specific men secured manumission remains unclear, but a cohort of at least fifteen veterans of the Natchez war did receive their freedom.[161] According to one historian, an official suggested manumissions for military service would encourage slaves to support the French and "will give others a great desire to deserve similar favors by material services."[162] In the years to follow, the black militia would shape the nature of black freedom on the coast. It would frequently be called into service, and select enslaved men would continue to access manumission through their ability to execute acts of devastating violence supporting the colonial regime.[163]

The return of captive and traumatized French women and girls pushed colonial officials to expend resources on a second institution—the Ursuline convent. In 1727, twelve French nuns had arrived in New Orleans with a unique charge: to found a convent and open a school for women and girls, including women and girls of African and indigenous descent. None of these Catholic devotees expected that, only a few years later, orphaned girls and widowed women, all Natchez survivors, would overwhelm their resources. Company officials turned to the Ursulines to provide relief for women and girls. Galvanized, the Ursuline nuns took in several of the orphaned girls, appointing sisters especially to their care, opened their school to the widowed women, and made plans to open "a house of refuge for women of questionable character."[164] In May 1730, eighty-five women, including at least three women of color, formed the Ladies' Congregation of the Children of Mary, a lay confraternity under the Ursuline convent. In appreciation of the Ursulines' expanded role at the outpost, colonial officials authorized a new set of buildings be built to house the confraternity, a complex that would include the Royal Hospital. For the next several years, the slaveowning Ursuline convent provided relief to orphaned girls and education to women, offering their services and succor "across race and status for years to come."[165]

The creation of two new institutions, one to reward black men and one to relieve white women, left black women nearly invisible at the intersection.[166] Enslaved black women would continue to labor in the war economy alongside the soldiers, officers, coopers, and gunsmiths who owned them. Or they would accompany their owners on campaigns as domestics, but without comparable access to free status. The Ursulines and affiliated lay confraternities like the Children of Mary offered aid to Native women and African women and women of African descent, but as subordinates within a relief project centering on French women and girls. Colonial authorities, sacred or secular, did not see black women as requiring special protection. Meanwhile many black women were still riding the long Middle Passage in Native territory, passing beyond New Orleans into slavery among the Choctaw or being sold to the British. Some ended their own lives.[167] As late as March 1731, one enslaved informant reported the state of black women, men, and children among the Choctaw. Six black women who belonged to the Company remained among black slaves still held by the Choctaw. An indeterminate number of women were part of a group of eighteen people who belonged to private owners. Seven women and men had died; four belonged to the Company and three were privately owned.[168]

Despite this intersection, women of African descent grew new womanhoods as well as new lives from the terror of *la traversée*. In June 1731, pushed to extremes and, perhaps, inspired by Natchez refusal, a black woman had celebrated the possibility of renaming herself Madame Périer. She told her friend, and, in the hushed but glittering tones of feminine conspiracy, they delighted and reveled in the possibility of freedom. This freedom (and their enjoyment of it) did not require emancipation, as the Bambara conspiracy did not mean freedom for all enslaved. It did not entail an end to hierarchy or even slavery. Her invocation of the honorific "Madame" still spoke to a claim of power, free status, authority, and womanhood. In this, she gestured backward to the free wives of the Bambara soldiers who "could not be forced to leave" as well as to property-owning stakeholders like Seignora Catti and even Marie Baude. The logic of *la traversée* fragmented African women and girls into Atlantic products, useful as fractured currency, producers of plantation goods and enslaved labor, receptacles for a host of monstrous fantasies and intimate violences. African women and women of African descent did not themselves inherit this logic or allow it to define their womanhood. However, there could also be no return to the continent of their birth or a free state of African womanhood predating slavery. The speculative Madame Périer looked to a future beyond bondage and constructed a new womanhood to meet it in community with other women. She was not the only one.

Articulated against race, property, and slave status, genders familiar in the Old World of the African continent took on new meanings. In other words, the ways enslaved Africans understood themselves as women, men, or children experienced an unprecedented onslaught as slave-ship captains, agents, and prospective slaveowners determined when to purchase, sell, or exchange slaves by the captives' size, musculature, and reproductive capacity. The kinds of violations enslaved Africans experienced on the coast, even as *captifs de case*, increased exponentially in the space of the slave ship. Womanhood took on a new meaning as the experience of bondage and commodification extended into intimate, kinship, and property relations in the New World. But even within the tortured logic of *la traversée* itself, African women, children, and men laid the foundation for new kinds of kinships, reformulations of intimacy, and polymorphous gendered reimaginings. In the years to come, the law, the militia, and the hospital would become critical spaces, ones where women of African descent would articulate a freedom resilient enough to bear the weight of their new gendered racial status.

Figure 10. Watercolor by Jean-Pierre Lassus, *Veüe et Perspective de la Nouvelle Orleans*, 1726. Courtesy of the Bibliothèque nationale de France, Paris.

Chapter 4

*

Full Use of Her:
Intimacy, Service, and Labor in New Orleans

We grant him his liberty in effect and full use of his wife to live with him save when the Company needs to employ her in its service.

—Représentation du M. Fleuriau and Decision du Conseil,
"Deliberations de Superior Council," 1725

In 1725, Suzanne, a *négresse*, moved with her husband to a plot of land just beyond the growing town of New Orleans. She'd been a slave belonging to the Compagnie des Indes (Company of the Indies), laboring on the Company's plantation, one of the trading company's attempts at promoting commercial agriculture. Before 1725, she would likely have labored alongside about twenty-five other women and men, drawn from ships that had begun arriving only six years earlier. From the perspective of the trading company, these were fragile years. The collapse of the Compagnie des Indes left a terrible taste in foreign investors' mouths, and the migration of settlers from France had slowed even as the importation of Africans increased. While at the Company plantation, Suzanne would have resided on one of the largest concessions in the colony, possibly in one of the *cabannes des nègres* "spaced here and there" across the river from New Orleans. With other bondspersons, she likely would have ridden or conducted pirogues back and forth across the river, traveling between town and the plantations at nearby Chapitoulas, or even as far as the White Earth and St. Catherine concessions at Natchez. She certainly would have gathered with other women, children, and men on Sundays when the population of the plantation nearly doubled, and enslaved and free alike made their way across the river for the *calinda* (a type of dance).[1] At these gatherings, she would have shared news and gossip with Africans and any Native or even European women, men, or children in attendance. She would have met old and made new friends.[2]

Suzanne's move from slave ship to plantation to something like domesticity signaled a perceptible change in status. Her husband, Louis Congo, had recently entered into a contract with the Superior Council of Louisiana. Louis would serve as the colony's executioner. Congo agreed to perform amputations, brandings, hangings, and whippings, to torture and break colonial subjects on the wheel on behalf of the Crown and colonial officials. His labor knew no racial boundaries. Settlers, *engagés* (indentured servants), and slaves of all races submitted to Congo's ministry. In return, Louis Congo was granted his freedom, land, rations—and Suzanne. Suzanne did not receive her freedom. Louis originally requested freedom for both of them in return for executing the grisly duties of empire. Although the 1724 *Code Noir*, revised and generated for Louisiana, permitted manumission, the Superior Council balked at the prospect of freeing two slaves. The officers of the council granted Louis "full use of his wife to live with him save when the Company needs to employ her in its service." Louis agreed and proceeded to rent his wife from the Compagnie des Indes.[3] As far as officials were concerned, Louis's request for "sa femme" had been honored. Suzanne's opinion on such matters was either not solicited or not recorded.

To fully appreciate black women's lives and labors in the wake of the long Middle Passage to the Gulf Coast, we must take a step back to explore the impact of a new gendered labor regime on the earliest arrivals. Even as the Gulf Coast became, for some, one stop among many points in the Atlantic slave trade, a growing population of women, children, and men remained in Louisiana, grappling with a world turned upside down. Viewed from the shores of the Mississippi River, slavery and freedom, gender and blackness, and intimacy and kinship took new forms. Use, possession, and forced labor beat new meaning into black skin once Africans found themselves in the Americas. To map the world that enslaved Africans entered as ships that carried them embarked from the West and West Central African coast means following them to the shores of New Orleans, a strange new world, and up the Mississippi River. As men like Salvert issued their regulations for proper behavior toward free African women at the Senegal *comptoirs*, an enslaved population of African descent was growing across the Atlantic. African women, children, and men moved through the devastating ungendering machine of *la traversée*, a process dominated by men in power who endeavored to transform people into *pièces d'Inde* for profit and consumption. With the monopoly of power on their side, colonial officials and slaveowners worked to tie free status to a legal fiction of manumission or release from bondage (*liberté* or *affranchissement*) they controlled. The boundary between slave and free sharpened. Meanwhile, as African women, men, and children emerged from the long Middle Passage, they fought to recover and re-create kinship ties, autonomy, safety, security, and some new sense of themselves in this strange new world. The New Orleans Atlantic world was one of overlapping diasporas and contingent freedoms. More than ever, safety and security required manumission, but manumission required intimacy with empire. For black men like Louis Congo, that often meant acceding to use, service, and possession as employees of the Company. For black women like Suzanne, that often meant use, service, and possession by men in power.

Africans on Native Ground Before 1724

Women of African descent along the Gulf Coast lived lives marked by isolation, scarcity, and the communal need to survive in a difficult environment. Until 1719, only a handful of African women and women of African descent lived and labored among a scattering of about a hundred waterlogged households crowded on the high ground at the river's edge. The settlement included a hospital, the barracks, and "half a wretched warehouse" that served as the church. Many of the trees along the natural levees, "sweet gum, hickory, cottonwood, magnolia, red maple, hackberry, and pecan," fell to residents making space for homes and subsistence garden plots or were used to provide wood for lodgings. Farther from the river's banks, cypress and Spanish moss remained, crowding and fencing in the settlement. Muddy paths and portages cut between these stands of trees and into the swamp, north toward the lake, and roughly southeast and northwest in either direction toward concessions lining the river. These concessions operated plantations and settlements, farms legitimately distributed by the Company or squatted upon by errant settlers and, later, even slaves. After the Company of the Indies acquired Louisiana, ships under Company employ began transporting French subjects and settlers without contracts as well as *engagés*, forced and semiforced penal labor, to the site. In 1721, Adrien Pauger, the royal engineer, would arrive and attempt to sort the haphazardly placed buildings onto a city grid, with limited success. The next year, a hurricane decimated the grid and forced multi-term Governor Jean Baptiste Le Moyne, Sieur de Bienville, Pauger, and other Company officials to begin again. This time, the Superior Council initiated a series of regulations compelling slaveowners to employ their slaves to hold back the river. Under threat of fines, slaveowners were asked to draft slaves as petty engineers constructing canals, ditches, and levees around and throughout the town.[4] Although the enslaved engineers were moderately successful, in New Orleans, water would always have its way; in ten years another hurricane would destroy what was created.[5]

The actual numbers of women of African descent before 1719 remain difficult to estimate.[6] In 1708, Nicolas de LaSalle conducted a census of inhabitants at Mobile, one of the earliest capitals of the region.[7] The census listed officers, soldiers, sailors, "canadiens," servants, priests, general laborers, cabin boys, *habitants*, women, children, and slaves. The "women" and "children" were listed without racial designation, although LaSalle described the eighty slaves listed as mostly *sauvagesses* (indigenous women enslaved to other inhabitants). LaSalle's census remains the only extant census preceding the more detailed census of the region, conducted between 1721 and 1723, by Diron d'Artaguette. Despite leaving little trace in the archive, it is likely that Africans, including black women, were among those present in the region before 1721. In 1709, Bienville and d'Artaguette were accused of flouting the official ban on slave trading with the Caribbean islands. Whether by accident or on purpose, the two officials sent a ship to Saint-Domingue that stopped in Havana, Cuba, "on pretext of looking for powder." While there, it picked up several slaves in what one historian described as the "first documentary evidence" of African slaves arriving in Louisiana.[8] Antoine Crozat, in his brief time as proprietary owner of the colony, held a contract to embark one slave ship per year from Africa to the Americas. Evidence from extant slave-ship registers suggests he never availed himself of his privilege, but by 1712, officials reported there were "ten blacks in all of Louisiana" from Mobile to Illinois.[9] In all likelihood *at least* ten Africans resided along the Gulf Coast alone, as colonists found their own ways of circumventing official decrees by smuggling.[10] Among this handful of slaves may have been black women, the first to reside in the region before the Compagnie des Indes began transporting slaves from the African continent.

As in *la traversée*, black women were already a metaphorical presence in the machinations of colonial and Company officials, who strategized ways to profit from their newest acquisition. As early as 1709, LaSalle, who complained of *coureurs de bois* engaged in intimate and domestic unions with Native women in his 1708 census, wrote to the Minister of the Marine. He asked the Crown to send Africans (*nègres*) of both sexes each year to supplement the enslaved Native population.[11] His reasoning was simple. Native workers "cause us trouble" and "are not appropriate for hard labor like the blacks." This presumption alongside an explicit call for Africans of both sexes outlined a set of official priorities—an intention to reproduce an enslaved population of hard laborers vis-à-vis the wombs of African women. Interesting enough, Bienville likewise tied the rise of an African laboring population to purging a resident and troublesome Native population. Between 1706 and 1708, he requested permission to trade Gulf Coast Native slaves for African slaves purchased from slaveholders, slave traders, and ships traveling from the Caribbean. Bienville's proposal suggested that a two-to-one trade of two Native slaves for one African would "do the colonists much good."[12]

Any African women and women of African descent in New Orleans may have found some uneasy camaraderie with Native women scattered among households at the time. The coast's integration into Mississippian indigenous slave-trading networks, dominated by Natchez, Choctaw, and Chickasaw traders, helped supply the French with their first bonded laborers.[13] Enslaved Native women, notoriously intransigent, continued to resist bondage by absconding into the frontier.[14] Two-thirds of indigenous slaves living in eighteenth-century Louisiana were female. Slavery, as it existed in New Orleans before the arrival of African slaves, was a gendered military affair involving domestic labor and sex acts without compensation. Until 1719, Native women bore the brunt of it.

The prominence of female slaves of Native nations among the eighty or so slaves counted in the 1708 census attested to their presence among the growing class of bonded laborers at New Orleans.[15] Women dominated the enslaved indigenous population around New Orleans—the same population Bienville wished to dispense with via trans-shipment Caribbean slave trades. Many of them lived as slaves, in concubinage to French men, or both. From the early sixteenth century in New Canada, French officials, settlers, and *coureurs de bois* trading fur along the river routes held and also traded Native people as slaves. Similar slaving occurred once the French moved farther south and along the Gulf Coast. Quinipissa, Houma, Acolapissa, Tchouacha, Chitimachas, and other *petite nations*, as the French called the smaller Native nations, made their home in the area around New Orleans. French officials authorized raids on these smaller groups, targeting the Chitimachas and Alibamons, in particular.[16] The Natchez, Chickasaw, and Choctaw, the largest and most heavily militarized nations in the area, engaged in their own traditions of slave trading and forced bondage well before the arrival of the French, by capturing and enslaving members of smaller groups in raids, or as prisoners of wars they engaged in with each other.[17] These three alternated between exchanging goods, raiding settlements, and forming alliances over time, splitting their loyalties between French, British, and Spanish colonial officials and individual traders.

Enslaving indigenous women occurred hand in hand with implementing and eventually nullifying *mésalliance* as a policy. Drawn from France's long-term engagements with indigenous nations farther north, *mésalliance* encouraged Catholic marriage and informal conjugal unions between Native women and French or French-Canadian men. For French officials, indigenous nations could be integrated into "the blood of France" through these sacred and secular ties. Crown and Church authorities in Quebec debated and challenged *mésalliance* long before the French arrived on the Gulf Coast.[18] By the eighteenth century, Catholic marriage and *mésalliance* existed uneasily alongside forced domestic and sexual labor. Bonded Native women's labor filled a need for labor and intimacy on the ground. As enslaving indigenous women grew commonplace, *mésalliance* as a policy rendered invisible the precarious position of the women involved. By 1713, Cadillac, then governor, described the "use of" Native women by French men as an illicit matter that kept the men "from going to confessional."[19]

In time, French governors in Canada reoriented to conceive of intimate relations between French men and Native women as a threat. French colonial officials and missionaries could not prevent French men from residing in the Native villages. Their everyday lack of control over sex acts between French men and free or enslaved Native women, and an inability to influence French men's decision to take or not take Native women as brides, forced officials to rethink *mésalliance* as a policy. Interestingly enough, *mésalliance* as a policy also underestimated Native women's own desires and strategic use of French men for their own purposes—a miscalculation that contributed to its failure. In 1715, Commissary Jean-Baptiste Dubois Duclos's description of why *mésalliance* did not work gestured to the same. Native women, he noted, did not stay with French men, never mind the union, except in one instance: only French men living in Native villages "in the manner of Savages" could keep them.[20] Native women desired to keep, as Duclos inferred, men with some connection to the French, but who could also be integrated into their own communities. By the 1780s, the adoption of Native dress marked New World French manhood in Illinois Country and Canada.[21]

Forced to restrategize colonizing a vast land with limited resources and ambivalent metropolitan commitment, French officials blamed *mésalliance*'s failure on the women themselves. By the time Bienville wrote to the Crown and suggested trading Native slaves for African, Catholic officials like Henri Roulleaux de la Vente, and colonial authorities like Antoine de la Mothe, Sieur de Cadillac, governor of New Canada, complained specifically about liaisons between French men and enslaved Native women. La Mothe charged fur traders and soldiers with keeping enslaved indigenous women for domestic labor, noting they "pretend they can't do without them for their laundry and for their food, and to keep house." Cadillac outright accused French settlers of enslaving indigenous women for sexual labor, suggesting laundering was cover for more lascivious practices.[22] Meanwhile, Gulf South nations participated in slave trading with French, British, and Spanish settlers almost immediately, supplying European colonists with Native and, as Africans arrived, black slaves. Indigenous women's recalcitrance and the region's integration with African slaving networks sped the failure of *mésalliance* as a policy and encouraged the transition to bonded labor.

Intimacy, Manumission, and the 1724 *Code Noir*

As the first ships from the African continent began to arrive, officials in Louisiana stood at the intersection of two French imperial discourses. On the one hand, *mésalliance* with Native women and integrating Native nations into the French empire lingered as policy and discourse. For the French minority on Native Ground, still relying on trade in supplies, fur, and the goodwill of surrounding Native nations, engagement with indigenous women as bondspeople or kin had become an everyday part of existence. On the other hand, French officials inherited a French Atlantic suspicion of intimate relations between African and European and an illicit taste for African women as violated and violable. Attempts to legislate intimate relations between white men and African women in the Antilles became key elements of a wider French Atlantic discourse, linking intimacy between the races to economic processes, and relations between white men and black women in particular to services exchanged. As slavery and slave trading spread across the Atlantic, French officials shaped official manumission policies with a concern with intimacy between races in mind.[23]

After 1685, the promulgation of an "edict concerning the enforcement of order in the Islands of the Americas," or *Code Noir*, did much of this work, institutionalizing slavery and slaveownership in the French colonies.[24] On the Atlantic African coast, French officials' preoccupation with relations between African women and European men made barely any headway. In the Caribbean, however, the French monopoly of power and control over military, legal, and social institutions begat a slave code preoccupied with surveilling and limiting the laboring and reproductive lives of enslaved Africans. The 1685 *Code Noir* did not ameliorate slavery—it defined the conditions of bondage according to French colonial priorities. Articles attempted to curb slaveowner excess by requiring owners to baptize slaves, provide a modicum of subsistence, and support elderly and infirm bondspersons. The edict also prohibited slaves from laboring on Sundays and forbade slaveowners from separating slave families by sale or forcing slaves to marry against their will.[25] The 1685 *Code Noir* also upheld the slaveowner's authority over the lives and bodies of those enslaved. It forbade priests from performing marriage rites for slaves without their owners' permission. Slaves could not bear arms or gather in public without written permission. The punishment for bondspeople who assaulted their masters, mistresses, or children was death. Corporeal punishment awaited runaways, if they should be captured, and was described in graphic detail. Colonial authorities also assumed authority to punish masters who maimed or killed their human property, but were encouraged to judge them "according to the circumstances of the atrocity" and empowered to forgive them without appealing to the king for grace.[26] In the words of Colin Dayan, "The Black Code designates slaves only to negate them."[27]

The *Code Noir* also created the category of the free person of African descent—only to negate it as well. The 1685 *Code Noir* emphasized and punished reproduction between free men of any race (*hommes libres*) and enslaved women. A free man who fathered a child with an enslaved woman and the enslaved woman's owner were both fined 2,000 livres in sugar. If the father was also the owner, the *Code Noir* empowered authorities to confiscate the slave and any children for the profit of the hospital, but "never to regain their freedom."[28] Men who knowingly fathered children with slaves would not be able to purchase the slaves' freedom. As for the free women and children of African descent already in the colonies by 1685, the *Code Noir* acknowledged their presence but as a subordinate population.[29] Free people of color born in the colonies and slaves freed from slavery (*affranchi* or *affranchie*) became French subjects, regardless of their place of birth. Article 59 of the *Code Noir* entitled them to "all the same rights, privileges, and liberties enjoyed by persons born free."[30] Regardless, free people of color were singled out from white colonists for harsher punishments. Article 39, which targeted those who harbored fugitive slaves, singled out freed slaves for a special tax of 3,000 livres of sugar if found guilty. Freed slaves were also admonished to "maintain a particular respect for their masters, their widows and to their children," and officials were empowered to punish *affranchis* more severely if found guilty of any crimes.[31]

For French colonists, especially trading-company officials in the Antilles, enforcing slave status also meant policing the boundaries and meaning of and access to freedom. The 1685 *Code Noir* defined the status of free black people and the policy whereby slaves gained their freedom. The 1685 *Code Noir* did not protect slaves and it did not prevent enslaved or free women of African descent from intimate violence. It established a coherent structure for protecting the Crown's investment in enslaved labor and established authority over its colonial subjects. And in doing so, officials yoked black women's reproductive labor to the production of slaves, the security of the colony, and the profit of empire. But if the *Code Noir* announced the king's policy toward blacks on paper, it hardly clarified black life in practice—particularly the intimate lives of black women. Just as intimate partnerships and sexual liaisons between African women and European men at the Senegal *comptoirs* confounded imperial officials' well-laid plans to regulate commerce, sex acts across race and status in the Antilles threatened imperial and local officials' ability to control the enslaved African population. From Company instructions to the creation of new currencies like the *pièce d'Inde*, a taste for black women as commodified, appropriated, and stolen found expression in the *Code Noir*.

The *Code Noir* endured multiple revisions as slaveowners, colonial officials, and imperial authorities in the Caribbean vacillated on how to manage colonies and slaves. In 1715, Saint-Domingue officially surpassed Martinique as the primary destination for French slave ships.[32] The brutality of slavery in Saint-Domingue defied imagination. Slaves were worked to death at a yearly mortality rate of 5 to 6 percent but exhibited a birthrate of about 3 percent.[33] As a result, the vast majority of slaves in the colony arrived from Africa and died before they could reproduce. Maroon societies developed in the hills of the Western

Province and along the border with Spanish Santo Domingo.[34] By the mid-eighteenth century, Martinique and Guadeloupe had become slave societies, and with a high rate of African slave importation, a dizzyingly high mortality rate, and a low fertility rate among female slaves, Saint-Domingue transitioned too.

Access to manumission in the Antilles began to close down as this process unfolded. In 1705, a royal edict admonished free people of African descent who aided maroons. Claiming that the 1685 article punishing *affranchis* assisting maroons did not do enough, the new edict mandated free people of African descent would "lose their liberty, to be sold with the family residing with them, at a profit to go to the Treasury of the Marine" for the crime.[35] In 1711, manumission in Martinique and Guadeloupe required approval from the governor and the intendant.[36] In 1714, the Superior Council at Cap Français in Saint-Domingue mandated perpetual bondage to all children of free men and enslaved women.[37] In 1733, Saint-Domingue punished white men for marrying across the color line by barring them from employment in the colony or from receiving officer commissions, ignoring the *Code Noir* article permitting enslaved women to be freed through marital unions.[38] More and more, free status did not exist beyond the bounds of extralegal protections of kinship, community, or ties to politically influential or wealthy patrons. Slaveowners who wished to manumit but wanted to avoid the cumbersome and expensive legal process allowed slaves to live like free people but without formal documentation as *affranchi sans l'être, libres de fait*, or *libres de savanne*.[39] *Affranchi sans l'être, libres de fait*, and *libres de savanne* were free in practice but not by law. These categories of unofficial freedom existed alongside formal manumission, but, without legal freedom, the *affranchi sans l'être* remained vulnerable to expulsion, dispossession, and reenslavement.

And yet African women and women of African descent who sought or secured their freedom pushed the acquisition and actualization of free status even further. Created for a New World context, the manumission act became a familiar instrument for African women and women of African descent in the Americas. Relocated to a place made profitable through the use and possession of their bodies, and designated as the means of bringing enslaved children into the world, black women incorporated securing manumission into their practices of freedom. Manumission necessitated intimate contact with institutions and men in power. In 1709, the Superior Council at Cap Français targeted *négresses* taken to France by their owners who claimed freedom as a result. Their "claims were not to be received" but those claims forced the council to reiterate a 1698 edict forbidding slaveowners from taking their bondspeople to France unless "they knew they would be loyal."[40] The 1711 edict requiring the governor and intendant to approve manumissions was partly in response to attempts by an enslaved woman named Babet to secure freedom granted her by interim intendant Vaucresson.[41] Enslaved women sought manumission through baptisms and inheritances as well, invoking kinship ties before priests and missionaries in order to circumvent colonial officials. At times, these diversions failed. Missionaries' own views of race, sex, and bondage sometimes led them to betray black women and their newborns or stigmatize African women as seeking sex across the color line, regardless of the women's own sexual decisions or white slaveowners' predations. In a 1722 statement filled with the language of use, labor, and possession, the Superior of the Jacobins in Saint-Domingue described sex between white men and black women as an "unfortunate commerce of impurity" and a "criminal coupling."[42] The Superior Council could also overturn decisions, even in testaments, rescinding the slaves' "pretended liberty" and reminding them manumission offered only a legal fiction of freedom.[43] Pretend or not, enslaved women and men continued to pursue formal freedom from bondage in creative ways, putting constant pressure on manumission ordinances and placing the boundaries of bondage in question.

In 1724, the year Marie Baude, the wife of Jean Pinet, stood before Company directors in Senegal, the Superior Council of Louisiana gathered in New Orleans to promulgate its own version of the *Code Noir*.[44] The Louisiana *Code Noir*, according to one historian, "constituted the most racially exclusive colonial law of the French empire."[45] It telegraphed the priorities of the largest slaveowners and highest-ranking officials in the colony. Louisiana governing elites Bienville, Jacques de la Chaise, Jacques Fazende, Antoine Bruslé, and Paul Perry incorporated the latest developments in jurisprudence from the Antilles, including discourses of race and gender.[46] The Louisiana *Code Noir* required that slaveowners seeking to manumit their slaves must ensure the slaves were twenty-five or older, not twenty as in the 1685 *Code Noir*. Manumissions now required the permission of the Superior Council to prevent masters from setting a price on their manumission and "causing slaves to steal and rob." Slaves could not receive gifts or inheritances, and thus no longer could be freed by being declared heirs in or executors of their owner's will, although the Louisiana *Code Noir* continued to allow slaves named as guardians of their owner's children to be treated as *affranchis*.[47]

With the Louisiana *Code Noir*, the Louisiana Superior Council codified a comprehensive and deliberate attack on sex across the color line. It discarded the arguably race-neutral terminology *hommes libres* and *esclaves* and introduced the terms *blancs* and *esclaves nègres*. It outright forbade "our white subjects of either sex from contracting marriage with the Blacks," and ordered all religious authorities to comply. The Louisiana *Code Noir* took its prohibition against interracial sex a step further when it forbade "blancs, Noirs *affranchis* or those born free from living in concubinage with the slaves." The only exceptions to the rule were black men (*hommes noir*) who married their slaves before engaging in concubinage or producing a child.[48] In short, the Louisiana *Code Noir* subjected intimate practices across race, status, and gender to an entirely new level of scrutiny. The owner of an enslaved woman who produced a mixed-race child was fined 300 livres, and the father, if he was not the owner, was fined as well. The woman and child were seized to labor in the hospital, never to be freed. Whereas the 1685 *Code Noir* waived the fine and seizure if the father married the slave (an act that freed both mother and child), in the Louisiana *Code Noir*, only free men of color were allowed the same exception.[49] The Louisiana *Code Noir* further circumscribed the liberty of free people of color. It forbade them from receiving donations or inheritances from whites, confiscating any property received for the profit of the hospital.[50] While the 1685 *Code Noir* levied a tax on free people of color who harbored fugitive slaves, the Louisiana *Code Noir* also ordered those unable to pay the tax to be sold for the profit of the colony and reenslaved.[51]

Superior Council officials, and the metropolitan authorities who ratified the Louisiana *Code Noir*, imagined—and then punished—African women according to a narrow sexual economy of bondage.[52] Only women of African descent were enslaved for sex with European men. Only their children were consigned to perpetual slavery for sex across the color line. The Louisiana *Code Noir* made no provisions for and did not distinguish between consensual or nonconsensual sexual activity. There was no stated punishment for free men in sexual relations with enslaved women that did not produce offspring. Free women of African descent with enslaved male lovers could not marry their partners and have them declared free. This exception applied only to free black men. All the while, in the French slave trade to Louisiana, a project of commodification and sexual access unfolded on slave ships and across letters between governors and the trading companies on both sides of the Atlantic.

The African women who survived *la traversée* as fractions of a *pièce d'Inde* or were born into bondage on the Gulf Coast entered a world where manumission offered little more than a legal fiction of safety and security.

Women and mixed-race children were among those most likely to be freed from bondage in colonies across the Atlantic world. However, Dominique Rogers, describing both the kinship and manumission practices of free women of African descent in the port of Cap Français, has argued that historians must retire the stereotype of women of color securing freedom through relationships to white men. In Cap Français, free women of African descent secured manumission, formed business partnerships, and created households with the help of other free women of African descent or others who were enslaved.[53] As early as the 1730s, Anne Dominique Acquiez, a free woman of African descent in the Southern Province parish of Aquin, operated a tavern where she sold goods to town residents. She also dealt in contraband, reselling goods pilfered from French ships. In 1768, Marion ditte Bin, a *négresse libre* living in Les Cayes, the same port in which Marie Baude found a brief respite from the sea some thirty years earlier, purchased a small boat from Pierre Cornier, a *mulâtre libre*, and engaged in interisland commerce. Marie Louis ditte Ruiq, a *négresse libre* also in Les Cayes, sold fabric from a shop in the city.[54] The image of the white male slaveowner bestowing manumission on grateful female slaves for "good and agreeable services" was a gendered and racialized legacy of slaveowning European travel writers' own lascivious assumptions. In Saint-Domingue, as in New Orleans, sexual availability to slaveowners did not, in and of itself, open the road to freedom. African women and women of African descent secured manumission for themselves despite the slaveowning and nonslaveowning whites around them (see Table 2).

The Louisiana *Code Noir* also reflected little of black women's intimate lives beyond the terrain of violence. Conception and childbirth evidenced certain sex acts, but did not foreclose possibilities of others. Enslaved women in the Gulf Coast, as in the Caribbean, resisted slavery and sought to control their own sexual and reproductive lives through abortion or infanticide, and by forming intimate and kinship ties to other women.[55] In an Atlantic world saturated by a taste for black women as violated and violable, it would be impossible to quantify the number of acts of sexual violence hidden from official notice as a result of black women's determination not to bring their children to term or to raise children in a world of slaves. These null values haunt the archive.

Table 2. Percentage of Female Slaves Among Total Slaves
Manumitted per Decade in Gulf Coast Louisiana, 1720–1810

Year	Female
1720	50%
1730	41%
1740	70%
1750	47%
1760	63%
1770	67%
1780	64%
1790	62%
1800	60%
1810	65%

Source: Adapted from "Freed Slaves, Louisiana, Gender Percent
by Decade," *Databases for the Study of Afro-Louisiana History and
Genealogy, 1699–1860*, CD-ROM (Baton Rouge: Louisiana State
University Press, 2000).

Null Values: Disappearing Bodies in Empirical Archives

Impossible acts of quantification marked the lives of enslaved and free women
of African descent, leaving null values, or empty spaces, in the census registers.
French colonial officials along the Gulf Coast occupied themselves with what
one scholar has described as "obsessive census-taking" as they attempted to
catalogue the varied and various populations along the Gulf Coast.[56] By track-
ing individuals across the colony, officials attempted to create a data set or
database of hierarchical, legible, interrelated subjects in service to the Crown.
They did so even as enslaved and free African women and women of African
descent engaged in practices antithetical to property and subjection, such as
securing manumission. For colonial elites, if black women could not be used
or possessed as laboring, sordid, or lecherous subjects, they received little or
no mention—but black women did not disappear. Black women labored to
secure livelihoods and spaces of safety for themselves and their kin. Their
actions, desires, and priorities shaped the meaning of freedom and transgressed
administrative priorities. Instead of pausing at empirical silence or accepting
it at face value, surfacing silence in the empirical, imperial archive as having a

value—a null value—imbues absence with disruption and possibility. In other words, instead of accepting documentation that, along with describing women of African descent as wicked and criminal had also often ignored them completely, the null value offers opportunity *before* reading along the bias grain for "marking this space of indeterminacy." It brackets "missing information and inapplicable information in a systematic way, independent of data type." Identifying archival silences as null values surfaces slaveowners and officials as responsible for missing and unacknowledged black life in the archive, but it resists equating the missing or inapplicable information with black death.[57]

Although plantation production in New Orleans slowed, the Caribbean plantation system remained ravenous. By 1715, Saint-Domingue surpassed Martinique as a sugar producer and in slave purchases.[58] Between the 1730s and the 1750s, New Orleans and other port towns of the French Atlantic became increasingly integrated with France and into a French Atlantic, linked by slavery, commodity production, and imperial administrative structures. In Saint-Domingue, after the failure of the Compagnie de Saint-Domingue (Saint Domingue Company), the Crown extended its authority over the entire colony. As a result, in the 1730s, Les Cayes, along with the rest of the Southern Province, joined the Western Province as territory administered by the council at Léogane. At the same time, plantations expanded across the west, and Port-au-Prince outstripped Petit Goave and Léogane as an urban hub. By 1752, the council at Léogane moved to Port-au-Prince, and Port-au-Prince joined Cap Français as an administrative node of the colony with its own Superior Council.[59] The French Crown might have declined to invest more resources in its Gulf Coast enterprise, but with plantation production experiencing brutal success so close to its shores, slaveowners in Louisiana could not help but try. In 1743, wealthy slaveowner Claude Joseph Villars DuBreuil and Etienne Dalcourt financed a single slave ship from Gorée to New Orleans, but sales from these captives failed to reinvigorate production.[60] Indigo and rice replaced tobacco as the plantation product of choice, but only for those with enough slaves and land to make the investment worthwhile.[61] Formally, New Orleans remained the center of administrative life, but the Natchez Revolt had broken the nascent plantation regime in Gulf Coast Louisiana. The colony had become a society with slaves.[62]

Preoccupied with property but endeavoring to account for the people living in time and space in New Orleans, colonial officials made curious decisions when quantifying black people.[63] Counting slaves, who as human capital represented property and people, happened most readily. Counting free people of African descent proved more tenuous. Counting the presence of maroons was impossible. In the decades following the Natchez Revolt, colonial officials counting people of African descent in the town revised and edited their rubrics for enumeration. The further from bondage black people appeared, the more officials avoided the confrontation of quantifying them. Census enumeration also failed to capture movement, a lived reality of Africans migrating between settlements and the town on a regular basis. While officials counted and recounted their numbers, asserting their power against the appearance and reappearance of insurgent subjects around them, Africans along the Gulf Coast outnumbered Europeans nearly two to one. Enslaved laborers and the handful of free people of color filled commercial and domestic roles left vacant by an unstable administration and a transient white population. The Compagnie des Indes even encouraged members of the Superior Council to replace white laborers with enslaved laborers on construction apprenticeships, particularly in the river trade, building levees, canals, and fortifications.[64] Marie Baude arrived in a town where enslaved Africans worked alongside each other in the markets on the levees; managed homes, inns, and taverns; and exchanged goods grown or made with Native traders and resident whites. Slaveowners also required mobile labor to maintain the undermanned and undersupplied settlement, and the New Orleans black population remained connected through kinship and intimacy to networks of black laborers across the colony.[65] Most enslaved people labored on farms and plantations within rowing distance of New Orleans, no more than ten to thirteen miles apart. Whether officials acknowledged it or not, New Orleans became an attractive meeting place and crossroads of black social and political life in the region.[66]

Officials especially failed to acknowledge or represent black women, enslaved or freed, in their census documentation on New Orleans. In 1726, Bienville conducted the first street-by-street, outpost-by-outpost population survey of the colony. The census, a surveillance document and official account of power, placed Africans in and around New Orleans, the colonial center of a disgraced French Atlantic coast, and only partially recorded the presence of black women and children in the city. The 1726 census did not count free Africans or people of African descent. Although Suzanne and her husband, Louis Congo, resided in the area as early as 1725, neither appear in official enumerations until 1727. That year, Congo was listed as head of a household along Bayou Saint-Jean.[67] When Suzanne's transgressive body finally makes an appearance in the archive, she does not appear in the census. She appears as a wife, newly registered, in the sacramental records of the parish.[68] Perhaps causal, perhaps coincidental, Suzanne appears one year after the Ursulines arrived in New Orleans with a mission to convert, educate, and proselytize European, African, and indigenous women and girls. The black population, infused with new members at regular intervals through the 1730s, remained heavily African, but natural reproduction began to increase after the 1740s. Across Louisiana, over half of those enslaved continued to be listed in family units.[69]

When officials did chart black life in New Orleans, they acknowledged bodies and property but not these more complex lifeways. Bienville's 1726 census provides a closer examination of how administrators mapped the black population of the city.[70] In it, New Orleans' enslaved black population was unevenly distributed. People of African descent lived alone or in pairs among the households of the town. Occasionally, people of African descent lived in clusters of five or more, within dense pockets of community, connection, and dissent. The French-era home of St. Martin on Chartres Street became one such cluster. Some thirty-three enslaved black people lived along Chartres Street (present-day Chartres Street from present-day Bienville to present-day St. Peter). However, seventeen of them lived and worked in the household of Raymond de St. Martin de Jauriguebery. In less than a decade, with the aid of enslaved labor, St. Martin would own a plantation along the bayou running from the ramparts to Lake Pontchartrain, along present-day Bayou Road, cultivating tobacco, rice, and corn.[71] The census acknowledged this wealth in people and land. The next largest cluster of black people that officials identified existed at the wharves, or the Rue du Quay (present-day Decatur Street). Twenty-one enslaved Africans lived and worked on the waterfront, in the hospital, or on the levee. As enslaved labor, it made sense for men like Pauger, engineer and mastermind behind the grid system structuring the city, to own and direct black workers in construction, fortifying buildings, engineering and repairing levees, and loading and unloading materials. However, the four enslaved black laborers who Pauger claimed resided with him on the Rue du Quay paled in comparison to the numbers of laborers he further requisitioned from area slaveowners.

Along with the wharves, most enslaved were identified as living on one of the four streets parallel to and extending back from the riverfront—Rue de Quay, Rue de Chartres, Rue de Conde, and Rue Royale—and were never more than a muddy stroll away from colonial administration or commercial activity.

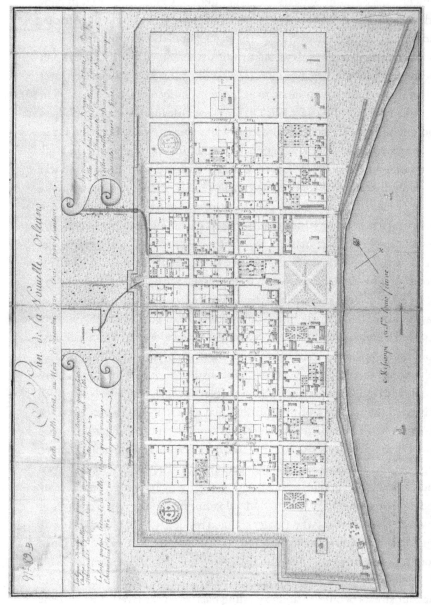

Figure 11. New Orleans, 1731. By Gonichon. In the nineteenth century, Congo Square would replace the cemetery. Courtesy of Archives nationales d'outre-mer de France, Aix-en-Provence.

Another cluster of fourteen enslaved women, men, and children living on Rue Royale (present-day Royal Street) and the dozen or less living in homes on Conde, Bienville, St. Anne, St. Pierre, and Bourbon were identified as living alone or in pairs in the homes of their owners. Four black slaves lived with Thomas Dezery, a carpenter, on Royale. Carpenters, coopers, and other artisans employed enslaved laborers in their workshops and could afford the cost of purchasing and supporting enslaved laborers. Another four enslaved black laborers lived on Royale with the widow Candel and her two children. Three black slaves lived with François Fleuriau, the *procureur général* (attorney general), along with his wife and sister on Rue de Bienville. Several others were listed as living and laboring alone in various capacities: in the homes of various Company employees like St. Quintin and Danville, for the Capuchin priests, enslaved to Superior Council members like Jean René de Fazende, or belonging to an array of middling settlers like Sieur Bru (a cashier), Bodson (a smith), and Lazon (captain of a small ship) and his wife.[72] For individual colonists, purchasing, feeding, and housing enslaved labor remained the costly privilege of Company officials or their political allies, Company employees with cash or credit to spare, and artisans. As a result, where Company employees clustered, enslaved property did as well. And where property clustered, census takers took notice.

Contrary to the tentative accounting in the 1726 census, New Orleans had already become the center of a black diaspora. By that January, ten slave ships had disembarked, with some twenty-three hundred slaves. Distributed to buyers throughout the region, most African women, men, and children found themselves transported to labor on plantations upriver from New Orleans like Natchez. With a few dozen to a hundred slaves residing among the European and Native residents of the Mobile, Natchez, Natchitoches, and Balize outposts, only New Orleans could count more slaves than even the concessions at Chapitoulas—all combined, nearly eight hundred women, men, and children of African descent resided in the city. Meanwhile, nearby plantations like Chapitoulas and land belonging to French-Canadians like the Chauvin brothers, Dubreuil, and Bienville himself amassed the largest numbers of slaves. The next largest enslaved African population lived and worked along the right bank of the river, on plantations owned by the Mandeville, Darby, Coustillhas, Dalcour, Carrier, Raguet, Tixerant, and Trudeau families. These African women, children, and men would map with their feet, arms, and legs the indeterminacy at the heart of the census rolls, as they moved between homes and outposts, traveling by land and water. Movement was a fact of everyday life for enslaved and free people of African descent in the colony.

A 1726 watercolor of the riverfront by Jean-Pierre Lassus visualizes the everyday presence of African laborers and the seeming absence of African women (Figure 10). Taken from across the King's Plantation across the river from town, Africans can be seen cutting cypress trees, tending fires, and killing snakes and alligators. African men labor alongside Native men (pictured in a boat and rowing southwest up the river) and European men (also painted in a boat, rowing toward the town and flying a flag). The occupations available to enslaved women—in the kitchen, at market, in the hospital, and sometimes in the field—placed them shoulder to shoulder with enslaved men, Native women, and *les petites blancs* (*engagés, forçats, coureurs de bois*, soldiers, settlers, and more) as all scrambled to survive on a crescent of land. The watercolor, *Veüe et Perspective de la Nouvelle Orleans*, is the only extant representation of the town during the French period. African women do not appear in it. Not until 1737 did an official census differentiate between enslaved women and men. And yet women, enslaved and free, remained a presence in the town and countryside.

Despite their absence from the census register, enslaved and free women in and around New Orleans gave birth and raised children, founding a new generation of African descent in Louisiana. As in Senegal and the Antilles, African women and women of African descent adopted baptism as one practice of freedom that might respond to the crisis of how to protect, nurture, and mother children in a foreign place. According to Emily Clark, in the sacramental records for St. Louis Cathedral in New Orleans, beginning in 1731 and continuing through 1732, 1733, and 1744, some 377 individual baptisms of slave infants or children were performed.[73] Black women and girls consistently dominated the numbers of those baptized in the 1730s, outpaced by black men in the 1740s, an affront to their archival erasure. As enslaved women secured manumission, and as baptized women and girls grew to adulthood, they stood as godparents to the children and adults around them. The number of godparents of African descent sponsoring enslaved godchildren jumped from 2 percent to 21 percent between 1733 and 1750. The number rose to almost a quarter of enslaved baptisms by 1760. In these fusions, the knitting of new kinships, the "feminine face of Afro-Catholicism" in New Orleans, began to emerge.[74] Although the numbers of those being baptized or sponsoring at the baptismal font remained small, small did not mean insignificant.[75] Among those baptized was Nanette, an enslaved domestic owned by Claude DuBreuil. DuBreuil's wife and daughter-in-law both became Children of Mary. Nanette would have at least four daughters, all of them baptized. At least two (Cecile and Marianne) would go on to sponsor multiple other women, children, and men of African descent. Cecile's great-granddaughter would be Henriette Delille, the founder of the black confraternity Soeurs de Sainte Famille (Sisters of the Holy Family).[76]

The Ursuline complex itself became another cluster of black life and a distinctly feminine one. By the 1720s, a hospital of a kind existed to service soldiers, settlers, and enslaved. After their arrival in 1727, the Ursulines assumed management of the company hospital, including "any nègres and négresses, animals, furniture" in use.[77] By April 1728, Sister Marie-Madeleine Hachard reported "our little community increases day by day, we have twenty boarders, of which eight today made their first communion, three ladies also board, and three orphans that we took through charity." Hachard also reported that the Ursulines supported seven enslaved boarders "to instruct for baptism and first communion" as well as a "great number" of "négresses and sauvagesses." These day students received instruction for two hours a day.[78] At least two of the boarders were girls, ages six and seventeen, sent to learn Catholic doctrine. These girls stayed to serve the Ursulines in the little house they were renting on the corner of Chartres and Bienville streets. Hachard, in fact, thought it important to remark on the strong presence of Africans in New Orleans, noting the nuns had grown accustomed to seeing black people (*noirs*). Apparently, this familiarity happened quickly. By 1734, they owned a plantation across the river and were actively participating in buying, selling, and hiring out *pièces d'Inde* of their own.[79]

The Ursuline complex expanded in response to the Natchez Revolt. In 1734, construction on a formal convent, boarding house, and royal hospital, also under their management and all on the eastern edge of the outpost, was completed. In that complex, downriver from town, the Ursuline nuns, their enslaved laborers, and free and enslaved women of color all lived and worked. An additional Hospital for the Poor, the first of two hospitals for the poor established in the French era, was founded formally in 1735 out of a bequest and occupied the house at Chartres and Bienville streets.[80] At both locations, enslaved women washed linens, cleaned, cooked, and otherwise supported the colony's medical institutions. The Royal Hospital employed at least one black surgeon and both hospitals used slave labor. Sometime after 1743, officials erected a second hospital, near the cemetery just beyond the north ramparts, placing the hospital near the cemetery, the brickyard, and the Place des Nègres.[81]

Even as the Ursulines evangelized to enslaved women and girls, experienced baptism, and labored on their plantations, African women and children of African descent continued to fall through the cracks of inconsistent enumeration, null values that refracted official anxieties about how to demarcate black life in the town, including free black life. In 1732, Marie, a *négresse libre*, who owned a house on Rue Bourbon, appeared on the census but not in the final counts the census takers produced that year.[82] Xavier, however, did. Described as a *mulâtre libre*, he was designated a head of household just up the road from Marie. Along with Xavier, officials counted six residents in the city and described them as "*mulâtres*," the first year the term appeared as a census category. Five of those six resided in white households. Although, by 1732, the shifting dynamics of blackness, enumeration, and colonial power acknowledged *mulâtres* as a population important enough to catalogue, *affranchis* remained obscured.[83] Along with Marie and Xavier, officials also listed Simon and Scipion, free men of color, but under the subheading of "men carrying arms."

Gendered racial categories like *négresse, mulâtresse,* or even *sauvagesse* also did not accurately count or account for African or indigenous womanhood. These categories evidenced colonial attempts at social control, acts of power meant to discipline, surveil, police, and shame women of African descent.[84] For colonial officials, the emergence of a racial vocabulary in New Orleans reflected power struggles over how to characterize sex, gender, blackness, and freedom. In 1726, two years after Bienville signed the Louisiana *Code Noir*, a four-year-old boy named Pierre died. The priest who interred him labeled him a "mulâtre," and Pierre became the first child so labeled in the colony.[85] It took another eight years for the priests to use the feminine variant of *mulâtre* to describe a person of African descent. In 1732, Catherine became the first child described as a "mulâtresse" in the sacramental registers of the parish.[86] Only eight years old, Catherine had died and been buried in New Orleans. A year later, Marie, described as a *mulâtresse* but the daughter of a *sauvagesse*, was baptized as a slave.[87] Sacred authorities incorporated *mulâtresse* as a racial category nearly twelve years after the start of the slave trade. And yet Catherine could not have been the first child of mixed ancestry born in the colony or the first child of mixed-African descent baptized or buried there, and Marie did not fit neatly into the categorization of *mulâtresse*.

Free people of African descent received no separate distinction in censuses taken between 1732 and 1763, resulting in their numbers being continually undercounted.[88] The 1737 census contained no category for *mulâtre* or *mulâtresse*, *affranchi* or *affranchie*, although two years later, Bienville led a contingent of black men and boys to war against the Chickasaw. Fighting alongside him was a contingent of fifty men described specifically as *affranchis*.[89] In 1763, a year after the secret transfer of Louisiana from France to Spain and six years before the Spanish military arrived to claim their prize, the first census to document categories of race and status was completed.[90] Three years later, despite some imperial attention from a new sovereign, black subjects who were not enslaved still did not appear in transparent or uniform fashion in official documentation. According to historian Jennifer Spear, census takers "scattered them throughout the census" and the totals still "fail to account for any of those residents identified as free people of African descent."[91]

In a riverine and ocean-bound imperial world obsessed with bondage and mastery, free and freed black women along the Gulf Coast could not be easily assimilated or consumed as a viable population by the census-taking apparatus. It is possible to see their absence as evidence of either their perceived nonexistence or lack of importance, or inferior data-collection practices. It is also possible, however, to hear in the register's silence the ecstatic shout of black freedom practices transgressing colonial desires, black people forming maps of kin between towns and countryside, black women loving each other into free states that could not be counted by census officials, much less managed by imperial entities or recorded on manuscript pages.[92] And in an already distorted archive of black life, African women and women of African descent at multiple intersections of status, race, and gender constituted a disappeared population. Empty spaces and miscalculations by the census-taking apparatus resulted from officials who failed or refused to account for the uncertain and transgressive existence of women like Suzanne, women living as free, freed, and fugitive subjects.

Full Use of Her: Intimacy, Service, and Labor

A population of women, children, and men free or freed from bondage existed as early as the 1720s, appearing in flashes and instances wholly beyond the colonial censuses. In 1722, four years after the founding of New Orleans, three years after the opening of the French slave trade, and eight years before Marie Baude's arrival, colonial officials in Louisiana began remarking on a specifically free black presence in the colony. The free black population that did emerge as worthy of comment by colonial authorities was male, employed by the colony, and engaged in the everyday labor of maintaining (or disrupting) the colonial order. In 1722, Laroze, a "free negro," was convicted of stealing from Company stores. He was flogged and sentenced to prison for six years.[93] The next year, Joseph Chaperon filed a complaint against the locksmith Le Roy and his *négresse* wife, whom he suspected of stealing "goods and money" from his plantation.[94]

Some men of African descent arrived in Louisiana as free men. In 1724, a free negro named Raphael Bernard approached the Superior Council about his labor contract with M. Jean Baptiste Faucon Dumanoir. Raphael hired himself out to Dumanoir around 1719, in France, at the rate of 200 francs a year in silver, plus clothing. Since their arrival in Louisiana, Dumanoir had failed to provide him with his stated earnings. Raphael maintained, although he'd treated Dumanoir with "fidelity and affection," Dumanoir had not done the same. In fact, Dumanoir "treated him with rigor." He asked the Superior Council to grant restitution in the form of funds to return to France and to order Dumanoir to return a trunk that belonged to him. The Superior Council granted him 100 francs and permitted Raphael to change his service, a decision that would have freed him from his obligation to Dumanoir and allowed him to return to France. Sometime before 1725, Jean Baptiste Raphael arrived from Martinique as a free man. In 1727, John Mingo, like Raphael, arrived as a free man of color, this time from the British colonies. He hired himself out to the Bernard Cantillon concession.[95] In 1736, Scipion, a free black man, hired himself out for one year to François Trudeau. Scipion agreed to serve as a rower, traveling upriver between Illinois Country and Louisiana, or otherwise serve Trudeau. In return, Trudeau agreed to pay Scipion 200 livres "in proportion to his needs."[96] Few slaveowners formally manumitted their bondspeople from slavery during these years. In 1728, the Superior Council confirmed the wishes of an officer, Major Cazeneuve, who died granting freedom to two slaves of unspecified genders, on the condition they serve Jean Roussin and his wife, two settlers at Natchez, over a period of two years.[97]

Before 1729, only a handful of women of African descent described as free or freed appear in documents in New Orleans. Along with the wife of Le Roy, in 1724, a free woman of color named Magdelaine Debern complained to the Superior Council about a head tax applied to free blacks from which mulattoes had become exempt. According to historian Alice Dunbar-Nelson, Debern won an exemption from the tax for free blacks as well as mulattoes.[98] After 1729, some free women and girls of color appeared in connection to the Ursuline convent. In October 1729, a Native woman of the Osage nation, freed by Viard dit François, a settler at Natchitoches, attended school with the Ursulines. Viard purchased her from Caddo slave traders. In addition to her freedom, he left her a hundred pistoles and requested she be schooled in Catholic doctrine.[99] Colonial officials approved the manumission and she was sent to the Ursulines for schooling. Fleuriau, when he approved the manumission, invoked the 1724 *Code Noir* against the Osage woman's inheritance. According to Article 52 of the now five-year-old document, slaves were not allowed to receive inheritances. The council confiscated the pistoles and donated them to the hospital. Her indigenous descent did not protect her from the rapidly evolving slave laws or help her secure formal manumission.[100]

Despite her official slave status, Suzanne's part-time autonomy as the wife of Louis Congo would have made her one of Marie Baude's few "free" contemporaries. In November 1725, Fleuriau delivered a representation to the Superior Council, arguing for the importance of an executioner in New Orleans, who would serve the entire colony. He noted that Louis Congo, a "slave belonging to the Company," performed a previous execution very well. However, to continue doing so, Louis made multiple demands. He requested his freedom and that of his wife. He also requested a full ration of rice, flour, and alcohol ("*boisson*") for himself ("*pour lui seullement*") and a plot of land. Although a slave of the Company, Louis requested the plot of land he and his wife already labored on. Fleuriau described Louis's habitation as "*fort et robuste*," capturing both the quality of Louis's work and the fertility of the land, but the description might also have applied to Congo himself, an intimate and intrusive sizing up of Louis's strength and physical form. Louis's request to be given the plot of land he labored on suggested something of the ownership Africans felt over the physical land itself—even if it was land they worked as slaves.

Fleuriau, the Superior Council member advocating for the appointment, might have been taking a cue from practices occurring in Saint-Domingue when he suggested a negro executioner would be one solution to the colony's personnel issues. Fleuriau needed to find bodies to do the unpleasant work of empire. The security of the colony demanded it. The situation was so critical that both he and the Superior Council were willing to employ a man of African descent in an abhorrent position that, in theory, transgressed the color line.[101] They were even willing to free him to do so. At the exact same time, these anxious patriarchs balked at outright manumitting a woman of African descent of no obvious threat or seeming interest. Although French colonial authorities found themselves in a foreign land, juggling new imperial social relations, with limited access to trustworthy personnel, Fleuriau still described the dual emancipations as a hardship, noting "it is a lot to ask the Company to lose two slaves at once." After being granted, among other things, "full time use" of his wife "who remains a slave of the Compagnie des Indes," Louis Congo began his employ as the colony's executioner.[102] From 1725 to 1737, Louis proceeded to "whip, brand, amputate, and torture subjects" in the name of the king and across race and status boundaries.[103] Louis may even have crossed paths with Jean Pinet, who was occasionally employed as an interpreter for Bamana slaves brought before the Superior Council.

For men of African descent like Congo and Mingo, freedom or the semblance of it entailed use by colonial authorities or slaveowners and conducting the grisly business of empire. This martial and masculine labor was not unique to Louisiana. Along Senegal's coast, *laptots* and *gourmettes* participated in the business of slaving as sailors, translators, and agents for either African or European factors. Bamana slave soldiers guarded the *captiveries* and the forts, protecting commercial operations through force of arms. Unique to the Americas, however, was the offer of freedom that accompanied such labor, an offer with special salience in a new land where the majority of Africans arrived as slaves. Congo joined contemporaries like Andre Senegal, who gained his freedom by serving as colonial executioner at Cap Français in Saint-Domingue. The majority of executioners appointed in Saint-Domingue, thirteen out of twenty, were elevated from the rank of slave.[104] Congo also participated in a larger French imperial project of sowing discord between European, African, and indigenous subjects. In a bloody paradox, a key avenue to freedom available exclusively to enslaved men of African descent required them to maintain the imperial structures that first enslaved them.

In contrast, Suzanne's consent, her desire for Congo, or even her desire for freedom do not make themselves apparent in Congo's indexing of her alongside alcohol, land, and rations. Congo's desires, though mediated through the consternation of Compagnie des Indes officials, do, however, make themselves legible. When Congo listed his demands, the privileges he required from officials in exchange for serving as the colonial executioner, he included freedom for Suzanne, his wife, on the list. Congo outlined more than the terms of his employment in his negotiation for freedom. He also aggregated the terms of black male freedom in eighteenth-century New Orleans. In his estimation, a free wife, self-sufficiency, reparations, and a means to imbibe for his own pleasure would be enough to lubricate his entrance into free status and the business of death. When officials refused and revised his demands, they responded in kind and outlined what they feared most—not black male freedom, which could be harnessed to serve colonial power, but black female freedom, including the loss of female slaves' reproductive labor. And as with Congo, nowhere do officials consider or discuss Suzanne's wish for relocation or desires, her intended "use of" her(self). For Congo as for the Compagnie des Indes, to preserve colonial power and in exchange for a dreadful freedom, Suzanne needed to remain commodified, consumed, and consumable, a line in a register. And, ultimately, the Company wielded the final say when it denied Congo full claim of what free white men were allowed—a woman and her dependent labor.

Around the same time period, another woman, Thérèse, also found herself the subject of marriage and labor negotiations. In 1726, John Mingo, a fugitive slave fleeing bondage in South Carolina, arrived in New Orleans. Two years later, Mingo entered into a work contract with Jonathan Darby, the director of the Bernard Cantillon concession. In exchange for his labor, Mingo would be allowed to "redeem" Thérèse, an enslaved woman belonging to the concession, as well as any children she bore, once he'd paid the price of her value of 1,500 francs. As he worked, Mingo would be allowed to invest and pay down the value of his wife with the wages Darby would give him, and Darby would provide Thérèse with "rice, corn, beans, and so many sweet potatoes," lodging, and clothing in the meantime. The contract with Mingo also officiated a marriage, authorized by Darby, with Thérèse, who he was quite in love with (devant amoureux)."[105] The contract went so far as to secularize the marriage bond between Mingo and Thérèse, placing the power to authorize marriage in Darby's hands and not in the hands of ecclesiastical authorities—an everyday reality of marriage for enslaved and free Africans. Like Suzanne, Thérèse's consent, desires, or intent all disappear from the negotiation, leaving only her presence as a consumable and productive item of exchange. Written into an additional promissory note was a clause allowing someone (the name has been rubbed clean) to rent Thérèse from Darby until they had paid the funds owed Darby for her freedom or to exchange her for a *"négresse esclave pièce d'Inde"* of the same value.[106]

Mingo did not remain with Darby. Not long after, he took a new position with a man named Chavannes as a *commandeur* (slave driver). In return, Mingo would be paid 300 francs a year, receive 8 percent of the plantation's produce, and earn a jug of brandy each month. In addition, Chavannes agreed to hire Thérèse as a domestic for an additional sum of 200 francs a year, an amount that would be paid to Darby until her full purchase price was paid off.[107] In November 1730, Mingo reported to the Superior Council that Darby "makes difficulties" and was withholding pay. Darby claimed he was not, that something may have been lost in the translation between them from French to English. With Thérèse's manumission, safety, mobility, and the autonomy of her marriage to Mingo tied tightly to his work contracts, more than wages were under dispute. Thérèse may in fact have been the leverage Darby used in his favor, retaining her or restricting access to her in some fashion. The Superior Council ordered Darby to return Thérèse to her husband and said that Mingo must finish making his payments.[108]

Absconding from any kin or community he had formed in South Carolina, Mingo needed to find and make a new home in the heart of Gulf Coast slaveholding society.[109] Like Congo, Mingo's negotiations defined free black manhood as including subsistence, pleasure, and female companionship. Like Congo, Mingo agreed to perform difficult and potentially dreadful labor. As a *commandeur* on a plantation, Mingo's freedom required him to maintain discipline, enforce work patterns, and otherwise manage enslaved people. His gender facilitated his appointment as a slave driver, a position African women did not occupy. Thérèse, meanwhile, may have created and cultivated intimate and kinship ties of her own by the time she met Mingo. It is unclear whether those ties were strengthened or ruptured as she moved from plantation site to plantation site with Mingo, conscripted to labor as a domestic in a household near her husband, the slave driver. However, just as Mingo's mobility offered him access to new labor roles and positions of relative power, her movement alongside him put her in range of precarious circumstances—from the threat of reenslavement under Darby to the threat of intimate and personal physical violence in a slaveowner's household.

Skills or employment in positions of power like *commandeur* could change enslaved and free black laborers' circumstances completely, but often they were available only to men. A small percentage of enslaved women of African descent possessed skills marketable to their owners.[110] Some forms of labor that principally employed men might have employed women as well. Ship builders hired enslaved Africans and people of African descent to manufacture pitch, tar, and turpentine for ships. Farmers and herdsmen hired out for black men and women on permanent and seasonal bases to harvest crops, manage livestock, and work in construction. Other labor was more gender specific. Black women did not apprentice alongside European or free black male craftsmen. Craftsmen—coopers, blacksmiths, tanners—hired African men as apprentices and employees, passing on their craft in the face of plummeting European migration to the colony. An entire company of free men of African descent waged war for the French empire, and the military force employed by colonial officials included some 250 black men who remained enslaved. The uneven distribution of labor even gendered the character of the fugitive freedoms taken by maroons. Beyond the indigo-growing areas around the town, labor requiring massive numbers of slaves grew more diffuse, more open for negotiation and collaboration. There, lumber mills employed enslaved laborers to harvest wood from the cypress swamp and did not shy away from employing runaways, whether truants or habitual maroons.[111]

Suzanne and Thérèse may have enjoyed some manner of freedom, but its terms were murky, their laboring lives hidden somewhere at the margins of the archive. Officials did not draft enslaved women into positions of colonial punishment or enlist them in paramilitary forays. On the one hand, this spared them from participating in spectacles and displays of violence on behalf of slaveowners and colonial officials. African women participated in farming, gardening, and frontier trading, particularly the frontier-exchange economy with *coureurs de bois* and indigenous agents, selling goods in small markets along the levee and through commercial ties across race and status with colonists.[112] A select few labored as free or enslaved at the hospital managed by the Ursulines, and these positions may have been without restitution in return for their freedom. Others likely participated in even more clandestine spiritual and medical economies of healing, magic, and midwifery. These spaces allowed enslaved women to accrue small amounts of resources, creating opportunities for self-sufficiency and autonomy. On the other hand, black men retained greater access to employment for the colony, a gendered division of labor that enslaved African men used to maintain and secure freedom on the Gulf Coast.

For African women and women of African descent, securing manumission and exercising liberty required a stunning amount of figurative and literal contact between their bodies and empire. French colonial authorities could not exist without individuals participating in and complicit with the workings of the colony. Governed first by trading companies and royal officials, New

Orleans political power shifted as francophone landowning emigrants and the children of emigrants took over the Superior Council—ironically at the same time the colony was transferred to royal governance. French administrators required colonists, indentured servants, European forced migrants, and African slaves to fill much-needed labor roles. As a result of this demand, Jean Pinet, a gunsmith deported from Senegal for murdering a local mulatto sailor, would be offered a new commission as a gunsmith and occasional Bambara translator in Louisiana. The same desperate search for laborers led officials to offer enslaved men freedom and positions as soldiers and sailors, and even, in at least one man's case, as a colonial executioner. In contrast, the labor demanded of women of African descent would place them in a different kind of jeopardy and relationship to securing freedom.

* * *

For African women and women of African descent arriving and laboring in New Orleans and its environs, manumission, conquest, colonial conflict, and war were linked in uncomfortable and devastating ways. For black men and boys, whose labor could be used in gendered and racialized ways against both white colonial subjects and rebelling Native nations, a kind of release from slavery was possible, if precarious and dangerous. From Louis Congo to John Mingo, working for the colony or slaveowners meant risking their lives and relinquishing years of their labor to indiscriminate masters. These practices underwrote the shift in 1729, when officials sanctioned a black militia in response to the Natchez Revolt. In the years to come, neither Périer nor Bienville shied away from using black male executioners like Congo against whites convicted of crimes, Native allies against absconding and maroon Africans, or black soldiers against indigenous enemies.[113] Black men's freedom would continue to be intimately bound to their use, possession, and forced labor for slaveowners and by colonial institutions.[114]

Black women's freedom was likewise bound to their intimate and kinship relationships—claimed, forced, enjoyed, and otherwise—with institutions and men in power. Scholars have read Louis Congo's contract as also a contract of manumission on Suzanne's behalf. It is easy to interpret Congo's request for "*sa femme*" as affirmation that Congo and Suzanne were married, perhaps even through mutual consent and agreement. Congo certainly claimed her as his wife. However, Congo and Suzanne did not register their marriage for at least another three years. While Congo received his freedom through his contract with the Company, it is a more accurate interpretation to recognize the considerable limits placed on Congo's free status. Like freed black executioners across the Caribbean archipelago, Congo risked losing *his* freedom should he decide to leave his gruesome appointment. In his marriage register, he was not described as *affranchi*, the new and modern French Atlantic designation for a freed slave, but simply as the "negro executioner."[115] Congo held this position for the next twelve years, and for the duration of his appointment, he suffered multiple threats on his life as both enslaved and free people across race singled him out for assassination.[116]

In the face of *la traversée* and the *pièce d'Inde*, use, possession, and forced labor came to mark the intersection of blackness and womanhood in a different way. Manumission itself became tinged with the specter of forbidden sex. The illicit nature of freedom unfolded even in written texts like the 1724 *Code Noir*. Suzanne's and Thérèse's relocations, read against the grain, offer brief and unambiguous narratives of women freed de facto through the labor of their husbands. Taking seriously, however, what scholar Marisa Fuentes has described as the "mutilated historicity" of enslaved and free women of African descent in the archive, reading their experiences along the bias grain reveals a much grayer reality.[117] Nuances appear in the everyday fact of his freedom and not hers, her lack of control over her own mobility and her body, and the menace of husbands' contractual obligation to slaveowners or Company officials. For these women, the daily, lived reality of practicing freedom required more than a contract, more than a link to a powerful man. The specter of force in their commodified and ambivalent intimate ties to their husbands muddies their manumissions with the colony's, slaveowners', and their husbands' power to possess them.

For African women and women of African descent, manumission became one tool among many in the struggle for safety, security, and autonomy. Other practices would need to be cultivated and created to make freedom free. The *Code Noir* mandated work stoppages on Sundays and feast days. On those occasions, women, men, and children who understood themselves as Bambara, Wolof, Mandingo, Senegal, Congo, and creole or born in the Americas gathered, crossing paths, folkways, and systems of belief. Moving by way of Bayou Saint-John, the Mississippi River, or the King's Plantation, or walking through town, black people remapped New Orleans into a network of sites marked by the sound of the kora and drums, the sight of couples dancing *calinda*, the touch of hands in fellowship, and the clamor of African languages.

In these fusions of music and spirit, black women, children, and men from a motley array of homelands gathered information from each other about the place they now resided in and the places from which they had come. They constructed an epistemology, a way of understanding their being in the New World, and were not afraid to call the supernatural into being on their behalf. Through dance and song, they beseeched spirits and deities for favor, protection, and restitution. They encouraged ancestors to speak across time and space by using those in attendance—by possessing them. After 1730, partly in response to the Natchez Revolt, officials ordered a series of fortifications built around the town, separating it on three sides from the surrounding cypress swamp. These wooden palisades were haphazard, at best, and were never constructed, at worst, into the 1760s. They did not matter. Walls stopped no one. In fact, just beyond the northwest ramparts, adjoining a burial ground, free and enslaved Africans forged a new gathering space, adding it to the broader constellation of spaces large and small where black freedom was being practiced. Officials would eventually describe this space at the back of town as the Place de Nègres or Place Congo—Congo Square.

Chapter 5

⌒𝑛⌒

Black Femme:
Acts, Archives, and Archipelagos of Freedom

> Charlotte, a mulâtresse owned by Sr. d'Erneville having disappeared and gone
> to Sr. Batard's residence on the pretense of asking Sr. Batard's assistance
> to bring her before Governor de Vaudreuil to obtain his pardon, was arrested
> on petition of Sr. d'Erneville by a sergeant's platoon.
> —Records of the Superior Council of Louisiana, 1751

In May 1751, Charlotte asked to speak with the governor's wife. The evening
had not gone her way. A *mulâtresse* slave, Charlotte had spent the day looking
for Sieur Pierre Louis Batard. Batard, recently arrived from Martinique and
captain of the ship *L'Elizabeth*, had promised Charlotte that he would be able
to arrange an audience with the wife of the governor, Madame de Vaudreuil,
née Jeanne-Charlotte de Fleury Deschambault. When Batard sent her word
that the audience had been permitted, she rushed to his home to find him.
Charlotte waited in his home through the early morning hours and into the
evening. Batard, however, never appeared. Now, Charlotte had run out of
options. A platoon sent by her owner dropped by to inspect the home. With
the help of one of Batard's compatriots, Charlotte hid in the absent mariner's
bedroom, beneath some mosquito netting, but a second investigation of the
home found her out. Now she stood before the soldiers on the brink of arrest,
a girl about seventeen years old and a runaway slave.

Caught, Charlotte appealed to the soldiers' patience, sympathy, and even
their sense of greed. She insisted she simply needed to wait for Batard to return,
that a pardon from the governor's wife was imminent. She asked to speak with
Madame de Vaudreuil herself. She offered them the 100 livres she had in her

possession if they would leave her be. She described the abuse she would suffer at her owner's hands, if they apprehended her now, as a fugitive, for he "would have her whipped unmercifully." Despite it all, the soldiers arrested her. Even if they felt any empathy for her position, they also would have known her owner well. Chevalier Pierre Henri d'Erneville had survived the wars against the Natchez and the Chickasaw, eruptions of violence that had shaken the colony to its core. Charlotte, however, also knew her own owner well, perhaps better than they. He was, after all, her father.

Charlotte did not receive her freedom that day, but her life encapsulated the contradictions that intimacy, kinship, and black freedom begot in the decades between the Natchez Revolt and the transfer of the colony to Spain. Charlotte, perhaps the daughter of a woman born on the African continent, was barely an adult, but like other girls her age, she learned to navigate a precarious and changeable terrain of status, gender, and race. When caught, Charlotte did not appeal to d'Erneville for leniency, neither as her owner nor as her father. If she appealed to her still-enslaved mother for release or relief, there is no record of it. Charlotte also did not appeal to the governor, although acts of *liberté* or legal acts of manumission required approval from the governor and intendant to be official. Charlotte understood the inner workings of the colonial apparatus that bound her. She knew her case was precarious at best, in part because her father and owner was a man of distinction. To circumvent him, Charlotte appealed to the most powerful *woman* in the colony in her bid for freedom. For Charlotte, her freedom was a project that only another self-identified woman could understand.

Scholars have already provided comprehensive histories of the journey from slavery to freedom in New Orleans, Saint-Domingue, Martinique, Guadeloupe, Cuba, and the Dominican Republic.[1] This chapter, therefore, focuses on key elements of African women's and women of African descent's practices of freedom in the New World—securing their bodies, defending their mobility, and protecting their legacies. For slaveowners, freedom for people of African descent would never be free. Slaveowners did their best to make manumission processes an ordeal, reminding free people of color of the respect owed to their former masters and other white colonial subjects. The long and grueling Atlantic crossing shocked and impressed upon those in bondage that something had changed. Africans entered a New World where chattel slavery based on African and indigenous descent dominated social relations in ways it could not in West Africa. Between 1731 and 1769, enslaved and free black women, children, and men in New Orleans moved farther from coastal Senegambia in their lifeways, social patterns, and everyday lived experiences, and proximally closer to patterns of black diasporic and archipelagic life taking shape in the eighteenth-century Caribbean. And in this new world, black people remained in bondage more than they secured freedom.

African women and women of African descent—above and beyond any act of conferred *liberté*—understood themselves as having all of the rights and subjectivity that officials attempted to reserve for *hommes libres*. These women interpreted slave codes, pursued manumission acts, and returned again and again to the Superior Council when their freedom became contested. They showed up in defense of themselves and each other. They sought joy and pleasure, gave birth and lost children, and endured the everyday toil of their laboring lives. The freedom that African women and women of African descent desired transgressed and transcended the boundaries of the manumission act. On the Gulf Coast, black women practiced a freedom rooted in their relationship to African descent, their sense of themselves as women, and their capacity to belong to themselves and each other. Mutable and dexterous, black women flouted use and possession to seek out new arrangements of kin. They demanded a promiscuous accounting of blackness as future possibility and femme as stealing a bit of sweetness for themselves. This interpretation of freedom was excessive and fugitive, beyond the bounds of colonial law and convention. Like the practice of freedom engaged in by women on the Atlantic African coast, it too was distinctly African as well as creole or born-of-this-place, but it was not identical. This was a diasporic and archipelagic black femme freedom, one attuned to the epistemological dilemma familiar to people of African descent scattered by slavery across the Atlantic world—how did we get here, what is this place, and what does it mean to live?

An Archive of Black Women's Freedom

An archive of black women's freedom begins to be constructed in earnest only after the Natchez Revolt. In January 1730, while on its way back to France, the captain and crew of *L'Annibal* must have breathed a sigh of relief. They had survived two slave revolts—one on the Gambia River and one at Saint-Domingue. They had sold their enslaved cargo, leaving them free to return to Europe quickly. And they had avoided what appeared to be a brutal conflict brewing in the colony of Louisiana. The ship log bore witness to the disorder unfolding a sea away: "The *sauvages* have made carnage in that place, and have killed 200 whites."[2] Word of the conflict spread to the Caribbean and to Europe quickly. Following the rebellion, the Compagnie des Indes (Company of the Indies) relinquished its charter, the transatlantic slave trade to the colony effectively ended, and exiled Governor Bienville returned to Louisiana.

For the duration of the French occupation of the coast, even legal manumission remained elusive and contested as black women, men, and children pressed their claims on recalcitrant owners. Their stories—of which women like Suzanne, Charlotte, and Marie Baude became a part—illuminated the stubbornness of bondage and the ambiguity of official claims to freedom. For black women, the choices grew much more complicated. Arriving alongside black men, African women and women of African descent did not find themselves redistributed among the artisan class of coopers and blacksmiths. They did not have ready access to the same appointments offered men like Louis Congo or the slaves freed for battling the Natchez. As a result, African women and women of African descent navigated a more intimate and illusory economy of manumission, one where a kind of autonomy might come through "full use" of them by their husbands (as with Suzanne) or require years of deliberate and aggressive petitioning, as in the case of Marie Charlotte. Freedom also might entail the loss of property and social prestige, as in the case of Marie Baude.[3]

From an African householder and propertied wife of a Company employee in a community of women of similar wealth, race, or status, Marie Baude, upon arrival in New Orleans, transformed into the unpropertied and nameless "*la femme Pinet.*" Only when Jean complained to Company officials, did the governor acknowledge anything untoward might have occurred with her enslaved property. When Jean admonished Balize officials for not sending her captives ahead, to resolve the matter, the governor solicited advice from directors in Paris. In the meantime, Jean and Marie's slaves remained in possession of the Company. In June 1729, following another unanswered petition from Jean, the Superior Council acknowledged the slaves had been sold but agreed to compensate Jean for half the value of the slaves and forgive both the *tarif* and the cost of Marie Baude's passage to Louisiana.[4] Jean demanded the Company finance the voyage of another group of his slaves. No response from the Company to this request has survived. Marie Baude retired with Jean Pinet to a home he built for them and, for the most part, disappeared from the archive. Marie Baude may have disappeared from the record, but one of her slaves emerged in the same moment. Louise Bertiche, a *négresse* slave belonging to "Jean Penet," had been "confiscated to Charity Hospital" in compliance with an unnamed ruling of the Superior Council. It was unusual for enslaved people to describe themselves or to be described using European first and last names. More telling, Louise shared a last name with Marie Bertiche, a prominent Senegambian *mulâtresse* and many times a godmother at Saint-Louis.[5]

In 1731, the year the Compagnie des Indes relinquished its control of Louisiana to the French Crown, Jean Pinet lived with his unnamed wife, five black slaves or servants, and one white servant downriver from the city.[6] He owned a lot in town on the block bounded by St. Pierre and Royale.[7] In 1733, Bienville returned to the helm of colonial governance and inherited its charred diplomatic relations with Native inhabitants. For the next fifteen years, Bienville combined negotiation with Choctaw allies, continued suppression of Natchez insurgents, and outright military attacks on the British-allied Chickasaw in an effort to secure French colonial control over the region. In 1736, 1738, and 1739, Bienville would attempt to violently subdue the Chickasaw. These campaigns employed black men as soldiers and as labor, including slaves freed for their service. Yet none of these campaigns succeeded. Jean Pinet, as a gunsmith, may have witnessed some of this, as he continued to labor in the town. However, his work must have taken a toll. In 1735, former Governor Étienne de Périer asked Bienville to nullify Jean's compulsory service out of respect for his "infirmities." Bienville agreed. Sometime during the next two years, Jean Pinet passed away.[8] By November 1739, Bienville had agreed to negotiate a truce with Chickasaw leaders and end the fighting. A relative peace reigned in the colony, for a time.

Women's intimate and kinship ties to the black men who secured their freedom through their work for the colony continued to lead to their own manumission. François Tiocou, describing himself as of the Senegal nation, fought against the Natchez and received his freedom as a result. His wife, however, remained the property of Charles de St. Pierre Chevalier de St. Julien. In June 1737, after St. Julien failed to return from the Chickasaw wars, Tiocou appealed to the Superior Council to claim items from his estate. He claimed, first, that St. Julien owed him 450 francs for back wages. Second, he noted that the St. Julien estate still owned his wife, Marie Aram. He asked the Superior Council to have the back wages deducted from the price of his wife and to prevent the heirs of the estate from selling her, "urging that she remain in the employ of the estate until he could redeem her completely."[9] The action granted,

Marie Aram appears to have been placed with the Hospital for the Poor, what would become Charity Hospital of New Orleans. A few weeks later, Tiocou signed a contract with S. Raguet, director of the hospital, and Fr. Phillippe, a Capuchin priest, pledging himself to labor for the hospital without pay for a total of seven years in return for the freedom of his wife. During that time, he would receive no wages and he could not leave the colony. At the end of this period, she would be free and "considered as the other legitimate wives married to the subjects of the King." Seven years later, Tiocou appealed to the Capuchin priests, as well as Governor Vaudreuil, for Marie Aram's freedom. The priests remarked on both Tiocou and Marie Aram serving the hospital "well and faithfully" over the course of seven years and on her "good services rendered to the hospital."[10]

Black women laboring for colonial officials like Superior Council members also sometimes found ways to secure their freedom. In 1732, Jean-Baptiste Chavannes, a former council member, petitioned to free Marie Angelique dit Isabelle, *négresse*, for her "fidelity, services, and in payment."[11] Chavannes purchased Marie Angelique from the Compagnie des Indes and paid in cash. His petition contained his receipt from the Company. Périer and Salmon, as governor and intendant, approved the manumission a month later. Jeanneton, the *négresse* slave of another Superior Council member, François Trudeau, secured her manumission. In 1737, Trudeau freed Jeanneton, one of over thirty slaves laboring for him, in exchange for her serving him "with zeal and fidelity" over the past twenty-six years. The manumission came with conditions. Jeanneton, Trudeau's slave since 1714, the majority of his time in Louisiana, would need to continue in his service until he died. Bienville and Salmon approved his manumission.[12]

In 1733, Marie, Jorge, and their son, Zacharie, lived in New Orleans as enslaved property of Bienville. What arrangements had been made for them in the absence of their owner remain unclear. That October, after Bienville returned, he filed documents freeing Marie and her husband, Jorge, for "good and faithful service" over the previous twenty-seven years. As property of Bienville since 1705, Marie and Jorge would have been among the first enslaved black men and women in the colony. Bienville freed them both, but retained ownership over her son. Two years after Bienville granted her freedom, Marie returned to the Superior Council to file emancipation paperwork on behalf of herself and her husband, suggesting some question might have come up about her free status.[13] Zacharie would not be freed for another ten years—on the eve of Bienville's departure from the colony. In 1743, Bienville freed Zacharie, the son of "Old Marie," on the condition he continued to serve him or his designee for another five years. In exchange, Zacharie would be supported, in sickness and in health, in Bienville's name, and thereafter he would be free to enjoy the privileges of all free men, "with due respect for his master and his descendants; whom he shall always consider his protectors."[14] As with Marie and her family's freedom from Bienville, enslaved women and children could find their freedom granted in the wake of soldiers' and officers' arrivals and departures from the colony. In August 1736, an enslaved Native woman and her daughter found their freedom after the departure of their owner. Their owner, Rebout, returned to France, leaving them with another settler, Calixte Descairac. Descairac had spent the last few years in the colony as an inspector of tobacco, a position Périer granted him in exchange for slaves. Rebout left instructions to free both of them, which Descairac did not do until his own death in 1738, and he later sued Rebout for the cost of their upkeep.[15]

As Company officials and employees embarked on military campaigns, some used the moment before their departure to free slaves they owned. Those freedoms did not come carte blanche or en masse. Enslaved women and children, in particular, found access to freedom via these peculiar instances of intimate labor and claims of intimate care made by their former owners. Sometime before October 1735, Marie Charlotte and her daughter Louise, both *négresses*, were freed by their owner, the aforementioned St. Julien of Cannes Brulées, upon his departure for the Chickasaw wars. He freed the two women, the daughter and granddaughter of Calais dit Gaigne, another enslaved woman he owned, for "good and agreeable services" rendered. Like Bienville, St. Julien cautioned that the freedom they now enjoyed required them to "pay the respect they must always have for Whites." St. Julien understood the gravity of his departure—the possibility of dying and what might happen to Marie Charlotte's or Louise's emancipation when his creditors and heirs divided his property among themselves postmortem. To prevent anyone from remanding Marie Charlotte or Louise back into slavery, St. Julien attempted to account for debts he owed against the Compagnie des Indes and other settlers. He signed his act of manumission alongside S. Henri and S. Aufrere, his witnesses.[16]

St. Julien did not return. In October 1735, Marie Charlotte and Louise found their freedom under dispute. S. d'Ausseville, the council member in charge of managing successions in the colony, claimed that St. Julien owed three times as much as he claimed in his estimate. Settling the deceased's debts required d'Ausseville to sell Marie Charlotte and Louise.[17] In addition, he pointedly corrected Marie Charlotte's racial designation from *négresse* to *mulâtresse*, and stated neither the governor nor the intendant approved St. Julien's act of manumission, a requirement of manumission outlined in the *Code Noir*. In correcting Marie Charlotte's racial designation, he drew on a generation of stigma against mixed-race enslaved women securing freedom through their intimate and kinship ties to white men by suggesting that Marie Charlotte was of some kin to St. Julien, possibly his daughter.[18] As a member of the Superior Council, he claimed for himself the right to decide race and sexual codes of body and behavior. Instead of freedom, Marie Charlotte was sent to live and presumably labor for the Ursulines at their convent in New Orleans with no mention of Louise, her daughter. For two years, the mother and daughter remained with the Ursulines, who were nothing if not efficient bookkeepers. In July 1737, Sister St. André, the Mother Superior, charged S. d'Ausseville some 450 livres to maintain "a mulâtresse belonging to" the St. Julien concession.[19]

Marie Charlotte understood clearly the injustice done. Sometime before 1743, she appealed to the Superior Council for her freedom. She based her appeal on the 1724 *Code Noir*, the same code that d'Ausseville manipulated to deny her freedom. Under Article 20, slaves could appeal for their freedom if their owners had improperly fed, clothed, or otherwise provided for them. The ability to make such appeals may have provided just enough access to colonial authorities to enable her to tell her story. In November 1743, Fleuriau petitioned Vaudreuil and Salmon for Marie Charlotte's freedom. He outlined the fraudulent behavior of d'Ausseville, who, in the meantime, had been caught attempting to manipulate the sales of property of other successions for his own profit and benefit. Fleuriau stated that d'Ausseville's claim that the St. Julien estate could not cover its debts was false. As the manumission was "in writing, under private seal, before witnesses," it should be considered valid. He requested Marie Charlotte be granted her manumission and the d'Ausseville heirs paid 1,500 livres in compensation from the d'Ausseville estate.[20]

Her manumission granted, Marie Charlotte lashed out. In February 1745, claiming that "it is not just that a free person [*personne libre*] should have been kept in slavery through a trick," Marie Charlotte sued d'Ausseville. She described her outrage in terms of slavery, her right to labor, and her right to compensation. She stated d'Ausseville "stealthily suppressed the manumission." She demanded wages from d'Ausseville, 1,500 livres to reimburse her former owner for her freedom, and back wages of 20 livres for every month he held her illegally.[21] Like Marie Charlotte, Janeton, Pierre Garçon dit L'Eveillé's slave, also knew her way around the *Code Noir*. L'Eveille granted Janeton her liberty in 1736, only to cancel it. A year later, Janeton threatened to leave him—and then did. When she was captured after eight days as a maroon, she declared to officials of the Superior Council that her owner not only had promised her freedom, but also had impregnated her. Not having received her liberty, she demanded to be confiscated from him. Article 6 of the *Code Noir* dictated just such punishment for L'Eveille's behavior. Both Marie Charlotte and Janeton knew or gestured to knowing something of the black codes that circumscribed their status—and they were determined to use every tool at their disposal, even their own bodies, to secure some safety and security for themselves.[22]

As with Marie Charlotte, Catherine found her and her family petitioning the Superior Council for their freedom to be honored after their owner died in the Chickasaw wars. In August 1738, Captain Jacques Coustilhas drafted a will before his departure, freeing Catherine, a Wolof slave; her husband, Louis Connard; and their four children, Jeannette, Baptiste, Marguerite, and "little Louis" in the event of his death.[23] He too named Calixte Descairac as the executor of his estate, who appears to have kept them as his slaves or otherwise failed to liberate them until his death a month later. Coustilhas died in the Chickasaw wars, but Descairac did not free them immediately. Descairac also failed to mention their quasi-free condition, even when he dictated his will to the Royal Notary, although he took the time to gift a cow to Catherine, a *négresse* "belonging to Sr. de Coustilhas." Not until the following March, when Louis Connard petitioned the Superior Council directly to recognize their freedom as drafted in Coustilhas's will, did their *affranchissement* become a reality.[24]

Marie, an eleven-year-old slave, gained her freedom when Joseph Meunier manumitted her on his departure for the first Chickasaw wars. In 1736, Joseph Meunier freed Marie for "her affection and her services," "not knowing if he would return."[25] Meunier survived and returned, only to depart for a second set of Chickasaw wars, hoping to "ply his trade in all the work necessary for the army."[26] Before he left, he filed a nuncupative will with the Superior Council that freed another nine of his slaves, among them Françoise, Manon, another enslaved man, and six children, including three girls. Meunier requested his heirs "raise them [the children] in the fear of God, with the greatest possible gentleness."[27] Two of his slaves, however, he took with him to war, requesting one and a half rations for himself, as well as an enslaved man and woman.[28]

Meunier survived again, leaving the fate of the nine slaves freed by will on hold. In July 1744, he and his wife freed two: Françoise and her six-year-old son, for their good and agreeable services and care during his illness.[29]

African women and women of African descent in New Orleans who practiced freedom sought safety from the terrors of slavery for their children, and they nurtured communities of enslaved and free Africans against the death-dealing demands of slaveowners and officials. When the Natchez Revolt forced colonial officials to scale back attempts to forge a plantation empire, black women experienced a necessary change of pace. After 1731, miscarriage, infant mortality, disease, resale, and overwork eased enough for the enslaved black female population to begin to reproduce, though the enslaved population was not self-sustaining. Black slaves continued to suffer from high mortality rates. In the 1740s, the ratio of children under fifteen to women of child-bearing age among the enslaved only grew to about 1.5, only slightly better than the rate in Saint-Domingue (1.3) or Guadeloupe (1.24) at the height of their plantation regimes.[30] But some African women and women of African descent who gave birth did see their children survive. The *Code Noir*, on paper, protected family units from being separated and sold. The edict did not guarantee enslaved communities could survive the breakup of plantations, estate sales, or slave-owner caprice, but it did create a structure for slaveowners to catalogue and enumerate enslaved Africans. As a result, 51 percent of slaves recorded in Louisiana were listed in hetero-biological family units.[31]

The birth of children among enslaved women became another opportunity to press for manumission. African women and women of African descent used Catholic Church officials' ambivalence about manumission for their own benefit. In 1713, Antilles law prohibited priests from declaring slaves free at baptism without proof of the same. By the 1730s, the Crown felt compelled to reiterate its prohibition on priests baptizing slaves as free people, stating that those baptized must have proof of their freedom, and also targeting children and women of African descent specifically for special approbation. Priests were further forbidden from recording the children of women of color in the book of baptisms for free persons without proof that the mother was a free woman of color. Lacking evidence, priests were instructed to write the names of those newly baptized slaves only in the book for slaves.[32]

In New Orleans, free-by-baptism manumissions existed somewhere in the gap between imperial permission for release from bondage and individual slaveowners' prerogative to manumit their property. To be marked as free in the baptism register provided enslaved people official evidence of having been granted freedom by their owners in a context where formal acts of *liberté* (which required certification by the governor and intendant) were more difficult to acquire. By 1745, instances of free-by-baptism manumissions began to appear in New Orleans. Françoise, baptized in March of that year, was marked as free in her register, although her mother was a *négresse* slave. Françoise's father, though anonymous, was white, a distinction that continued to confound the clerics' attribution of slave or free.[33] That same November, Marie Louise secured her status as a free person of color when Vincent Le Porche filed a statement with the Superior Council. Submitted in the register the day before his marriage to Marie Françoise Pauque of Point Coupée, he declared Marie Louise was "not a slave but should enjoy complete liberty, being the daughter of a Frenchman."[34] White paternity, however, did not guarantee freedom. Within a few months of Françoise's baptism, another Marie, also the *mulâtresse* daughter of an anonymous white father, was baptized as a slave.[35]

By 1751, priests began to note some version of proof in the registers, but evidence included simply taking French fathers like Louis Rançon at their word when he claimed to have secured freedom for his three-day-old son, Louis François. Young Louis and, likely, his mother, Marie Jeanne, a *négresse*, belonged to the commander of the Swiss troops.[36] Nine years later, Marie Jeanne's other child by Louis, a daughter, would also be baptized as free. Proof, however, or the requirement of proof, was inconsistently enforced. In 1766, Marie Joseph, daughter of Angelique, a *négresse* slave, was baptized as free in this same manner. Angelique secured this statement of free status without clear approval from her owner, but the priest still declared the one-month-old child a *mulâtresse libre*.[37] In 1769, as Alejandro O'Reilly established formal Spanish control over the Gulf Coast and introduced the Spanish Cabildo to the residents of New Orleans, Jacqueline, a *mulâtresse* slave belonging to Jacques Lemelle, saw her daughters baptized as free.[38] Perhaps fugitives' strategies for securing manumission through sacramental sanction and gentle subterfuge traveled across the Caribbean sea from Martinique, Guadeloupe, and Saint-Domingue. By 1777, the Superior Council of Saint-Domingue at Cap Français found itself reiterating, once again, that priests could not declare slaves freed through baptism without proof. Regardless of whether this route to freedom arrived in New Orleans from the Antilles, mothers of African descent used it on behalf of their children despite their own enslaved status.

Along with maneuvering their children into free status at the baptismal font, securing freedom for themselves or their children in the wake of their owners' deaths grew into a practice and strategy. The strategy first became legible along the Gulf Coast in the manumission of enslaved women, children, and men by soldiers departing the colony or en route to fight in the Chickasaw wars. Fearing death, men dictated last wills and testaments declaring their enslaved property free in the event of their death or submitted writs to the Superior Council freeing bondspersons immediately before their departures. Witnessing these acts, executed most often by Company-affiliated European men on behalf of enslaved blacks from a range of genders and ages, Africans and people of African descent seized on a manumission-by-will as a way out of bondage. In 1740, Jeanneton elicited a promise of freedom for herself and her daughter, Marie Jeanne, from her owner, Bernard Jaffre dit la Liberté, who willed them free as long as she worked for the hospital for two years. In 1746, Charlotte of Senegal secured a promise from her owner, Antoine Meuillion, to free her whenever he died or left the colony. He willed her and her two children free in 1767.[39] Marianne secured the promised manumission of her two sons, Joseph and Pierre, held by Pierre Boyer, in 1745 when he willed them free.[40]

Slaveowners, executors of estates, white female widows, and enterprising investors likewise grew more adept at challenging testaments. In 1765, when twelve-year-old François became free upon the death of Madame St. Hermine, the executor of the estate repurchased him, and his freedom was denied because of debts.[41] A few years later, Marie Claude Bernoudy did not protest her husband's manumission, in his will, of Marie, a *négresse* slave, and her son François, despite his confession that he was the child's father. The widow Pechon drew the line, however, at the bequest of 3,200 livres to be paid in currency or in slaves her husband left to his son. "It is difficult," she stated in her petition to the Superior Council, "to guess what ground, income, or inheritance an *enfant mulâtre* born out of wedlock this illegitimate (*ci illegitimé*), between the ages of 10 and 11 years of age at the most could have to acquire such property."[42] Jeanneton served two years in the hospital, only to have Liberté's widow attempt to block her and her daughter's freedom. In 1742, Bienville granted them their freedom, and the widow settled, finally, for a portion of their value, nearly twenty years later.[43] Promises made in testaments could be broken, delayed, or deferred for a variety of reasons, but women of African descent used every tool available to secure manumission.

Women of African descent who were determined to secure manumission for their children and themselves plagued officials in New Orleans just as they did in surrounding islands. Whether enslaved people secured freedom through intimacy with their owners, at the baptismal font, after their owners' deaths, or through petitions to colonial authorities directly, manumissions emerged from enslaved insistence on rejecting the logic of bondage. Manumission (and manumitted people) confirmed to women of African descent the lie of *partus sequitur ventrem*. It ripped off the slaveowner's veneer. For if manumission existed, slavery was contingent, structural, and imposed, not natural, hereditary, or reproductive. Black women's practices of freedom expanded beyond the manumission act, encompassing an array of strategies, including running away, finding allies, and making political appeals.[44] Even when these attempts failed, as in Charlotte's hunt for an audience with the governor's wife, they make it apparent that African women and women of African descent understood freedom as more than escaping slavery. Freedom for black women meant stealing themselves back from their owners, creating spaces for safety, protecting and teaching kin, and girding themselves with allies against further violation. These efforts required a fugitive, maroon practice and deep care for each other, "the black heart of our social poesis."[45] As Marie Charlotte made clear in her appeal, black women knew slavery was a trick and "it was not just that a free person should have been kept in bondage through a trick."

In 1743, Pierre de Rigaud, Marquis de Vaudreuil, succeeded Bienville as governor. Members of the Superior Council, which was increasingly dominated by slaveowning colonists born in or with ties to the Americas, had fewer illusions about quick plantation profits and were less inclined to return to France or resettle in the Caribbean.[46] After the Chickasaw wars, violence between French and Native nations slowed. Committed—or resigned—to life in Louisiana, a white francophone, landowning elite struggled to carve a sense of mastery out of a fractious population. By the 1750s, military campaigns and departures no longer inspired emancipations. As avenues for manumission through men's departure from the colony closed down, black women's struggle to enact a more expansive meaning for freedom continued.

A Stick Between Her Legs: Intimate Violence in a World of Slaves

By securing manumission and defending it, African women and women of African descent engaged in a critical labor on behalf of themselves and the complex black communities forming around them. But black women knew they and their kin continued to navigate a world of violence, regardless of whether they received their freedom papers. Securing acts of *liberté* did not vanquish these codes and customs, and free status alone did not protect black women's bodies. Officials enacted imperial intimate violence on African women and girls, constructing them in law and official discourse as objects of use, possession, and sexual infiltration. On the ground, African women and women of African descent experienced these discourses as everyday confrontations between themselves and other Atlantic subjects—European men and women, men of African descent, soldiers and *engagés*, members of indigenous nations. Intimate violence—both the acts themselves and the threat of their possibility—saturated black women's encounters in the bedrooms they slept in, in the fields they labored in, on the streets they walked, and on the waterways that cut through the town. Steeped in an ever-evolving hierarchy of status following the mother, racial difference, and imperial encounter, these devastating clashes revealed axes of racial, sexual, and status difference. In other words, the intimate and kinship relations begot by slaving proved so volatile, that who could be used or possessed, whose service could be compelled or forced, became matters of sex and proof of power.

Violence between the enslaved and free husbands and wives of African descent occurred, sometimes with murderous results. In 1723, Company officials sentenced an enslaved man to be executed by strangulation for murdering his wife. One of the first sentences of capital punishment for a slave, officials decreed he would be baptized first. His owner would also be compensated for the loss.[47] A few years later, Maxama, a Bambara slave, stabbed his wife "several times without provocation."[48] In the 1740s, an enslaved man called Baraca of the "Poulard" nation beat his wife, Taca, also a slave, to death. According to witness testimony, Taca claimed Baraca often insulted and beat her. Antoine Flatague, a Bambara and a fellow *commandeur* (slave driver), claimed Taca admonished Baraca for his behavior in Flatague's presence on the evening she was killed. When he arrived at Baraca's cabin, after encouraging him to share a smoke, Baraca complained to Flatague that Taca was seeing a man named Mamouroux. Baraca forbade her from seeing him, but she continued to do so. When Taca heard this, she charged her husband with violent jealousy. "Baraca is always beating me because he is jealous. . . . Why are you angry, since you saw nothing; why always scold and beat your wife without reason?"[49] Baraca, in response, grabbed a stave from a pail and struck her on the head. Then he fled. Flatague rushed for help. He found René Antoine Millet, the overseer of the plantation, who sent to the hospital for the surgeon. Taca remained alive for hours as the surgeon attempted to bleed her as a curative. The surgeon, however, was unsuccessful. She died that morning from her wounds. During her autopsy, the surgeon discovered blood in her brain. Baraca hid away from the plantation through the next day with the aid of "Indians" he met near another plantation and was caught as he returned to the King's Plantation in search of a pirogue to cross the river.

Taca's refusal to abide by her role as wife or domestic laborer incited Baraca's act of violence. In his defense, Baraca complained that she would not cook dinner for him, even though he had requested it, and that she "had a stick between her legs and he was afraid she would hit him with it." The Superior Council condemned him to death by strangulation and a public hanging in the square. His body hung in the Place d'Armes for a full day to set an example for others.[50] The Superior Council did not specify whether the example was meant to warn bondspeople from running away, from fatally assaulting each other, or from engaging in fatal acts against enslaved women. They did not need to. The dead and swinging body of the African man, material evidence of colonial violence, terrorized on these multiple registers; the creak of the rope could be heard by both enslaved and free, *petits* and *grands*, young and old who passed the square on their daily rounds. For women and girls of African descent, Baraca's crime and punishment would have served as gory evidence of their own vulnerability to personal and public violence, and confirmation that a growing codex of slave law might avenge their deaths as property belonging to others, but did little to save their lives.

Refusal was a practice of freedom that would be taken up again and again by African women and women of African descent, who were marked by their gender and race as exploitable by multiple classes of colonial society, including lower-class white men like soldiers, artisans, and sailors. On a June day in 1758, Louison and Babet, both enslaved *négresses*, went to the river near the Ursuline convent to wash linens. Louison belonged to the Crown, and Babet to the Ursulines, but both at the time were working for the town hospital. Laboring among the ill and infirm were women like Marie Charlotte, whose freedom claims had been circumvented; enslaved property confiscated by the Company like the slaves of Marie Baude; and temporary indentures like Marie Aram, who worked for years as her free black husband labored to purchase her. These people turned the hospital into a rich crossroads of experience and information. Louison and Babet would have encountered women like these as they completed daily rounds of laundering, cooking, and cleaning. They may have recognized each other as members of a laboring community. Most likely, they would have known whose freedom was precarious, whose freedom remained to be fulfilled, and who were consigned to servitude. The hospital, in other words, already a site of physical exhaustion, frustration, and suspended animation, would also have been a space for sharing information, strategy, and tactics—a space where a black female counter surveillance network brewed.[51]

Hospital labor included laundry duties, a grueling task requiring physical strength, strong stomachs, and attention to detail, especially when washing the soiled linens of the hospital. Laundry was their task that day, and Louison and Babet walked to the riverbank with pounds of fabric in their charge, engaged in a labor common to their race and gender, and one that left them exposed to the gaze, taunts, and attention of anyone wandering the riverbank at the same time. Paired up and, thus, stronger in number, they remained vulnerable, but the river, as the nearest source of fresh, if gritty, water, served as a gathering place for Africans in town. Louison and Babet joined others at the river, including other enslaved women with their own washing to do and passersby on their way about town.

On that day, a soldier named Pierre Antoine Pochonet interrupted them. Drunk and belligerent, Pochonet hassled them as they went about their work. Pochonet went so far as to pull Babet aside. Whatever he said to her, he was not pleased with her response. Witnesses would later suggest he made sexually suggestive remarks. Louison, reminiscent of Marie Baude, claimed later she did not hear what was said between Babet and Pochonet. If Babet rebuffed his sexual overtures, Pochonet did not take the woman's refusal lightly. She saw Pochonet strike Babet in the stomach in response and begin to beat her. Louison rushed to defend her companion, "screaming so loud that they attracted the attention of the people in the hospital."[52] Infused with liquid courage, Pochonet lashed out at both women. The bayonet shredded her arms and body, piercing Louison in the collarbone and Babet in the sternum, according to the surgeon of the hospital.[53] At one point, Pochonet stopped his assault long enough to order Louison to her knees to beg his pardon. Louison did so, but Pochonet did not stop. He continued to cut her arms and body despite her physical obeisance.

The screaming drew the attention of everyone at the river and beyond. Joseph Badon, an eighteen-year-old surgeon, and Baptiste, an enslaved black surgeon and Louison's husband, ran out of the hospital to stop the attack.[54] A black boy ran away from the scene and into the hospital pharmacy where François, a black slave, was working. François joined Badon and Baptiste. Pochonet turned on everyone who attempted to defuse the fight. Pochonet sliced Baptiste's hand before being subdued by the men and others, many of them enslaved and free blacks who arrived on the scene who "dragged [him] into the hospital yard."[55] When the altercation ended, Baptiste, Louison, and Babet all found themselves in the hospital and Pochonet had been arrested by the officials. All three were wounded and bleeding, but neither woman was expected to live. In the investigation that followed, it became evident Pochonet left a trail of braggadocio and brutality in his wake that day and in the moments leading up to his interaction with Babet. François, described as a creole *nègre*, met Pochonet in his walk to the river "as he was returning from the waterfront with a purchase of plums." Pochonet demanded some of the fruit. When François refused, Pochonet drew his bayonet and tried to strike him with it, but François escaped.[56] Manon, an enslaved *négresse*, was washing clothes with two other *négresses* near the barracks when Pochonet approached them. He ordered them to wash a handkerchief for him. They refused to wash his things and Pochonet chased them down with his bayonet. When they escaped into the river, he "trampled upon the clothes lying on the bank" before running off.[57] The Ursulines and the hospital stood just downriver from the barracks.

In a world of limited options, black women used refusal as a practice of freedom that rejected the intimate violations slavery allowed. Pochonet's aggressive demand for labor and sexual attention endeavored to shame and dominate Manon, Louison, and Babet specifically as laboring women of African descent. All three women refused him, Babet, perhaps, most intimately. In rejecting him, the women refused to be bullied into doing more work, allowing him sexual access, or performing subservience. Alerted by the sound of their screams, a broader community of support rushed to their aid, with children helping to sound the alarm, and men, including Louison's own husband, mobilized in an attempt to save the two women's lives. Their defense, its immediacy and urgency, contrasted in a powerful way from the response the Ursulines gave to the near murder of their enslaved laborer. Faced with the option of giving testimony against Pochonet, Reverend Mothers Xavier and Magdeleine replied they would not. After all, "if they could, they would like to save his life and that they would prefer to lose their negresses rather than do anything against charity toward their fellow men."[58] The Ursulines' largesse did not save Pochonet. On 28 June 1752, he was ordered to be executed for the murder of

Louison and Babet who, by that date, two weeks after their encounter with Pochonet, had both died.[59]

As a practice of freedom, African women and women of African descent across New Orleans modeled refusal and defense, especially of those whom they claimed as kin. In 1745, Fanchon, a free *négresse* and wife of another free man of color, Raphael, narrowly missed being attacked by a sword when she entered a dispute between her husband and the carpenter/cabinetmaker S. Charles Le Moine. After her husband tussled with Le Moine over an adze Le Moine borrowed from her husband, Fanchon took matters into her own hands. Entering Le Moine's house, she attempted to retrieve the adze herself. Le Moine managed to bar her from his house by brandishing his sabre, calling her *une coquine*, a slur for prostitute. Fanchon fired back, calling him a *putain*, another slur related to sex work and "nothing but an engagé" or indentured servant. She dared Le Moine to attack her "if he was brave enough" and promised him he would pay what he owed.[60] She sent her children after Le Moine as he passed their home on his way to work, and they followed him and pelted him with rocks. Fanchon and her family harassed Le Moine into such a state of distress, he finally asked the Superior Council to intervene.

Fanchon's flagrant refusal to be cowed by Le Moine saturated her rebuke. Emboldened, perhaps, by her own free status, she took up the discourse of use and possession and turned it against Le Moine. She revealed and expressed a matrix of beliefs about her world, including that the tool owed to her husband was also owed to herself, *sa femme* or the wife, and as a part of their household. As such, it was in her power to demand collection. She understood kin to be a resource for safety, security, and, in this instance, restitution. When her attempt to secure her property was thwarted, Fanchon mobilized her kin, her children, to participate in the collection process, offering them a robust tutorial in restitution and dissent. She fully comprehended the sexually charged insult leveled at her by Le Moine and returned slurs and barbs of her own that trafficked in the same tropes of use and possession. By making choices like these, fleeting and ephemeral, Fanchon joined Manon, Louison, and Babet and other women of African descent engaged in refusal as a practice of freedom. In physically defending themselves and each other, as Louison did, black women also risked their own lives to fight for their kin. In their practices of refusal and defense, whether as tired wives balking at cooking a meal, harassed laundresses refusing to clean more clothes, or free black wives defending their households, black women rejected the notion that licentiousness and subservience was the sum total of their gender and race. Refusal mattered enough to African women and women of African descent that they risked their lives to engage in it.

These knots and tangles of sex, labor, and domination extended into the ribald world of insults, barbs, and slurs used between men as well. Pochonet's attempt to dominate along his intoxicated walk from the canteen to the convent, with all of its explicit and implicit sexual overtures, can be set against another street brawl that occurred five years earlier. In May 1747, Etienne Larue strolled past the hospital. Larue was a pilot and arrived most recently from Saint Louis on the coast of Saint-Domingue on the ship *L'Unique*. He was also a free African man, born in Senegal and likely never enslaved. His father, Sieur (Sr.) Larue, operated a shipping and transportation business out of Saint-Louis. Sr. Larue owned ships and employed *matelots*, enslaved and free, to take goods between *escales* up and down the Senegal River, between Saint-Louis and France, and between the West African coast and the Antilles. Larue began work as a Company employee at least by the 1720s. In 1722, Company officials at Galam paid him one slave for labor completed.[61] By the 1730s, he married a *mulâtresse* named Marie Thomas and continued to captain ships for trading companies.[62] Etienne Larue walking along New Orleans' riverfront, at twenty-two years old, may have been the product of their union. He was also a product of the Atlantic world created first through free African labor on Senegambia's coast, and then through continued African enslaved and free labor in New Orleans, Saint-Louis in Senegal, and Saint Louis in Saint-Domingue.

When he, a free African man born and raised in a community of free Africans, the son of a free African man of significant wealth and status, passed three soldiers on his stroll, it would have been normal for him to tip his hat. He did. New Orleans, however, was not Saint-Louis and late 1740s New Orleans even less so. One of the soldiers, offended, responded, "Bonsoir, Seigneur Nigritte." Combining the noble title "Seigneur" with the racialized and infantilizing diminutive *nigritte* was meant to offend, belittle, and put Larue in his proper place as a black child, subservient and beneath the notice of adult white men. Larue, apparently, did not miss a beat in his response: "Bonsoir, Jean Foutre." The insult Larue offered did more than incense the soldiers because he refused to be humiliated by their dismissal. With "Jean Foutre," Larue flung an explicitly sexual and sodomic insult, one meant to offend, belittle, and implicate the other man in sexual intercourse with men.[63] A physical altercation ensued, with the soldiers slapping Larue and Larue fighting back. M. Tixerant, an officer, spotting the battle, broke up the melee by beating

back Larue with the scabbard of his sword. Somewhere in the tussling, Larue
fired his pistol at the three soldiers. The gunshots ended the fighting, but soldiers placed Larue in irons and sent him to jail.[64]

In the types of insults both Fanchon and Larue wielded, illicit sex acts and
sexual violence collided with race, status, and bondage. Sexually charged insults
troubled and expressed gender, race, and sexual practices. Insults also proved
promiscuous—anyone at any level of society could access their repertoire and
their threat. When his autonomy, masculinity, and racial status were challenged,
Larue returned with a slur alleging his adversary engaged in illicit, penetrative,
possessive sexual activity. Fanchon insulted Le Moine as engaged in sexual labor
and her derision toward *engagés* gestured to the saturation of sexual politics
with servitude—as an *engagé*, Le Moine was both used and possessed by someone in mastery over him. But the power of the slurs hinged on sex acts that
threatened penetration, violation, and transgression. They suggested potential
feminization and trafficked in the metaphorical and real dangers that lurked
in the lives of women of African descent—even when women of African descent
were not the ones wielding them.

Beyond the Manumission Act: Black Femme Freedom

When women and girls like Charlotte, Marie Charlotte, Louison, and Fanchon
engaged in practices of freedom that exceeded the manumission act, they created black femme freedoms. On the one hand, the *Code Noir* created a structure
to secure freedom from bondage. Slaveowners contested this process. Officials
limited it further through a series of commodificatory acts.[65] On the other
hand, colonial officials, slaveowners, and husbands, buttressed by legal and
social power, claimed more than the physical labor of their slaves. They presumed intimate access to the bodies, labor, and lives of everyone around them.
This presumption did not stop at the manumission act. It trickled out beyond
white male elites to *petit blancs* and even enslaved men who used intimate
violence to prop up their own dominance over the lives of African women and
girls. Black femme freedom, a fluid plurality, describes actions, expressions,
and excretions that moved beyond the fractional flesh of *la traversée* and the
container of the manumission act. Black femme freedom points to the deeply
feminine, feminized, and femme practices of freedom engaged in by women
and girls of African descent. In the practice of refusal, whether in rejected labor

demands or sexual advances, and even refusal to concede to officials in manumission disputes, black women and girls claimed ownership over themselves. Their claim superseded that of their owner; it even rejected claims of their bodies or labor by their husbands. Black women created black femme freedoms by stepping into the fray on each other's behalf. They raised sons brazen enough to throw rocks at white soldiers and daughters who knew enough of the *Code Noir* to demand officials recognize a "trick." They troubled the position of *sa femme*, yet also took up the status of woman and wife as identities worth defending. Black femme freedoms emerged in these interstices as black women exploited every tool at their disposal on behalf of themselves and their kin.

Invoking black femme instead of (black) women or womanhood remembers the slipperiness of the category of woman in a multilingual world of slaves.[66] The Ursuline nuns' casual dismissal of the violence against Louison and Babet offers only one of many reminders that womanhood did not always entail care or community across lines of race or status. In eighteenth-century New Orleans, gender formation and desire bucked stable nomenclature, but the architectural outline of honorable widows, masterless mistresses, libertine *sauvagesses*, and wicked *négresses* was clear. Black femme captures the distinction between New Orleans white womanhood in formation and women at other levels of society. Black femme pushes even further, into a framing of blackness embracing the promiscuous and polymorphic arrangements of femininity and feminine desire that enslaved and free created out of impossible circumstances. Through *la traversée*, the *Code Noir*, and their own lust, slaveowners and colonial officials did their best to prime black flesh for plantation production. Black women, aware of these reformations, kept sticks between their legs and refused to allow slaveowners the last word on their femininity.

A life-sustaining definition of blackness emerged out of black women's survival, the survival of their children, the creation of self-sustaining communities across African origins, racial nomenclatures, and the precarity of bondage. This represented no small feat. Anne Gusban fought for her born-of-this-place children in a Senegambia where Europeans lacked the monopoly of power. African women and girls who survived *la traversée* mothered born-of-this-place children in colonial societies that marked them as commodities and consumable unto their death. As a self-propagating African-descended population emerged along the Gulf Coast, African women mothered black children on a different continent, in a terrifying context, with only the knowledge and

tools they had at hand. Becoming black hurt. It fused heartbreak with dislocation, mourning, and dispossession, especially after 1730, when the forced migration that had forged a link between West Africa and Gulf Coast Louisiana and
laid the foundation for black life and culture in the region ended. Becoming
black also healed, as women, children, and men cast nets of chosen kin, community, and relation across, over, and around each other.

Black femme freedom evinced the genesis, contradictions, and complica-
tions of blackness, intimacy, and freedom as these crossed into the New World.
Marie Baude experienced these herself. As an African woman married to a
French man and residing at Saint-Louis, her status as a free woman, a property
owner, and the daughter of a white man did not prevent Pierre LeGrain from
issuing his sexually explicit threat. The murder that followed, as her husband
took up arms to defend her honor or his own pride, the severity of the attack,
and Pinet's disregard for LeGrain's body as "just a mulâtre" broadened the
terrain of violence surrounding Marie Baude. Eighteenth-century Atlantic
societies on the African and American sides of the ocean became sites of contestation and physical conflict, driven by the brutality of colonial expansion
and the slave trade. African women and women of African descent like Marie
Baude, who resided in ports like Saint-Louis and Gorée as those places transformed into Atlantic-era slaveholding societies, lived in the everyday shadow
of possible violation as the rules of engagement fell under violent negotiation.
Threatened with sexual violence, Marie Baude did (or did not) witness her
husband kill a man, and then followed that same husband to a foreign land
where she lacked kin and community. Both the threat of and possible freedom
from intimate violence undergirds Marie Baude's inconceivable choices; her
loss of status, property, and, finally, archival trace undergirded her diasporic
reality.

Black femme also troubles the "over-expression of heterosexual desire"
attributed to women of African descent in the Atlantic world, calling attention
to the intimacy that accompanied kinships like the one between women like
Louison and Babet.[67] Black and woman of color feminists use the term "femme"
to define "a Black and queer sexual identity and gendered performance rooted
in embodying a resistive femininity."[68] Using black femme in the context of
women of African descent's practices of freedom in the eighteenth century
surfaces foundational strains of this resistive femininity and intimacy between
women. In a setting where assault and rape, brandings and burnings, and broken
limbs and dismemberment awaited black women who refused to submit to

their owners or defied the men around them, daring to form intimate bonds with women was a strategy for survival. In the eighteenth-century context, black femme freedom articulates the audacity of a freedom that dared to reach past masculinity and empire for satisfaction. It infuses black women's choosing of each other with carnal and erotic stickiness. Omise'eke Tinsley, in her study of women loving women in the Caribbean, used the phrase "thiefing sugar," with its dual invocation of thievery and sweetness, "to imagine brown women keeping sweetness among themselves." Noting the ways the French *Code Noir* mandated corporeal punishment for enslaved Africans who stole sugar cane, Tinsley turns the colonial order (law, police, forced labor, and deprivation) on its head to highlight the pleasurable disruption "of refusing to imagine [each other] as commodifiable natural resources for someone else to survey or claim."[69] Meditating on black femme freedoms created by women and girls of African descent who refused the use and possession mandated by slaveowners and husbands, who reached past the manumission act into new forms of selfhood, an array of disruptive possibilities for black womanhood emerge.

Geographies of Pleasure and Spirit

African women and women of African descent in New Orleans took advantage of the changing material conditions of their owners and etched geographies of black freedom that overflowed law and colonial intent. Charlotte did more than run away from her father and owner. She combined flight, appeal, allyship, and willfulness in her defiant bid to escape bondage. She demanded to be heard. While she may have been found in a man's bed, she requested an audience with a woman, one with as much power as possible—the governor's wife. Considering the plans Charlotte wove to get to the governor's wife, Charlotte must have chosen her target with care. Whether Charlotte endeavored to tell a story of violence will never be clear. Her political awareness, however, rises to the surface, despite her inability to secure an audience or manumission at that time.[70] Demanding to be heard by someone in power, seeking out a powerful woman, attempting to secure allies in men like Batard, offering bribes, and fleeing the scene as she had fled from her owner—each of these represented practices of black femme freedom engaged in by women and girls of African descent. Moving beyond the manumission act as a practice of owning oneself required claiming political and physical space, and reclaiming the physical body for all of its pleasures.

Almost immediately upon arrival on the Gulf Coast, Africans found themselves appropriated, moved, captured, and commanded according to colonial officials' or slaveowners' demands. They also immediately cultivated alternative ways of thinking about their bodies, time, and space. Stephanie Camp, describing the resistance strategies of the enslaved in the antebellum South, noted the ways the enslaved shaped a rival geography or "alternative ways of knowing and using plantation and southern space that conflicted with planters' ideals and demands."[71] Along the Gulf Coast, geography and environment were slaves' allies. The river became a portal between those enslaved in town and the black majorities residing on plantations. Africans navigated the channels, portages, and streams on errands for their owners and at times laboring for themselves. The cypress swamps above and below the town hid maroons of black and Native descent, men and women absconding from slaveowners and plantations across the region. In a symbiotic relationship with local slaveowners, maroons felled cypresses for white landowners, visited enslaved kinfolk in secret, and continued to use New Orleans itself as a space to congregate. By organizing gatherings and sharing space together, enslaved and free people of African descent constructed a rival geography out of the kinds of intimacies they desired and kinship they wished to keep.

Sunday dances and market spaces became gathering points for people of African descent, slave and free, across society. In 1726, Le Page du Pratz, manager of the plantation across the river from New Orleans, described the *calindas* thrown by black women, men, and children from across the region, even noting the pirogues Africans used to navigate back and forth to town.[72] Although Du Pratz claimed to have ended the gatherings and destroyed the pirogues, people of African descent continued to appropriate Sundays for their own marketing and play. On these days, enslaved and free turned the colonial geography inside out, transmuting spaces marked by violence into opportunities to meet kin, secure livelihoods, and play. The area that would become known as Congo Square emerged in these years. Along with the plantation across the river, Africans gathered beyond the rear ramparts, near the portage Bayou Saint-Jean and St. Peter's Cemetery.[73] Indigenous traders long used this area for exchange and festivals of their own. When Chevalier Charles Morand built a brickyard on Bayou Saint-Jean, this area also gained a concentrated black presence. By the 1730s, Morand employed some forty "*negroes* and *negresses*." By 1747, about twelve cabins had been built along Bayou Saint-Jean for "negroes of the Brick-yard."[74] With the combined indigenous and African presence, situated as it was on the edge of the maroon-inhabited cypress swamp, but linked by the portage to the elusive waterways behind the town, this area became a prime location for clandestine gatherings of all kinds.

Africans and people of African descent did not limit their gatherings to the back of town or to large dances. In the courtyards and private homes, enslaved women brought community together. In September of 1746, Jeannette, a *négresse libre*, stood before the Superior Council to be reprimanded. Jeannette hosted nighttime gatherings of slaves and servants. As a free woman of African descent, Jeannette did not risk nearly as much as the enslaved who participated in these "assemblies." Article 13 of the 1724 *Code Noir* forbade slaves belonging to different masters to assemble at any time, day or night, and threatened whippings, brandings, and death if the offenders were caught.[75] However, Jeannette would have known how tenuous and contingent her freedom and her privileges truly were. She would have known this well before she invited and catered to the Africans and indigenous women and men, and poor white women and men, who appeared at her gatherings. And yet she persisted. Now, summoned before the Superior Council, Jeannette waited as colonial officials "reprimanded and admonished her" for her behavior, ordering her not to repeat her mistake or risk further penalty.[76] Within a year, Jeannette would be con-demned to return to slavery as punishment and payment for back debts.

Black pleasure played a central role in the logic of black femme freedom. The communal labor of Louison and her kinswoman Mama Comba offer an example of this.[77] Mama Comba, a fifty-year-old "Mandinga" slave belonging to the Capuchins, lived at the Hospital for the Poor. Mama Comba labored at the hospital, likely alongside Marie Jeanne, an Arada slave, but work was not the only thing that filled her days and nights. On multiple evenings, Mama Comba joined Louison, also fifty years old, at her home in the garden of S. Cantrelle, for community dinners. Together with others enslaved, Mama Comba and Louison ate a *gombeau* or gumbo, complete with pilfered filé, shared origin stories, and flirted and enjoyed each other.[78] Louison and Louis were known lovers, as were Cezar, another attendee, and his wife, Marie Anne. Comba, however, may have taken the younger Louis as a lover as well at some point. The gathering gained its power from the kinship generated around it—those who stole to make the meal possible, the lovers who met for time together, the time spent preparing the meal, the gastronomical pleasures of eating flavorful food. Engaging in sensual intercourses recovered commodified bodies from the machinery of bondage and remembered histories that lay beyond *la traversée*. At Louison's dinners, the Senegambian heritage among the Gulf Coast's enslaved community was also on full display. Comba noted several Bambara in attendance and described herself as a Mandinga. Another woman in the group went by the name Fatima, a name common in both Muslim and Senegambian society at the time.[79] Fatima prepared the gumbo. Even the decision to cook gumbo gestured to foodways across the Atlantic, to the soupi-kandia of Senegal and green-sauce gumbos of Benin.[80]

As Jeannette, Comba, and Louison found, the erotics of feeding the black body for joy and pleasure came with deadly risks. Pleasure intersected with what officials would have perceived as criminal activity. Maroons attended. At least two of the dinner's participants stole a pig to share together, and the filé itself was acquired by dubious means.[81] Cezar and Louis, two Bambara attendees, would later be apprehended and executed by colonial officials for maroonage and theft. Louison would be forced to watch the execution of her lover, Louis, alongside Mama Comba as punishment. Black networks of pleasure and play came with a price. They also came with their own systems of accountability and standards for inclusion. Another community of feasting and dancing risked exposure and punishment when they confirmed that an enslaved man, Francisque, attended their dance events with laundry he had stolen. In 1766, Francisque, an English slave from Philadelphia, had appeared at a series of dances, spent money on the drummers and the women in attendance, but later refused to pay for eggs he purchased and stole earrings from one of the group's members. When Francisque was accused of theft, the male members of the group stepped forward to witness against him. As Sophie White noted, "His ostentation at the dances appeared to have evoked feelings of resentment" and feelings in the men that "they were being shown up to their female audience."[82]

The river would also, as Manon, another Louison, and Babet found, become a node of the black femme geography. During the height of French immigration and enslaved forced migration, the riverfront churned with the activity of enslaved and indentured African, Native, and European workers. Thanks to the drafting of men and boys at the point of disembarkation by Jacques Fazende, a Superior Council official, it was also a black masculine space. Women would also have occupied it as well, using the waters for the grueling labor of washing, laundering, and peddling. Not far from the river, on the Place d'Armes or parade ground where members of the militia and soldiers in the garrison drilled, and executions and corporeal punishment were administered, enslaved and free black peddlers joined indigenous and white traders engaged in market work. Their petty commerce stretched the black geography even farther, from the riverbanks to the church. These transgressions mattered. For enslaved and free African women and women of African descent in town, this ebb and flow of everyday black life, work, and pleasure marked their everyday lives.

Black femme geographies, pleasure, and appeals for freedom often existed in excruciating tension with each other. Charlotte's flight from her owner-father offers not only a lesson in the audacity of fugitivity, but an alternative, erotic mapping of slavery and freedom. For an adolescent girl in the bed of a sailor, seeking safety from violence may have been inextricable from seeking pleasure, sensation, and escape. Her relations with Batard, as inscrutable as they appear in the archive, also rupture what we can assume about consent and desire. Taca's actions likewise recall a practice of freedom invested in the pleasuring body. When Baraca complained to his comrade that she was seeing another man, Taca did not deny it. She complained to their guest about Baraca's jealousy. Her suggestion to them both, that if Baraca did not witness it, perhaps it did not happen, refused to concede a crime on her part. Taca was unapologetic, as unapologetic as Charlotte. In her critique of Baraca's behavior toward her, Taca also challenged his right to physically harm her as a result of his inability to control his own emotions. Given the archive's silence on her consent to being part of this marriage, Taca offered a rubric for intimate justice that attended to her erotic freedom.

Marie's fugitive flight offers another example. A runaway creole *négresse* belonging to M. Tixerant, she nearly found herself in irons before the Superior Council.[83] In March 1748, the group of fugitives she had been part of was captured in Havana, Cuba. In 1738, they were taken by deserting soldiers from the area around Bayou Saint-Jean. Whether Marie left willingly or found herself kidnapped by the soldiers with hopes of selling her for a profit in a colony far away remained unclear. Ten years later, Marie evaded recapture, but the testimony of the other prisoners troubled the Superior Council. Marie, according to her fugitive kinfolk, continued to live as a free person in Havana. Manuel and John, two of the recaptured fugitives, reported that they had seen Marie alive and well as a street vendor selling bananas and other items. Although Marie was still married to a man in Louisiana named François, she also had a new husband in Havana, a carpenter named André. François, meanwhile, was still alive and in Louisiana as were three of her children: Charlot, her son, and two daughters, Jeanne and Babet.[84] Marie, stolen property and a fugitive slave, in the ten years since fleeing or being taken from the Gulf Coast, and in the face of family separation, had somehow found her way to a different kind of freedom in Cuba. She evaded capture and did not return to life as a slave in New Orleans. Perhaps Marie found pleasure, financial security, or relative safety by remaking herself as a *casta,* as the Spanish described free people of African descent in their colonies. Or perhaps the journey home, a journey that risked taking her across open seas, as well as from a state of freedom and into one of unfreedom and punishment for maroonage, proved too difficult to risk. Like Charlotte, her status, race, gender, age, and kinship ties placed particular constraints on the options available, elicited different desires, and presented different opportunities, shaping her black femme freedom in particular ways.

Even the body itself served as a node in the black femme geography. Sister Marie-Madeleine Hachard noted to her superiors that "if it were the fashion here, the *negresses* would wear beauty marks on their faces."[85] By the eighteenth century, the beauty mark, and most especially artificial beauty marks (*mouches*), had become a trademark associated with high femininity, sexuality, and fashion in France. On the other side of Hachard's off-hand jibe were black women and girls who carried themselves with no small amount of womanly affectation.[86] The experience of black women and girls among the Ursulines would have been instructive. On the one hand, the Ursulines centered proselytizing, educating, and providing relief for women and girls, regardless of race. Women of African and indigenous descent resided with the Ursulines almost immediately upon their arrival and continued to do so through the eighteenth century. The Ursulines, however, did not balk at owning slaves as labor or as property, nor did they abstain from leasing multiple plantations, including one across the river from town.[87] The Ursulines were women of their time and slaveownership accompanied free white womanhood in the Atlantic world.

By the 1730s, African women and women of African descent had taken advantage of the Ursuline complex as an important space of contestation for enslaved and free, particularly those exposed to Catholic doctrine. The *Code Noir* required that slaveowners baptize their slaves, but few owners obeyed. Those who did took advantage of the occasion of Masses that occurred on Easter and Pentecost Eve, bringing hundreds of enslaved laborers to be initiated in the mysteries of the faith. In what Emily Clark and Virginia Meacham Gould describe as "religious creolization," African women and women of

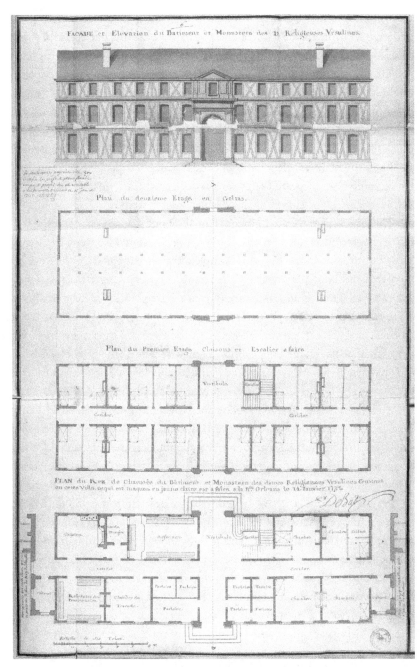

Figure 12. Facade and elevation of the Ursuline Convent. By Alexandre de Batz, 1735. Courtesy of Archives nationales d'outre-mer de France, Aix-en-Provence.

African descent took advantage of the Ursuline nuns' determination to teach and convert women across race and status.[88] For some, particularly those recently arrived from the Senegal, Benin, or Congo coasts, regions with years of exposure to French and Portuguese missionaries, Catholic rites of baptism might have been familiar. Whether they were practitioners of Islam, vodun, other African religions, or Catholicism, African women and women of African descent would have understood their roles as mothers and women to be very much tied to cultivating and passing on spiritual knowledge and protection. For those unfamiliar with Catholicism, exposure to a social and spiritual iconography that suggested safety and security within a broader community of filial responsibility may have been especially attractive.

The founding of the first Hospital for the Poor in 1735 expanded the free black geography as free and enslaved people circulated between the Royal Hospital, situated in the Ursuline complex, and the Hospital for the Poor on Chartres and Bienville streets.[89] The Ursulines continued to treat enslaved Africans belonging to the king, and enslaved and free continued to be employed by the Capuchin priests who managed the Hospital for the Poor. As black laborers and patients circulated between the two locations, they created a network of healing, labor, and rumor. Louise Bertiche, who might have been one of Marie Baude's slaves, labored in the Royal Hospital until her purchase in the 1730s by M. Belille. In the 1740s, Marie Louise and her daughter found themselves in manumission limbo at the Royal Hospital when their owner died and the executor of his estate placed them there, despite a will freeing them. Jeanneton, in contrast, found herself laboring at the Hospital for the Poor after her emancipation by will, working for two years as part of the terms of her *affranchissement*.

In 1751, frustration with the freedom that enslaved people exhibited led the governor to issue a set of regulations, a police code, to control the movement, marketing, and networks of African and indigenous women, children, and men throughout the outpost. In the 1740s, a combination of Choctaw raids, enslaved and free black cattle rustling, and the presence of maroons in the swamps and forest beyond and between outposts created white settler panic reminiscent of the Natchez days.[90] Settlers upriver fled their farms for New Orleans in fear. Almost thirty years after the promulgation of the *Code Noir*, the 1751 police code attempted to restore order and placate white colonists. Concern over the rival geography enslaved and free Africans had created suffused Vaudreuil's edict. Articles 21 through 23 condemned assemblies of enslaved, and punished

free men and women of all races who allowed the same. The governor empowered soldiers to surveil black peddlers as they entered market spaces by checking
them for passes from their owners. Article 10 singled out free black men and
women as harboring slaves in their homes. In a turn of phrase drawn from
centuries of sexualizing black freedom practices across the Atlantic, the article
admonished free people of African descent for harboring slaves "in order to
seduce them and excite them to plunder their masters and lead a scandalous
life." The punishment for offering maroons shelter reminded all people of
African descent of the legal fiction of manumission—for harboring slaves, free
black men and women would lose their freedom and become slaves of the
king.[91] Vaudreuil did not limit his concerns to free and enslaved African and
Native residents. French and Swiss soldiers were allowed to sell liquor at shops
of their own, but these shops were segregated from each other. Settlers from
outside of the city and all other vagrants were instructed to leave town completely and return to their farms.

Black pleasure economies were not altruistic. The stakes were too high and
the risk of death or reenslavement too stark. Creating and maintaining a black
geography required resources. Black women stepped up to the project of sustaining their own kinfolk. Small commerce, provisioning, and a local trade-
barter system, which had long prevailed as a matter of survival, became the
custom and practice as support from France fizzled. The frontier-exchange
economy, begun for survival and convenience between black and indigenous
slaves, itinerant traders, and French settlers, continued to provide one of the
primary means of subsistence. As fortunes waned, more and more slaveowners
divested from any responsibility they may have felt toward provisioning for
their laborers. Instead, masters encouraged and even required enslaved and
free black laborers to support themselves through gardening, hunting, and
craftsmanship. The *Code Noir* required enslavers to offer black laborers Sunday
off as a Catholic holiday only, but this requirement went unenforced. Africans
used Saturday and Sunday to hire themselves out, raise their own crops (including cotton and tobacco for trade and cash), or otherwise spend time working
on their own accounts. In New Orleans, where work ceased for a midday break,
Africans could be seen using "their two hours at noon to account by making
faggots to sell in the city; others sell ashes, or fruits that are in season."[92] Louison
herself, along with hosting dinners, sold cakes and other treats around the city.
Sundays also became opportunities for Africans from the plantation districts
to travel to New Orleans, trade on the levee, or gather just north of town at

Bayou Saint-Jean.[93] Between the haphazard houses that made up the heart of town and along streets sometimes little more than streams themselves, laborers of African descent from the plantations' growing regions met kinfolk and made community with enslaved and free black residents living along the river.

Black femme geographies were not egalitarian. The work of cooking, baking, laundering, and ironing fell primarily to enslaved black women. While men and boys also served as domestics in the plantation district, the role of domestic or *domestique*, particularly in the area around the town, became the more exclusive space of African women and women of African descent. In many cases, women filled multiple roles for themselves, their households, and their owners, serving as cooks, ironers, laundresses, and seamstresses at the same time. As these roles suggest, the grueling and largely anonymous labor of sustaining slaveholders' households often fell to women. In the same way, as Mama Comba, Louison, and Fatima demonstrated at their dinners, the labors of hospitality, cooking, and creating pleasurable space in the rival geography also fell to women. The gendered dimensions of hospitality might have accompanied distinctions based on age. Mama Comba's honorific of "Mama" may have been an honorific and mark of elder status as acknowledged by those who knew her.

Differences created by ethnicity may also have shaped membership within and among geographies. Several of those who gathered for Louison's and Mama Comba's feasts were Senegambian. When women of African descent along the Gulf Coast fused African ethnicity with Atlantic-wide racial nomenclature, they grappled with what African descent would mean. These reformations were promiscuous. Some women and girls articulated ethnic identifications while others described themselves through broader characterizations like "born in Guinée" or "creole." All engaged in the intellectual work of regenerating old and generating new ways of knowing the world around them. African knowledges and imperial pressures shaped practices of freedom in Guadeloupe, Martinique, Saint-Domingue, and Cuba as well. In struggling with these questions of place, history, and community, Africans on the Gulf Coast existed in an intimate relationship or "common unity" with Africans on coasts, in ports, and across hinterlands of the Caribbean archipelago.[94]

Difference created by enslaved, fugitive, or free status may have mediated entrance into black geographies. Louis smoothed his way into Mama Comba's and Louison's dinners by claiming he was traveling from his owner on a pass, a rationale that potentially eased concerns about the danger his fugitive status might bring to their space. In contrast, free women of African descent like Jeannette claimed the right to gather, host gatherings, and own their own labor, a tangible distinction from those who remained enslaved. Geography and mobility, the illicit and fugitive purview of the enslaved, became an indulgence of free status. Whatever the rubric of inclusion, black femme geographies had membership criteria of their own as black women made active claims on whom to trust and whom to labor for—in other words, whom they would claim as kin. These rubrics, particularly distinctions based on gender and status, would shape intimate and kinship ties in the decades to come.

* * *

Caught at the intersection of diaspora and empire, women generated a null archive of inconsequential marks and laboring *pièces d'Inde*. Extraordinary, then, that black women and a black feminine presence can be gleaned from the archives at all. But African women and women of African descent do appear in the archive where they exceeded the bounds of colonial power. Intimacy and kinship structured the ways black women and girls encountered slavery, but intimate and kinship ties also offered resources that could be mobilized on their own behalf. In petitions and appeals, in refusal and defense, in constructing black femme geographies, in embodied pleasure and desire, black women created black femme freedoms. These glimmerings, ephemeral when they appeared and contingent on violence as they were, lay atop an ocean of behaviors, strategies, and epistemologies that were not beholden to French Atlantic ideologies of race, sex, and bondage. Out of a practice of black femme freedom, African women and women of African descent marshaled the audacity to challenge those who presumed mastery—whether imperial authorities or their husbands—over and over again.

When the Gulf Coast abruptly transitioned from French to Spanish governance, African women and women of African descent turned to these practices of freedom to take advantage of change where they could. Returned to her master and father, Charlotte remained d'Erneville's slave for another twenty-two years—through the Seven Years' War and the transition of Louisiana from French to Spanish rule. During that time, she had a son, acquired slaves of her own, and owned and ran her own household, despite her state of bondage. With Spanish administration came access to new institutions like notaries and the imposition of new slave laws meant to bring Louisiana into conformity with the rest of Spanish America. In 1771, d'Erneville took advantage of looser Spanish rules around testaments and manumission. He went before a notary to register his last will and testament. In it, he granted Charlotte, now Carlota, her freedom "for great love of them and for services" but required her to serve him until her death. Perhaps dissatisfied with that qualification, three years later, Carlota purchased her freedom from d'Erneville outright for 400 pesos. The teenage girl caught in the bed of a ship captain trying to find her way to freedom would live another thirty years, into the American-inflected nineteenth century, and die with a house and some land, having freed her son, willed at least one slave their manumission, and owned several others.

Freedom continued to come most readily to those with intimate relationships to power, but the spaces where power resided grew more diffuse. Kinship between free and enslaved people grew more fraught and more complicated. The transition to the Spanish period triggered an immediate and concentrated change in the free community of African descent along the Gulf Coast. The official designation of free people of African descent as *libres* and *castas* brought new strategies for securing manumission and new ideas about the customary rights available to enslaved, formerly enslaved, and those born as free. Spanish officials also introduced a new archipelagic innovation into Louisiana. Imported from Cuba, *coartación* offered a process of mediated self-purchase. If women and girls like Charlotte already practiced freedom through legal and extralegal strategy, woman-loving kinships, black femme geographies, and embodied pleasure, then the introduction of *coartación* created an explosion of new opportunities to do so. After 1762, the number of free people of African descent rose dramatically as both enslaved and free used the change of regime to make the case for individual and collective cases for freedom. With the expansion of manumission came new tensions as freed and free African women and women of African descent fought for the right to acquire, inherit, and bequeath property on behalf of themselves and their kin. The battle over legacies had begun.

Chapter 6

༄

Life After Death:
Legacies of Freedom
in Spanish New Orleans

It is true that I lived in public, notorious and familiar concubinage and many years with Pedro Moris and during this time had three children aforementioned... and that this citizen Moris did call them his children and them to him "Father" and that he provided for them and for me all that was necessary for their life and more after their death.

—"Court Testimony," *María Tereza,*
grifa libre v. Perine Demazillier, parda libre, New Orleans, 1789

In January 1789, in New Orleans, a free woman of color named María Teresa initiated legal proceedings against Pelagia "Perine" Dauphine dit Demasillier, another free woman of color living in the city.[1] According to María Teresa, two years earlier, Pedro Maurice Dauphine, a free man of color and Perine's brother, passed away in his home. Before he died, Maurice drafted a nuncupative will, or a will-by-voice. He made provisions for his three children with María Teresa, bequeathing all of his property to their two daughters and one son, also named Pedro. Through a series of unfortunate events, possession of Maurice's property fell to Perine Dauphine, his sister and godmother of one of the children. Perine, however, refused to relinquish her brother's estate. With Don Antonio Méndez representing her, María Teresa accused Perine of "avarice" and behaving "against the natural law and will of the testator." She asked the officers of the Cabildo to respect Maurice's final wishes and to force Perine to yield Maurice's effects to his children.[2]

Over the course of the case, María Teresa solicited testimony from myriad white New Orleans businessmen and city leaders. She asked them to attest to both Maurice's "love and affection" for the children and the strength of her claim. In return, Perine convened a panel of surgeons and deployed Atlantic constructions of race as biology and blood quotients against María Teresa. She sought to disprove Maurice's paternity by asserting the children of "that *grifa libre*" were too phenotypically African to be the children of her lighter-skinned, *pardo* brother. Both women crafted arguments rooted in their sense of paternal and filial obligation, obligations themselves shaped by inheritance practices and the circulation of property. By 1793, when the New Orleans Cabildo presented its decision, several of New Orleans's wealthiest householders had been asked to testify, the paternity of María Teresa's children was under dispute, and a provocative debate on the science and propriety of race mixture had ensued.

African women and women of African descent transitioned into the Spanish period with a practice of freedom that defied enslavers' attempts to safeguard free status for themselves. A small community of free people of African descent emerged from bondage during the first half of the eighteenth century, remaining integrated spatially and socially with other enslaved and with whites. Free Africans, born across the ocean and in the Americas, creole slaves, and *affranchis* recently escaped from bondage lived and labored in a complicated and motley community. Owning property distinguished some free people of color, but most free people of African descent acquired very little property through inheritance, donations, or gifts, acts of property, exchanges barred them by the 1724 *Code Noir*. Receiving manumission left many formerly enslaved in precarious positions. The introduction of Spanish colonial law changed this. Over the second half of the eighteenth century, Spanish officials permitted Africans and people of African descent to secure manumission through a process called *coartación*, to inherit and receive donations or gifts, and to do so through notarial statements instead of requiring formal authorization from the colonial governor. The change broadened enslaved people's access to freedom even as property acquisition—including enslaved labor—created new layers of difference among and between free people of African descent.

After 1769, death rites of inheritance became as important as manumission to free women of African descent protecting and defending their progeny. Determined to establish family on their own terms, women like María Teresa and Perine Dauphine drew on several criteria to define the boundaries of kinship, from formal bonds like Catholic marriage and godparenthood, to informal bonds created through the intimacy of charity and care. As they had with the Superior Council, African women and free women of African descent continued to petition Spanish Cabildo officials for their rights to freedom and property, and to defend legacies of property. Legacies of property, rooted in tangled kinship and intimate ties, became legacies of freedom as free women of African descent received and transferred property that would allow them to subsist, maintain households, purchase manumissions of other kin, and build wealth across generations. The possibilities and boundaries of kinship, always more than the birthrights of heredity, legitimacy, and bloodline, came into sharp relief as conflict arose over issues of property, debt obligation, gifts, and inheritance. María Teresa and Perine's altercation, each woman's persistence in clarifying the links and boundaries between them, mirrored the changing nature of race and status in the city. Each woman's testimony outlined her criteria for claiming kinship—and therefore freedom—in Atlantic New Orleans.

Buen Gobierno: Castas, Congas, and Pañuelos

In 1769, six years after France transferred Gulf Coast Louisiana to Spain, Governor Alejandro O'Reilly's "Ordinances and Instructions," or the "Code O'Reilly," introduced Spanish law and administrative structure to the colony.[3] The Superior Council was abolished and replaced with its Iberian counterpart, the Spanish Cabildo. Replacing French law and the French Superior Council with the laws and legal structure of the Spanish empire led to a series of changes favoring enslaved and free people of African and indigenous descent. Spanish officials abolished slavery for indigenous women, men, and children. Although slaves claiming indigenous descent continued to be held in bondage in Louisiana into the 1790s, enslaving Native nations ceased to be permitted and *sauvages* were no longer distinguished from Africans in Louisiana's official Spanish census after 1771.[4] Spanish structure also reintroduced and reinforced the office of the *escribano* (notary public). A familiar office across the French and Spanish empire, in the Spanish Caribbean, and, now, in Spanish Louisiana, the *escribano* registered acts for residents across race. Spanish legal traditions also replaced the 1724 *Code Noir*, which had barred free people of African descent from inheritances, exchanging property, or receiving donations, and

free black and white residents from manumitting slaves without imperial permission. Under the French, manumissions were official only after being
approved by the governor and intendant, infringing on any slaveowner's ability
to choose to free slaves. Now, for the first time, enslaved Africans and people
of African descent along the Gulf Coast required only their owner's signature
on an act from a notary for their legal freedom to be valid.

Spanish officials also recognized enslaved access to manumission through
a process of formal self-purchase called *coartación*.[5] Like so many things in
New Orleans, a single, linear origin story for *coartación* does not emerge from
the archive. *Coartación* arrived in New Orleans from multiple directions. The
first request for a *carta* (act) of manumission under the Spanish came on March
1771, in a request by the "elderly negro" Bautista from his owner, Joseph Meunier.
It was approved at 30 pesos. The second request was made by Juana Catalina,
a "mulata," for a *carta* from the estate of her former owner, Destrehan.[6] When
Governor O'Reilly arrived on the shores of the Gulf Coast, he employed a
contingent of free *pardo* and *moreno* soldiers brought from Havana. Two
enslaved runaways, Manuel and John, were apprehended in Louisiana after
absconding for ten years in Cuba as key to spreading the use of *coartación*.[7]
Some slaveowners may even have brought *coartación* to Louisiana themselves,
and used it to offer manumission to their human property in ways they would
not have been able to do under the French. However it arrived, *coartación*
circulated among enslaved and free people of African descent as a strategy for
securing freedom for loved ones and freeing themselves. Within a few years,
Spanish officials attempted to reverse course and stem enslaved enthusiasm
for *cartas de libertad*, but these refusals registered too late. In *coartación*, Africans and people of African descent uncovered a formal, bureaucratic outlet
for nearly three decades of frustrated appeals for manumission. There would
be no stemming the tide.

Coartación enabled slaves to bypass slaveowner authority in accessing acts
of manumission. In Louisiana, a slave could request an appraisal and receive
an estimated manumission price, or a *carta*. As *coartado* slaves, men, women,
and children in bondage could purchase their freedom by working toward the
value on the *carta* or request a third-party purchase for the same amount.
Coartación offered slaves a bureaucratic means for accessing manumission and
made it difficult for slaveowners to change prices or retract offers of freedom.
Coartación also made it easier for slaves to secure freedom through third-party
purchase. Informed by their experience in Havana, Spanish officials made the

decision to administer Louisiana's free population of African and indigenous descent with legal equanimity—a matter of good bureaucracy and careful governance. However, these protective provisions of Spanish law became reality only through petitions, requests, and civil cases initiated by slaves and free people of color themselves.[8] Using Gwendolyn Midlo Hall's database of slaves freed during the French, Spanish, and American periods in Louisiana, Jennifer Spear suggests an average of forty-four slaves were freed each year of Spanish rule, and it took "only four years under the Spanish for the number of manumitted slaves to surpass all those freed during five decades of French rule." According to the database, approximately 160 slaves were freed under the French. These numbers describe manumissions, not the total population of free people of color.

The Code O'Reilly brought Louisiana into parity with policies across the Spanish empire in other ways as well. Spanish occupation added new dynamics of race and status to the colony. Officials introduced corporate categories of race called *castas* in an attempt to divide and control the colonial population. Long implemented by Spanish administrators across Spanish America, the *sistema de castas* (*castas* system) created new legal distinctions of race based on gradations toward and away from whiteness.[9] Bracketed by *negro/ negra* (African or black) and *blanco/blanca* (white), the *castas* system distinguished mixed-race individuals by the amount of presumed African, European, and Native descent. The new vocabulary of race and gender included terms like *moreno* or *morena pardo* or *parda, grifo* or *grifa, cuarteron* or *cuarterona*. Used in official documents by priests, secular officials, and individuals themselves, *casta* designations telegraphed social position as well as family histories of intimacy, race, and property (see Table 3 for a list of common *casta* designations).

The introduction of the *sistema de castas* coincided with the shifting terrain of African origin. In 1777, officials reopened the Atlantic slave trade to the colony, leading to a fresh influx of enslaved women, children, and men from the African continent. African arrivals to the coast remained sporadic through the end of the eighteenth century. In 1782, officials opened slave trading with the French Antilles, closed it in 1791 after the outbreak of the Haitian Revolution, then reopened it for two years before closing it until 1800. Official sanction of the slave trade aside, Spanish officials often turned a blind eye to illegal slave trading. In sum, between 1772 and 1803, over 9,500 African women, children, and men arrived from Jamaica, Dominica, Martinique, Saint-Domingue, and

Table 3. Casta Designations Used in Late Eighteenth-Century Louisiana

Race	Derived from the Parental Combination Below
Blanco/Blanca	Blanco/Blanca + Blanco/Blanca
Negro/Negra	Negro/Negra + Negro/Negra
Moreno/Morena	Blanco/Blanca + Negro/Negra
Pardo/Parda	Blanco/Blanca + Moreno/Morena
Cuarteron/Cuarterona	Blanco/Blanca + Pardo/Parda
Grifo/Grifa	Pardo/Parda + Moreno/Morena; or African ancestry + Indian ancestry

Source: Kimberly S. Hanger, *Bounded Lives, Bounded Places: Free Black Society in Colonial New Orleans, 1769–1803* (Durham, NC: Duke University Press, 1997), 15–16.

Cuba, as well as West and West Central Africa.[10] New Orleans' enslaved population tripled during the Spanish period. As Hall argues, the Gulf Coast population re-Africanized with the arrival of women, children, and men who described themselves as "Congo," "Senegal," and "Nâgo." It also re-creolized in spectacular archipelagic and diasporic fashion as enslaved people arrived who also described themselves as creole, black, English, *de Martinique*, and more. The *sistema de castas* imposed a new racial order on these varied forms of black and African identity, incentivizing some and stigmatizing others.

The *sistema de castas* was notoriously imprecise. It did not foreclose or promise access to material resources and social standing in colonial New Orleans. It did not certify race mixture. Sacred and secular officials noted *casta* designations on case-by-case bases using criteria that shifted over time. Scholars have shown that *castas* in Spanish America functioned less as a concrete system of racial identification and more as a set of assumptions based on genealogy and phenotype as well as free status, family reputation, marriage, property ownership, and adherence to Catholic sacraments.[11] However, *casta* did matter when and where slaves and free people of African descent interacted with imperial institutions. Free men of color in the militia served in separate *pardo* and *moreno* companies, with higher levels of social distinction given to the men in the *pardo* company. *Grifo/a* and *indio/a* slaves petitioned for their freedom, using the Spanish ban and their *casta* designation to their advantage. High-prestige marriages sometimes required writs of *limpieza de sangre* to prove either partner was free of the "impure blood" of "Moors, Jews, Mulatos, and Indians."[12] On the ground, as between María Teresa and Perine Dauphine, *casta* designations played a role within communities of African descent themselves.

New Orleans' growing free population of color was overwhelmingly female as enslaved and free women of African descent responded to changing Spanish jurisprudence. Between 1771 and 1803, over nine hundred slaves freed themselves, loved ones, and other kin through self-purchase and third-party purchase in New Orleans.[13] Some eight hundred slaves gained their freedom *graciosa* (without conditions). A handful of owners required years of continued service or fidelity.[14] By 1788, the year of the great New Orleans fire, nearly 40 percent of the city's black population was freed or free born.[15] Women and children secured manumission more often than men, and free women of color consistently outnumbered men, sometimes as much as two to one, in New Orleans censuses.[16] Most manumitted women purchased their freedom or found a third party to subsidize their self-purchase. Another two-fifths of female slaves manumitted during the Spanish period secured freedom *graciosa* from their owners. The vast majority of women freed described themselves or were described as *negra* or *morena* and moved quickly to distribute estates, small and large, across legitimate, natural, and illegitimate heirs. Between 1771 and 1803, 260 *morena* slaves and 180 *pardas* were freed *graciosa*, compared with 86 *morenos* and 148 *pardos*. During the same time period, 242 *morena* slaves and 49 *pardas* purchased themselves, compared with 116 *morenos* and 26 *pardos*. Only in third-party purchases did male slaves of any *casta* compare—93 *pardo* slaves were freed against 91 *pardas*. However, a quarter more women were freed by self-purchase overall—104 *morena* slaves were freed by third-party purchase, compared with only 56 *moreno* slaves.[17]

Coartación and other changes to manumission law were not intended to ameliorate slavery for Africans and people of African descent but as acts of good governance (*buen gobierno*). In the grand Atlantic contest between European powers, France's tenure in the Antilles had been brief. Spain, the benefactress of Columbus's voyage across the Atlantic and *reconquistadora* of the Iberian Peninsula from the North African Almoravid empire, was the true grand dame of the Atlantic world. Almost three centuries after Spanish conquistadors established outposts across the Northern and Southern Hemispheres, Spanish imperial might remained the scourge of French and British imperial dreams. In that time, Spain had honed an approach to the conquered and enslaved in their midst. As early as 1542, Dominican friar Bartolomé de las Casas argued against enslaving indigenous peoples. By the end of the sixteenth century, Spanish officials had appropriated the *Siete Partidas*, a thirteenth-century corpus of legal and social practices promulgated by King Alfonso X *el Sabio* (the Wise), and they used it to guide policy toward enslaved Africans and conquered Native empires. By the 1760s, African and indigenous subjects of the king had what historian Jane Landers described as corporate and hierarchical identities, defined in law and practice as subordinate to whites but with customary rights even in contradistinction to each other.[18]

Establishing and enforcing Spanish rule brought these approaches to Louisiana. It also went hand in hand with sending a message of mastery and dominance to slaveowners and francophone white elites in Louisiana. O'Reilly's arrival followed an abortive rebellion by French colonists protesting the transfer of Louisiana to Spain. The "Revolt of 1768," led by twelve of "the most influential men in the colony," failed to unseat the Spanish, but O'Reilly still executed the leaders on his arrival.[19] The disintegration of the Superior Council and creation of the New Orleans Cabildo, for French whites, occurred on top of the spilled blood of these rebels. Spain did not intend to create a system of bondage more palatable to African or indigenous women, children, and men, but the difference between the French and Spanish regimes created opportunities for contestation.

The black femme freedoms, or freedoms forged beyond the manumission act that African women and women of African descent staked out during the French administration, fractured after the transition to Spanish governance. African women and women of African descent's intimate and kinship practices tangled with an African-descended population infused with new arrivals, the *sistema de castas*, *coartación*, a growing free population of color, and a new legion of imperial officials. Practices of freedom in the form of legal and extralegal strategy, claiming kin, and enjoying rival geographies of embodied pleasure and spirit became legacies black women shared and paid forward. As newcomers of African descent arrived and were forced to navigate the diasporic and archipelagic crossroads of the Gulf Coast, strategies for securing manumission continued to be exchanged, recalibrated, and applied to new circumstances with verve. But after 1769, black women manipulated new forms of legal manumission and articulations of blackness and womanhood that complicated the meaning of free status and, with it, the meaning of freedom. Slaveholding society continued to expose African women and women of African descent to a particular and peculiar physical and intimate violence premised on sexual access and labor use. These barbarisms did not cease when black women received *cartas de libertad* any more than they had upon being declared *affranchies*. At the same time, confronted by outsiders of white and black descent, Africans and people of African descent considered carefully whom to define as kin, how to protect themselves and others, and what responsibilities free status entailed.

Magdalena's altercation with Pedro La Cabanne, a white carpenter, refracted some of these tensions.[20] In 1778, Magdalena, a *mulâtresse* slave, stood in the courtyard of her owner, Nicholas Perthuis, "making a great noise and crying" and covered in blood. Magdalena, though a slave, lived in a cabin in the same courtyard as her owner. The separate living space provided her with freedom of movement, both for herself and others whom she hosted at her home. For a time, Pedro La Cabanne, nicknamed Titon, had been one of her guests and her lover. Magdalena reported to Perthuis and, later, to Cabildo authorities, that while she sat on Perthuis's steps, Titon appeared before her. He begged her to allow him sexual favors "as she had been accustomed to do before." In his desire for her "he had not eaten, nor slept nor drunk for three days." Magdalena, unmoved by his entreaties, told him "that all of that had passed and that she did not wish to have anything more to do with him." When he continued to pressure her, she went into her home to escape him. Unrelenting, Titon went into another dwelling adjoining the courtyard—the home of the free negress Fanchon. That evening, Fanchon was hosting friends of her own, San Juan and a free man of color, Pedro Mulato de la Baye. Titon, according to Magdalena, secreted his way through Fanchon's home, "jumped the fence," and came back to Magdalena's home, "throwing himself on his knees" to plead with her. She continued to refuse, closing her door to him. Titon entered her home through her window, again throwing himself on his knees before her. Titon continued to pursue Magdalena, chasing her with a hatchet at one point, before finally sneaking back into her home later that evening and stabbing her while she lay beside another man, the ship captain Claudio Chabote.

Magdalena's practice of freedom saturated the rapid escalation of violence she experienced with Titon. Although she participated in some form of intimate engagement with Titon in the past, Magdalena, a slave, reserved her own right to declare "all that had passed." Like an increasing number of enslaved and free women of color in the town, she took advantage of her separate living quarters to quite literally shut the door on Titon's entreaties. Her practice of freedom incorporated an erotic practice, perhaps with Titon, but in this instance with the man Chabote, who spent the evening with her and suffered an assault by Titon with the same weapon that wounded Magdalena. Magdalena's practice of freedom also influenced her interaction with Fanchon. After Titon entered her home through Fanchon's window, Magdalena went to Fanchon's house "to complain to her because she let Titon in." Magdalena judged Fanchon's actions as a failure of Fanchon's ability to control her space and, as a result, the safety of other courtyards. Magdalena also claimed a kinship in this complaint, placing a responsibility on Fanchon to protect her that Fanchon betrayed by allowing Titon access. When Titon chased Magdalena with a hatchet, it was to Fanchon's house that she ran. Whether, how much, and how explicitly Fanchon reciprocated this claim, Fanchon understood Magdalena's outrage. When barricading the door, with Magdalena safely inside, Fanchon chastised Titon, saying, "It was very shameful to persecute a woman so and enter her house." Fanchon, like Magdalena, understood the demand and coercive intention Titon pursued against Magdalena in gendered terms, as affronts to a woman's control of her body, space, and right to refusal. Blackness and distinctions in free and slave status further undergirded Titon's attack and Magdalena's vulnerability. It was Fanchon, the free negress, who received an apology later, when Titon appeared at her home and "asked to be excused for his boldness in pursuing the mulâtresse to her house." Magdalena, in contrast, received a knife wound.

In the undertow of complex shifts within the population of African descent, black women continued to identify freedom as including more than legal manumission. Freedom, and its practice, required the embodied pleasure of taking up space with their bodies, engaging with kin and community, and wresting the resources to control their own lives. Hosting dinners and dances and participating in markets and illicit economies made sumptuous through black femme affectation were practices of freedom that continued into the Spanish period. The assumption of the Spanish notary public in New Orleans allowed free women of African descent to formalize some of their business practices, some of which operated in the Spanish period much as they had in the French period. Women like Juana, born in Guinea and now a *morena libre*, owned a dry-goods store with a white man named Pedro Viejo.[21] Margarita Trudeau, a free *morena*, also sold retail, using it to purchase her son from her former owner.[22] The dances that Le Page du Pratz so feared in the 1720s had continued. Described by Spanish officials as *tangos, congas*, and *Congos*, dances and gatherings occurred in the plazas or squares around the city, on the Place d'Armes (now Plaza de Armas) or parade grounds, and in the back of town.

Where play happened, often commercial exchange followed, as black pleasure practices linked dance, fellowship, subsistence, and commercial exchange in a reciprocal loop. At least one area in town came to be described as the Conga del Mercado, a black or African market where enslaved and likely some free women of color sold their wares. Indigenous and European traders participated in marketing as well, including street selling and staffing market stalls, but official and colloquial descriptions of these spaces of exchange as black also telegraphed the heavy African-descended presence in the frontier-exchange economy under the Spanish.[23]

By the 1780s, Spanish officials' desire for *buen gobierno* led them to condemn black pleasure practices as a threat to order. In 1784, the Cabildo attempted to centralize dances and markets under more formal authority. Officials authorized the construction of a permanent market, centrally located and near the river. Those wishing to sell their wares were forced to purchase permits and fined for marketing without them. The Cabildo empowered the *mayordomo de propios* (city steward or treasurer) to collect fees and fines from those caught in the act.[24] Two years later, Governor Miró issued a sweeping edict, his inaugural *bando de buen gobierno* for the "successful and safe administration of justice" in the colony as a whole. Miró's 1786 *bando* forbade commerce of any kind on feast days (Sundays and other holy days), the same days most available to enslaved as free days for their own use and labors. He also restricted the time available for dancing (the "tangos o bailes de los Negros") on those days until after vespers, or evening prayer. He forbade gambling, lotteries, and games of any kind outside of designated times and places. He prohibited merchants from selling alcohol to those enslaved or to "indios." Landlords could not rent rooms to enslaved people without proper notice from their owners. In a tactic reminiscent of the French *Code Noirs*, the Spanish defined spaces of black freedom in New Orleans only to surveil, curtail, and negate them.[25]

Black femme pleasures came under special scrutiny as causes of disorder. Miró singled out for special approbation those living in "concubinage" and promised to punish them with all of the "strength and vigor of the law." In the event this admonishment did not properly implicate women of African descent, he followed this promise with an article dedicated to the pernicious effect that women of African descent had had on the colony. "The idleness of the Negras Mulatas and the quarteronas libres," Miró declared, implicate the entire population. Such women subsisted "on their libertinage, without virtue, and for this I reprimand them to separate from vice and order them to labor." Miró noted that he'd become familiar with these women in his brief time in the colony. *Mulatas* and *cuarteronas* "did not hide their crimes," amusing themselves and reveling in their "*mal vivir.*" If they did not renounce their ways, Miró threatened to have them removed from the province. Miró interpreted black femme affectation, or black women's performance of womanhood and femininity, as women of African descent exhibiting "too much luxury in their bearing." So much so, the governor included an additional edict in his *bando*. He noted that recent practices of hair texture and styling employed by African women and women of African descent were "losing their usefulness." To correct this, Miró ordered "that the Negras Mulatas, y quarteronas can no longer have feathers nor jewelry in their hair." Instead, the *bando* mandated that women of African descent "must wear [their hair] plain (*llanos*) or wear *pañuelos*, if they are of higher status, as they have been accustomed to." *Pañuelo* was the Spanish word for *tignon* or headwrap.

The manner in which the 1786 *bando*, described decades later as implementing the *tignon* law, tightened restrictions on dress, play, and pleasure placed women of African descent in New Orleans in archipelagic and diasporic conversation with women of color elsewhere in the Caribbean. During the eighteenth century, sumptuary laws (laws targeting dress, play, and other pleasure practices) for free people of African descent spread across the French Antilles.[26] Many of these laws targeted black femme presentation and activities specifically. In Saint-Domingue, officials "gave orders to stop the balls of the mulâtresses and negresses."[27] By 1774, Cap Français officials required free people of African descent to wear red ribbons on their heads. Five years later, their edicts also forbade free women and men of color from wearing certain garments and fabrics altogether.[28] Spanish officials across the Americas were no more lenient. When in 1784, the Real Audiencia, the high court in Santo Domingo, issued the *Codigo Negro Carolina* to govern enslaved and free people of African descent, an entire section was devoted to preventing free people of color from using "pearls, emeralds or other precious stones; gold, or silver, in metal or embroidery, in their costumes and decoration"; ordering *negras libres* and *pardas* not to wear *mantillas* (a lace headpiece worn by elite Spanish women) and forcing them to use *pañuelos* instead; and forbidding castas of either gender from carrying either "a sword or cane, [or] a chevron hat of gold or silver" or "wear[ing] silk clothes."[29] The 1785 *Codigo Negro* became the foundation for the 1789 *Real cedula*, a corpus of slave law that governed the Spanish Americas until 1795.[30] Sumptuary laws did more than restrict Africans and people of

African descent from the top down. They invited invasive intimacy, empowering everyday white women as well as men to enforce a presentation of subjection
on free and enslaved blacks. In 1780, two Saint-Domingue free women of color,
Marianne and Françoise, were sentenced to stand on display in the market
with an iron collar around their necks, holding a sign that read, "*Mulâtresses*
insolent toward white women." Their crime was speaking sharply to the white
women who had called out to them as they passed in all of their finery. The
white women had said, "Look at these rotten pieces of meat! They deserve to
have their lace cut flush with their buttocks and to be sold on the fish table in
the Clugny Market!"[31]

The audacity of taking sensual and physical pleasure in their own dress,
body, and hair made African women and women of African descent the targets
of imperial misrule. In other words, for Spanish imperial authorities, black
women's affect and styling no longer distinguished them by class, *casta*, or
status as distinct from each other or as inferior from women of European
descent. The 1786 *bando* reminded the colony, but women of African descent
in particular, that their very existence in and through their womanhood was
an offense. The *bando* attempted to prevent African women and women of
African descent from, as scholar Lisa Ze Winters noted, "all that might produce
pleasure outside the purview of the dominant society: the rituals of femininity,
the comfort of friendship, the nurturing of family."[32] In other words, black
women had created new ways of reaffirming their own humanity that responded
to their needs, not solely to the desires of colonial officials, slaveowners, or
even recalcitrant lovers. According to Médéric-Louis-Élie Moreau de Saint-
Méry, *mulâtresses affranchies* circumvented laws requiring them to go barefoot
by adorning themselves with flowers. They headed out to dances, at times
matching their dress to that of "a good friend who is a confidante, the woman
she cannot do without."[33] The emergence of sumptuary laws did not stop black
femme presentation or intimacy. Black women in New Orleans with feathers
in their hair shared in these archipelagic acts of self-expression and pleasure
while their would-be masters struggled to keep up with their practice of
freedom.

This pace sped forward, regardless of Miró's *bando* and related prohibitions.
Charlotte, the young *mulâtresse* who sought freedom in the bed of a ship captain,
did not allow opportunities created under Spanish administration to pass her
by. Now Carlota "Derneville," she took her father's name and purchased her
freedom in 1773 on a *carta* worth 400 pesos.[34] Two years later, she agreed to

hire herself out to Santiago Landrieu in exchange for the freedom of her twenty-one-year-old son, Carlos. Carlota practiced her freedom aggressively. In 1787, in the wake of the *bando*, she paid 30 pesos for a license to operate a tavern. When the great New Orleans fire swept the town in 1788, she lost some 2,000 pesos' worth of property, but by 1795, she owned rental properties across the city. In addition to rental income, Carlota continued to operate her tavern, paying her license fees in 1799 and 1800. When she wrote her will in 1801, Carlota owned a house and one slave she granted manumission, and she named a niece, Carlota Wiltz, as her heir.[35] Charlotte was not alone. In 1795, the official census listed seventeen free black women secondhand dealers (*revendeuses*) and eleven shopkeepers (*marchandes*).[36] Women of African descent who did not own or control their own retail spaces continued to find opportunities to rent or labor for those with goods to sell. Women like free *morena* Perina Armesto worked for shop and stall owners.[37]

At the same time, it should come as no surprise that these opportunities fell disproportionately to women of African descent with free status, who had more control over their time and movement and the ability to own slaves of their own. For enslaved women securing manumission and for free women of African descent reclaiming time, financial resources, and purchasing property of their own, leaving legacies to future generations became a possibility. Defining freedom as property ownership, however, did not guarantee manumission for all enslaved women, children, or men, or safety and security for all enslaved or free women of African descent. Enslaving other women of African descent and children created the means for free women of African descent to engage in necessary labor, access credit, and distinguish themselves from the enslaved around them. As Magdalena and, years later, María Teresa discovered, a practice of freedom that centered kinship claims, embodied pleasure, and safety and security existed uneasily and unevenly in a world where free status, *casta* designation, and property ownership, including ownership of slaves, increasingly played a significant role in securing black women's legacies of freedom.

Kinship and Inheritance in Atlantic New Orleans

More than a question of inheritance, the case of *María Tereza, grifa libre v. Perine Demasillier, mulata libre* was a dispute between two women over the meanings of and obligations to family in late eighteenth-century New Orleans.

Their legal battle exemplified the ways free women of color constructed kinship beyond biological ties, gradations of race, and bonded status even while seeking redress from institutions defining race and kinship in limited ways. Scholars such as Virginia Meacham Gould, Gwendolyn Midlo Hall, Kimberly Hanger, and Jennifer Spear have outlined how free people of color in late eighteenth-century New Orleans, though not enslaved, remained bound by French and Spanish social and legal constructions of gender, *casta*, status, and marriage.[38] Litigious and savvy, free people of African descent in New Orleans took advantage of laws, as well as gender and racial constructions, promising to protect their property and familial ties. As women of African descent defending themselves and their kin in a patriarchal, imperial slaveholding city, María Teresa and Perine Dauphine used their roles as mother and consort, sister and householder, respectively, to add legitimacy to their individual sides of the case. The two women's actions offer a vivid and rare portrait of the extent to which some free people of color in the city used law, property, and constructions of race to create as well as disrupt kinship ties.

In New Orleans, registering testaments allowed free people of color to protect property and community after their death. Across the eighteenth-century Atlantic world, free Africans and people of African descent used property to build protective networks of real and fictive kin. Living and laboring in societies structured around Atlantic slave trading, plantation slavery, and bonded labor, free people of color grew acutely aware of their proximity to disease, poverty, war, and violence. They balanced these uncertainties by establishing livelihoods and acquiring property. Where fortunate enough to accumulate material goods of their own and retain them over the course of their lives, free people of color used succession to control and distribute goods within kinship networks. Historians of New Orleans describe ways inheritances and donations provided an economic base for the rise of the robust free community of color that would emerge in the nineteenth century.[39] However, property and inheritance did more than build productive futures for people of African descent. Death, so pervasive in late eighteenth-century slaveholding societies, offered opportunities to augment family units. As scholars such as Dylan Penningroth, Vincent Brown, and Tiya Miles have shown for other locales, by deciding and debating how and who would actually receive material goods, individuals debated how and who belonged in familial networks.[40] Free people of color in New Orleans practiced a kinship that would not be assumed or foreclosed by biological and legal boundaries. Choices made over whom to gift to and how to divide estates redefined entire networks and revealed the fluid and complex structure of free black family life.

The inheritance practices of New Orleans' free community of color drew on a longer history of French interaction in the French Caribbean. The much-revised 1685 *Code Noir*, promulgated by the French Crown to administer its Caribbean colonies, included language permitting people of African descent to be named sole legatees, executors of estates, or guardians of children.[41] By 1703, officials in Martinique prohibited this practice, and the French metropolitan government prohibited French men from marrying women of African descent and bequeathing their patents of nobility to them.[42] Some twenty years into the French occupation of the Gulf Coast, the French and French-Canadian elites of the Louisiana Superior Council no longer viewed inheritance as a universal death rite. In 1724, they passed the Louisiana *Code Noir*, which prohibited enslaved and free people of African descent from receiving inheritances, seizing their property. Aware of the proliferation of unions between the French and those of indigenous descent as well, the Superior Council went further and restricted indigenous women from receiving bequests from their French husbands.[43] Preventing inheritance made it difficult for free African and Native women, children, and men in New Orleans to protect or recirculate property after a loved one had died.

Despite these restrictions, Africans and people of African descent accumulated some limited property. Company employees of color, the Natchez veterans, their wives, and other people of color who secured their freedom in the first decades of the eighteenth century immediately began to establish themselves within Gulf society through property acquisition. As early as 1722, Scipion, who later hired himself out, received a lot on present-day St. Philip Street. His neighbors were the free *nègre* Jacquot and Jacquot's free wife.[44] In 1727, Suzanne lived with Louis Congo and another couple on Bayou Road, perhaps pooling resources for support and perhaps for company.[45] In 1731, Marie, a *négresse*, owned property on Bourbon Street, between Anne and Dumaine streets.[46] Simon and Scipion, free men of color, owned property along the banks of the river just outside of town.[47] By 1749, Genevieve Junon, a free negress, owned property on Ursulines Street. Eleven years later, she sold it to another free negress named Maria Juana.[48] Etienne Larue or his descendants owned a house and lot on Dauphine and Toulouse streets. In 1757, Jeannette owned a lot on Bourbon. Jacqueline (Jeanne) Lemelle owned multiple lots on Dauphine as well by the 1770s.[49] Other people of color resided in households adjoining their employers. In 1731, a domestic of Monsieur Duoy resided on Rue Royale.[50] Finally, as in Gorée and Saint-Louis, some Africans and people of African descent lived independently of their owners. A slave belonging to Mezelliers lived on Rue Royale, down the street from the domestic of Monsieur Duoy.

Manumission-by-will, as it emerged in New Orleans in the 1740s and 1750s, set the stage for further property acquisition by free women and children of African descent. In one of the earliest bestowals of property in a will, François Deserboy left his personal effects and any surplus cash on his account to a *négresse* owned by M. Larou. Deserboy explained the gift was "for her faithful care of him while he was sick."[51] Two years later, when Marie Louise, an Osage slave, was freed and granted 100 pistoles in a will written by Viard dit François, the Superior Council annulled the inheritance on the basis of the *Code Noir*. In 1747, Marianne and her two sons received 300 piastres and cattle from a white man, Claude Vignon dit La Combe, whom she lived with. By the 1760s, when François, María's son by Comte Pechon, found his inheritance of property contested by the widow Pechon, officials had ceased to be surprised or shocked by the act of bequeathing property alongside freedom. In 1739, Isabella, formerly a slave of the Compagnie des Indes (Company of the Indies), sold a lot at 45 Royale to Sr. Claude Villers Dubreuil, contractor for public works, for the sum of 600 livres in cash. Isabella became the property of Jean-Baptiste de Chavannes after he purchased her from the Company.

Unfortunately, even after freedom, black women's ability to cobble together livelihoods varied. As women and children came to be freed more often than enslaved men, they entered into freedom with different repertoires. As slaves, many free women of African descent had not described themselves and were not described as skilled compared to enslaved men. When Jacques received his freedom, he entered into a new status with the skills of a jewelry maker, trained by his owner, Dominique Brunel.[52] On rare occasions, free women of African descent received gifts of property at manumission. When Marianne and her three sons emerged from bondage, they did so with no remarked-upon skills, but they did inherit 300 piastres and cattle.[53] For the most part, black women struggled to shape new circumstances with little aid from their former owners and no way to secure property for future generations.

In comparison, at Saint-Domingue, officials appear to have ignored these restrictions, and free people of color continued to receive gifts, donations, and property from residents of all races. Property ownership spread among the island's *gens de couleur libres*. Residents circulated material wealth within and across kinship networks comprising largely people of color, building family lineages using inheritance and marriage. Free testators of color even attempted to bequeath freedom to enslaved friends and family members, incorporating manumission requests and obligations into their wills.[54] In 1777, María Juanita, a *mulâtresse libre*, charged her heir, Guillaume Pourveur, a *mulâtre libre*, with purchasing her son, Pierre, a *griffe* slave also in the city. She added provisions. If Pierre died before the will went into effect, María Juanita charged another *libre* named Guillaume with securing the freedom of Pierre's three children—Martine, Pierre Louis, and "another *petite fille*." She also revoked Guillaume's inheritance should he fail in his mission naming Pierre Marion, a Nâgo *nègre libre*, the replacement executor and heir. If either Guillaume or Pierre Marion died before the will went into effect or died in the process of freeing Pierre or the children, María Juanita passed the task on to the *nègre libre* Blaise Breda. Across the archipelago, Africans and people of African descent incorporated inheritance into a broader practice of freedom, recognizing its potential to create and confirm kin, or, as one scholar noted of Saint-Domingue, establish "communities of property" well beyond white patronage.[55]

The new laws arriving by way of Cuba heavily influenced legacies and freedom in New Orleans.[56] Iberian laws long distinguished between offspring born of different unions and extended succession rights to all heirs through partible inheritance. Children of Catholic unions were declared legitimate or legitimated if the couple married after the child's birth. Unmarried parents could also recognize children born outside of marriage as "natural," as long as the parents' union did not violate other ecclesiastical or imperial laws.[57] Illegitimate children or those conceived out of wedlock and between persons prohibited from marrying or having children could make no legal claim on paternal estates.[58] Full inheritance privileges fell automatically to legitimate children as forced heirs, but natural and even illegitimate children often received close to one-fifth of the parental estate. In places such as Cuba, free people of color were permitted to receive and bequeath property within these guidelines and from testators of all races.[59] With the implementation of Spanish law in New Orleans, these inheritance practices became the basis for testaments registered before notaries. Free people of color could now legally exchange property between each other and whites, receiving gifts, donations, and inheritances. And they took active advantage of the opportunity to direct property toward their descendants.

Table 4. Population of New Orleans, Louisiana, 1771–1805

Year	Whites	Free People of Color	Slaves	Total
1771	1,803	97	1,227	3,127
1777	1,736	315	1,151	3,202
1788	2,370	820	2,131	5,321
1791	2,386	862	1,789	5,037
1805	3,551	1,566	3,105	8,222
Total	11,846	3,660	9,403	24,909

Source: Kimberly S. Hanger, *Bounded Lives, Bounded Places: Free Black Society in Colonial New Orleans, 1769–1803* (Durham: Duke University Press, 1997), 72. The population data above are based on colonial censuses that likely undercounted the total number of free people of color. For example, Hanger notes (184n11) that, in 1770, militia rosters listed 61 free *pardos* and 283 free *morenos* bearing arms in and around New Orleans.

Only two years after the implementation of the Spanish Cabildo, Janeton had already used her free status, access to the Spanish notary, and relaxed restrictions around inheritance to transfer property to the kinfolk of her choice, in this instance, her only daughter. In June 1771, Janeton La Liberté filed her last will and testament. She described herself as a native of Senegal and a Catholic. She was a *negra libre*, formerly enslaved and living at English Turn. In 1741, she'd married Luis, a negro. She married him voluntarily, lived with him, and together they built a life. All that she now owned ("todo el caridad y bienes que yo tengo") she accumulated with Luis, including having a daughter named Maria Juana. In 1750, Janeton married a *negro libre* named Zacaria, but she did not acquire any goods or property with him. In her will, she described this property—a half lot on St. Ursula Street (present-day Ursulines) with a small house built on top of it, and land near English Turn and bordered by land owned by "el nombrado" Reynaud on one side and land owned by the *negro libre* Pedro Tomas, her daughter's husband. Janeton owned it all, she stated, debt-free. In addition, she owned four cows, which she willed with the lot and land to her daughter, Maria Juana Tomas. Janeton then named Simon, *mulato*, as the executor of her estate, and asked that Juan Baptiste, *mulato libre*, fulfill those duties in Simon's absence. In 1801, when Maria Juana Tomas wrote her will, she passed the same half lot and house on to her six living children and one grandchild.[60]

Testaments such as these, near impossible during the French period, became more common after Spanish occupation of the Gulf Coast. In August 1794, for example, María registered her will, describing herself as "de nación Congo, natural de Guineau." More than likely, she arrived in New Orleans as a slave and secured her freedom under *coartación*.[61] María told the notary recording her testament that she was unmarried and had "neither ancestors nor dependents" to serve as heirs. Nonetheless, she described a network of important people in her life and distributed her effects accordingly. She named a third party, Santiago Masó, her universal heir.[62] Santiago had been missing from the city for several years. In the event he was found dead, María left her effects with Constansa Flor, a free woman of color. She also left furniture to Constansa and donated various items to a slave named Fransin, as well as the free daughter of Mariana Goudreau, *negra libre*. Like many free testators of color, she named a white resident, Julien Vienne, the executor of her estate. María's renunciation of ancestry may have been a rhetorical flourish meant to suggest she did not know or chose not to identify a mother or father an ocean away. Born in Africa and living in Spanish New Orleans, María instead reconciled old kinship claims and forged new ones with chosen kin living in various states of bondage, as well as across color and gender.

Exploring a cross-section of fifty-two testaments like María's, a complex picture emerges.[63] Black women, many of them African, drove inheritance practices. By gender, thirty-six free women of color, including sixteen black female testators, registered testaments compared to sixteen free men of color.[64] Nearly half of all testators registered as *nègres, négresses, negras,* or *negros*. One-fifth of testators claimed they were "born in Guinea," although few declared more specific birthplaces. Others, like Ana Marta, a *mulata libre*, were descended from slaves freed during the French period.[65] Registrants described owning property that ranged from jewelry to slaves. When Mariana Meuillon named her natural son, Bautista Meuillon, her only heir, she bequeathed him silverware, lots and houses in New Orleans, land upriver, and a *morena bozal* (African slave) also named Mariana.[66] Testators also used wills to confirm and collect debts using webs of credit and physical goods to build and confirm connections to each other. Even testators possessing nothing material of their own accumulated and claimed financial obligations to men and women across race and status.[67] Before her death in 1786, Isabel, *mulata libre*, stated several individuals owed her between 16 and 57 pesos, including Madame Favre Daunoy; Ursula, *negra libre*; and Francisca, *mulata libre*. Isabel noted "various others" owed her "various amounts" but that she could not recall them all in the moment.[68]

As free people of color used their wills to clarify a range of intimate relationships, testaments became confessionals. Many designated one or more of
their children natural and legitimate, as their heirs, regardless of sex or bonded
status.[69] Agustín Malet, a free man of color and a militia officer in the *pardo*
company, left his estate to his three children. When one more daughter was
born after the will was written, the siblings agreed to share everything equally.[70]
But free people of color made decisions to include or exclude estranged family
members, offspring born out of wedlock, and children or partners from past
partnerships. In 1802, Pedro Demouy, a free man of color, had eight slaves in
his household. According to his will, he owned four. The other four belonged
to his domestic partner, Juana, as community property and should pass to their
five children together. Pedro noted he had lived "la vida viciosa" with Juana
for twenty-three years, but he married her the day he registered the testament.[71]
Henrique Sambas of Senegal was legally married to María, another free woman
of color, but his four children out of wedlock inherited his estate of land, horses,
mules, cattle, and three slaves. The eldest daughter remained a slave.[72] Marion
Dubreuil, *mulata libre*, originally included her eight natural children, three by
Bautista, *negro libre*, in her will. Six months later, she amended her will to
include two more natural children as co-heirs.[73]

As in Saint-Domingue, free people of color in New Orleans used their
testaments to free other slaves. These decisions exposed fault lines in kinship
networks. In 1779, the shoemaker Juan Bautista registered a will reminding
his mother to "fulfill the promise she made" to buy his son Luis's liberty. Though
married to María Juana Piquery, *mulata libre*, Juan Bautista claimed Luis as
his "one spurious son" by another unnamed *negra* slave.[74] Andrés Cheval's wife
and two of his children were still slaves when he registered his testament. In
his 1790 will, Cheval asked his executor to exchange a slave he already owned
for the freedom of his daughter and set aside additional funds to free his son.
He made no request to free his wife.[75] Jean-Baptiste Hugon declared that he
had "freed all of his children from slavery," except his daughter Genoveva, a
slave in Opelousas. Hugon requested she be freed from slavery after his death
and included her with his five other children as his universal heirs.[76] In 1800,
Santiago, *negro libre*, agreed to pay his natural son Carlos Meunier's debt and
left his legitimate son, Estevan Perrault, over 800 pesos to free his grandson
by another daughter.[77] These funds may not have been enough. A year later,
Santiago registered a second version of the will, authorizing his executor to
sell land he owned in the city to raise the money to buy his grandson.[78]

Free people of color did not automatically name direct offspring as heirs. Testators also designated grandchildren, nieces, siblings, parents, and god-parents as part of their legacy. A wealthy free woman of color, Francisca Montreuil, left an estate worth over 7,000 pesos to her three children—Carlos, María Genoveva, and Agata—and three grandchildren.[79] Married thirty-five years earlier, Angelica had two children who predeceased her. She named her two grandchildren, María and Juan Bautista, her universal heirs.[80] Bellehu-meur, with no natural heirs, named his godmother, Felicidad Juana María, *mulata libre*, as his universal heir.[81] María Teresa Cheval never married and had no living children, parents, or grandparents. She named her two sisters, Mariana and Catalina, and Bernardo Yzurra, her business partner, as her heirs.[82] Those without direct descendants made other claims of kin. Margarita Momplessir, unmarried when she wrote her testament and with no children, left thirteen slaves representing three generations of one family to three women—Catalina, a *morena* slave; and Eufrosina Dimitry and Francisca Momplessir, both *libres*.[83]

Over time, succession could tie generations together. María Belair, a free woman of color, married Luis Daunoy, a free man of color, but had two natural daughters by another man. In her will, she included them when she divided her estate—one-fifth to each of them, the rest to her son with Daunoy, also named Luis. María's daughter Martona died immediately after her. Martona's will passed her share of María's estate on to her own six natural children.[84] With generations of property and livelihoods at stake, contesting, obstructing, or rejecting wills meant contesting legacies, memories, genealogies, and affec-tions, exposing fractures within webs of kin.

María Teresa, *Grifa Libre*

In 1789, when María Teresa, *grifa libre*, took Perine Dauphine, *parda libre*, to court, Perine operated in a discreet network of moderate wealth and social privilege. Perine was the daughter of Marie Thomas, a *negra libre*, and "M. Dauphine," an unnamed member of the white Dauphine family.[85] During the 1780s, Maurice and Eugenio, Perine's brothers, were more active in commercial transactions than Perine or their fourth sister, Carlota Thomas, *mulâtresse libre*.[86] In 1786, Eugenio, Maurice, and Don Juan Pedro Dauphine appear as creditors of Don Antonio Babini.[87] Juan Pedro was the only white Dauphine to appear alongside Maurice and Eugenio in the archives and may have been related to them.[88] Along with building a house in the city, Maurice owned at least one slave, Eufrosina, an epileptic woman whom he attempted to return to her previous owner. For her part, Perine's relationship with white property owner Don Francisco Demasillier became serious enough for her to claim his last name on legal documents without apparent dispute and for Demasillier to name her as one of his beneficiaries.[89] However, the 200 moneda corriente Demasillier left her did not provide much security. After Demasillier's death, Perine took over managing Maurice's estate and paid his debts. She and Eugenio completed construction on the house and even successfully returned Eufrosina to her original owner. Perine may not have formally owned any property of her own, but she did have access to Maurice's modest but significant holdings.[90] Her social prestige emanated as much from sibling connections to two propertied, skilled free men of color as it did from her role as consort to a wealthy, but deceased, white male householder.

In contrast to Perine, María Teresa was much less financially secure. María Teresa's *casta* designation, *grifa libre*, identified her as a woman of African and possible Native descent.[91] However, throughout deliberations, she also identified herself or was identified as a *mulata* and *negra libre*, suggesting that a slippage occurred between *casta* designations in practice.[92] María Teresa provided no surname during the trial, nor was one recorded, a common practice for slaves and the recently freed. Beyond these faint traces, María Teresa's life becomes difficult to discern until 1789, when she presented herself before the Cabildo as an impoverished, unmarried mother of three. Her poverty became her justification for bringing the inheritance case to the attention of the Cabildo, and the lack of clear documentation about her may support this claim. Like so many free women of color, María Teresa and Perine faced the lived reality of navigating a patriarchal slaveholding society where sex and property configured patronage and protection. In such a context, a lucrative inheritance was key to sustaining both of their livelihoods.

María Teresa's request to the Cabildo appeared simple. María Teresa declared that in 1787, before Maurice died, he drew up a nuncupative will leaving everything to his three children with her—Pedro, Margarita, and Sesamie. Three white New Orleans householders, Don Juan Bautista Rio Seco, Don Luis Mollier, and Don Geronimo Lachiapella, witnessed the "will by voice." Perine knew all of this, María Teresa claimed, because Maurice named Don François Demasillier, Perine's deceased consort, the executor of the estate. In

1788, Demasillier died and the estate fell to Demasillier's executor, Don Joseph Dusseau Lecroix, who placed decisions about Maurice's estate in Perine's hands.[93] María Teresa, meanwhile, initiated proceedings to recover her children's inheritance immediately after Demasillier died, but a fire in 1788 destroyed those documents. To "right this wrong," María Teresa asked Don Almonester y Rojas, the presiding judge, to summon the three original witnesses and Don Fernando Rodriguez, an *escribano* at the time of Maurice's death, to testify to the truth of her claim.

A month later, Perine responded, representing herself. She argued that María Teresa did not file the correct documents and was not the guardian of the three children. Therefore, according to Perine, María Teresa had no right to bring such a suit against her. She insisted the case be immediately dismissed. A small exchange ensued through the Cabildo clerk as the two women sent petitions back and forth. María Teresa's petition sidestepped Perine's question of her guardianship. She asserted that she simply wanted the best for her children. Complying with Maurice's last wishes honored him and put their children in the best financial position possible. She asked the court to dispense with Perine's counterpetitions as rooted in "avarice" and to compel Perine to secure an attorney so the case could proceed.[94] Almonester y Rojas agreed with both women. He declared María Teresa the *tutora* (guardian) of the three children and commanded Perine to respond to the accusations being made against her.[95] Perine continued to rely on a combination of temporizing and technicality to circumvent María Teresa's claim. María Teresa repeated her petition twice before Perine hired a legal representative. When she finally presented Don Estevan de Quiñones as her *procurador* (defender), she registered another protest against María Teresa's "false claim to the goods" and insisted that Maurice had bequeathed his property to her.[96] In June, when it appeared María Teresa would not meet her deadline to present her case, Perine sent admonishing petitions to the Cabildo, noting that only a few days remained for the other woman to gather her evidence.

Nine days later, María Teresa appeared before the Cabildo with Don Geronimo Lachiapelle, one of the witnesses to the will. Almonester y Rojas asked Lachiapelle whether he knew the parties involved, whether what María Teresa claimed was true, whether the evening proceeded as she described, and, finally, whether Maurice named the three children his universal heirs.[97] Lachiapelle corroborated María Teresa's testimony. Lachiapelle confirmed he was called to the house of the "mulato Maurice and in the company of Don Francisco

Rodriguez, the recently deceased [Rio Seco] and the witness Don Luis Molière."
He confirmed that Maurice did intend the inheritance to go to her children
by him. Perine attempted to cast doubt on Lachiapelle's statement, asking him
why he would witness the will, given "the great debilitation of his [Maurice's]
accident and quasi-consciousness." Lachiapelle, however, stated that although
he and the other witnesses arrived to find Maurice unable to complete a written
testament because of his condition, "Don Fernando Rodriguez repeated three
times . . . whom . . . he [Maurice] wanted to name his heirs" and each time Maurice repeated that it was "to my children." Rodriguez asked a fourth time whether
the testament was in the form that Maurice wished and Maurice confirmed
that it was. The second living witness, Don Luis Molière, described Maurice's
last moments. Molière stated that Maurice called the three children to him on
his sickbed and, before the witnesses, "declared them his legitimate or natural
children." He did this although "the sickness was plainly immobilizing."
Molière stated that "these were his last wishes, to give his inheritance to the
three children, which he did not name, but who after were called to the room
of the sick man and declared so in the presence of the eyewitnesses as was
custom."[98]

María Teresa also introduced testimony from Don Fernando Rodriguez, the
Cabildo *escribano* at the time of Maurice's death. According to Rodriguez, four
or five days before Maurice died, he sent a *negra* to summon Rodriguez from
his home. Rodriguez arrived and "found him in his bed." Maurice, according
to Rodriguez, explained, "I called you to authorize my will but I don't want
anyone to know [until after my death]." As *escribano*, Rodriguez had to authorize and record testaments. However, he explained to Maurice he could not
authorize a will without witnesses.[99] "Seeing that the declared was sick," Rodriguez suggested "finding three witnesses close to the house." With witnesses
in place, Maurice acknowledged María Teresa's three children and declared
them his universal heirs. In fact, when the children were called into the room,
Maurice recognized the children for those gathered. According to Rodriguez,
he "knew the three as his children and when called 'Father' he responded." By
describing how Maurice assumed paternity, Rodriguez corroborated María
Teresa's claim: "And thus," concluded Rodriguez, "I can state what was repeated
by the deceased Maurice, that he is four times sure and was seen by the witnesses that this is the testament [and the testament] is in the state he wished."[100]
Because Rodriguez regarded the gathering as a provisional meeting, and given
the secrecy of Maurice's request, he did not file the proceedings as was

customary for an *escribano*. Instead, he struck the meeting from the record and left Maurice's home with the witnesses.[101]

Over the next month, María Teresa gathered testimony describing Maurice's affection for the children, his public acknowledgment of them, and his willingness to provide financial support. She traveled from the city to the countryside and the royal barracks, soliciting statements from some of New Orleans' distinguished gentlemen—Don Santiago Hubert, wealthy landowners Don Pedro Caselard and Don Augustin Macarty, and Spanish military officer Don Nicolas Favre Daunoy. At least two, Caselard and Macarty, supported their own free consorts of color, Carlota Wiltz and Céleste Perrault, respectively.[102] In asking several of New Orleans' esteemed *blanco* residents to confirm the "paternal love and affection" Maurice showed toward his three children, María Teresa may have been cognizant of the authority white male property owners possessed in the eyes of the Cabildo judges. All of the men testified to the same. María Teresa and Maurice participated in a public, long-term relationship, and they had produced three children together. Maurice acknowledged all of their children. When the children called him "Father," he responded. Maurice also provided them with "all that was necessary for life and also necessary after his death." Some of the men interviewed issued their own opinion on the matter. In his testimony, for example, Macarty described Maurice and María Teresa's relationship as a "public and notorious concubinage." However, none of the witnesses contested the veracity of the nuncupative will, the paternity of the children, or, ultimately, the legitimacy of María Teresa's claim.[103]

Faced with such formidable witness testimony, Perine Dauphine submitted a provocative counterargument to the Cabildo. She requested the presence of three New Orleans doctors: Don Estevan de Pellegrue, doctor of the Royal Hospital; Don Santiago Le Luc, surgeon for Charity Hospital; and the surgeon Don Juan Cenas. These doctors, Perine stated, "know the three children" and would be able to expound "on the knowledge that they have of the natural course of procreation." Drawing on the logic of the *sistema de castas*, Perine invoked Atlantic-wide assumptions of race, color, and legitimacy. The doctors, she stated, would show "that the union of a *mulato* with a *grifa* does not produce a *negro*." In fact, the coupling of a *mulato* with a *grifa* should produce a "*mulato claro*" or a lighter-skinned *mulato*—not a *negro* "or others that resemble those that have been made from very inferior unions." María Teresa had not produced any such *mulato claros*. As such, these could not be Maurice's children. In fact, Perine continued, "The three referred to bastards are naturally distinct one from the other in color, fashion, semblance, and hair" and may have different fathers altogether. Since María Teresa's three children could not be her brother's, they also could not have a claim to his estate, and Perine asked the case be dismissed, with María Teresa ordered to pay any court costs.[104]

Perine willingly invoked the *sistema de castas*, purity of blood, fears of amalgamation, and natural science in her defense. Her actions redefined her network of kinship by excluding María Teresa and the three children from it. By calling on three surgeons, a novel and striking maneuver, she also circumvented Iberian and French Atlantic inheritance practices that emphasized myriad forms of legitimacy, offers of financial support, and community witnesses. Instead, she endeavored to build a paternity claim rooted in nature, reproduction, biology, and racial heredity. This construction of kinship, entirely modern and hyperrationalized, relied on corporeality, examination, observation, and science. To better prepare their testimony, the doctors collected the children and examined them before reporting their findings to the judge. Physical characteristics like phenotype, hair texture, facial features, and body composition became evaluating markers, more convincing than lived experience or distinguished white men's honorable testimony.

There is no reason to doubt Perine believed her statements to be true. During deliberations, Perine was described or described herself as either a *parda* or *mulata*. By implying the amount of mixture among María Teresa's children made them inferior to her *pardo* brother and, by association, herself, Perine outlined a larger tension between the two women. Perine may have resisted María Teresa's claim because she opposed incorporating an unpropertied woman from a lesser *casta* into her kinship network. Her willingness to use race mixture, reproduction, and blood to secure a decision in her favor suggests that Perine understood the legal and social resonance of *casta* and race in colonial New Orleans.

The surgeons did not disappoint Perine, but their testimony took a subtle and unexpected turn. When the doctors Pellegrue, Le Luc, and Cenas appeared before the Cabildo, they interpreted the inheritance case as part of a much larger social problem, one related to race mixture but not limited to it. Their concern centered on legitimacy, specifically obeying the Catholic sacrament of marriage. The surgeons condemned acts of concubinage that made paternity "always difficult to resolve." And they emphasized the importance of honoring God "who blessed the human species with infinite variety," but before whom "the laws of legitimacy and reproduction are 'inflexible.'" They waxed eloquent on the mixing of the races as "horrible plagues on the society" that create "inflexible" racial anomalies. María Teresa was scolded for having "created the scandal" in the first place by producing children outside of Catholic marriage and having no appreciation for *casta* boundaries.[105]

The doctors expounded on the physical characteristics of María Teresa's children, noting Pedro's and Sesamie's hair textures, skin colors, body types, and features as being, in Pedro's case, of a *mulato*, and in Sesamie's, of a *negra*.[106] The third, Margarita, was described as not resembling the first two at all, having skin color akin to Sesamie but much darker than Pedro. "A *mulato*," they noted, "does not produce a *negro* in their union with a *negra grifa*, but definitely a *grifo* much lighter than that *grifa* [María Teresa], less light than the *mulato* that is the father of a purer state, proceeding the mother, and of hair like the father." The doctors concluded that the races of potential fathers did differ.[107] Margarita was the daughter of a *mulato*, while Pedro's father was white and Sesamie's was a *negro*.[108] However, the surgeons finished by reminding the Cabildo, regardless of their *casta*, the children remained "bastards" by virtue of their conception outside of "holy matrimony." For the surgeons, Catholic marriage was the most important requirement for legitimacy. The sacraments of marriage defined fatherhood and "without the sacrament of marriage or approval of the [Catholic] Religion," Pellegrue, Le Luc, and Cenas could not state with certainty that the three children *were* Maurice's.

María Teresa wasted no time petitioning for new witnesses—Perine Dauphine and Don Juan Cenas. María Teresa sent each questions to recenter the role that guardianship played in interlocking networks of kinship. María Teresa asked Perine to explain the whereabouts of the children up until this point. Perine's response revealed the three children had been living with her since the night of the 1788 fire.[109] When asked why, Perine answered that she accepted them into her home "because she is their godmother; and also for Charity." The children remained in Perine's home even when María Teresa's guardianship became a court matter; when the surgeons collected them for examination, they collected them from Perine. By Perine's incorporating the children into her home after a major disaster and being a godmother, María Teresa suggested that Perine had already accepted María Teresa and her children into her kinship network. Charity, Catholic rituals of belonging in the form of godparentage, and physical cohabitation worked against Perine's claim that María Teresa's children were not also her brother's. When María Teresa asked Don Juan Cenas to testify, she again reminded the Cabildo of the role that public expressions of financial support and social belonging played in determining kinship and property. María Teresa asked Cenas whether it was true that Maurice Dauphine brought him his sick children, whether the children Cenas treated were the same ones in question, and whether Cenas could confirm the deceased paid for the visit and medicines prescribed. Cenas confirmed all of the statements, adding that "just as a father would, and that he [Maurice] called them his children, and that he knew them, worked with them and assisted them as though they belong to him."[110]

María Teresa and Perine Dauphine built cases for Maurice's inheritance by making various assumptions about the practice of kinship. According to María Teresa, Maurice was the children's father because he publicly claimed them and provided for them on a regular basis. His willingness to provide support extended beyond his death in the form of a nuncupative will witnessed by three of New Orleans' white male heads of household. Perine Dauphine, by contrast, defended her case by relying on biological assumptions about race and status rooted in the colonial logic of reproduction and the *sistema de castas*. Where María Teresa's argument for the inheritance emerged from the experiential struggle of maintaining family and community, Perine's counterargument relied on legal precepts and racial constructions. From her attempts to have the "groundless" case dismissed on legal technicalities to arrival of the surgeons, Perine's refusal to relinquish Maurice's inheritance to María Teresa suggested she too was using succession to draw boundaries and maintain connections between kin but did not consider either María Teresa or her children part of that network.

María Teresa lost her case. In December 1789, Don Almonester y Rojas ruled María Teresa did not prove the legitimacy of her children, invalidating her children's claim to Maurice Dauphine's estate. However, in order "to best administer justice," Almonester y Rojas ordered a public auction of Maurice's goods, one-sixth of which would be paid to María Teresa as guardian of his three "bastard children." Almonester y Rojas also ordered María Teresa to pay all court costs and fees. María Teresa asked to appeal the case to the tribunal in Havana. Perine issued her customary protest, but Almonester y Rojas allowed the appeal to proceed.

Over the following year, María Teresa's appeal stalled. According to Méndez, María Teresa fell "gravely ill of labor and fatigue" while attempting to care for herself and her three children. María Teresa requested more time to appeal and for relief from court costs, claiming insolvency.[111] She was granted both.

In late 1791, with no word from the appellate court in Havana, Perine began petitioning the court for a resolution. In response, Méndez admitted María Teresa had been absent from the city for several months, and he had no correspondence from his client. He asked Don Pedro de Marigny, the new presiding judge, to enforce the original decision and proceed with an auction of the estate.[112] Six months later, in mid-1792, Marigny agreed. María Teresa, last seen at Mobile, was ordered by the commandant there to comply with the auction. In June, María Teresa reappeared in New Orleans to name Don Antonio Budanquier and Josef Fernandez, a carpenter, her representatives for the appraisal and auction. She disappeared again, however, and was not present for the final auction. She petitioned the Cabildo only once more, afterward, to accuse Perine and her brother Eugenio of not disclosing, estimating, or selling all of Maurice's property. According to María Teresa, they failed to appraise or sell Maurice's furniture or his land outside of the city, in the suburb of Monplaisir. The same day, a receipt for the land was entered into the record, in Eugenio Dauphine's name.[113]

Perine, forced to sell her brother's property at public auction, purchased it back at the same auction. As a free mother of color and guardian of three children with no property to speak of, María Teresa could mobilize neither the energy nor the resources to continue pursuing her case. She may have moved back to Mobile, perhaps following her own kinship networks or in search of a livelihood. However, at least one of her children remained in New Orleans—and reappeared in a community of property forged by Perine Dauphine. In 1797, a few years after the auction and perhaps encouraged by the recent trial, Perine registered her first testament. In it, she bequeathed clothes, kitchen items, a slave, a large bed, and over 300 pesos to "María, grifa libre, the daughter of my deceased brother Mauricio." She also left another 300 pesos to "Eugenio, Mauricio's son, her brother."[114]

Over the next two decades, through Atlantic revolutions and imperial reorganization—including the end of the Haitian Revolution and the incorporation of Louisiana into the United States—Demasillier-Dauphin property holdings continued to expand. Perine Dauphine lived into the 1810s and registered a second will before passing away in 1816. Her final estate included several slaves, a house, furniture, specie, and land—property enough for her heirs to remain self-sufficient. But Perine never married and claimed no children. Instead, like free people of color before her, her final testament was evidence of a matrix of kinship obligations defying biology, blood, race, and status. She freed several of her slaves in her will, including Sophie, a *négresse*, "in return for the *bon services* she has given me," and left 1,000 piastres for Sophie's daughter, Luisa, to claim at her majority. She named Silvaine and Thomas, the children of Marie Maurice Thomas, *mulâtresse libre*, as her universal heirs.[115] If Maurice's children remained in New Orleans or alive, Perine made no mention of them and made no provisions for them or their children.[116] But Perine did leave behind a namesake, a goddaughter born in 1795 named Pelagia Marta Dauphin. In the baptism register, Pelagia's mother was listed as "Marta Dauphin, *grifa libre*, deceased." Her father was listed as "unknown." Perine's final testament circumvented biological kin to create new generational ties, and in doing so she charted new paths for future wealth. In 1816, Silvaine, Perine's heir, filed a petition to take control of the land above the city left to her by Perine Dauphine—the same land claimed by Perine from her brother Maurice in the case against María Teresa.[117]

* * *

Archipelagic questions of intimacy and kinship were activated by the ways in which property circulated in a world of slaves. Over the second half of the late eighteenth century, with the introduction of Spanish law, free people of color's relationship to inheritance and property materialized as testators of color wrote wills, named heirs, and made decisions meant to shape lives after their own deaths. In the legal battle between María Teresa and Perine, these relatively new inheritance and property rights defined links and boundaries between families and within the free community of color. Both María Teresa and Perine viewed inheritance as a customary right and understood the structures of property, race or *casta*, and status well enough to mobilize support in their own favor. María Teresa plied her case with a multitude of testimonies from wealthy white businessmen and property owners. Perine's defense, in return, pivoted on the science of race and race mixture to disprove paternity. In the end, the surgeons' preoccupation with the legitimacy of holy matrimony and Catholic sacraments of marriage held greater authority before the Cabildo. María Teresa and Perine both made choices suggesting neither biology nor legitimacy told the full story of kinship relations in the slaveholding city.

   African women and free women of African descent in the second half of the eighteenth century secured greater access to freedom and property acquisition, and with it the right to inherit and exchange property. They determined their own heirs and distributed property with self-conscious regard for the role those heirs played in their past. They judged the impact distribution of property would have on their imagined communities after their deaths. In this, African women and women of African descent practiced freedom in ways that moved beyond present-day considerations. They imagined entire futures of freedom and left legacies with those futures in mind. The free communities of color that emerged from these decisions owed their existence to broad networks of distributed property, financial obligation, and kinship bonds that transgressed intimate, biological, or racial designations. In their struggles with each other, free women of African descent elaborated on what role property accumulation and inheritance should play in defining kinship and kinship's future in their lives. In this, María Teresa and Perine Dauphine's conflict was a quintessentially New Orleans conflict.

The free community of color, imperial law, and free people of color's relationship to property in the city would change again with integration into the United States and the Saint-Domingue refugee migration. Litigious and savvy, where the law created space for building property or kin, free people of color took advantage. But Anglo-American traditions of law and race offered few opportunities to enslaved or free people of African descent. Women like Perine Dauphine, a free *parda*, and well positioned to retain and expand her property holdings through donation or inheritance claims, would begin to see their opportunities and livelihoods curtailed in a variety of ways. Inheritance and property would continue to play a role in shaping the dynamics of race and freedom in Atlantic New Orleans, but it would play a special role in communities of African descent under assault and struggling to continue to create sustainable legacies of freedom across generations in an American New Orleans.

Conclusion

⟡

Femmes de Couleur Libres
and the Nineteenth Century

... in return for the good services she has given me.
—Pelagia Dauphine Demazillier, last will and testament, 1814

By 1816, the year Silvaine, Perine Dauphine's heir, claimed land in the new
suburbs just above New Orleans, the meaning of freedom in New Orleans
changed a great deal. In fact, the meaning of freedom across the entire Atlantic
world had changed. In August 1791, enslaved Africans in Saint-Domingue's
Northern Province rose up. Fields of sugar cane went up in flames. Plantation
production and civil governance fell into disarray. War, the great leveler, created homeless refugees out of hundreds of women, children, and men from
all levels of society. Many fled the island, fearing for their lives and mourning
their plantation wealth. Many others joined the fray, particularly black men
and boys. From the formerly enslaved to the *ancien libres*, those remaining on
the island fought to secure a thing called freedom for themselves. Of those
who departed, the migration of Saint-Domingue residents created a refugee
triangle that extended from revolutionary Saint-Domingue, to the island of
Jamaica just west of Les Cayes, to Cuba's eastern province, Santiago de Cuba,
north of Port-au-Prince. The Haitian Revolution's refugee diaspora did not
end in the Caribbean. From Saint-Domingue, slaveowners and nonslaveown-
ers, of African and European descent, traveled as near as New York and Philadelphia, and as far as France, seeking safe harbors and opportunities to begin
their lives again.[1]

The revolutionary violence sparked by the slaves of Saint-Domingue
reshaped the Atlantic world. In 1801, Napoleon Bonaparte negotiated the return

of Louisiana to France from Spain. When slave and colonial revolt in the Antilles continued unabated, Bonaparte sold Louisiana to the new American Republic, an account negotiated during Thomas Jefferson's tenure. In 1803, France formally transferred Louisiana, more than doubling the landmass of the United States. Less than a year later, despite having relinquished his obligations along the Gulf Coast, Bonaparte lost his war for Saint-Domingue. Saint-Domingue became the free republic of Haiti and slavery was abolished. The antislavery and anticolonial insurgency did not remain within Saint-Domingue's boundaries. Both Guadeloupe and Martinique experienced fierce moments of revolutionary violence that threatened to end France's overseas empire. France scraped by, retaining control of both, but the loss of Saint-Domingue proved to be a devastating one for the Crown's holdings in the Americas. The Haitian Revolution destroyed France's most lucrative overseas venture. Slave trading from West and West Central Africa to the French Caribbean all but ceased. When, in 1807, the British Parliament passed a law banning the slave trade, the United States followed suit by adhering to its 1808 ban, and England deployed its considerable navy to enforce the proposed end of Atlantic slave trading. The Atlantic slave trade did not end for nearly fifty years, sustained by the rise of coffee production in Cuba and Brazil, but something fundamental had shifted in the Atlantic world. Something irreparable had broken open, and ideas of slavery and freedom would never be the same.

Making *Femmes de Couleur Libres*

Ocean waters brought Africans in French slave ships to New Orleans' shores. Gulf waters brought a new Atlantic African diaspora to the edges of the city. Sylvaine's New Orleans was a different city for free women of color. It was very different from the collection of planks and boards that Marie Baude encountered on her arrival almost a century before. It was different even from the rough outlines of town and swamp that Charlotte (now Carlota) witnessed emerge under the Spanish administration. Encroaching American influence even before the 1803 Louisiana Purchase created fault lines in New Orleans even as "Kaintucks" and other English-speaking migrants brought aggressive economic expansion to the port. Anglo-Americans, many of them Southerners, looked at the Mississippi Delta in the same manner the French had, once upon a time—a strategic site for their dreams of expansion west into Mexico or south into the Caribbean—but found themselves, like the Spanish, captivated, titil-lated, and afraid of the populations they encountered. U.S. officials were unsure how to govern a population composed of French, Spanish, and Creole speakers of African descent, all protective of their property and self-conscious of their rights.[2] How could one manage mobile and self-confident slaves, some carrying *cartas de libertad*, aware of their rights and personhood? Most confusing of all were the Gulf Coast African women and women of African descent whose rich expressive, material, and economic practices defied white Anglo-American expectations of both black servitude and female propriety.

The Louisiana Purchase and the Haitian Revolution marked an even deeper change in the terrain of black life in the city. With access to new land for devel-oping plantations, Anglo-Americans migrating south and west demanded enslaved labor. From 1801 to 1810, more than 50,000 Africans arrived in Charles-ton, primarily from West Central Africa.[3] New Orleans became the port of call for a significant number of these women, children, and men who were routed to or through the town along with the bales of cotton they produced. By 1810, creole slaves, or those born in the Americas, were the minority in Louisiana, at only 45 percent of the enslaved population. Meanwhile, the Haitian Revolu-tion sparked waves of migrations of whites and free people of color with slaves and property in tow to Jamaica, Cuba, and the Gulf Coast, proving that slavery would reinvent and remake itself in new places. As a francophone city with close ties to Saint-Domingue, New Orleans received a large number of émigrés during the first wave of revolt in the colony. In 1808, Bonaparte invaded Spain, and the Spanish government retaliated against the many French subjects who'd made Cuba their home. The following March, Spanish officials in Cuba issued a proclamation expelling all French citizens without Spanish spouses from the island. Between May 1809 and January 1810, over nine thousand men, women, and children arrived in New Orleans.[4] In July 1809, the mayor of New Orleans reported that "people of all descriptions . . . have arrived here from the Island of Cuba" and "there are about one thousand on their way up the river and about the [sand]bar with respect to whom there is as yet no official return."[5]

The 1809–10 refugee migration of people of African descent to New Orleans was predominantly adult women and children. Most refugees arrived from southeastern Cuba, embarking from the ports of Santiago de Cuba and Bara-coa.[6] Among the mass of whites, free people of color, and slaves, the majority of those arriving were people of African descent. By January 1810, over six thousand free people of color and slaves arrived in New Orleans, compared to fewer than three thousand white refugees.[7] A large number of arrivals were free and enslaved women of color and their children. According to one official count, among free and enslaved refugees of color, the 1,341 adult women eclipsed the 660 free and enslaved adult men, as well as the 975 free and enslaved children. Among free people of color, more free women of color arrived than both free men and children of African descent, but free children of color followed more closely behind. About 640 free women of color compared to 620 free children of color found themselves disembarking from ships and into the city of New Orleans.

In comparison, the only demographic of refugees to exceed free women of color was the 769 adult white men.[8] White men outnumbered white women nearly two to one, and more white men arrived than white women and children combined. Factors contributing to the gender imbalance among migrants varied. Free men of color and enslaved men might have found themselves more readily and willingly drawn into the conflict in Saint-Domingue, and remained—or were killed before they could leave. In New Orleans, official anxiety over an in-migration of free black men contributed to the female majority as officials did their best to enforce laws requiring free men of color and boys over the age of fifteen to leave the territory. Some free people of color needed no official encouragement to leave, building new lives in other spaces.[9] The rival geography forged in the eighteenth century continued to be drawn and redrawn into the nineteenth century, and it continued to include cities and ports from Cuba to New Orleans to Mexico to Trinidad to the western territories that would become California.[10]

African women and women of African descent, who spent years under Spanish rule negotiating a system of customary rights from their owners and Cabildo officials, found themselves facing new imperial masters once again. The privileges accrued by enslaved and free people of African descent during the Spanish regime began to erode as soon as the United States took over. As the French and Spanish attempted before them, U.S. territorial officials used force of law, edict, and code to extend its power over enslaved and free blacks it deemed unruly. In many instances, the United States simply extended and enforced punitive measures that the Spanish had attempted, such as restricting the mobility of free people of color. In an 1806 "Black Code," the territorial government went further. It tightened access to manumission and declared free blacks could not "conceive themselves equal" to whites, effectively nullifying the system of *coartación* that had been in place for a generation.[11] In a gesture similar to that made by Saint-Domingue officials who required free people of color to take African names, Louisiana officials passed a Civil Code in 1808 requiring free people of color to identify themselves on documents with abbreviations like "f.p.c." (free person of color), "f.w.c." and "f.c.l." (free woman of color), "f.m.c." and "h.c.l." (free man of color).[12]

The loss of privileges, however, did not occur all at once and people of African descent made their own demands on the new stewards of the Gulf Coast. In 1810, Adéle, an enslaved woman, sued her owner for freedom on the basis of her ancestry as a mulatto. The New Orleans Supreme Court ruled in her favor, declaring that "mulattoes" were to be regarded as free while "negroes" were to be presumed slaves, unless proven otherwise.[13] The free black militias continued to muster and fought to retain their nonwhite officers with differing success. But by 1812, when Louisiana transitioned from a territory to a state, delegates submitted a constitution that left free people of color unprotected by remaining silent on their citizenship status and declared its entrance into the Union as a slave state. By happenstance, it also tore democracy from the hands of white laborers, nonslaveholders, and anyone without enough wealth to meet the property requirement for the franchise.[14]

The wicked freedom that African women and women of African descent produced in the wake of Atlantic slaving flowed, like a river, around these new changes. The archipelago had arrived in New Orleans, and alongside this new influx of free people of African descent, African women and women of African descent continued to use what they could to build ties within and across kinship networks. In this instance, baptism, inheritance, and marriage already existed as institutions and rituals familiar to people of African descent. In New Orleans, St. Louis Cathedral, particularly under the stewardship of Pere Antoine Sedella, became a site for protection and consolidation, one where free people of African descent flocked. In nineteenth-century New Orleans, black women's intimate arrangements ranged from work in brothels, boarding houses, and other pleasure spaces to common-law unions with white and free men of color to formal Catholic marriages arranged between free families of African descent.[15] Intimacy with powerful and privileged men continued to be a strategy deployed by African women and women of African descent, only this time it wasn't *mariage à la mode du pays* that came under scrutiny. By the twentieth century, some observers described informal conjugal ties between free women of African descent and white men in New Orleans as *plaçage*. Potentially more fiction than fact, fascination with *plaçage* extended an eighteenth-century archipelagic fixation on the freedoms sought by wicked *negresses* and lustful quadroons into a later era.[16] Meanwhile, U.S. federal, state, and city officials attempted to restrict free women of color's authority. In response, free women of color sent petitions, took current and former slave-owners to court, and continued to confront civic authorities in lawsuits and court cases through the Civil War. In other words, the arrival of Saint-Domingue refugees did not mark the emergence of practices of freedom or of an insurgent free black community or of black women's struggle for safety, security, and pleasure on the Gulf Coast. African women and women of African descent had started that journey a century earlier.

At the same time, enslaved Africans continued to arrive in New Orleans and plantation production expanded in the region as never before. The fissures that emerged between free people of African descent and enslaved people grew larger during the nineteenth century, but they began in the *sistema de castas* and struggles over property that occurred during the Spanish era. The arrival of free people of African descent with enslaved property in tow and the expansion of slaveholding among free people of color both laid the foundation for tensions over the meaning of freedom for decades to come. Free African women continued to purchase and reap the advantages of enslaved labor, using enslaved women as domestics, laundresses, cooks, and seamstresses or employing them in boarding houses, hiring them out, or offering them as credit. In 1811, when slaves rose up on the German Coast in the largest slave rebellion to occur in the United States, free militiamen of color helped put down the revolt. Enslaved Africans, however, also had practices of freedom of their own. Dancing, drumming, feasting, drinking, and ostentatious displays of style and defiance continued in the nineteenth century, infused by African arrivals from Saint-Domingue and the continent. In 1817, a city ordinance confined drumming to the back of town, an area of the city just beyond the ramparts. In 1819, Benjamin Latrobe found himself drawn to the sound of drums and discovered a crowd of five to six hundred in the Place des Nègres, or Congo Square. He noted, "In the first were two women dancing. They held each a coarse handkerchief extended by the corners in their hands, & set to each other in a miserably dull & slow figure, hardly moving their feet or their bodies. The music consisted of two drums and a stringed instrument." Moving their bodies with gravitas, the women carved space for embodied pleasure, spiritual connection, and time with kin out of the Americanizing geography of the city, and they brought a swath of women, men, and children of diasporic origins and bonded statuses with them in their black geographic project. As Latrobe witnessed, "all those who were engaged in the business seemed to be blacks."[17]

Into these changes and continuities, these ebbs and flows, girls like Sylvaine Dauphine became *femmes de couleur libres*, cultivating kin and property, part of a complicated and circular legacy of freedom that began along Senegal's coast and extended deep into the United States. Perine, meanwhile, died without claiming any natural children of her own, but like free women of color before her, her kinship networks survived her death. Like generations of women before her, Perine imagined her bequest to include more than biological kin or property that might wash away in the next fire or storm. Perine owned three slaves, a home, and land when she died. It was property enough for her heirs to remain self-sufficient. Although the location of her lots is not described, if located in Bayou Saint-Jean, the land would have bordered land sold by Claude Tremé to French-speaking white and free property owners of color—a significant number of them Saint-Domingue refugees.[18] Sylvaine now owned property in the midst of what would become a prosperous free community of African descent. Between Sylvaine, her heir, and a goddaughter, Pelagia Marta Dauphine, Perine's postmortem kin included women who could carry on practices of freedom—with their tensions and complexities, successes and failures—long after her death.[19]

Wicked Flesh: Black Women, Intimacy, and Freedom in the Atlantic World unravels the complex lives that African women and women of African descent created in the Atlantic world. *Wicked Flesh* follows black diasporic women from their first interactions with European traders along the Senegambian coast, across the Atlantic as they grappled with the rise of Atlantic slave trading and the development of slavery, through the Caribbean archipelago to the riverside *comptoir* that would become an American city named New Orleans. Between 1685 and 1816, New Orleans transformed from a few shacks dotting the muddy high ground on the bend of a continental river into a major Atlantic city. The spread of plantation slavery across French settlements overseas powered this transformation, but African women's labor sustained it. From its founding in 1718, French imperial provenance relied on enslaving African women, men, and children, forcibly transporting them overseas, and maintaining people of African descent in subordinate positions relative to whites. French colonial officials, trading-company administrators, and slaveowners were ruthless and used every means available to create legal, political, and conceptual linkages between blackness and bondage. From the 1685 *Code Noir* to restrictions on property ownership, French Atlantic officials never fully welcomed free people of color. The transfer of power to the Spanish eased some of the restrictions on free people of African descent, but also introduced new forms of exploitation and domination, including reopening the African slave trade, *coartación*, and the *sistema de castas*. African women and women of African descent struggled, with varying degrees of success, to navigate these changes. This struggle and their practices of freedom refused the imposition slavery, race, gender, and colonialism placed on their lives, bodies, reproduction, kinships, and sexuality. It laid the foundation for nineteenth-century emancipation struggles to come.

Any study of New Orleans necessarily confounds disciplinary boundaries. For scholars of colonialism and empire, New Orleans' trajectory, in moving from outpost to city, and passing from French to Spanish back to French and then to U.S. administration, suggests the limits of metropolitan reach and the impact of eighteenth-century warfare. For scholars of the Atlantic African diaspora, New Orleans was the site of one of the few concentrated streams of Senegambian forced migration, multiple slave rebellions, multiple white refugee migrations, a cosmopolitan slave and free population, and a cacophony of African and Afro-Atlantic expressive, material, and visual cultural activity. For historians of the United States, the addition of New Orleans to the new nation as a major port city immediately after the Louisiana Purchase shifted the geography of slavery and the future of the nation. Until emancipation, New Orleans hosted the busiest domestic slave market in the nation alongside the wealthiest, most literate, and, according to one scholar, most radicalized free population of color in the United States.[20] New Orleans' role in antebellum U.S. society on the road to the Civil War is well beyond the scope of this story, but these seeming contradictions have a longer history, one rooted in and routed through diasporic practices of freedom and autonomy generated by enslaved and free people of African descent.

The rise of free populations of African descent across the Atlantic world in the eighteenth century relied on the determination and creativity of African women and women of African descent. *Wicked Flesh* diverted from Senegal right before the Seven Years' War, a global conflict that embroiled both Saint-Louis and Gorée. As part of their truce, France and Britain negotiated their access to the African coast, splitting administration of Saint-Louis (by the

British) and Gorée (by the French). The truce barely held, and the two European powers alternately conquered and relinquished the *comptoirs* through 1817, when, in the wake of Napoleon's defeat, France formally reoccupied the entire coast.[21] In the imperial tug-of-war over the *comptoirs*, some *habitants* and Company employees began to migrate to France. Others traveled south to British-controlled Gambia. Those who remained used shifting imperial administrations to make new alliances.

Although women dominated the Saint-Louis and Gorée property rolls, Charles Thevenot and other male traders stepped forward as representatives of African residents, the wealth created by their wives and slaves bolstering their standing.[22] Free African women and men continued to demand that the French and British hire their dependents, domestics, and slaves as laborers, formalize their property rights (including slaveownership), and permit slave trading.[23] By the 1760s, the era in which enslaved women in New Orleans struggled to have their freedoms recognized by Louisiana officials, Saint-Louis and Gorée were dominated by the sons and daughters of African trading families made wealthy by decades of trade. By the 1780s, as Carlota established her property investments, as María Teresa created her family with Maurice Dauphine, and as Perine argued with contractors over her brothers' labors, the descendants of unions between African women and European men at the Senegal *comptoirs* began to describe themselves as *métis*, consolidating themselves into a political bloc that would dominate commerce and politics in the region well into the nineteenth century.[24]

The *métis* survived the Haitian Revolution, which decimated plantation production at Saint-Domingue, encouraging French mercantile interests in Africa to transition to gum and peanuts as "legitimate trade."[25] They continued to hold court in homes and at *folgars* even as French economic priorities shifted, as *métis* at Saint-Louis and Gorée lost their lauded position with the French to Trarza Moors who controlled Mauritania and North African gum-trade routes. *Habitants* also found themselves struggling against French abolitionists to keep their enslaved property, a key source of their wealth. Paradoxically, as *métis* commercial power waned, the *signares'* mystique in the French imaginary grew. But the descendants of the *signares* continued to have real, flesh-and-blood lives beyond these fantasies, through the tumult of France's West African empire and the rise of Senegal as an independent nation. If that story is complicated by slaveownership and property, by violence and negotiation, by colonialism and assimilation, it is also a story of the audacity of African women's determination to claim autonomy for themselves. It was this audacity that led, in 1994, to the founding at Gorée of le musée de la Femme Henriette-Bathily, the first museum dedicated to women on the African continent. The founder, poet, editor, and activist Annette Mbaye d'Erneville, was an artist in her own right. She was also the many-times granddaughter of Charles Jean-Baptiste d'Erneville, Pierre Henri d'Erneville's Louisiana-born son and Charlotte/ Carlota's half-brother.[26]

In other words, the history of African women and women of African descent who landed in New Orleans offers only one thread of an experience, insurgence, and recalcitrance that spread oceanwide. In Saint-Louis and Gorée, African women plied their trades, worked for trading companies, and built lives in the same *comptoirs* where slavery and forms of unfree labor resided. Free African women participated in trade with Europeans through long-standing practices of hospitality, aesthetics, and pleasure, as well as by navigating practices of patronage that gained them status and position in a patriarchal, coastal world. In Le Cap, Les Cayes, Havana and across outposts of the Caribbean, enslaved women emerged from slavery and helped bring others into freedom, participated in inter-island and intra-island trades, and accrued wealth to pass on to their kin. As enslaved women secured manumission, organized gatherings, participated in Catholic rituals, formed kinship networks, and acquired property and wealth, they challenged the racial and gendered labors that slaveholding society demanded of them. At the front lines of slave trading, imperial change, and Atlantic warfare, African women and women of African descent pursued opportunities that bolstered their households, expanding the meaning of freedom and thus the meaning of black womanhood beyond flesh and slave codes, contracts and manumission acts.

As the nineteenth century dawned over New Orleans, the augmentation of the free community of color with *femmes de couleur libres* from Saint-Domingue coincided with new forms of Anglo-American repression, reshaping the trajectory of black New Orleans. Among migrants themselves, the memory of the Haitian Revolution and their migration to New Orleans reverberated across generations. In 1940, when interviewed by Works Progress Administration employees about life in Louisiana and asked "to start at the beginning," Zoe Posey described her great-great-grandmother as having "lived durin' the revolution in San Domingo." Her grandmother, she said, was a free woman of color "born in Montenegro [Cuba]," and her grandmother arrived in Louisiana from Saint-Domingue with the Duplantiers. "Miss Julie Duplantier was her godmother," Posey stated, "She [my grandmother] was Catholic to the backbone."[27] While the migrants shaped black womanhood in the city in significant ways, black women's community building has an even longer history. A generation before the migration from Haiti, women of African descent were creating intimate and kinship networks that laid the foundation for the free communities of color that formed across the city in the nineteenth century. And in New Orleans, a black femme practice of freedom would appear again and again, returning like the hurricanes, reminding the city of its exquisitely femme, African-descended origins, and of what it owed to black women's labors, past and present.

Henriette Delille and Marie Laveau, two of the most famous women to emerge from nineteenth-century New Orleans, represent a long struggle, a convergence of diasporic flows from Senegambia and archipelagic flows from the Antilles to the Gulf Coast. In 1812, Henriette Delille was born to Maria Josefa Diaz, the several-times granddaughter of Nanette, the African woman enslaved in DuBreuil's household and baptized at St. Louis Church by the women who would help found the Children of Mary, the Ursulines' first laywomen's confraternity. Diaz was the child of a European father and a woman of African descent, what would come to be described as a *placée*, but Delille rebuked the system to commit herself to Catholic practice.[28] Delille would go on to found the Sisters of the Holy Family, formalizing a tradition of Catholic involvement that women of African descent helped shape in New Orleans over a century earlier. Delille's legacy of freedom through Catholic practice and safety from the predations of men of either race continues to be remembered by members of that confraternity into the present day.

In 1801, Marie Laveau, a free mulatto girl, was born to Marguerite Henry, a free *mulâtresse*, and Charles Laveau, a free carpenter of color. Marie's great-grandmother, Catherine, enslaved in 1756 in the household of Henry Roche dit Belaire, came of age in the generation just after the Atlantic slave trade. She, her daughter, and Marie's mother all gained their freedom in the shifts attending Spanish expansions of manumission. Marie, born in soon-to-be-American New Orleans, was baptized by Father Sedella and married Jacques Paris, a Saint-Domingue refugee and free man of color. Working from her grandmother Catherine's home at 152 St. Ann Street, Marie began to hold feasts, ceremonies, and consultations, creating a spiritual community that came to be associated with vodun. Marie herself gained renown as a "voodoo Queen" and practitioner of magical arts. And although described as hailing from Saint-Domingue, she only married into that archipelagic stream—Marie Laveau was very much a product of the Gulf Coast, a daughter of New Orleans' Atlantic world. The press reviled her as a "notorious hag" who presided over "unrestrained orgies"— in other words, a nineteenth-century *femme de mauvaise vie*—but Marie remained feared, legendary, multiplicitous (she and her daughter were often viewed interchangeably by past and contemporary enthusiasts), and super-natural well past her death in 1881.[29]

Although these iconic examples represent a deep well of black life and community formation, African women and women of African descent appear only in fits and starts in slavery's archive. Local memory of Rose Nicaud, for example, is strong in the present day, but there is almost no archival trace of this enslaved woman who purchased her freedom by selling coffee and pralines on the streets of the Marigny and French Quarter.[30] The black femme freedoms that enslaved and free women of African descent cultivated, their practices that placed them at marketplaces and squares throughout the city selling food and drink, often appear only as null values, empty, blank spaces—except in the memory of black women in the city. And where the presence of African women and women of African descent should be undeniable (as it was in life) at the French Market, on the riverfront, at the hospital, in the Ursuline convent, or in the streets themselves, no monuments mark their presence. Only at Congo Square, in a sculpture reproduced from an 1886 sketch by Edward Kemble, does a femme-presenting figure with African features still dance.[31]

The stories of individual enslaved women and less wealthy (or less infamous) women of African descent remain difficult to uncover, much less celebrate. Through the prodigious labor of scholars Rebecca Scott and Jean Hébrard, the life of Rosalie Vincent, the "Poulard" grandmother of Edouard Tinchant (a free man of color and delegate to the state constitution convention after the Civil War), became known. Her freedom papers, recovered from archives around the world, allowed her story to be told and appear exceptional, but Rosalie, enslaved in Senegambia, taken to Saint-Domingue, and part of the flow of refugees that landed in Louisiana, lived a typical life for a woman of her ancestry in the eighteenth and nineteenth centuries. These stories seem extraordinary because they appear in an archive structured to erase them. Rosalie, Seignora

Catti, Marie Baude, Charlotte, María Teresa, Perine, and others provide an arc of black womanhood as a practice of freedom that laid the foundation for the freedom dreams of the nineteenth and twentieth centuries. The idea of human freedom rooted in embodied, social, spiritual, and interconnected belief in humanity's possibilities emerges in African women and women of African descent's confrontation with its utter opposite—racial slavery and imperial violence. As individuals, these women and others existed and evidenced the extraordinary possibilities that surfaced amid overwhelming odds. As part of a deeper well of women, communities, practices, strategies, failures, and terrors that shaped the meaning of freedom and a faith in the possibility of emancipation, these women are only part of the story–the part we are able to witness.

It is from these deeps, deeper than exceptional names and silent registers, that black women remember their mothers, daughters, godmothers, and aunts. Black communities remember each other, in family whispers, at altars, and at communion. Historians, bound by archives, may scrape dusty folios for sources, may question whether women and girls will appear or worry that when they do appear, they emerge as legends, myths, and motifs representing more than themselves. That is not the intellectual tradition this book was written in. *Wicked Flesh* was written in the tradition of "that event, and this memory."[32] Where history becomes memory, where practice becomes ritual, where black women find life after death, black women remember black women. This book was written in that tradition, in honor of the daughters—and the Mothers—of New Orleans.[33]

Postscript

what is the nature of the saint? the holy woman?
what does she dream when she lies down on her bed?
do her nightly visions follow?
does she sit down to table for cold fish and coffee each morning
like the rest of us?
does she never crave a man
heavy with the smell of the docks, the river?
does she bind up her breasts with white linen

washed soft beneath the hands of a good older woman?
has she *never* craved a man?
what does she dream at night upon her bed
having fed us all with visions through the day?
do her dreams then turn in and to her own in the night?
and when I pass her on the street
what is such a woman to me?

        —Brenda Marie Osbey, "Faubourg Study: Blood," 1995

Archives and Databases

ᝍ

ANS	Archives nationales du Sénégal
CAOM	Centre des archives d'outre-mer
Afro-Louisiana	*Databases for the Study of Afro-Louisiana History and Genealogy, 1699–1860* (Baton Rouge: Louisiana State University Press, 2000)
HNOC	Historic New Orleans Collection
LOC	Library of Congress
LHC	Louisiana Historical Center
LHQ	*Lousiana Historical Quarterly* (New Orleans: Louisiana Historical Society, 1917–1961)
NONA	New Orleans Notarial Archives
NOPL	New Orleans Public Library
RSCSJR	Records of the Superior Council of Louisiana and Spanish Judicial Records of Louisiana, as indexed in *Louisiana Historical Quarterly*
RSCL	Records of the Superior Council of Louisiana
SJRL	Spanish Judicial Records of Louisiana
MPA	Rowland Dunbar and Albert Godfrey Sanders, eds., *Mississippi Provincial Archives*, 5 vols. (Jackson: Mississippi Department of Archives, 1911)
SDNA	Saint-Domingue Notarial Archives
SLC	Sacramental Records of the Archdiocese of New Orleans, St. Louis Cathedral
VCS	Vieux Carré Survey, Historic New Orleans Collection
Voyages	Voyages: The Trans-Atlantic Slave Trade Database and Inter-American Slave Trade Database (http://slavevoyages.org)

Notes

ᴄᴍ̇

Abbreviations for names of archives and databases are located in the "List of Archives and Databases."

Introduction

1. Unless otherwise indicated, translations in this text are by the author. Translating eighteenth-century racial terminology from multiple languages and into twenty-first-century parlance is a precarious process. Terms varied across empires and language groups or, as in the case of the French imperial *nègre* or *négresse* (African or black man or woman with no race mixture) or *mulâtre* or *mulâtresse* (African or black man or woman with a white/European mother or father), gestured to gender and race mixture but were often used haphazardly in practice. Where specificity is unavailable, I use "black" or "black diasporic" (lowercased) to refer to African people or people of African descent, regardless of their status or race mixture. When uppercase "Black" appears, it gestures to the Pan-African nationality and shared sociality of people of African descent. Overall, however, I have shied away from this usage in this text as limiting when applied to an early modern context where ethnicity and lineage organized individuals' relationship to their blackness. This is a history of diasporic identities still in formation. Unless otherwise noted, "African" describes individuals born on the African continent, whether they resided in Africa or the Americas. Where more detail is needed or available, individuals are described by their racial designation and any other markers accorded them in the sources. This attention to identification may produce a more tedious narrative and the reader may encounter terms that are seen as pejorative in the present day (i.e., *négresse, Bambara*). Reusing eighteenth-century vocabulary is meant to capture the tenor and use of such terminology by officials, slaveowners, and the women themselves, even where derogatory. Ultimately, *Wicked Flesh* is concerned with troubling the biopolitical emphasis on blackness and exploring the racial math of those consistently deemed to reside on the wrong side of the human. See also Alexander G. Weheliye, *Habeas Viscus: Racializing Assemblages, Biopolitics, and Black Feminist Theories of the Human* (Durham, NC: Duke University Press, 2014).

2. For the purposes of this study, Gulf Coast Louisiana, or lower Louisiana, is bounded on the east by Pensacola, Florida; on the south by the Gulf of Mexico; on the west by eastern Texas; and on the north by Natchez (Fort Rosalie). See Antoine Simon Le Page du Pratz, *The History of Louisiana* (London: T. Becket, 1774), 107, 118. The north and west boundaries were under constant dispute throughout the eighteenth and nineteenth centuries, but the geography of the Mississippi Delta and the geopolitics of French, British, and Spanish interaction created a Gulf Coast society roughly conforming to these limits. "Gulf Coast" in this study is distinguished from "Gulf South,"

which includes Florida to the east, Texas as far as San Antonio and Laredo to the west, and Charleston, South Carolina, to the north. See Richmond F. Brown, "Introduction," in *Coastal Encounters: The Transformation of the Gulf South in the Eighteenth Century*, ed. Richmond F. Brown (Lincoln: University of Nebraska Press, 2007), 1–6.

3. For early work on free people of color, see David W. Cohen and Jack P. Greene, eds., *Neither Slave nor Free: The Freedman of African Descent in the Slave Societies of the New World* (Baltimore: Johns Hopkins University Press, 1974); David Barry Gaspar and Darlene Clark Hine, eds., *Beyond Bondage: Free Women of Color in the Americas* (Urbana: University of Illinois Press, 2004). For work on African women in slaveholding West and West Central Africa that studies their relationship to slavery and free status, see Pernille Ipsen, *Daughters of the Trade: Atlantic Slavers and Interracial Marriage on the Gold Coast* (Philadelphia: University of Pennsylvania Press, 2015); Vanessa S. Oliveira, "The Gendered Dimension of Trade: Female Traders in Nineteenth Century Luanda," *Portuguese Studies Review* 23, no. 2 (2015); Kristin Mann, *Marrying Well: Marriage, Status and Social Change Among the Educated Elite in Colonial Lagos* (Cambridge: Cambridge University Press, 1985); Lorelle D. Semley, *Mother Is Gold, Father Is Glass: Gender and Colonialism in a Yoruba Town* (Bloomington: Indiana University Press, 2010); Richard Allen, *Slaves, Freedmen, and Indentured Laborers in Colonial Mauritius* (New York: Cambridge University Press, 1999).

4. Katherine McKittrick, "Mathematics Black Life," *Black Scholar* 44, no. 2 (2014): 16–28; Jennifer L. Morgan, "Partus Sequitur Ventrem: Law, Race, and Reproduction in Colonial Slavery," *Small Axe: A Caribbean Journal of Criticism* 22, no. 1 (2018): 1–17; Marisa J. Fuentes, *Dispossessed Lives: Enslaved Women, Violence, and the Archive* (Philadelphia: University of Pennsylvania Press, 2016).

5. Sue Peabody and John D. Garrigus, eds., *Slavery, Freedom, and the Law in the Atlantic World: A Brief History with Documents* (Boston: Bedford / St. Martin's Press, 2007), 31; Joan Dayan, "Codes of Law and Bodies of Color," *New Literary History* 26, no. 2 (1995): 283–308. Until the 1685 *Code Noir*, most slave codes emerged from local councils and governing bodies. The first slave code written in the Americas was the *Ordenanzas para el sosiego y seguridad de los esclavos negros*, compiled by the Audiencia of Santo Domingo in 1528. The first laws stating that status would follow the mother were passed in 1662 in the Virginia Colony. The 1685 *Code Noir* was formally titled *L'Édit royal de mars 1685 touchant la police des îles de l'Amérique française*.

6. Manumission as a process remains largely understudied. For work on manumission in the Americas more broadly, see Rosemary Brana-Shute and Randy J. Sparks, eds., *Paths to Freedom: Manumission in the Atlantic World* (Columbia: University of South Carolina Press, 2009); Rebecca J. Scott and Jean M. Hébrard, *Freedom Papers: An Atlantic Odyssey in the Age of Emancipation* (Cambridge, MA: Harvard University Press, 2012); Orlando Patterson, "Three Notes of Freedom: the Nature and Consequences of Manumission," in Brana-Shute and Sparks, *Paths to Freedom*, 15–30; Hans W. Baade, "The Gens de Couleur of Louisiana: Comparative Slave Law in Microcosm," *Cardozo Law Review* 18 (1996): 535–86.

7. On freedom as emerging from black women's wombs, see Jessica Millward, *Finding Charity's Folk: Enslaved and Free Black Women in Maryland* (Athens: University of Georgia Press, 2015). See also Sasha Turner, *Contested Bodies: Pregnancy, Childrearing, and Slavery in Jamaica* (Philadelphia: University of Pennsylvania Press, 2017); Jennifer L. Morgan, *Laboring Women: Reproduction and Gender in New World Slavery* (Philadelphia: University of Pennsylvania Press, 2004). Although free white women also passed their status on to their children by men of color, they are not the focus of this study. First, they were a numerical minority for much of the eighteenth century in the sites under study. Second, this study focuses on black women and the myriad ways they

defined and redefined the meaning of freedom. In early modern travel writing, letters, and laws, black women, not black men, embodied much of the monstrosity, licentiousness, and misrule that characterized Atlantic slavery. White women did not share this embodiment on either side of the Atlantic. Black women's reproductive labor was likewise tied to slavery in ways that white women's reproductive labor was not. Black women's actions against bondage, as a result, take on special significance and require special attention. That said, white women's intimate encounters in both Senegambia and the French Antilles with men of African descent remain understudied.

8. On slavery and social death, see Orlando Patterson, *Slavery and Social Death: A Comparative Study* (Cambridge, MA: Harvard University Press, 1982). On challenges to social death as the moniker of the slave or blackness, see Vincent Brown, "Social Death and Political Life in the Study of Slavery," *American Historical Review* 114, no. 5 (2009): 1231–49; C. Riley Snorton, *Black on Both Sides: A Racial History of Trans Identity* (Minneapolis: University of Minnesota Press, 2017); Christina Sharpe, *In the Wake: On Blackness and Being* (Durham, NC: Duke University Press, 2016). On the problem of freedom or seeking a free state before slavery, see Saidiya V. Hartman, *Scenes of Subjection: Terror, Slavery, and Self-Making in Nineteenth-Century America* (Oxford: Oxford University Press, 1997).

9. My definition of intimate relations draws on Ann Stoler's geography of intimate domains ("sex, sentiment, domestic arrangement, and child rearing"), which, she argued, "figure[s] in the making of racial categories and in the management of imperial rule." Ann Laura Stoler, "Tense and Tender Ties: The Politics of Comparison in North American History and (Post) Colonial Studies," *Journal of American History* 88, no. 3 (2001): 829. See also Jennifer M. Spear, *Race, Sex, and Social Order in Early New Orleans* (Baltimore: Johns Hopkins University Press, 2009).

10. See also historian Earl Lewis's charge to see African American history as emerging from "overlapping diasporas." Earl Lewis, "To Turn as on a Pivot: Writing African Americans into a History of Overlapping Diasporas," *American Historical Review* 100, no. 3 (1995): 765–87. Rae Paris, *The Forgetting Tree: A Rememory* (Detroit: Wayne State University Press, 2017).

11. *Wicked Flesh* employs a range of source material from archives around the world. Travel narratives, notarial records, church registers, and civil and criminal court records found in France, Senegal, and Louisiana describe the range of activities and complicated kinship networks that African women and women of African descent participated in. French colonial officials maintained extensive records of their eighteenth-century ventures overseas, much of it housed at the Centre des archives d'outre-mer in Aix-en-Provence, France. A small amount of material relating to the same time period was also available at the Archives nationales du Sénégal in Dakar, Senegal. New Orleans' many research institutions, including the Historic New Orleans Collection, the New Orleans Notarial Archives, the New Orleans Public Library, and the Louisiana Historical Center at the Louisiana State Museum, provided a considerable amount of material used for this book. Additional material relevant to the time and places under discussion was found in the African Americana Collection at the Library Company of Philadelphia and in the French Colonial Collection at the Library of Congress in Washington, DC.

12. Fuentes, *Dispossessed Lives*, 78.

13. See also Jennifer Morgan's call for a "disruption poetics" in histories of the Middle Passage; Anjali Arondekar's call for "narratives of retrieval" that challenge narratives of historical recovery; and Saidiya Hartman's use of "critical fabulation" and an "archive of the exorbitant." Jennifer L. Morgan, "Accounting for 'the Most Excruciating Torment': Gender, Slavery, and Trans-Atlantic Passages," *History of the Present* 6, no. 2 (2016): 184–207; Anjali Arondekar, *For*

the Record: On Sexuality and the Colonial Archive in India (Durham, NC: Duke University Press, 2009); Hartman, *Scenes of Subjection*; Saidiya Hartman, *Wayward Lives, Beautiful Experiments: Intimate Histories of Social Upheaval* (New York: W. W. Norton, 2019).

14. James F. Searing, *West African Slavery and Atlantic Commerce* (Cambridge: Cambridge University Press, 1993), 17–18.

15. Mark Hinchman, *Portrait of an Island: The Architecture and Material Culture of Gorée, Sénégal, 1758–1837* (Lincoln: University of Nebraska Press, 2015), 40–41.

16. Robin Blackburn, *The Making of New World Slavery: From the Baroque to the Modern, 1492–1800* (New York: Verso, 1998), 280; Philip P. Boucher, *France and the American Tropics to 1700: Tropics of Discontent?* (Baltimore: Johns Hopkins University Press, 2008).

17. John D. Garrigus, *Before Haiti: Race and Citizenship in French Saint-Domingue* (New York: Macmillan, 2006), 23–29; Philip D. Curtin, *The Rise and Fall of the Plantation Complex: Essays in Atlantic History* (New York: Cambridge University Press, 1998), 95; Richard Dunn, *Sugar and Slaves: The Rise of the Planter Class in the English West Indies, 1624–1713* (Chapel Hill: University of North Carolina Press, 1972), 21–42; Malick W. Ghachem, *The Old Regime and the Haitian Revolution* (Cambridge: Cambridge University Press, 2012), 35–40; Bernard Moitt, *Women and Slavery in the French Antilles, 1635–1848* (Bloomington: Indiana University Press, 2001), 3–6.

18. Jean-Baptiste Labat, *Nouveau voyage aux isles de l'Amérique* (La Haye: P. Husson, 1724), 2:133–35. In 1724, ambiguously discussing either the unification of the colonies or *partus sequitur ventrem* or both, Labat noted, "Depuis cette Ordonnance, les Mulatres sont tous esclave; & leurs maitres ne peuvent être contraints de quelque manier que ce soit, de les vendre a ceux qui en sont les pères, sinon de gré à gré" (Since this ordinance, the *mulâtres* are all slaves and their masters cannot be constrained in any manner whatsoever to sell them to those who are their fathers, unless by mutual agreement).

19. David P. Geggus, "The Major Port Towns of Saint Domingue in the Late 18th Century," in *Atlantic Port Cities: Economy, Culture and Society*, ed. P. Liss and Franklin Knight (Knoxville: University of Tennessee Press, 1991), 91, 93, 112n2. In 1788, 35 percent of the exports to France and 38 percent of slave ships arriving in Saint-Domingue went through Le Cap; in the same year, Port-au-Prince handled 26 percent of the exports to France and received 25 percent of the ships to the island.

20. On ungendering and theorizing "flesh," see Hortense Spillers, "Mama's Baby, Papa's Maybe," *Diacritics* 17, no. 2 (1987): 65–81.

21. "In 1718, the regency government of the duke of Orléans established the town of Nouvelle Orléans one hundred miles above the mouth of the Mississippi River." Thomas N. Ingersoll, "Free Blacks in a Slave Society: New Orleans, 1718–1812," *William and Mary Quarterly* 48, no. 2 (1991): 174. Jean-Baptiste Le Moyne, Sieur de Bienville, was named Company director.

22. Craig E. Colten, *An Unnatural Metropolis: Wresting New Orleans from Nature* (Baton Rouge: Louisiana State University Press, 2006), 3; Pierre Margry, *Premiére formation d'une chaine de postes entre le fleuve Saint-Laurent et le Golfe du Mexique (1683–1724)* (Paris: Maisonneuve Frères & Ch. Leclerc, 1883), 5:599–608. Beginning in 1699 with a French outpost at Biloxi Bay, the French established a series of forts along the Gulf Coast. New Orleans was especially attractive because of "an old Indian portage to a series of huge lakes" linking the Gulf to the Delta. Thomas N. Ingersoll, *Mammon and Manon in Early New Orleans: The First Slave Society in the Deep South, 1718–1819* (Knoxville: University of Tennessee Press, 1999), 6.

23. For more on southeastern Native nations, particularly in colonial Louisiana, see Guillaume Aubert, "'The Blood of France': Race and Purity of Blood in the French Atlantic World,"

William and Mary Quarterly 61, no. 3 (2004): 439–78; Spear, Race, Sex, and Social Order; Daniel H. Usner, American Indians in the Lower Mississippi Valley: Social and Economic Histories (Lincoln: University of Nebraska Press, 2004); Daniel H. Usner, Indians, Settlers, and Slaves in a Frontier Exchange Economy: The Lower Mississippi Valley Before 1783 (Chapel Hill: University of North Carolina Press, 1992); David Wheat, "My Friend Nicolas Mongoula: Africans, Indians, and Cultural Exchange in Eighteenth-Century Mobile," in Brown, Coastal Encounters; Sophie White, Wild Frenchmen and Frenchified Indians: Material Culture and Race in Colonial Louisiana (Chapel Hill: University of North Carolina Press, 2013); White, Voices of the Enslaved: Love, Labor, and Longing in French Louisiana (Chapel Hill: University of North Carolina Press, 2019); George Edward Milne, Natchez Country: Indians, Colonists, and the Landscapes of Race in French Louisiana (Athens: University of Georgia Press, 2015); Kathleen DuVal, The Native Ground: Indians and Colonists in the Heart of the Continent (Philadelphia: University of Pennsylvania Press, 2011).

24. Kimberly S. Hanger, Bounded Lives, Bounded Places: Free Black Society in Colonial New Orleans, 1769–1803 (Durham, NC: Duke University Press, 1997). In 1762, Louis XV transferred Louisiana to Spain but French law (and French control) continued until Spanish administrators took definitive, military control in 1769 after crushing a small revolt by French landholders. R. E. Chandler, "Ulloa's Account of the 1768 Revolt," Louisiana History 27, no. 4 (1986): 407–37.

25. See Wilma King, The Essence of Liberty: Free Black Women During the Slave Era (Columbia: University of Missouri Press, 2006); Gaspar and Hine, Beyond Bondage; Erica Armstrong Dunbar, A Fragile Freedom: African American Women and Emancipation in the Antebellum City (New Haven, CT: Yale University Press, 2008); Adele Logan Alexander, Ambiguous Lives: Free Women of Color in Rural Georgia, 1789–1879 (Fayetteville: University of Arkansas Press, 1991); Suzanne Lebsock, The Free Women of Petersburg: Status and Culture in a Southern Town, 1784–1860 (New York: W. W. Norton, 1985); Diane Batts Morrow, Persons of Color and Religious at the Same Time: The Oblate Sisters of Providence, 1828–1860 (Chapel Hill: University of North Carolina Press, 2002); Amrita Chakrabarti Myers, Forging Freedom: Black Women and the Pursuit of Liberty in Antebellum Charleston (Chapel Hill: University of North Carolina Press, 2011); Virginia Meacham Gould, "Urban Slavery, Urban Freedom: The Manumission of Jacqueline Lemelle," in More Than Chattel: Black Women and Slavery in the Americas, ed. David Barry Gaspar and Darlene Clark Hine (Bloomington: Indiana University Press, 1996), 298–314; Virginia Meacham Gould, ed., Chained to the Rock of Adversity: To Be Free, Black and Female in the Old South (Athens: University of Georgia Press, 1998); Millward, Finding Charity's Folk; Loren Schweninger, "Property Owning Free African-American Women in the South, 1800–1870," Journal of Women's History 1, no. 3 (1990): 13–44.

26. Brenda Marie Osbey, "Madhouses," in All Souls: Essential Poems (Baton Rouge: Louisiana State University Press, 2015), 14–19.

27. Angela Davis, "Reflections on the Black Women's Role in the Community of Slaves," Massachusetts Review 13, no. 1/2 (1972): 81–100; Darlene Clark Hine, "Lifting the Veil, Shattering the Silence: Black Women's History in Slavery and Freedom," in Hine Sight: Black Women and the Re-construction of American History (New York: Carlson Publishing, 1994), 3–26; Deborah G. White, Ar'n't I a Woman? Female Slaves in the Plantation South (New York: W. W. Norton, 1985).

28. A sample of this work follows. For West and West Central Africa, see Claire C. Robertson and Martin A. Klein, eds., Women and Slavery in Africa (Portsmouth, NH: Heinemann, 1983); Gwyn Campbell, Suzanne Miers, and Joseph C. Miller, eds., Women and Slavery: Africa, the Indian Ocean World, and the Medieval North Atlantic (Athens: Ohio University Press, 2007); George E. Brooks, Eurafricans in Western Africa: Commerce, Social Status, Gender, and Religious Observance from the Sixteenth to the Eighteenth Century (Athens: Ohio University Press, 2003); Philip J. Havik,

Silences and Soundbites: The Gendered Dynamics of Trade and Brokerage in the Pre-colonial Guinea Bissau Region (Münster: Lit Verlag Münster, 2004). For the United States, see White, *Ar'n't I a Woman?*; Stephanie M. H. Camp, *Closer to Freedom: Enslaved Women and Everyday Resistance in the Plantation South* (Chapel Hill: University of North Carolina Press, 2004); Morgan, *Laboring Women*; Thavolia Glymph, *Out of the House of Bondage: The Transformation of the Plantation Household* (Cambridge: Cambridge University Press, 2008); Tera W. Hunter, *Bound in Wedlock: Slave and Free Black Marriage in the Nineteenth Century* (Cambridge, MA: Harvard University Press, 2017); Deirdre Cooper Owens, *Medical Bondage: Race, Gender, and the Origins of American Gynecology* (Athens: University of Georgia Press, 2017); Stephanie E. Jones-Rogers, *They Were Her Property: White Women as Slave Owners in the American South* (New Haven, CT: Yale University Press, 2019). For the Caribbean, see Hilary Beckles, *Natural Rebels: A Social History of Enslaved Black Women in Barbados* (New Brunswick, NJ: Rutgers University Press, 1989); Barbara Bush, *Slave Women in Caribbean Society, 1650–1838* (London: Heinemann, 1990); Arlette Gautier, *Les soeurs de Solitude: La condition féminine dans l'esclavage aux Antilles du XVIIe au XIXe siècle* (Paris: Éditions Caribénnes, 1985); Moitt, *Women and Slavery in the French Antilles*.

29. Gwendolyn Midlo Hall, *Africans in Colonial Louisiana: The Development of Afro-Creole Culture in the Eighteenth Century* (Baton Rouge: Louisiana State University Press, 1995). Hall also helped pioneer the use of databases to create data visualizations that shed light on the lives of enslaved and free people of African descent—a strategy now seen as cutting edge among humanists researching Atlantic slavery. Read more at https://www.ibiblio.org/laslave/introduction. php. The book was accompanied by *Databases for the Study of Afro-Louisiana History and Genealogy, 1699–1860*, a website and CD-ROM compilation of databases, maps, graphs, and images.

30. Hall, *Africans in Colonial Louisiana*; Ibrahima Seck, *Bouki Fait Gombo: A History of the Slave Community of Habitation Haydel (Whitney Plantation) Louisiana, 1750–1860* (New Orleans: University of New Orleans Press, 2014); Emily Clark, *The Strange History of the American Quadroon: Free Women of Color in the Revolutionary Atlantic World* (Chapel Hill: University of North Carolina Press, 2013); Emily Clark, Cecile Vidal, and Ibrahima Thioub, eds., *New Orleans, Louisiana, and Saint-Louis, Senegal: Mirror Cities in the Atlantic World, 1659–2000s* (Baton Rouge: Louisiana State University Press, 2019).

31. Cécile Vidal, *Caribbean New Orleans: Empire, Race, and the Making of a Slave Society* (Chapel Hill: University of North Carolina Press, 2019); Cécile Vidal, ed., *Louisiana: Crossroads of the Atlantic World* (Philadelphia: University of Pennsylvania Press, 2013); Spear, *Race, Sex, and Social Order*; White, *Wild Frenchmen and Frenchified Indians*; White, *Voices of the Enslaved*; Hanger, *Bounded Lives, Bounded Places*. See also Aubert, "'Blood of France'"; Caryn Cossé Bell, *Revolution, Romanticism, and the Afro-Creole Protest Tradition in Louisiana, 1718–1868* (Baton Rouge: Louisiana State University Press, 2004); Gilbert C. Din, *Spaniards, Planters, and Slaves: The Spanish Regulation of Slavery in Louisiana, 1763–1803* (College Station: Texas A&M University Press, 1999); Rashauna Johnson, *Slavery's Metropolis: Unfree Labor in New Orleans During the Age of Revolutions* (Cambridge: Cambridge University Press, 2016); Usner, *Indians, Settlers, and Slaves*.

32. At the same time, this book also contributes to scholarship on blackness and French empire. For brilliant examples of this work for later periods, see Lorelle Semley, *To Be Free and French: Citizenship in France's Atlantic Empire* (Cambridge: Cambridge University Press, 2017); Robin Mitchell, *Vénus Noire: Black Women and Colonial Fantasies in Nineteenth-Century France* (Athens: University of Georgia Press, 2019); Annette K. Joseph-Gabriel, *Reimagining Liberation:*

How Black Women Transformed Citizenship in the French Empire (Urbana: University of Illinois Press, 2019); Maboula Soumahoro, *Le triangle et l'hexagone* (Paris: L'Éditions de la Découverte, 2020); and Félix Germain, Silyane Larcher, and T. Denean Sharpley-Whiting, eds., *Black French Women and the Struggle for Equality, 1848–2016* (Omaha: University of Nebraska Press, 2018).

33. Joseph C. Miller, "Domiciled and Dominated: Slaving as a History of Women," in *Women and Slavery: The Modern Atlantic*, ed. Gwyn Campbell, Suzanne Miers, and Joseph C. Miller (Athens: Ohio University Press, 2007), 284–312. Research compiled by Claire Robertson and Martin Klein profiled the predominance of women as slaves in Africa, their importance to household production, and the many roles women throughout the African continent played as enslaved laborers, slaveowning and property-owning wives, and heads of households across the continent. Robertson and Klein, *Women and Slavery in Africa*.

34. Morgan, *Laboring Women*. In the words of historian Stephanie M. H. Camp, women's history "changes what we know and how we know it." Camp, *Closer to Freedom*, 3.

35. Gautier, *Les soeurs des Solitude*; Dominique Rogers, "Les libres de couleur dans les capitales de Saint-Domingue" (diss., Université de Bordeaux III, 2001); Moitt, *Women and Slavery in the French Antilles*. See also Myriam Cottias, "Gender and Republican Citizenship in the French West Indies, 1848–1945," *Slavery and Abolition* 26, no. 2 (1995): 233–45; Joan Dayan, *Haiti, History, and the Gods* (Berkeley: University of California Press, 1995); Doris L. Garraway, *The Libertine Colony: Creolization in the Early French Caribbean* (Durham, NC: Duke University Press, 2005); Karol K. Weaver, *Medical Revolutionaries: The Enslaved Healers of Eighteenth-Century Saint Domingue* (Urbana: University of Illinois Press, 2006).

36. For scholars doing this work, see Daina Berry and Leslie Harris, eds., *Sexuality and Slavery: Reclaiming Intimate Histories in the Americas* (Athens: University of Georgia Press, 2018); Gwyn Campbell and Elizabeth Elbourne, eds., *Sex, Power, and Slavery* (Athens: Ohio University Press, 2014); Colin (Joan) Dayan, "Erzulie: A Women's History of Haiti," *Research in African Literatures* 25, no. 2 (1994): 5–31; Omise'eke Natasha Tinsley, "Black Atlantic, Queer Atlantic: Queer Imaginings of the Middle Passage," *GLQ: A Journal of Lesbian and Gay Studies* 14, no. 2 (2008): 191–215; Amber Jamilla Musser, "Queering Sugar: Kara Walker's Sugar Sphinx and the Intractability of Black Female Sexuality," *Signs: Journal of Women in Culture and Society* 42, no. 1 (2016): 153–74; Treva B. Lindsey and Jessica Marie Johnson, "Searching for Climax: Black Erotic Lives in Slavery and Freedom," *Meridians: feminism, race, transnationalism* 12, no. 2 (2014): 169–95; Lisa Ze Winters, *The Mulatta Concubine: Terror, Intimacy, Freedom, and Desire in the Black Transatlantic* (Athens: University of Georgia Press, 2016). See also work in progress produced by members of the Queering Slavery Working Group, co-organized by Jessica Marie Johnson and Vanessa Holden, at http://qswg.tumblr.com.

37. LaMonda Horton-Stallings, *Funk the Erotic: Transaesthetics and Black Sexual Cultures* (Urbana: University of Illinois Press, 2015), 16.

38. Jeri Hilt, "There Are No Survivors Without Scars," *Bitch Media* (26 August 2015), https://bitchmedia.org/article/there-are-no-survivors-without-scars (accessed 20 September 2019).

39. Lawrence N. Powell, *The Accidental City: Improvising New Orleans* (Cambridge, MA: Harvard University Press, 2013); Ned Sublette, *The World That Made New Orleans: From Spanish Silver to Congo Square* (Chicago: Lawrence Hill Books, 2008).

40. *Purchased Lives: New Orleans and the Domestic Slave Trade, 1808–1865*, exhibition at the Historic New Orleans Collection (17 March–18 July 2015); Brentin Mock, "The Movement That Made New Orleans Take 'Em Down," *CityLab* (29 May 2017), https://www.citylab.com/

politics/2017/05/the-man-who-knocked-down-robert-e-lee/528378/ (accessed 4 May 2019); Take
'Em Down Nola, *Roots Rising: The Take 'Em Down NOLA Zine* (New Orleans, LA: n.p., 2019).

41. Clyde A. Woods, "Do You Know What It Means to Miss New Orleans? Katrina, Trap
Economics, and the Rebirth of the Blues," *American Quarterly* 57, no. 4 (2005): 1005–18.

42. David Scott, "That Event, This Memory: Notes on the Anthropology of African Diasporas
in the New World," *Diaspora: A Journal of Transnational Studies* 1, no. 3 (1991): 261–84.

Chapter 1

Source of epigraph: Julien Dubellay to Messieurs le Directeurs de la Compagnie des Indes, 25
May 1724, C6 8, fol. 5, CAOM. "À l'égard des femmes de Bambaras, elles sont libres, ainsi je ne
pourray les forceur de suive leurs maris, je les y engagera cependant au possible."

1. Boubacar Barry, *Senegambia and the Atlantic Slave Trade* (New York: Cambridge University Press, 1998), 100. Jean Barbot's narrative is a fraught one, with original accounts and
elements borrowed from earlier published accounts of the West African coast, but it is still
useful, particularly where scholars have analyzed it for original content. This description of
Catti draws on the 1732 English translation published after Barbot's death and on the original
journal as cross-referenced, translated, and republished by P. E. H. Hair, Adam Jones, and
Robin Law. See P. E. H. Hair, Adam Jones, and Robin Law, eds., *Barbot on Guinea: The Writings
of Jean Barbot on West Africa 1678–1712* (London: Hakluyt Society, 1992), 122–25. The reference
to her stature and wealth (i.e. a gift of a horse of significant value) is original. Barbot, in Hair
et al., *Barbot on Guinea*, 90–91. On using Barbot, see Robin Law, "Jean Barbot as a Source for
the Slave Coast of West Africa," *History in Africa* 9 (1982): 155–73; P. E. H. Hair, "Barbot, Dap-
per, Davity: A Critique of Sources on Sierra Leone and Cape Mount," *History in Africa* 1 (1974):
25–54.

2. In this narrative, Barbot also described Catti as a "Portuguese Christian." In the 1732 narrative, Barbot described Catti as "a black lady of a good presence and a very jovial temper, widow
to a Portuguese of note." Barbot, in Hair et al., *Barbot on Guinea*, 135n6.

3. In the 1732 narrative, Barbot notes it as "a fine mat," which guests sat around "with our legs
across, after the Moorish fashion." Barbot, in Hair et al., *Barbot on Guinea*, 135n6.

4. Barbot, in Hair et al., *Barbot on Guinea*, 124–25.

5. The concept of an "Atlantic Africa" was first developed by Africanists as a way to challenge the absence of African continental history from histories of the "Atlantic world" and to
describe ways African history connects to, influences, and must be centered in Atlantic and
African diaspora history. See Robin Law and Kristin Mann, "West Africa in the Atlantic Com-
munity: The Case of the Slave Coast," *William and Mary Quarterly* 56, no. 2 (1999); J. Lorand
Matory, *Black Atlantic Religion: Tradition, Transnationalism, and Matriarchy in the Afro-Brazilian
Candomblé* (Princeton, NJ: Princeton University Press, 2005); John Thornton, *Africa and
Africans in the Making of the Atlantic World, 1400–1800* (New York: Cambridge University Press,
1998); James H. Sweet, *Recreating Africa: Culture, Kinship, and Religion in the African-Portuguese
World, 1441–1770* (Chapel Hill: University of North Carolina Press, 2003); James H. Sweet,
"Reimagining the African-Atlantic Archive: Method, Concept, Epistemology, Ontology,"
Journal of African History 55, no. 2 (2014): 147–59; Mariana Candido, *An African Slave Port in
the Atlantic World: Benguela and Its Hinterland* (New York: Cambridge University Press, 2011);

Jessica A. Krug, *Fugitive Modernities: Kisama and the Politics of Freedom* (Durham, NC: Duke University Press, 2018).

6. Pernille Ipsen, *Daughters of the Trade: Atlantic Slavers and Interracial Marriage on the Gold Coast* (Philadelphia: University of Pennsylvania Press, 2015); Kristin Mann, *Marrying Well: Marriage, Status, and Social Change Among the Educated Elite in Colonial Lagos* (Cambridge: Cambridge University Press, 1985); Kwabena Adu-Boahen, "Abolition, Economic Transition, Gender and Slavery: The Expansion of Women's Slaveholding in Ghana, 1807–1874," *Slavery & Abolition* 31, no. 1 (2010): 117–36; Vanessa S. Oliveira, "The Gendered Dimension of Trade: Female Traders in Nineteenth Century Luanda," *Portuguese Studies Review* 23, no. 2 (2015); George Brooks, "A Ñhara of the Guinea-Bissau Region: Mae Aurelia Correia," in *Women and Slavery in Africa*, ed. Clare Robertson and Martin Klein (Madison: University of Wisconsin Press, 1983), 295–319.

7. In contemporary Senegal, hospitality or *teranga* (in Wolof) is taken very seriously and continues to be a defining feature of everyday social life.

8. Barbot, in Hair et al., *Barbot on Guinea*, 135n6. Hair and his coeditors offer this candid reflection on Barbot's disgust.

9. Peter Mark, *"Portuguese" Style and Luso-African Identity: Precolonial Senegambia, Sixteenth–Nineteenth Centuries* (Bloomington: Indiana University Press, 2002); George E. Brooks, *Eurafricans in Western Africa: Commerce, Social Status, Gender, and Religious Observance from the Sixteenth to the Eighteenth Century* (Athens: Ohio University Press, 2003). On Africans influencing the European "culture of taste," see Simon Gikandi, *Slavery and the Culture of Taste* (Princeton, NJ: Princeton University Press, 2011).

10. Prosper Cultru, *Histoire du Sénégal du XV siècle à 1870* (Paris: Emile Larose, 1910), 115–16. On LaCoste's embezzlement, see La Courbe's mention and Cultru's notes in Michel Jajolet de la Courbe, *Premier voyage du sieur de La Courbe fait a la Coste d'Afrique en 1685* (Paris: E. Champion, 1913), 270.

11. La Courbe, *Premier voyage*, 78–81.

12. James F. Searing, *West African Slavery and Atlantic Commerce* (Cambridge: Cambridge University Press, 1993), 16, 43; Abdoulaye Bara Diop, *La famille Wolof: Tradition et changement* (Paris: Karthala Editions, 1985), 22–23; Barry, *Senegambia and the Atlantic Slave Trade*, 52, on the Linger Yaasin Bubu; Brooks, *Eurafricans in Western Africa*, 150–51, on the woman known alternately as Marie Mar, Maguimar, and La Belinguere, a wealthy trader and woman of high status who traded with the British at St. James Fort in the Gambia and was written into account books as "Belinger, Queen of Barra." "Belinguere" may be a Portuguese derivation of *lingeer* or *linger*, the honorific ascribed to royal officials.

13. Brooks, *Eurafricans in Western Africa*, 134. Brooks argues that Wolof women did not benefit much from interacting with Europeans because of the male-centered hierarchy.

14. Diop, *La famille Wolof*, 183–85. As Searing notes, in the origin stories of royal lineages of Senegambia, conflict and competition between the children of royal wives played key roles in the rise and fall of kings and kingdoms. Searing, *West African Slavery*, 15–16. In the present day, African feminists have critiqued polygyny, the practice of taking multiple wives, as exploitative. See Penda Mbow, "L'Islam et la femme Sénégalaise," *Éthiopiques: Revue socialiste de culture négro-africaine* 66–67 (2001): 203–24; Mariama Bâ, *Une si longue lettre* (Dakar: Les Nouvelles Editions Africaines, 1980). Others have argued that the state should do more to protect women in polygynous marriages. See Loretta E. Bass and Fatou Sow, "Senegalese Families: The Confluence of Ethnicity,

History, and Social Change," in *African Families at the Turn of the 21st Century*, ed. Yaw Oheneba-Sakyi and Baffour K. Takyi (Westport, CT: Praeger, 2006), 83–102.

15. Searing, *West African Slavery*, 93–164; Barry, *Senegambia and the Atlantic Slave Trade*, 78; Brooks, *Eurafricans in Western Africa*, 61.

16. Searing, *West African Slavery*, 207.

17. The Wolof of Kajoor established commerce with the Portuguese in the sixteenth century. The French first begin to discuss Fort Saint-Louis in 1660. See Hilary Jones, *The Métis of Senegal: Urban Life and Politics in French West Africa* (Bloomington: Indiana University Press, 2013); Boubacar Barry, *Le royaume du Waalo: Le Sénégal avant la conquête* (Paris: Karthala Editions, 1985), 18, 90–91; Mamadou Diouf, *Le Kajoor au XIXe siècle* (Paris: Karthala, 1990), 76–79.

18. Ibrahima Thiaw, "Digging on Contested Grounds: Archaeology and the Commemoration of Slavery on Gorée Island, Senegal," in *New Perspectives in Global Public Archaeology*, ed. Katsuyuki Okamura and Akira Matsuda (New York: Springer, 2011), 132. Thiaw relates a story from an unpublished manuscript by Pierre-Andre Cariou: in 1445, when the Portuguese attempted to land at Gorée, they were chased back by local warriors wielding poisoned arrows. Thiaw describes this as inaugurating the first contact between Africans and Europeans. Thiaw, "L'espace entre les mots et les choses: Mémoire historique et culture matérielle à Gorée (Sénégal)," in *Espaces, culture materielle et identites en Senegambie*, ed. Ibrahima Thiaw (Dakar: CODESRIA, 2010), 25.

19. Jones, *Métis of Senegal*, 24; Brooks, *Eurafricans in Western Africa*, 50, 59. Brooks defines *lançados* as Portuguese men living within African communities and *tangomãos* as *lançados* who participated more fully in African social life via the clothing they wore, systems of belief (amulets, divination) practiced, and rites of passage (circumcision, scarification) participated in, including marriage. See also Jean Boulégue, *Les Luso-Africains de Sénégambie, XVI–XIXème siècles* (Dakar: Université de Dakar, 1972).

20. Richard Jobson, *Discovery of the River Gambia and the Golden Trade of the Aethiopians*, ed. Charles G. Kingsley (England: Teignmouth, 1904), 35–40; Brooks, *Eurafricans in Western Africa*, 50.

21. See, for example, Walter Hawthorne's discussion of Balanta "insiders" (women, youth) seeking out trade opportunities with Europeans. Walter Hawthorne, *Planting Rice and Harvesting Slaves: Transformations Along the Guinea-Bissau Coast, 1400–1900* (Portsmouth, NH: Heinemann, 2003).

22. Jones, *Métis of Senegal*, 23; Mbaye Guèye, "La traite négrière dans l'arrière-pays de Saint-Louis," in *Saint-Louis et l'esclavage: Actes du symposium international (Saint-Louis, 18, 19 et 20 Décembre 1998)*, ed. Djibril Samb (Dakar: Université Cheikh Anta Diop, 2000), 21; Richard Campanella, "Fluidity, Rigidity and Consequence: A Comparative Historical Geography of the Mississippi and Sénégal River Deltas and the Deltaic Urbanism of New Orleans and Saint-Louis," *Built Environment* 40, no. 2 (2014): 186–87.

23. La Courbe, *Premier voyage*, 28. See also Searing's description, which he translated to "never make love without a price." Searing, *West African Slavery*, 99.

24. Guèye, "La traite négrière," 21.

25. M. Wallons, profile et plan de l'isle de Gorée, March 1723, Dépot des fortifications des colonies 22B, CAOM.

26. Raina Croff, "Village des Bambaras: An Archaeology of Domestic Slavery and Urban Transformation on Gorée Island, Senegal, A.D. 17th–19th Centuries" (Ph.D. diss., Yale University,

2009), 61, 77–78, 101–2, 107; Ibrahima Thiaw, "Every House Has a Story: The Archaeology of Gorée Island, Sénégal," in *Africa, Brazil and the Construction of Trans-Atlantic Black Identities*, ed. Livio Sansone, Elisée Soumonni, and Boubacar Barry (Trenton, NJ: Africa World Press, 2008), 54. See also Ousmane Sene, "Urbanisation, urbanisme et architecture dans l'ile de Gorée aux XVIIIe et XIXe siècles" (mémoire de maîtrise, Université de Dakar, 1972).

27. Thiaw notes that even maps themselves depicted increased integration by the late eighteenth century as the African presence at Gorée grew. Thiaw, "Digging on Contested Grounds," 130.

28. Rochefort was among several seaside French towns that soldiers, sailors, and settlers traveled from: La Rochelle, Rouen, Dieppe, Rochefort, Nantes, and Bordeaux. Rochefort, however, was unique. In the 1670s, Rochefort joined Brest as one of two naval centers established specifically for the purpose of supporting France's military interests at sea. See Gilles Havard and Cécile Vidal, *Histoire de l'Amérique française* (Paris: Flammarion, 2003), 125, 144; Philip P. Boucher, *France and the American Tropics to 1700: Tropics of Discontent?* (Baltimore: Johns Hopkins University Press, 2008), 169. The Company listed "Jean Pinet, Armurier" at Gorée was due a credit of 177 livres and 10 sols. Pinet's credit was comparable to masons, blacksmiths, and other artisans on the island (whose credit ranged from 87 to 400 livres) but higher than sailors and cabin boys (30–50 livres). For comparison, the same document listed 8,000 livres due to the then-governor of Gorée, François Duval. Estat des appointements qui sont deüs aux Employez de la Compagnie des Indes à la Concession du Senegal par les Comptes arrestez par Mr. Brüe Directeur et Commandant general le 30 Avril 1720, C6 6, fol. 2, CAOM.

29. "There are very few clues indicating such differentiation in archaeological patterns of uses of space or in the material." Thiaw, "Every House Has a Story," 54. See also Croff, "Village des Bambaras."

30. Thornton, *Africa and Africans*, 17.

31. David Boilat, *Esquisses sénégalaises: Physionomie du pays, peuplades, commerce, religions, passé et avenir, récits et légendes* (Paris: P. Bertrand, 1853), 441–46; Jean-Baptiste-Anne Raffenel, *Voyage dans L'Afrique Occidentale: Comprenant l'exploration du Sénégal* (Paris: Arthus Bertrand, 1846), 79–86; Barry, *Senegambia and the Atlantic Slave Trade*, 46, 78; Michael David Marcson, "European-African Interaction in the Precolonial Period: Saint Louis, Senegal, 1758–1854" (Ph.D. diss., Princeton University, 1976), 22–23.

32. Sixty-four black slaves were working at Gorée, seventy at Saint-Louis, and another two hundred or so more during trading season. Règlement concernant la concession du Sénégal, 8 October 1734, C6 11, fol. 43, CAOM.

33. François Saugnier, *Relations de plusieurs voyages á la Côte d'Afrique, á Maroc, au Sénégal, á Gorée, á Galam* (Paris: Chez Gueffier jeune, 2005), 184–85, 302–4; Guèye, "La traite négrière," 32, on *pileuses* and *rapaces*. Although Guèye notes *rapaces* were women, Searing argues that *rapaces/rapasses* were children being trained in the trade. I would argue *rapaces* (and its female derivation, *rapardilles*) is an age category used across status in the slave trade along Senegal's coast.

34. Boilat described the scene: "Drums began to sound from on board in the midst of rifle fire and the songs of the laptots . . . who, as if they need to reward themselves for all the difficulties of the voyage, leap about and vary their melodies with new accents . . . will plant their flags in the middle of the streets, and invite the women and the girls to dance. Five or six griots arrive in haste with their large drums; everyone celebrates, dances, sings, eats and drinks until all that has been earned at the risk of life has been spent." Boilat, *Esquisses sénégalaises*, 445–46. See also Searing,

West African Slavery, 125–27, who notes that Boilat may have exaggerated the antics of the *laptots*, but was likely correct about the festivities themselves.

35. Searing, *West African Slavery*, 96–98.

36. Aissata Kane Lo, *De la signare à la diriyanké sénégalaise: Trajectoires féminines et visions partagées* (Dakar: L'Harmattan Sénégal, 2014), 19, 1. Transcultural adornment could go both ways: African men along the coast were also reported wearing European clothing. La Courbe, *Premier voyage*, 193.

37. Lo, *De la signare*, 125. Lo describes the material culture of the *signares*, particularly the use of cotton cloth, imported and spun locally. Lo argues that local traditions of head adornment and hairstyling inspired the *mouchoir de tête*, a tradition of head covering particular to the worshippers of Islam. See also Jones, *Métis of Senegal*, 36.

38. Mark, *"Portuguese" Style*; Mark Hinchman, *Portrait of an Island: The Architecture and Material Culture of Gorée, Sénégal, 1758–1837* (Lincoln: University of Nebraska Press, 2015); Thiaw, "Digging on Contested Grounds."

39. Carson Ritchie, "Deux textes sur le Sénégal (1673–1677)," *Bulletin de l'Institut fondamental d'Afrique Noire* 1, Series B (1968): 326–28.

40. Lo, *De la signare*, 190–92; Brooks, *Eurafricans in Western Africa*, 216–17.

41. Lo, *De la signare*, 189–90. The *mbootay* would evolve into a mechanism for cooperative economics and microfinance by the nineteenth and twentieth centuries. Similar models emerged across the diaspora, including *susus* in the Caribbean and community banking in the United States. See Peter James Hudson, "On the History and Historiography of Banking in the Caribbean," *Small Axe: A Caribbean Journal of Criticism* 18, no. 1 (1 March 2014): 22–37; Elsa Barkley Brown, "Womanist Consciousness: Maggie Lena Walker and the Independent Order of Saint Luke," *Signs* 14, no. 3 (1989): 610–33.

42. George E. Brooks. "The Signares of Saint-Louis and Goree: Women Entrepreneurs in Eighteenth-Century Senegal," in *Women in Africa: Studies in Social and Economic Change*, ed. Nancy J. Hafkin and Edna G. Bay, 19–44 (Stanford, CA: Stanford University Press, 1976), 34–36; Brooks, *Eurafricans in Western Africa*, 211–12; Jones, *Métis of Senegal*, 35–36; Lo, *De la signare*, 65–68, 83–87; Karen Amanda Sackur, "The Development of Creole Society and Culture in Saint-Louis and Goree, 1719–1817" (Ph.D. thesis, School of Oriental and African Studies, University of London, 1999), 148–53.

43. Sackur notes that the wives of the Brak of Waalo told La Courbe, "Surtout elles estimoient les femmes [en France] heureuses en ce que les maris n'en avoient qu'une et n'estimoient rien tout le reste en comparaison de celà" (Above all they esteemed the women in France happy in that their husbands had only one [wife] and esteemed/valued none of the rest in comparison to her). Sackur, "Development of Creole Society and Culture," 154–55.

44. Diop, *La famille Wolof*, 244–45; Bass and Sow, "Senegalese Families," 87; Searing, *West African Slavery*, 15–17.

45. Lo, *De la signare*, 66; Brooks, *Eurafricans in Western Africa*, 221. Although Lo and Brooks suggest *signareship* began with enslaved women, these origins are challenged by present-day descendants of *signares* who state that their descendants arrived to trade at the *comptoirs* as free Africans. Jones, *Métis of Senegal*, 28–29.

46. Jones writes, "It is impossible to determine exactly when the practice of *mariage à la mode du pays* ceased to exist. Metis families did not leave their own descriptions of their marriage ceremonies in the late nineteenth century. While the status of signare continued to exist after

1850, Christian families in Saint Louis increasingly opted for Church weddings rather than the informal unions of their ancestors." Hilary Jones, "From Mariage à la Mode to Weddings at Town Hall: Marriage, Colonialism, and Mixed-Race Society in Nineteenth-Century Senegal," *African Historical Studies* 1 (2005): 36. See also Jones, *Métis of Senegal.*

47. Estat des appointements, fols. 2–3. Paula's is the earliest reference I've found in French documents of a woman of African descent with the honorific *signare.* Forthcoming work by Lindsey Gish promises to uncover even earlier references.

48. Marie-Hélène Knight-Baylac, "La vie à Gorée de 1677 à 1789," *Revue Française d'Histoire d'Outre-Mer* 57, no. 4 (1970): 399–400; Searing, *West African Slavery*, 106–7; Brooks, *Eurafricans in Western Africa*, 215–16; Jones, *Métis of Senegal*, 36.

49. Estat de ce que les dits Employez doivent a la dit Compagnie par les comptes attestez par le dit Sieur Brue le 30 Avril 1720, 30 April 1720, C6 6, CAOM, 2; St. Robert to the Compagnie des Indies, 18 June 1724, C6 9, fols. 61–62, CAOM.

50. Malietal is also described as "Maure" (Moor). "Andre Rapasse" is listed as "de Monsieur Hardouin" or belonging to Monsieur Hardouin, but in the list of "Negres Libres." He may be hired out, a dependent of Hardouin, or a slave, just not a slave belonging to the Company. Facture des marchandises, estancils et autres effets chargez du magasin du Senegal par ordre de Monsieur Julien Dubellay, Directeur et Commandant General sur le Brigantin Le Fier Capitaine Mr. La Rue, 20 August 1724, C6 8, fol. 3, CAOM; Facture des Marchandises chargées du Magazin du Senegal par orde de Monsieur Julien Dubellay, Directeur, 28 October 1724, C6 8, fol. 2, CAOM.

51. Rolle des passagers venus de France par la frigatte le Prothée commande par Monsieur Hautier arrivée au Senegal, 16 November 1724, C6 8, fol. 2, CAOM.

52. Julien Dubellay to Messieurs le Directeurs de la Compagnie des Indes, 25 May 1724, C6 8, fol. 5, CAOM.

53. Act de naissance, 5 November 1730, no. 16, *État Civil de Saint-Louis du Sénégal*, CAOM (hereafter, *État Civil*); Act de mariage, 12 June 1731, no. 55, *État Civil.*

54. Philip D. Curtin, *Economic Change in Precolonial Africa: Supplementary Evidence* (Madison: University of Wisconsin Press, 1975), 39. Curtin estimates that 86 percent of the men were slaves; he does not provide estimates for the women. During the eighteenth century, the white female population at Saint-Louis and Gorée was negligible. A small handful of white women appear in marriage records of the *État Civil* and are listed as natives of Paris and Bretagne. In 1758, John Lindsay, traveling through West Africa and remarking on married life at Saint-Louis and Gorée, noted that "the French suffer'd no white women to be sent thither—Nor do I think it would be wrong to follow their example." John Lindsay, *A Voyage to the Coast of Africa in 1758* (London: S. Patterson, 1759), 78. Saint-Louis and Gorée were also garrisoned French outposts, not settled French colonies (as in the Americas), and would have been less attractive to voluntary settlers, whether individual women or families. White female missionaries also do not appear to have had a presence in eighteenth-century Saint-Louis or Gorée. Not until after 1817 with the arrival of missionizing European women, through orders like the Soeurs de Saint-Joseph de Cluny, did a white female presence become significant. Jones, "Mariage à la mode," 41, 67; Mamadou Diouf, "The French Colonial Policy of Assimilation and the Civility of the Originaires of the Four Communes (Senegal): A Nineteenth Century Globalization Project," *Development and Change* 29, no. 4 (1998): 681. On the Soeurs and their founder, see Geneviève Lecuir-Nemo, *Anne-Marie Javouhey: Fondatrice de la Congrégation des Soeurs de Saint-Joseph de Cluny, 1779–1851* (Paris: Karthala, 2001).

55. Curtin, *Economic Change*, 40.

56. Curtin, *Economic Change*, 40.

57. Pierre Cariou, "La rivale inconnue de Madame de Sabran dans l'ile de Gorée," *Bulletin de Institut Fondamental d'Afrique Noire* 45, Series B (1950): 13–15.

58. On the "House of Slaves" and its complicated history and memory, see Ana Lucia Araujo, *Shadows of the Slave Past: Memory, Heritage, and Slavery* (New York: Routledge, 2014), 58–64.

59. For an overview of artists' depictions of *signares*, see George E. Brooks, "Artists' Depictions of Senegalese Signares: Insights Concerning French Racist and Sexist Attitudes in the Nineteenth Century," *Genéve Afrique / Geneva Africa* 18, no. 1 (1980): 75–90. Postcolonial depictions of *signares* range from poetry published by the first president of Senegal to popular histories. See Léopold Sédar Senghor, "Chants pour signare," *Nocturnes* (Paris: Éditions du Seuil), 1961; Jean-Luc Angrand, *Céleste ou le temps des signares* (Sarcelles: A. Pépin, 2006). For an example of *signares* "self-fashioning" in Saint Louis, see Ferdinand de Jong and Judith Quax, "Shining Lights: Self-Fashioning in the Lantern Festival of Saint Louis, Senegal," *African Arts* 42, no. 4 (2009): 38–53.

60. Jong and Quax, "Shining Lights."

61. Lisa Ze Winters, *The Mulatta Concubine: Terror, Intimacy, Freedom, and Desire in the Black Transatlantic* (Athens: University of Georgia Press, 2016), 34.

62. Boulégue, *Luso-Africains*, 24; Brooks, *Eurafricans in Western Africa*, 213; Searing, *West African Slavery*, 39.

63. Paul E. Lovejoy, *Transformations in Slavery: A History of Slavery in Africa* (New York: Cambridge University Press, 2000), 3–6; Barry, *Senegambia and the Atlantic Slave Trade*, 102–6; Martin A. Klein, *Slavery and Colonial Rule in French West Africa* (New York: Cambridge University Press, 1998), 243–46, on how *jaam* were seen as lacking honor; James F. Searing. "'No Kings, No Lords, No Slaves': Ethnicity and Religion Among the Sereer-Safèn of Western Bawol, 1700–1914," *Journal of African History* 43, no. 3 (2002): 407–29; Andrew F. Clark, "'The Ties That Bind': Servility and Dependency Among the Fulbe of Bundu (Senegambia), c. 1930s to 1980s," in *Slavery and Colonial Rule in Africa*, ed. Suzanne Miers and Martin A. Klein (London: Frank Cass, 1999).

64. I have also seen the slave warrior classes of the Wolof called the *tyeddo*. I choose to use *ceddo*, drawing from Martin Klein's usage. Martin A. Klein, *Slavery and Colonial Rule in French West Africa* (New York: Cambridge University Press, 1998), 8–9.

65. Searing notes rising demand for these items may have kept the export of slaves to the Americas lower, even if the circulation of slaves within Senegambia continued. Searing, *West African Slavery*, 30. See also Walter Hawthorne, "Nourishing a Stateless Society During the Slave Trade: The Rise of Balanta Paddy-Rice Production in Guinea-Bissau," *Journal of African History* 42, no. 1 (2001): 1–24; James L. A. Webb Jr., "The Horse and Slave Trade Between the Western Sahara and Senegambia," *Journal of African History* 34, no. 2 (1993): 221–46; Martin A. Klein, "Slaves, Gum, and Peanuts: Adaptation to the End of the Slave Trade in Senegal, 1817–48," *William and Mary Quarterly* 66, no. 4 (2009): 895–914; James F. Searing, "Aristocrats, Slaves, and Peasants: Power and Dependency in the Wolof States, 1700–1850," *International Journal of African Historical Studies* 21, no. 3 (1988): 475–503.

66. On slavery, property, and capital in Africa, see Jane I. Guyer and Samuel M. Eno Belinga, "Wealth in People as Wealth in Knowledge: Accumulation and Composition in Equatorial Africa," *Journal of African History* 36 (1995): 91–120; Igor Kopytoff and Suzanne Miers, eds., *Slavery in Africa: Historical and Anthropological Perspectives* (Madison: University of Wisconsin Press, 1977); Claude Meillassoux, *The Anthropology of Slavery: The Womb of Iron and Gold* (Chicago: University of Chicago Press, 1991).

67. Muslims being sold as slaves to Europeans was one of the complaints that led to the 1770s Toorodo *marabout* movement. Barry, *Senegambia and the Atlantic Slave Trade*, 102–6.

68. Martin A. Klein, "Women in Slavery in the Western Sudan," in *Women and Slavery in Africa*, ed. Claire C. Robertson and Martin A. Klein (Portsmouth, NH: Heinemann, 1983), 72–73, 50.

69. Joseph C. Miller, "Domiciled and Dominated: Slaving as a History of Women," in *Women and Slavery: The Modern Atlantic*, ed. Gwyn Campbell, Suzanne Miers, and Joseph C. Miller (Athens: Ohio University Press, 2007), 286.

70. Searing, "Aristocrats, Slaves, and Peasants," 480.

71. Lovejoy, *Transformations in Slavery*, 31–33.

72. Searing, "Aristocrats, Slaves, and Peasants," 480; Diouf, *Le Kajoor*, 57–59; David P. Gamble, *The Wolof of Senegambia* (London: International African Institute, 1967), 44–46.

73. Klein, "Women in Slavery," 78.

74. Boulègue, *Luso-Africains*, 24.

75. On slavery and kinship, see Guyer and Belinga, "Wealth in People"; Ibrahima Thioub, "Stigmas and Memory of Slavery in West Africa: Skin Color and Blood as Social Fracture Lines," *New Global Studies* 6, no. 3 (2012).

76. Boulègue, *Luso-Africains*, 63.

77. For a French discussion of Bambara slaves, see Julien Dubellay to Messieurs le Directeurs de la Compagnie des Indes, 25 May 1724, C6 8, fol. 5, CAOM; Pierre Charpentier to Nicolas Deprès de St. Robert, 12 October 1722, C6 7, fol. 4, CAOM; Facture des marchandises, estancils et autres effets chargez du magasin du Senegal par ordre de Monsieur Julien Dubellay, Directeur et Commandant General sur le Brigantin Le Fier Capitaine Mr. La Rue pour porter a Arguin et remettre au Sr Delamotte garde magasin au d. lieu, 20 August 1724, C6 8, fol. 3, CAOM. See also Croff, "Village des Bambaras," 24.

78. Peter Caron, "'Of a Nation Which the Others Do Not Understand': Bambara Slaves and African Ethnicity in Colonial Louisiana, 1718–1760," *Slavery and Abolition* 18, no. 1 (1997): 101–2; Searing, *West African Slavery*, 107; André Delcourt, *La France et les établissements français au Sénégal entre 1713 et 1763* (Dakar: Institut fondamental d'Afrique noire, 1952), 130–31. Caron challenges Gwendolyn Midlo Hall's assertion that "Bambara" as an ethnic identity made its way across the Atlantic among Africans enslaved in Louisiana. Hall makes this claim in *Africans in Colonial Louisiana: The Development of Afro-Creole Culture in the Eighteenth Century* (Baton Rouge: Louisiana State University Press, 1992), 43–46, and in *Slavery and African Ethnicities in the Americas: Restoring the Links* (Chapel Hill: University of North Carolina Press, 2007), 97–100. On the other hand, scholars of the Atlantic African diaspora and African history, including Michael Gomez, James Sweet, Randy J. Sparks, Paul Lovejoy, and David Trotman, argue that attempts to prove or disprove African ethnicities based on Western standards of ethnicity as stable units of identity do not fit with the elasticity and fluidity of ethnicity in African contexts or self-conscious ethnic identity formation as Africans crossed the Atlantic under duress. See James H. Sweet, "Mistaken Identities? Olaudah Equiano, Domingos Álvares, and the Methodological Challenges of Studying the African Diaspora," *American Historical Review* 114, no. 2 (2009): 279–306; James H. Sweet, *Domingos Álvares, African Healing, and the Intellectual History of the Atlantic World* (Chapel Hill: University of North Carolina Press, 2011); Randy J. Sparks, *The Two Princes of Calabar: An Eighteenth-Century Atlantic Odyssey* (Cambridge, MA: Harvard University Press, 2004); Paul E. Lovejoy and David V. Trotman, eds., *Trans-Atlantic Dimensions of Ethnicity in the African Diaspora* (London: Continuum, 2003).

79. Pierre Charpentier to Nicolas Deprès de St. Robert, 12 October 1722, C6 7, fol. 2, CAOM.

80. St. Robert to les Directeurs de la Compagnie des Indes, 14 October 1720, C6 6, CAOM; Delcourt, *La France*, 235–36.

81. St. Robert to les Directeurs de la Compagnie des Indes, 24 May 1721, C6 6, fol. 3, CAOM.

82. Memoire sur la concession du Senegal: Nouvel arrangement touchant la concession du Senegal, 8 October 1734, C6 11, fol. 47, 11, CAOM. Officials observed some seventy Africans worked for the Company as *"nègres domestiques, compagnons, ouvriers, ou gens de peine."* The memoire also notes that some Africans working for the Company are called *gourmettes*, while the others are called Bambara but "those are mainly slaves." In addition to *gourmettes* and Bambaras at the *comptoir* for four to five months of the year, the island and surrounding land hosted some 230 *laptots* who also worked the trade and were understood to be free.

83. "Les garsons mulatres ont été emploiés au service pour ouvrier ou matelots, mais toujours come maitres, étant nés de françois et non come esclaves, quand meme leur mere eut été esclave" (The mulatto boys were employed in the service as laborers or sailors, but always as masters, being born of French [men] and not as slaves, even though their mother had been a slave). Michel Adanson, "Mémoires d'Adanson sur le Sénégal et l'île de Gorée," ed. Charles Becker and Victor Martin, *Bulletin de Institut Fondamental d'Afrique Noire* 42, no. B4 (1980): 736.

84. St. Robert to les Directeurs de la Compagnie des Indes, 18 June 1725, C6 9, fol. 20, CAOM. St. Robert ordered some twenty Bambaras embarked on *L'Afriquain* on a trading expedition to Ouidah.

85. La Courbe, *Premier voyage*, 109, 111.

86. According to the Trans-Atlantic Slave Trade Database, between 1726 and 1775, across 242 voyages, 48,856 slaves embarked on slave ships from Galam, Gorée, Joal, or Saloum River, Portudal, Saint-Louis, or French Africa (Gorée or Senegal). Of those, 42,337 disembarked (i.e., survived the voyage). Voyages, http://slavevoyages.org/voyages/xKEevv8h (accessed 11 January 2018).

87. St. Robert to Messieurs les Directors de Compagnie des Indes, 15 July 1722 and 8 August 1722, C6 7, CAOM; St. Robert to the Compagnie des Indies, 24 May 1721, C6 6, fols. 2–3, CAOM. See also Hall, *Africans in Colonial Louisiana*, 68.

88. Marisa J. Fuentes, *Dispossessed Lives: Enslaved Women, Violence, and the Archive* (Philadelphia: University of Pennsylvania Press, 2016), 27–30, 37–38.

89. British factor Charles Wheeler described it to William Smith, in William Smith, *A New Voyage to Guinea*, 2nd ed. (London: J. Nourse, 1745), 266.

90. Jean René Antoine, *Voyage fait par ordre du Roi en 1771 et 1772* (Paris: Imprimérie Royale, 1778), 158–59. See also Barbara Bush, "'Daughters of Injur'd Africk': African Women and the Transatlantic Slave Trade," *Women's History Review* 17 (November 2008): 673–98.

91. Croff, "Village des Bambaras," 17–22.

92. Dubellay to Messieurs le Directeurs de Compagnie des Indes, 25 May 1724, fol. 5; Delcourt, *La France*, 130–31.

93. By 1718, the 1685 edict was being reprinted by French jurists under titles that included the phrase "Code Noir." See *Le code noir ou Edit du roy servant de reglement pour le gouvernement & l'administration de justice & la police des isles françoises de l'Amerique, & pour la discipline & le commerce des negres & esclaves dans le dit pays* (Paris: Veuve Saugrain, 1718), 2–12. For a version of the *Code Noir* annotated to compare eighteenth-century versions against the 1687 copy registered with the Superior Council of Guadeloupe (the only extant copy of the 1685 edict), see Jean-François Niort and Jérémy Richard, "L'Édit royal de mars 1685 touchant la police des îles de l'Amérique

française dit 'code noir': Comparaison des éditions anciennes à partir de la version 'Guadeloupe,'" *Bulletin de la Société d'Histoire de la Guadeloupe* 156 (2010): 73–89. See also Louis Sala-Molins, *Le Code Noir, ou Le Calvaire de Canaan* (Paris: Quadrige, 1987). The discussion of the 1685 *Code Noir* that follows is based on the Niort and Richard study of the 1687 copy and cited hereafter in the notes as *Le Code Noir*.

94. Article 13, *Le Code Noir*; Jennifer L. Morgan, *Laboring Women: Reproduction and Gender in New World Slavery* (Philadelphia: University of Pennsylvania Press, 2004).

95. Article 55–6, 9 *Le Code Noir*. Masters twenty years of age or older could free their slaves inter vivos or upon their death.

96. Article 59 protected the rights of free and freed slaves ("Octroyons aux affranchis les mêmes droits, privilèges et immunités dont jouissent les personnes nées libres"). However, a number of restrictions in the *Code Noir* itself contradicted this. Article 39 singled out *affranchis* (freed slaves) and fined them 3,000 livres of sugar for harboring runaways. Article 58 required *affranchis* to respect the authority of their former masters, and ordered them to be punished more severely for crimes. See also Sala-Moulins, *Le Code Noir*, 168, 198–201.

97. See Mbaye Gueye, "From Definitive Manumissions to the Emancipation of 1848," in *The Abolitions of Slavery: From L. F. Sonthonax to Victor Schoelcher, 1793, 1794, 1848*, ed. Marcel Dorigny (Oxford: Berghahn Books, 2003).

98. Abdoulaye Ly, *La Compagnie du Sénégal* (Paris: Karthala, 1993), 261, 257, 259–60. These plans never came to fruition.

99. This changed after 1848 with the abolition of slavery in the Antilles and renewed French interest in Senegal, especially in the gum trade as a legitimate trade. For manumission in nineteenth-century Senegal, see Mamadou Badji and Ibrahima Thioub, eds., *Captivité et abolition de l'esclavage dans les colonies françaises ouest-africaines: Analyse juridique, historique et anthropologique* (Dakar: Crédila, 2015); Emily S. Burrill, "'Wives of Circumstance': Gender and Slave Emancipation in Late Nineteenth-Century Senegal," *Slavery & Abolition* 29, no. 1 (2008): 49–64; Gueye, "From Definitive Manumissions"; Bernard Moitt, "Slavery and Emancipation in Senegal's Peanut Basin: The Nineteenth and Twentieth Centuries," *International Journal of African Historical Studies* 22, no. 1 (1989): 27–50.

100. Règlements de la Compagnie Royalle du Senegal et Costes d'Affrique, 14 March 1721, C6 6, fols. 4, 6, 9, CAOM.

101. Règlements de la Compagnie Royalle du Senegal et Costes d'Affrique, 14 March 1721, fol. 9; Delcourt, *La France*, 97. The *règlement* does not specify what would constitute "better" slaves. It is possible non-Catholic (Muslim) slaves practicing traditional religions may have been more attractive to Company directors as captives than Catholic or Christian slaves.

102. Any French person who caused a slave's injury or death would receive a fine.

103. John D. Garrigus, *Before Haiti: Race and Citizenship in French Saint-Domingue* (New York: Macmillan, 2006), 41; Jean-Baptiste Labat, *Nouveau voyage aux Isles de l'Amérique* (La Haye, France: Chez Husson, 1724), 2:133–35.

104. Léo Élisabeth, *La société martiniquaise aux XVIIe et XVIIIe siècles: 1664–1789* (Paris: Karthala, 2003), 241; Doris L. Garraway, *The Libertine Colony: Creolization in the Early French Caribbean* (Durham, NC: Duke University Press, 2005), 204; Aubert, "Blood of Race in France," 461.

105. Léo Elisabeth, "The French Antilles," in *Neither Slave nor Free: The Freedman of African Descent in the Slave Societies of the New World*, ed. David W. Cohen and Jack P. Greene (Baltimore: Johns Hopkins University Press, 1974), 139; Élisabeth, *La société martiniquaise*, 237-8, 240, 466.;

Guillaume Aubert, "'The Blood of France': Race and Purity of Blood in the French Atlantic World," *William and Mary Quarterly* 61, no. 3 (2004): 461–63.

106. La Courbe, *Premier voyage*, 26.

107. André Brüe, "Premier voyage du Sieur André Brüe au long des Côtes Occidentales d'Afrique (1697)," in *Histoire générale des voyages*, ed. C. A. Walckenaer (Paris: Lefèvre, 1826), 2:91; Searing, *West African Slavery*, 100; Brooks, *Eurafricans in Western Africa*, 132–34.

108. La Courbe, *Premier voyage*, 25; Ritchie, "Deux textes," 294–98.

109. Ly, *La Compagnie du Sénégal*, 260.

110. Ritchie, "Deux textes," 309–10. "Mores" (derived from "Moors") was a generic term used by the French to refer to either North Africans or Muslims or both. In the seventeenth century, *mestis* or *métis* connoted mixed culture or mixed race. For the French, it came to have more specific, racialized definitions in both Senegal and across the Atlantic.

111. Ly, *La Compagnie du Sénégal*, 263–64; La Courbe, *Premier voyage*, 26, 28, 105.

112. Reglements de la Compagnie Royalle, fols. 3–4, 6, 7, 10. Drinking, quarreling, and slander were prohibited.

113. Reglements de la Compagnie Royalle, fols. 3–4, 6, 7, 10.

114. Julien Dubellay to Messieurs le Directeurs, 25 May 1724, C6 8, fol. 5, CAOM.

115. Conseil Supérieur to Messieurs les Directeurs de la Compagnie des Indes, 2 August 1737, C6 11, fol. 22, CAOM.

116. Conseil Supérieur to Messieurs les Directeurs de la Compagnie des Indes, 2 August 1737, fol. 22.

117. Adanson, Becker, and Martin, "Mémoires d'Adanson," 736.

118. Diouf, "French Colonial Policy," 671–96; Thiaw, "Digging on Contested Grounds," 132. Diouf identified four *djinn* or *rab* for four towns: Maam Kumba Bang (Saint-Louis), Maam Kumba Castel (Gorée), Maam Kumba Lambaay (Rufisque), and Lëk Daawur (Dakar), each with followings in coastal towns of Senegal.

119. *Rab* can possess adherents across gender. On *rab* and gender in Senegal, see Fatou Sow, "Gender Relations in the African Environment," in *Engendering African Social Sciences*, ed. A. Imam, Amina Mama, and Fatou Sow (Dakar: CODESRIA, 1997); Cheikh Ibrahima Niang, "Understanding Sex Between Men in Senegal: Beyond Current Linguistic and Discursive Categories," in *Routledge Handbook of Sexuality, Health and Rights*, ed. Peter Aggleton and Richard Parker (New York: Routledge, 2010), 116–24; András Zempleni, "La thérapie traditionnelle des troubles mentaux chez les Wolof et les Lebou (Sénégal): Principes," *Social Science & Medicine* 3, no. 2 (1969): 191–205; Rachel Mueller, "The Spirits Are My Neighbors: Women and the Rab Cult in Dakar, Senegal" (thesis, Macalester College, 2013).

Chapter 2

1. Deposition de Marie Baude, femme de Pinet (Jean), armurier au Sénégal, "Affaire criminelle," mémoire, 1724, COL E 336ter, CAOM (hereafter, "Affaire criminelle"), fol. 3. Many thanks to Guillaume Aubert for pointing me toward this document. The first scholarly treatment of Marie Baude was as "la femme Pinet," the *mulâtresse* wife of Jean Pinet, in Gwendolyn Midlo Hall, *Africans in Colonial Louisiana: The Development of Afro-Creole Culture in the Eighteenth Century* (Baton Rouge: Louisiana State University Press, 1995), 128. Since then, Marie has appeared in

work by Peter Caron, Jennifer Spear, and Lisa Ze Winters, who offers the most transatlantic analysis outside of the one presented here. See Peter Caron, "'Of a Nation Which the Others Do Not Understand': Bambara Slaves and African Ethnicity in Colonial Louisiana, 1718–1760," *Slavery & Abolition* 18, no. 1 (1997): 11–12; Jennifer M. Spear, *Race, Sex, and Social Order in Early New Orleans* (Baltimore: Johns Hopkins University Press, 2008), 80, 90; Lisa Ze Winters, *The Mulatta Concubine: Terror, Intimacy, Freedom, and Desire in the Black Transatlantic* (Athens: University of Georgia Press, 2016), 185n2.

2. African feminists and scholars of African women's history insist that African women's experiences not be measured against the experiences of European women or through binaries of gender transplanted from the West. Instead, scholars like Awa Thiam, Ayesha Imam, Fatou Sow, and Aminata Diaw-Cisse argue that analyzing African women means centering the social construction of gender, incorporating diverse and conflicting definitions of African identity, and acknowledging a multiplicity of oppressions and their impacts on women's lives. Rokhaya Fall-Sokhna and Sylvie Thiéblemont-Dollet, "Du genre au Sénégal: Un objet de recherche émergent," *Questions de communication* 16 (2009): 159–76; Ayesha Imam, Amina Mama, and Fatou Sow, eds., *Engendering African Social Sciences* (Dakar: CODESRIA, 1997); Awa Thiam, *La parole aux négresses* (Paris: Denoël-Gonthier, 1978); Esi Sutherland-Addy and Aminata Diaw, eds., *Women Writing Africa: West Africa and the Sahel* (New York: Feminist Press, 2005). Historians Hilary Jones, Nwando Achebe, Paulla Ebron, and Lorelle Semley draw on theories of gender and performance to describe the construction of gender in an African context, arguing ideas of gender that have emerged over time draw from constructions indigenous to African society, even as they refract constructions of gender imposed from the outside. Hilary Jones, *The Métis of Senegal: Urban Life and Politics in French West Africa* (Bloomington: Indiana University Press, 2013); Nwando Achebe, *The Female King of Colonial Nigeria: Ahebi Ugbabe* (Bloomington: Indiana University Press, 2011); Paulla A. Ebron, "Traffic in Men," in *Gendered Encounters: Challenging Cultural Boundaries and Social Hierarchies in Africa*, ed. Maria Grosz-Ngate and Omari Kokole (New York: Routledge, 2014); Lorelle D. Semley, *Mother Is Gold, Father Is Glass: Gender and Colonialism in a Yoruba Town* (Bloomington: Indiana University Press, 2010).

3. In Senegal, the details of the interaction between the *curé* (or other official) and the resident registering the act are unclear. Information from Saint-Domingue suggests the person registering the act answered a general template of questions about birth date and place, names of the mother and father, race and sex of the child, parents, and godparents and witnesses. That information could be contested by the registering official and anyone present. For example, demographer Jacques Houdaille noted a godfather who refused to sign a baptism register because it listed him as a "quarteron" instead of a "tierceron." The *curé* left a note in the margin registering the protest. Jacques Houdaille, "Trois paroisses de Saint-Domingue au XVIIIe siècle," *Population* 18, no. 1 (1963): 105–6, 105n.

4. In France, the *registres paroissiaux* became the *État Civil* or civil registers after 1792. In Senegal, a similar transition did not occur until 1830 when the Napoleonic Code was implemented in the region. See Hilary Jones, "From *Mariage à la Mode* to Weddings at Town Hall: Marriage, Colonialism, and Mixed-Race Society in Nineteenth-Century Senegal," *African Historical Studies* 38, no. 1 (2005): 37.

5. Reglements de la Compagnie Royalle du Senegal et Costes d'Affrique, 14 March 1721, C6 6, fol. 9, CAOM.

6. Louis Henry, "Une richesse démographique en fiche: Les registres paroissiaux," *Population* (French ed.) 8, no. 2 (1953): 282. See also Michel Fleury and Louis Henry, *Des registres paroissiaux a l'histoire de la population: Manuel de dépouillement et d'exploitation de l'état civil ancien* (Paris: L'Institut National d'Études Démographiques, 1956). In theory, registering a baptism, death, or marriage required a fee but it is not clear which fees were charged, how much, or whether a fee was consistently applied at either Saint-Louis or Gorée.

7. Pierre Lintingre, "La mission du Sénégal sous l'ancien régime," *Afrique Documents* 87 (1966): 207; Nathalie Reyss, "Saint Louis du Sénégal et l'époque précoloniale: L'émergence d'une société métisse originale, 1658–1854" (thèse de doctorat, Sorbonne, 1983), 219–20. In 1686, four Franciscans arrived at Saint-Louis: Pères Gaby, Tartary, Nison, and La Chaise. One remained at Saint-Louis for about a year before returning to France. The missionary priest they were replacing was on the verge of death himself. Priests and missionaries continued to arrive and fall ill or return to France within a year over the fifty years that followed. In all, sixteen missionaries or priests served in the entire Senegal concession. Joseph-Roger de Benoist, *Histoire de l'Église catholique au Sénégal: Du milieu du XVe siècle à l'aube du troisième millénaire* (Paris: Karthala, 2008), 64–65. On Catholic practices, missionary activity, and the chapel at Saint-Louis, see Benoist, *Histoire de l'Église Catholique*; Guy Thilmans, "L'église oubliée de Saint-Louis du Sénégal," *Outre-Mers Revue d'Histoire* 93, no. 350 (2006): 193–236; D. H. Jones, "The Catholic Mission and Some Aspects of Assimilation in Senegal, 1817–1852," *Journal of African History* 21, no. 3 (1980): 323–40; Jones, *Métis of Senegal*, 73–96.

8. Of 63 baptisms registered between 13 October 1730 and 5 September 1735, 33 were listed as female and 30 as male. This study focuses on the early decades of French contact at Saint-Louis and stops at 1735. The formal Saint-Louis *État Civil* continues through 1783: 790 baptisms were recorded. Acts de naissance, mariage, et décès, *État Civil de Saint-Louis du Sénégal*, 1730–1777, CAOM (hereafter, *État Civil*).

9. Acts de naissance, 10 March 1731, no. 49; 22 April 1731, no. 53; 24 June 1731, no. 56; 30 June 1731, no. 57, *État Civil*.

10. Act de naissance, 24 March 1731, no. 50, *État Civil*.

11. Act de naissance, 14 April 1732, no. 96, *État Civil*.

12. Act de naissance, 25 April 1732, no. 95, *État Civil*.

13. Fifteen acts for baptisms offered no specific birthplace. Of those fifteen, ten were listed as baptisms of slaves or those "belonging to" other residents.

14. Act de naissance, 22 June 1732, no. 105, *État Civil*.

15. Alexis de Saint-Lo, *Relation du voyage du Cap-Verd* (Paris: Chez François Targa, 1637).

16. Between 1730 and 1783, twelve marriages were recorded in Saint-Louis's parish registers. Only nineteen marriages were recorded from 1783 to 1809 and in 1818–19. Five marriages were recorded in Gorée from 1777 to 1824: *État Civil*. See also Michael David Marcson, "European-African Interaction in the Precolonial Period: Saint Louis, Senegal, 1758–1854" (Ph.D. diss., Princeton University, 1976), 19; Marie-Hélène Knight-Baylac, "La vie à Gorée de 1677 à 1789," *Revue française d'histoire d'Outre-mer* 57, no. 4 (1970): 414.

17. Act de mariage, 10 September 1733, no. 162, *État Civil*.

18. Act de naissance, 10 March 1731, no. 49, *État Civil*; Benoist, *Histoire de l'Église catholique*, 63.

19. Act de naissance, 19 October 1731, no. 75, *État Civil*.

20. Kimberly S. Hanger, *Bounded Lives, Bounded Places: Free Black Society in Colonial New Orleans, 1769–1803* (Durham, NC: Duke University Press, 1997), 105.

21. I have avoided assuming that the children of white-white unions had formally married parents, or that those without racial or African designations were white. However, if this is the case, there were four formal Catholic unions documented through baptism in registers, and four *mariages à la mode du pays*. The children of these unions were Michelle Angé (child of Pierre Anger and Angelique Bottemont), Marie (child of Antoine Flantre, a ship captain, and Marie Guerin); Olimpiate Radegonde (child of Jean Jacques Souttron and Catherine Andrieu); Françoise Madeleine (child of François Aubert and Comba Genne); Jacques Sebastien Boutelieu (child of Jean Boutilly and Angelique Bottemont); Antoine (child of Baptiste Durbey and Marie Combaceau); Barbara Arneau and Anne (children of Jacques Arnaud and Nanette Cornier); Michel Pierrette (child of Etienne le Prince and Marguerite Morel); Nicolas Anger (child of S. Avoland Denoist and an unlisted mother); and Elizabeth (child of François Marchais and Louis Aymond). Of the mothers, Nanette Cornier (*mulâtresse*) and Marie Combaceau (*négresse*) are explicitly identified in the register as people of African descent, while the name Comba Genne gestures to African descent. Marie Combaceau (Coumba Sow) was further identified "as de Pais de Fula" and also *chrestienne*. All of the children were sponsored by free African godparents. See Acts de naissance, 18 November 1733, no. 22; 10 March 1733, no. 49; 22 April 1733, no. 53; [n.d.] 1731, no. 54; 3 February 1732, no. 89; 25 April 1732, no. 95; 25 February 1733, no. 134; 2 July 1733, no. 159; 21 December 1732, no. 184; 12 February 1734, no. 192; 3 September 1734, no. 232, *État Civil*.

22. Jane I. Guyer and Samuel M. Eno Belinga, "Wealth in People as Wealth in Knowledge: Accumulation and Composition in Equatorial Africa," *Journal of African History* 36 (1995): 91–120.

23. Bernard Moitt, *Women and Slavery in the French Antilles, 1635–1848* (Bloomington: Indiana University Press, 2001), 81–83; Emily Clark and Virginia Meacham Gould, "The Feminine Face of Afro-Catholicism in New Orleans, 1727–1852," *William and Mary Quarterly* 59, no. 2 (2002): 409–48; Virginia Meacham Gould, "'A Chaos of Iniquity and Discord': Slave and Free Women of Color in the Spanish Ports of New Orleans, Mobile, and Pensacola," in *The Devil's Lane: Sex and Race in the Early South*, ed. Catherine Clinton and Michele Gillespie (New York: Oxford University Press, 1997). On missionaries in the French Atlantic, see Sue Peabody, "'A Dangerous Zeal': Catholic Missions to Slaves in the French Antilles, 1635–1800," *French Historical Studies* 25 (Winter 2002): 53–90; Cécile Vidal, "Caribbean Louisiana: Church, Métissage, and the Language of Race in the Mississippi Colony During the French Period," in *Louisiana: Crossroads of the Atlantic World*, ed. Cécile Vidal (Philadelphia: University of Pennsylvania Press, 2013), 125–46; Guillaume Aubert, "'The Blood of France': Race and Purity of Blood in the French Atlantic World," *William and Mary Quarterly* 61 (2004): 439–78; Spear, *Race, Sex, and Social Order*.

24. Clark, "Feminine Face," 424–25; Hanger, *Bounded Lives, Bounded Places*, 105–6.

25. Jones, *Métis of Senegal*, 37–38.

26. Jones, *Métis of Senegal*.

27. Acts de naissance, 18 November 1730, no. 22; 20 October 1731, no. 76; 15 April 1732, no. 97, *État Civil*. Olimpiate's baptism included Anne and Nicolas as godparents as well as Pierre Aubry and Marie Baude, *mulâtresse*, as witnesses.

28. Act de naissance, 22 June 1732, no. 104, *État Civil*.

29. Act de naissance, 22 June 1732, no. 105, *État Civil*.

30. Act de naissance, 13 October 1730, no. 2, *État Civil*.

31. By 1766, he would be described by British officials at Saint-Louis (and by himself) as the mayor and, in at least one account, would be holding Mass and church services in his and

Marie-Isabelle's home in the absence of a priest in the town. Lintingre, "La mission du Sénégal," 278; Thilmans, "L'église oubliée," 197–98; Marcson, "European-African Interaction," 57–58.

32. The nineteenth-century writer Abbé David Boilat was the *métis* son of a *signare* and born at Saint-Louis. He became a man of letters and occupied posts as a teacher, priest, and historian. In his 1840 study of Senegal society, he noted that Saint-Louis slaveholders rarely baptized their slaves and did so only to free them. In the first decades of the eighteenth century, slaveholding residents of the *comptoirs* did baptize their slaves on occasion and no acts of *liberté* have been uncovered. If manumission by baptism occurred in this earlier time period, baptized slaves may have been allowed to live as free in a manner similar to *libres de fait* or *libres de savanne* in the Antilles. See David Boilat, *Esquisses sénégalaises: Physionomie du pays, peuplades, commerce, religions, passé et avenir, récits et légendes* (Paris: P. Bertrand, 1853), 213. On *libres de fait*, see Bernard Moitt, "In the Shadow of the Plantation: Women of Color and the *Libres de Fait* of Martinique and Guadeloupe, 1685–1848," in *Beyond Bondage: Free Women of Color in the Americas*, ed. David Barry Gaspar and Darlene Clark Hine (Urbana: University of Illinois Press, 2004).

33. Acts de naissance, 16 February 1732, no. 91; 24 February 1732, no. 92, *État Civil*.

34. Acts de naissance, 19 December 1735, no. 290; 23 April 1779, no. 685, *État Civil*.

35. Messieurs les Directeurs de la Compagnie des Indes to Conseil Superieur du Senegal, 6 September 1736, C6 11, fol. 27, CAOM.

36. Devaulx to Compagnie des Indes, 14 June 1736, C 6 11. In another example, François le Luc, the Afro-European son of Pierre le Luc, petitioned for his father's property after Pierre's death. Reponse au memoire, 6 December 1736, fol. 2, CAOM.

37. Estat des appointements qui sont deüs aux Employez de la Compagnie des Indes à la Concession du Senegal par les Comptes arrestez par Mr. Brüe Directeur et Commandant general le 30 Avril 1720, 30 April 1720, C6 5, fol. 3, CAOM.

38. Memoire sur la concession du Senegal: Nouvel arrangement touchant la concession du Senegal, 8 October 1734, C6 11, fol. 57, CAOM.

39. Directeurs to Conseil, 6 September 1736, fol. 27.

40. Aissata Kane Lo, *De la signare à la diriyanké sénégalaise: Trajectoires féminines et visions partagées* (Dakar: L'Harmattan Sénégal, 2014), 65–67; George E. Brooks, *Eurafricans in Western Africa: Commerce, Social Status, Gender, and Religious Observance from the Sixteenth to the Eighteenth Century* (Athens: Ohio University Press, 2003), 211–12.

41. Abdoulaye Bara Diop, *La famille Wolof: Tradition et changement* (Paris: Karthala Editions, 1985), 244–45; Loretta E. Bass and Fatou Sow. "Senegalese Families: The Confluence of Ethnicity, History, and Social Change," in *African Families at the Turn of the 21st Century*, ed. Yaw Oheneba-Sakyi and Baffour K. Takyi, 83–102 (Westport, CT: Praeger, 2006), 87; James F. Searing, *West African Slavery and Atlantic Commerce* (Cambridge: Cambridge University Press, 1993), 15–17.

42. Lo, *De la signare*, 24–25.

43. André Delcourt, *La France et les établissements Français au Sénégal entre 1713 et 1763* (Dakar: Institut Fondamental d'Afrique Noire, 1952), 121.

44. Anne Gusban to Conseil de Gorée, 6 July 1737, C6 11, CAOM.

45. Gusban to Conseil de Gorée, 6 July 1737, fol. 2.

46. Conseil Supérieur de Senegal to Messieurs le Directeurs de la Compagnie des Indes, 25 May 1737, C6 11, fol. 23, CAOM.

47. Searing, *West African Slavery*, 96–98; Lo, *De la signare*, 14.

48. Rolle general des blancs et nègres au service de la Compagnies des Indes a la concession du Senegal les 1 May 1736, 1 May 1736, C6 11, CAOM.

49. Searing, *West African Slavery*, 93.

50. Lo, *De la signare*, 66. This is the historical memory that at least some descendants of *signares* at Saint-Louis retain. Drawing in part on interviews conducted within the *signare* community at Saint-Louis, Lo notes, "En choisissant de s'unir aux Europpéens, les femmes prenaient le risque de rompre, et de manière définitive, les amarres avec la société Wolof. . . . Toutefois, les profits qu'elles espéraient tirer de ces unions étaient tels que certaines firent le pari de la rupture, quitte à essuyer par la suite les pires railleries de la société ambiante" (By choosing to partner with Europeans, the women took the risk of breaking, permanently, their ties with Wolof society. . . . However, the profits they hoped to derive from these unions were such that some gambled on the rupture, and were subsequently left to suffer the worst kinds of jeers from society around them).

51. Michel Adanson, "Mémoires d'Adanson sur le Sénégal et l'île de Gorée," ed. Charles Becker and Victor Martin, *Bulletin de Institut Fondamental d'Afrique Noire* 42, no. B4 (1980): 736.

52. Adanson, "Mémoires d'Adanson."

53. Michel Adanson, Pièces instructives concernant l'Ile Goré voisine du Cap-Verd en Afrike, avec un project et des vues utiles relativement au nouvel établissement de kaiene, May–June 1763, C6 15, fol. 6v., CAOM. Adanson suggests that slaves seeking protection among the *habitants* may have been escaping famine or slavery in other areas, or simply hoping to alleviate their circumstances for a time.

54. Jacques Doumet de Siblas, Charles Becker, and Victor Martin, "Mémoire inédit de Doumet (1769)," *Bulletin de l'Institut fondamental de l'Afrique Noir* 36B, no. 1 (1974): 34.

55. Dénombrement des habitants natifs du Senegal et de ceux de Podor, Galam et Grande Terre, July 1781, 22G1, ANS.

56. Mark Hinchman, *Portrait of an Island: The Architecture and Material Culture of Gorée, Sénégal, 1758–1837* (Lincoln: University of Nebraska Press, 2015), 91.

57. "Deposition du nommé André," "Affaire criminelle," fols. 11–12.

58. "Deposition du nommé Charles le Fure," "Affaire criminelle," fols. 7–9.

59. "Deposition du Marie Baude," "Affaire criminelle," fols. 4–5.

60. Aisha K. Finch, *Rethinking Slave Rebellion in Cuba: La Escalera and the Insurgencies of 1841–1844* (Chapel Hill: University of North Carolina Press), 2015. On dissemblance and sexual violence, see Darlene Clark Hine, "Rape and the Inner Lives of Black Women in the Middle West," *Signs* 14, no. 4 (1989): 912–20.

61. In official documentation, Jean Pinet described himself as "natif de Rochefort." See Gilles Havard and Cécile Vidal, *Histoire de l'Amérique française* (Paris: Flammarion, 2003), 125, 144; Philip P. Boucher, *France and the American Tropics to 1700: Tropics of Discontent?* (Baltimore: Johns Hopkins University Press, 2008), 169.

62. "Affaire criminelle," fol. 1; Estat des appointements qui sont deüs aux Employez de la Compagnie des Indes à la Concession du Senegal par les Comptes arrestez par Mr. Brüe Directeur et Commandant general le 30 Avril 1720, 30 April 1720, C6 6, fol. 4, CAOM. The Company listed "Jean Pinet, Armurier" at Gorée as due a credit of 177 livres and 10 sols. Pinet's credit was comparable to other masons, blacksmiths, and other artisans on the island (whose credit ranged from 87 to 400 livres, and much higher than many sailors and cabin boys [30–50 livres]). For comparison, at the same time, a credit of 8,000 livres was due to the then-governor of Gorée, François Duval.

63. Another hint to the status both Baude and Pinet enjoyed is the use of the appellation "Sr." in official documentation. Sr. or "S." was short for "Sieur," an honorific reserved for men of property, wealth, or social status in the French colonies. As yet, there is no further information available on "S. Baude." The use of "Sr." in official documentation suggests the position Jean Pinet had at the Senegal concession, a position likely due in part to his conjugal tie to one of the island's African women.

64. St. Robert to Messieurs les Directeurs, 24 May 1721, C6 6, fol. 16, CAOM.

65. Presenting the marriage officiant a gift of an adolescent slave boy is a significant gift. It gestures to Marie Baude's and Jean's status within the island's hierarchy.

66. Searing, *West African Slavery*, 93–164; Boubacar Barry, *Senegambia and the Atlantic Slave Trade* (Cambridge: Cambridge University Press, 1998), 78; Brooks, *Eurafricans in Western Africa*, 61.

67. Brooks, *Eurafricans in Western Africa*, 61, 207. See also the memoire sur le departement de Gorée et le traité fait par M. Ducasse avec diverse Rois negres, June 1728, DPFC XIV Mémoires 76 no. 23, CAOM.

68. Voluire to the Ministry of the Marine, 6 May 1729 in Ser. B3 330, fol. 45; Voluire to the Ministry of the Marine, 23 May 1729, fols. 51–52, ANM. See also Hall, *Africans in Colonial Louisiana*, 92.

69. In 1721, Périer de Salvert issued instructions for French living at the *comptoirs*. They included, among other things, rules against "cohabitating" with "the *negresses*," selling resident Africans across the Atlantic, and interracial socializing (drinking together, dancing). Règlements de la Compagnie Royalle du Senegal et Costes d'Affrique, 14 March 1721, C6 6, CAOM.

70. Rolle general des blancs et negres au service de la Compagnies des Indes a la concession du Senegal les 1 May 1736, 1 May 1736, C6 11, CAOM; Searing, *West African Slavery*, 93.

71. Michel Jajolet de la Courbe, *Premier voyage du Sieur de La Courbe fait a la Coste D'Afrique en 1685* (Paris: E. Champion, 1913), 26, 28.

72. "Deposition du nommé André," "Affaire criminelle"; "Deposition du nommé Bazil," "Affaire criminelle," fol. 13. When written by French Company officials' perspectives, "Gambia" in official documentation may refer to an ethnicity or to the riverine region or the British fort on the Gambia. In this instance, it is difficult to tell which meaning French officials intended. However, the witness's name, "Basil" (written also as "Bazil" in documents), suggests he may have been connected or arrived at Saint-Louis from British-influenced trading networks and communities either in Gambia or elsewhere.

73. Acts de naissance, 27 January 1731, no. 87; 25 April 1732, no. 95; 1 September 1734, no. 226, *État Civil*. Guette was also spelled Guet.

74. Pierre Charpentier to Nicolas Deprès de St. Robert, 12 October 1722, C6 7, fol. 4, CAOM.

75. La Courbe, *Premier voyage*; St. Robert to Messieurs les Directeurs, 18 June 1725, C6 9, CAOM.

76. St. Robert to Messieurs, 18 June 1725, fol. 51.

77. Act de naissance, 1 August 1732, no. 107, CAOM.

78. Sr. Robert to Messieurs, 18 June 1725, fols. 30–31.

79. La Courbe, *Premier voyage*, 204. See also George E. Brooks, "The Signares of Saint-Louis and Goree: Women Entrepreneurs in Eighteenth-Century Senegal," in *Women in Africa: Studies in Social and Economic Change*, ed. Nancy J. Hafkin and Edna G. Bay (Stanford, CA: Stanford University Press, 1976), 34–36; Brooks, *Eurafricans in Western Africa*, 211–12. Two years later,

Hodges started a regional conflict when he attacked a woman companion of Maguimar or La Belinguere's at a party. According to La Courbe, Maguimar, a "certain Portugaise" and a woman of considerable status ("regaled splendidly") in the region, went to the English fort in the Gambia with her entourage. After drinking, "one of them quarreled with the English, apparently for some gallantry" and Hodges stabbed her ("coup de couteau"). The king of Barre (Niumi) arrested the *commis* and confiscated English goods as restitution. According to La Courbe, the reaction of the king was "a little extravagant," a response that might be squared with his description of Maguimar and her entourage as "women of mediocre virtue." La Courbe, *Premier voyage*, 270–71.

80. "Affaire criminelle," fols. 1–2.

81. Hartman asks, "What is required to imagine a free state or to tell an impossible story?" Saidiya V. Hartman, "Venus in Two Acts," *Small Axe* 12, no. 2 (2008): 10. See also Christopher Miller, *The French Atlantic Triangle: Literature and Culture of the Slave Trade* (Durham, NC: Duke University Press, 2008). On the "impossible story," see essays in Michel-Rolph Trouillot, *Silencing the Past: Power and the Production of History* (Boston: Beacon Press, 2012); and Laurent Dubois, "An Enslaved Enlightenment: Rethinking the Intellectual History of the French Atlantic," *Social History* 31, no. 1 (2006): 1–14.

82. Dominique Harcourt Lamiral, *L'Affrique et le peuple affriquain, considérés sous tous leurs rapports avec notre commerce & nos colonies* (Paris: chez Dessene, 1789).

Chapter 3

Source of epigraph: Cdt. Préville-Quinet, "Journaux du bord de *La Galathée*," Archives de la Marine, Service Hydrographique (hereafter, "Journaux du bord"), 4 JJ 16: 35 bis, 18 January 1729, Louisiana Colonial Records Collection, Library of Congress, Washington, DC. "Pris une mulâtresse passagere pour la Missisipi."

1. For an example of a passenger experience aboard a slave ship, see B. W. Higman, *Proslavery Priest: The Atlantic World of John Lindsay, 1729–1788* (Kingston, Jamaica: University of the West Indies Press, 2011).

2. "Journaux du bord," 18 January 1729; "Deliberations prives en l'assemblé des Directeurs," 29 June 1729, C13A 11, fols. 349–50, CAOM.

3. There is considerable debate on whether Gorée was an important port of embarkation for slaves being shipped to the Americas. This debate centers on research conducted by Joseph Ndiaye, former director of the "House of Slaves" in Gorée, and his claim that the building housed and funneled millions of slaves into the Atlantic slave trade. Economic historians of the slave trade, including Philip Curtin, David Eltis, and David Richardson, argue against this figure and against either Saint-Louis or Gorée playing a large role furnishing captives to the Americas. According to their research, Senegambian ports supplied only a few hundred slaves per year, in comparison to the tens of thousands shipped from ports in the Bight of Benin or West Central Africa. On the debate itself, see Ibrahima Thioub, "Regard critique sur les lectures Africaines de l'esclavage et de la traite Atlantique," *Historiens-Geographes du Sénégal* (special issue: *L'esclave et ses traites en Afrique, discours mémoriels et savoirs interdits*) 8 (2009): 15–28; Ralph A. Austen, "The Slave Trade as History and Memory: Confrontations of Slaving Voyage Documents and Communal Traditions," *William and Mary Quarterly* 58, no. 1 (1997): 229–44; Ana Lucia Araujo, *Shadows of the Slave Past: Memory, Heritage, and Slavery* (New York: Routledge, 2014), 58–64. For all of my figures

on slave trading between Africa and the Americas, I have relied on data from the Voyages database, and the numbers summarized most recently in Eltis and Richardson's published atlas. The database and atlas offer the most comprehensive statistics currently available on the transatlantic slave trade. According to the Voyages database, 102,945 enslaved Africans embarked from Saint-Louis, Gorée, or French Africa (Gorée or Senegal) on 536 total voyages. These figures would make the slave trade from Gorée 0.3 percent of the total slave trade; from Saint-Louis 0.7 percent of the trade; and from French Africa (Gorée or Senegal) less than 0.1 percent. For figures for Saint-Louis, Gorée, and French Africa from 1514 to 1866, see http://slavevoyages.org/voyages/lrKu6BNF; for percentages, see the summary tables of the trade at http://slavevoyages.org/voyages/ZiScLM3Q (both accessed 11 January 2018). The majority of French commerce in slaves was conducted from the ports of Ouidah, Malembo, and Loango. See David Eltis and David Richardson, *Atlas of the Transatlantic Slave Trade* (New Haven, CT: Yale University Press, 2010), 33.

4. Sowande' Mustakeem has argued against mystifying either the slave ship or the Middle Passage, calling for more work historicizing "the process of unmaking" begun in warehouses across the African coast and ending with disembarkation. Sowande' M. Mustakeem, *Slavery at Sea: Terror, Sex, and Sickness in the Middle Passage* (Urbana: University of Illinois Press, 2016), 5–7. See also Stephanie E. Smallwood, *Saltwater Slavery: A Middle Passage from Africa to American Diaspora* (Cambridge, MA: Harvard University Press, 2007).

5. Mustakeem, *Slavery at Sea*, 5–7. The mystification of the slave ship stems from horror of the trade, and the ship's ability to make that horror mobile and immobile, historical and ahistorical, all at once. Gilroy described the slave ship as "the living means by which the points within the Atlantic world were joined. They were mobile elements that stood for the shifting spaces in between the fixed places that they connected. Accordingly, they need to be thought of as cultural and political units rather than abstract embodiments of the triangular trade." Paul Gilroy, *The Black Atlantic: Modernity and Double Consciousness* (New York: Verso, 1993), 16.

6. Smallwood, *Saltwater Slavery*, 6.

7. Gomez argued that the first phase of the Middle Passage was not embarkation from the coast but the point of capture. Michael A. Gomez, *Exchanging Our Country Marks: The Transformation of African Identities in the Colonial and Antebellum South* (Chapel Hill: University of North Carolina Press, 1998), 155. Mustakeem, in *Slavery at Sea*, described the three phases of the Middle Passage as warehousing, transport, and delivery.

8. Jean-Baptiste Labat, *Nouveau voyage aux isles de l'Amerique* (Paris: G. Vagelier Pere, 1722), 4:446–50. Translation from James H. Sweet, *Domingos Álvares, African Healing, and the Intellectual History of the Atlantic World* (Chapel Hill: University of North Carolina Press, 2011), 44.

9. Voyages, Voyage ID# 33684, https://slavevoyages.org/voyage/database#searchId=3Spto3ma (accessed 8 March 2019); Carolyn Arena, "Indian Slaves from Guiana in Seventeenth-Century Barbados," *Ethnohistory* 64, no. 1 (2017): 65–90; Alan Gallay, *The Indian Slave Trade: The Rise of the English Empire in the American South, 1670–1717* (New Haven, CT: Yale University Press, 2003); Gabriel de Avilez Rocha, "Maroons in the Montes: Toward a Political Ecology of Marronage in the Sixteenth-Century Caribbean," in *Early Modern Black Diaspora Studies: A Critical Anthology*, ed. Cassandra L. Smith, Nicholas R. Jones, and Miles Grier (Cham, Switzerland: Palgrave Macmillan, 2018), 15–35.

10. Philip D. Curtin, *The Atlantic Slave Trade: A Census* (Madison: University of Wisconsin Press, 1969), 21–22; Patrick Manning, *The African Diaspora: A History Through Culture* (New York: Columbia University Press, 2010), 80.

11. Bernard Moitt, *Women and Slavery in the French Antilles, 1635–1848* (Bloomington: Indiana University Press, 2001), 3–4. Enslaved Africans were to work for a term of three years before being transported from the colony or sold.

12. Jean-Baptiste Labat, *Nouvelle relation de l'Afrique Occidentale* (Paris: Pierre-François Giffart, 1722), 4:232–33.

13. B. F. French, *Historical Collections of Louisiana and Florida* (New York: J. Sabin & Sons, 1869), 3:101–3.

14. Smallwood, *Saltwater Slavery*, 43.

15. Hortense J. Spillers, "Mama's Baby, Papa's Maybe: An American Grammar Book," *Diacritics* 17, no. 2 (1987): 65–81. On the gendered violence of selecting "aesthetically pleasing" slaves for the slave trade, see Mustakeem, *Slavery at Sea*, 39–40.

16. Mustakeem, *Slavery at Sea*, 38–40; Smallwood, *Saltwater Slavery*, 158–59.

17. Clarence J. Munford, *The Black Ordeal of Slavery and Slave Trading in the French West Indies, 1625–1715* (Lewiston, NY: E. Mellen Press, 1991), 2:307.

18. Munford, *Black Ordeal*, 2:426. Blenac, one of the architects of the 1685 *Code Noir*, chose eleven *nègres des choix* for himself from the *St. Jean d'Afrique* in 1714. Other examples are found in Munford, *Black Ordeal*, 2:422, 423, 425, 426.

19. Walter Johnson, "To Remake the World: Slavery, Racial Capitalism, and Justice," *Boston Review*, 20 February 2018, http://bostonreview.net/forum/walter-johnson-to-remake-the-world (accessed 9 March 2019); see also Walter Johnson, "Introduction: The Future Store," in *The Chattel Principle: Internal Slave Trades in the Americas*, ed. Walter Johnson (New Haven, CT: Yale University Press, 2008); Walter Johnson, *Soul by Soul: Life Inside the Antebellum Slave Market* (Cambridge, MA: Harvard University Press, 1999).

20. Joseph C. Miller, "Domiciled and Dominated: Slaving as a History of Women," in *Women and Slavery: The Modern Atlantic*, ed. Gwyn Campbell, Suzanne Miers, and Joseph C. Miller (Athens: Ohio University Press, 2007).

21. C. Riley Snorton, *Black on Both Sides: A Racial History of Trans Identity* (Minneapolis: University of Minnesota Press, 2017).

22. Eltis and Richardson, *Atlas*, 165. Between 1701 and 1807, in the slave trade from Senegambia to the Caribbean, female slaves were 33.1 percent of the trade; male slaves were 33.1 percent; children were 17.4 percent; and adults were 82.6 percent. One hundred and thirteen voyages provided data on gender; 104 provided data on age.

23. Eltis and Richardson, *Atlas*, 189.

24. *Relation très fidèle du voyage du Sr. François, directeur de la Compagnie royal du Sénégal et côtes d'Afrique, au Sénégal, Gorée, et lieux dépendants de la concession de la dite Compagnie, par le sieur Mathelot*, 1687, fol. 224v, Bibliothèque Nationale de France. See also Jean Barbot, *A Description of the Coasts of North and South Guinea* (London: Churchill Brothers, 1732), 5:530–31. On the Dutch raid, see Max Adrien Guérout, "La prise du fort d'Arguin par Ducasse en 1678 et ses répercussins sur les relations entre la Compagnie du Sénégal et les Maures," in *Saint-Louis et l'esclavage: Actes du Symposium international sur la traite négrière à Saint-Louis du Sénégal et dans son arrière-pays (Saint-Louis, 18, 19 et 20 décembre 1998)*, ed. Djibril Samb (Dakar: IFAN, Université Cheikh Anta Diop de Dakar, 2000).

25. Raina Croff, "Village des Bambaras: An Archaeology of Domestic Slavery and Urban Transformation on Gorée Island, Senegal, A.D. 17th–19th Centuries" (Ph.D. diss., Yale University, 2009), 13.

26. Proces verbal de la revolte des captifs arrivée a Gorée, 19 October 1724, C6 8, fol. 2, CAOM; Gwendolyn Midlo Hall, *Africans in Colonial Louisiana: The Development of Afro-Creole Culture in the Eighteenth Century* (Baton Rouge: Louisiana State University Press, 1995), 68.

27. Pruneau de Pommegorge, *Description de la nigritie* (Paris: Chez Maradan, 1789), 27–28. For examples of French ethnic typology of Africans in the trade, see Eugène Saulnier, *Une compagnie a privilège au XIXe siècle: La Compagnie de Galam au Sénégal* (Paris: Émile Larose, 1921), 14; Jean Mettas, "Pour une histoire de la traite des noirs française: Sources et problèmes," *Outre-Mers Revue d'Histoire* 62, no. 226 (1975): 41; Munford, *Black Ordeal*, 3:357n21. Europeans made broad generalizations about Africans including by region (i.e., "Senegal"), religion (i.e., "Moors"), or broadly as African (i.e., "Guinea"). On ethnicity and the slave trade, see Paul E. Lovejoy, *Transformations in Slavery: A History of Slavery in Africa* (New York: Cambridge University Press, 2000); Paul E. Lovejoy and David V. Trotman, eds., *Trans-Atlantic Dimensions of Ethnicity in the African Diaspora* (London: Continuum, 2003); Gwendolyn Midlo Hall, *Slavery and African Ethnicities in the Americas: Restoring the Links* (Chapel Hill: University of North Carolina Press, 2007); Ibrahima Seck, *Bouki Fait Gombo: A History of the Slave Community of Habitation Haydel (Whitney Plantation) Louisiana, 1750–1860* (New Orleans: University of New Orleans Press, 2014). Seck notes Wolof ("Senegal"), Fulbe ("Poulard"), and Moor ("Nard") were the most frequently documented ethnicities in Louisiana. Seck, *Bouki Fait Gombo*, 42.

28. Lovejoy, *Transformations*, 60–61.

29. Seck, *Bouki Fait Gombo*, 38. On Segu's history and politics, see Richard Roberts, *Warriors, Merchants, and Slaves: The State and the Economy in the Middle Niger Valley, 1700–1914* (Stanford, CA: Stanford University Press, 1987).

30. James F. Searing, "'No Kings, No Lords, No Slaves': Ethnicity and Rebellion Among the Sereer-Safen of Western Bawol, 1700–1914," *Journal of African History* 43 (2002): 407–29; James F. Searing, *"God Alone Is King": Islam and Emancipation in Senegal: The Wolof Kingdoms of Kajoor and Bawol, 1859–1914* (Portsmouth, NH: Heinemann, 2002).

31. Voyages, Principal Place of Slave Landing: Gulf Coast, Year Range 1516–1769, https://slavevoyages.org/voyage/database#searchId=yNnoZHjI (accessed 14 March 2019).

32. Voyages, Voyage ID #32041, https://slavevoyages.org/voyage/database#searchId=yNno ZHjI (accessed 14 March 2019).

33. The percentages are as follows: *La Néréide* (1721, 22.4 percent female), *La Fortuné* (1721, 21.1 percent female), *L'Afriquain* (1721, 29.1 percent female), *Le Duc du Maine* (1721, 34.7 percent female); *L'Expédition* (1723, 22.7 percent female), *Le Courrier de Bourbon* (1723, 40 percent female); *Le Mutine* (1725, 46.6 percent female), *La Flore* (1728, 10 percent female), *Le Saint Louis* (1730, 20.3 percent female).

34. Brenda E. Stevenson, "The Question of the Slave Female Community and Culture in the American South: Methodological and Ideological Approaches," *Journal of African American History* (2007): 84. Stevenson noted the importance of "slave female provenance, local prominence, and cultural presence" as categories of analysis. See also Morgan on slave-ship registers in Jennifer L. Morgan, "Accounting for 'the Most Excruciating Torment': Gender, Slavery, and Trans-Atlantic Passages," *History of the Present* 6 (2016): 184–207.

35. Simone Browne notes, "The violent regulation of blackness as spectacle and as disciplinary combined in the racializing surveillance of the slave system." Simone Browne, *Dark Matters: On the Surveillance of Blackness* (Durham, NC: Duke University Press, 2015), 42. Aimé Césaire used "thingification" or *chosification* to capture the fungibility of New World blackness. Aimé Césaire, *Discourse on Colonialism* (New York: Monthly Review Press, 2001).

36. Voyages, Voyage ID #33116, https://slavevoyages.org/voyage/database#searchId=yNnoZHjI (accessed 14 March 2019); Jean Mettas, Serge Daget, and Michelle Daget, eds., *Répertoire des expéditions négrières françaises au XVIIIe siècle* (Paris: Société Française d'Histoire d'Outre-Mer, 1984), 2:684–85. *Le Duc du Maine* transported 250 enslaved African women, men, and some children to Dauphine Island.

37. Voyages, Principal Place of Slave Purchase: Ouidah, Year Range: 1717–1721, https://slavevoyages.org/voyage/database#searchId=oeFSz2mJ (accessed 14 March 2019). In a few years, Ouidah would be conquered by the kingdom of Dahomey (1724) and en route to becoming one of the most active and important slave-trading ports in West Africa. See Robin Law, *Ouidah: The Social History of a West African Slaving "Port," 1727–1892* (Athens: Ohio University Press, 2004).

38. Hall, *Africans in Colonial Louisiana*, 63.

39. "Instructions pour le S. Herpin comandant du vaisseau *l'Aurore* destiné pour la traite des nègres à la coste de Guynee, July 4, 1718," in Elizabeth Donnan, *Documents Illustrative of the History of the Slave Trade to America* (Washington, DC: W. F. Roberts Company, 1930), 4:636–38. On gender and rice cultivation in Africa and the Americas, see Judith Ann Carney, *Black Rice: The African Origins of Rice Cultivation in the Americas* (Cambridge, MA: Harvard University Press, 2001). For a counterpoint, see David Eltis, Philip Morgan, and David Richardson, "Black, Brown, or White? Color-Coding American Commercial Rice Cultivation with Slave Labor," *American Historical Review* 115, no. 1 (2010): 164–71.

40. Carney, *Black Rice*; Edda L. Fields-Black, *Deep Roots: Rice Farmers in West Africa and the African Diaspora* (Bloomington: Indiana University Press, 2008).

41. Voyages, Voyage ID #32468, https://slavevoyages.org/voyage/database#searchId=yNno ZHjI (accessed 14 March 2019); Hall, *Africans in Colonial Louisiana*, 65–66; St. Robert to Messieurs les Directeurs de Compagnie des Indes, 20 March 1721, C6 6, fol. 15; CAOM.

42. Voyages, Voyage ID #32041, https://slavevoyages.org/voyage/database#searchId=yNno ZHjI (accessed 14 March 2019). A sailor is killed by a shark at Cabinda. Mettas et al., *Répertoire*, 2:240.

43. French, *Historical Collections*, 3:87.

44. Voyages, Voyage ID # 32473, https://slavevoyages.org/voyage/database#searchId=yNno ZHjI (accessed 14 March 2019); Hall, *Africans in Colonial Louisiana*, 65–66.

45. Mettas et al., *Répertoire*, 2:406, 2:557; St. Robert to Messieurs les Directeurs de Compagnie des Indes, February 1723, C6 7, CAOM; Dubellay to Messieurs les Directeurs de Compagnie des Indes, 1 June 1723, C6 6, CAOM; St. Robert to Messieurs les Directeurs, 24 May 1721, C6 6, CAOM; Memoire sur le Commerce, 23 March 1723, C6 7, CAOM.

46. Hall, *Africans in Colonial Louisiana*, 62, 64, 58; Mettas et al., *Répertoire*, 2:684, 687.

47. Until it was outlawed in 1715, Company directors, lieutenants, governors-general, and other highly placed officials in the French Antilles made a practice of confiscating the "most handsome" slaves from the rest of the cargo for their own purposes. Munford, *Black Ordeal*, 2:417–26.

48. Mettas et al., *Répertoire*, 2:575. After spending months along Senegal's coast securing captives at Saint-Louis and Gorée, the captain of *L'Annibal* died at Saint-Louis and the ship was forced to wait for a new one. *L'Annibal* finally departed for Louisiana and detoured at Cap Français, in Saint-Domingue. At Cap Français, the new captain also expired, for undeclared reasons, and the ship was again forced to wait before proceeding. As a result, *L'Annibal* embarked from Senegal with over three hundred slaves; only half arrived in Louisiana.

49. David P. Geggus, "The French Slave Trade: An Overview," *William and Mary Quarterly* 58, no. 1 (2001): 126–27.

50. French, *Historical Collections*, 3:101–3.

51. Hall, *Africans in Colonial Louisiana*, 64; Mettas et al., *Répertoire*, 2:240.

52. Hall, *Africans in Colonial Louisiana*, 67.

53. La Chaise to the Directors of the Company, 18 October 1723, C13A 7, HNOC, 51–88. See also *MPA*, 2:372–73; Mettas et al., *Répertoire*, 2:406; Hall, *Africans in Colonial Louisiana*, 67.

54. Mettas et al., *Répertoire*, 2:557.

55. "Les avoir exposées toutes les deux sur un canon pour être fustigées" (Had them both exposed on the cannon to be whipped). Mettas et al., *Répertoire*, 2:557.

56. Mettas et al., *Répertoire*, 2:557.

57. Mettas et al., *Répertoire*, 2:580. On the slave ship "the gendering of racial violence is highlighted, while women's leadership and resistance in insurrections is diagrammatically and textually absented." Browne, *Dark Matters*, 49.

58. Mettas et al., *Répertoire*, 2:581. A few days after the women attacked Bart, officials arrested another six slaves from *L'Annibal*, for security reasons.

59. Hall, *Africans in Colonial Louisiana*, 89.

60. Mustakeem, *Slavery at Sea*, 129.

61. On *rab* and djinn in Senegal, see Fatou Sow, "Gender Relations in the African Environment," in *Engendering African Social Sciences*, ed. A. Imam, Amina Mama, and Fatou Sow (Dakar: CODESRIA, 1997), 254–57; Mamadou Diouf, "The French Colonial Policy of Assimilation and the Civility of the Originaires of the Four Communes (Senegal): A Nineteenth Century Globalization Project.," *Development & Change* 29, no. 4 (1998), 671–96; Ibrahima Thiaw. "Digging on Contested Grounds: Archaeology and the Commemoration of Slavery on Gorée Island, Senegal," in *New Perspectives in Global Public Archaeology*, ed. Katsuyuki Okamura and Akira Matsuda, 127–38. (New York: Springer, 2011), 132.

62. By this point, Company officials were instructing ships like *La Mutine* to bypass Grenada to avoid exchanging slaves. The captain of *La Mutine* had stopped in Grenada anyway.

63. Mettas et al., *Répertoire*, 2:572; Hall, *Africans in Louisiana*, 72, on Adrien Pauger, the royal engineer, using slaves in public works.

64. On reading "along the bias grain" as historical practice, see Marisa J. Fuentes, *Dispossessed Lives: Enslaved Women, Violence, and the Archive* (Philadelphia: University of Pennsylvania Press, 2016).

65. *L'Aurore* was held before being allowed to embark because the governor needed the ship for transportation and supplies.

66. *La Diane* left Ouidah in October 1728 and suffered a similar fate as *L'Annibal* when the captain died at port and they were forced to wait for a new one before leaving Benin. Of about 460, 50 died en route.

67. Mettas et al., *Répertoire*, 2:576; Kenneth F. Kiple and Brian T. Higins, "Mortality Caused by Dehydration During the Middle Passage," in *The Atlantic Slave Trade: Effects on Economies, Societies and Peoples in Africa, the Americas, and Europe*, ed. Joseph E. Inikori and Stanley L. Engerman (Durham, NC: Duke University Press, 1992), 325–27; Sowande' Mustakeem, "'I Never Have Such a Sickly Ship Before': Diet, Disease, and Mortality in 18th-Century Atlantic Slaving Voyages," *Journal of African American History* 93, no. 4 (1 October 2008): 485.

68. La Chaise to the Directors, 18 October 1723, C13A 7, fols. 51–88.

69. Édouard Glissant, *Le Discours Antillais* (Paris: Gallimard, 1997).

70. Spillers, "Mama's Baby," 72.

71. The Compagnie des Indes Occidentales was based at L'Orient. Voyages, Voyage ID #32905, https://slavevoyages.org/voyage/database#searchId=yNnoZHjI (accessed March 14, 2019).

72. "Journaux du bord."

73. Délibérations du Conseil Supérieur de la Louisiana, 26 January 1726, C13A 9, fol. 329, HNOC.

74. In 1718, the French Crown granted the colony of Louisiana to the Compagnie d'Occident. Two years later, the Compagnie d'Occident was absorbed, with several other French trading companies, into the Compagnie des Indes. Cécile Vidal, "French Louisiana in the Age of the Companies, 1712–1731," in *Constructing Early Modern Empires: Proprietary Ventures in the Atlantic World, 1500–1750,* ed. Louis H. Roper and Bertrand Van Ruymbeke (Leiden: Brill, 2007), 148. See also Cécile Vidal, *Caribbean New Orleans: Empire, Race, and the Making of a Slave Society* (Chapel Hill: University of North Carolina Press, 2019).

75. Shannon Lee Dawdy, *Building the Devil's Empire: French Colonial New Orleans* (Chicago: University of Chicago Press, 2008), 150–53, on *forçats.* On white settlers and *engagés,* see Jerah Johnson, "Colonial New Orleans: A Fragment of the Eighteenth-Century French Ethos," in *Creole New Orleans: Race and Americanization,* ed. Arnold R. Hirsch and Joseph Logsdon (Baton Rouge: Louisiana State University Press, 1992); Lawrence N. Powell, *The Accidental City: Improvising New Orleans* (Cambridge, MA: Harvard University Press, 2013); Hall, *Africans in Colonial Louisiana,* 5. Exceptions to the gender distribution of settlers included the Ursuline nuns who first arrived in 1727 and the so-called *filles à la cassette* or "casket girls," presumably middle-class French girls sent with only a casket of belongings to serve as wives for settlers. Gayarre argues they arrived in 1728. Emily Clark, ed., *Voices from an Early American Convent: Marie Madeleine Hachard and the New Orleans Ursulines* (Baton Rouge: Louisiana State University Press, 2007); Charles Gayarre, *History of Louisiana* (New Orleans: F. F. Hanswell & Bros., 1903), 1:390.

76. Powell, *Accidental City;* Hall, *Africans in Colonial Louisiana;* Johnson, "Colonial New Orleans," 32–33.

77. Henry P. Dart, "The Legal Institutions of Louisiana," *Louisiana Historical Quarterly* 2 (1919): 92. New Orleans was founded in 1718 with sixty-eight colonists.

78. For more on John Law's Company, see Mathé Allain, *Not Worth a Straw: French Colonial Policy and the Early Years of Louisiana* (Lafayette: University of Southwestern Louisiana Press, 1988).

79. Recensement general des habitations et habitans de la colonnie de la Lousianne, 1726, G1 464, CAOM, no. 11.

80. Julius Scott, *A Common Wind: Afro-American Organization in the Revolution Against Slavery* (New York: Verso, 2018).

81. Philip D. Curtin, *Economic Change in Precolonial Africa: Supplementary Evidence* (Madison: University of Wisconsin Press, 1975), 39. There is no comparable census for Gorée. However, in 1767, a census counted 326 free and 768 slaves at Gorée. Curtin, *Economic Change in Precolonial Africa,* 41.

82. Michel Adanson, "Mémoires d'Adanson sur le Sénégal et l'île de Gorée," ed. Charles Becker and Victor Martin, *Bulletin de Institut Fondamental d'Afrique Noire* 42, no. B4 (1980): 738–41.

83. Morgan, "Accounting for 'the Most Excruciating Torment,'"; Barbara Bush, "'Daughters of Injur'd Africk': African Women and the Transatlantic Slave Trade," *Women's History Review*

17, no. 5 (2008): 673–98; Smallwood, *Saltwater Slavery*; Rhoda E. Reddock, "Women and Slavery in the Caribbean: A Feminist Perspective," *Latin American Perspective* 12, no. 1 (1985): 63–80.

84. Gilroy, *Black Atlantic*, 16; Marcus Rediker, *The Slave Ship: A Human History* (New York: Viking, 2007), 9. See also Simone Browne's discussion of the panopticon and the cross-section of the slave ship *Brooks* as carceral geographies that appear in the same historical moment (and in conversation with each other). Browne, *Dark Matters*, 31–62.

85. Gilroy, *Black Atlantic*, 16.

86. These distinctions appeared only in death, as the captain described the loss of each enslaved man, woman, adolescent (*rapasse, rapace, rapadille*), and "suckling infant."

87. "Journaux du bord," 21 August 1728, 15 November 1728. While anchored, Henry Pischot, a sailor from Dieppe, died, most likely from drowning, and one of the male slaves died.

88. Even the captain fell ill. Too sick to return to France, he relinquished command of the ship after reaching New Orleans.

89. The slaves were caught the evening of 7 January 1729.

90. Pierre de Vaissière, *Les origines de la colonisation et la formation de la société française à Saint-Domingue* (Paris: Bureaux de la Revue, 1906), 28–30. The Company failed in 1724.

91. John D. Garrigus, *Before Haiti: Race and Citizenship in French Saint-Domingue* (New York: Macmillan, 2006); David P. Geggus, "The Major Port Towns of Saint Domingue in the Late 18th Century," in *Atlantic Port Cities: Economy, Culture and Society*, ed. P. Liss and Franklin Knight (Knoxville: University of Tennessee Press, 1991).

92. "Recensement general de la colonnie de la Compagnie Royalle de St. Domingue fait au mois de may 1703," 15 May 1703, G1 509, fol. 12, CAOM.

93. "Etat des hommes, garçons, engagés, mulatres, et negres libres portants armes tiré des recensements du commence de Janvier 1718," G1 509, CAOM.

94. Jacques Houdaille, "Trois paroisses de Saint-Domingue au XVIIIe siècle," *Population* 18, no. 1 (1963): 93–110, 96, 98; "Récensement général des dependances des ressources des conseils superieurs du Petit Goave et du Cap pour l'année 1730," G1 509, CAOM. According to Houdaille, about 11 percent of these marriages were illegitimate and may have been interracial.

95. "Journaux du bord," 1 December 1728.

96. The seven crew members who disembarked were replaced by ten new ones. The name of at least one replacement sailor, François Sauvage de St. J——, suggests the possibility that some of the new crew members were of North American origin, perhaps of mixed race, Native, or African descent. At least one other, Bernard Riviere of Quebec, hailed from France's colonies in the New World.

97. "At two in the afternoon we viewed the island of la Balize in the 'bas du fleuve' . . . at three in the afternoon arrived a chaloupe with an officer named M. du Tisné [and] at four in the afternoon we were secured with a large anchor and I [Préville-Quinet] came a ground to survey the scene." "Journaux du bord," 18 January 1728. *Bas du fleuve* technically translates to "below the river" but along the Gulf Coast it referred to the swampy area between New Orleans and the mouth of the Mississippi River.

98. "Journaux du bord," 18 January 1729; "Etienne Périer and Jacques de La Chaise to the Minister of the Marine," 30 January 1729, C13A 11, fols. 315–16, CAOM. Périer lamented the loss of slaves to scurvy and placed the sickest ones on the first boat bound for New Orleans while the rest waited at Balize. All of the slaves, sick and well, would go to auction in three days' time.

99. "Périer and de La Chaise to the Minister of the Marine"; "Journaux du bord," 18 January 1729. There appears to have been some confusion and possible subterfuge among officials and officers over what to do about the slaves belonging to Marie Baude.

100. Marie-Madeleine Hachard, *Relation du voyage des dames religieuses Ursulines de Rouen a la Nouvelle-Orleans* (Paris: Maisonneuve, 1872); Emily Clark, *Masterless Mistresses: The New Orleans Ursulines and the Development of a New World Society* (Chapel Hill: University of North Carolina Press, 2007).

101. Hall, *Africans in Colonial Louisiana*, 34.

102. Ibrahima Seck, "Du Jolibaa au Mississippi, le long voyage des gens du Komo," *Mande Studies* 18, no. 1 (2016): 29–55. See also Seck, *Bouki Fait Gombo*.

103. Plantation agriculture would not develop in Senegal until the nineteenth century.

104. Marcel Giraud, *A History of French Louisiana* (Baton Rouge: Louisiana State University Press, 1974), 5:393; Patricia Kay Galloway, "Natchez Matrilineal Kinship: Du Pratz and the Woman's Touch," in *Practicing Ethnohistory: Mining Archives, Hearing Testimony, Constructing Narrative* (Lincoln: University of Nebraska Press, 2006), 97–109; Gordon M. Sayre, "Natchez Ethnohistory Revisited: New Manuscript Sources from Le Page du Pratz and Dumont de Montigny," *Louisiana History* 50, no. 4 (2009): 417.

105. According to the Trans-Atlantic Slave Trade Database, slaves from ships landed between 1719 and 1723 totaled 2,254. Voyages, https://slavevoyages.org/voyage/database#searchId=yNno ZHjI (accessed 14 March 2019).

106. Between 1721 and 1723, Bernard Diron d'Artaguette, inspector general of the colony, identified over eight hundred black slaves across the Louisiana colony, from outposts along the coast, the river (including New Orleans), and farther north into Illinois Country. He counted only eighty-nine black slaves and another eleven indigenous slaves residing within the boundaries of the town itself. Bernard Diron d'Artaguette, "Recensement des habitans et concessonnaires de la Nouvelle-Orléans, et lieux circonvoisines, avec le nombre de femmes, enfans, domestiques françoises, esclaves neigres, esclaves sauvages, bestes a corne, et cheveux," census, 21 November 1721–22, G1 464, CAOM; Powell, *Accidental City*, 54.

107. James F. Barnett, *The Natchez Indians: A History to 1735* (Jackson: University Press of Mississippi, 2007), 78–81; Hall, *Africans in Colonial Louisiana*, 99–100; Périer to Maurepas, 18 March 1730, *MPA*, 1:61–70.

108. In 1722, as part of restitution for damages incurred during the second Natchez war, Tattooed Serpent, the war chief, sent Natchez warriors and two African slaves to rebuild buildings at St. Catherine. Antoine Simon Le Page du Pratz, *Histoire de la Louisiane* (Paris: Chez de Bure, 1758), 1:199–200; for context on Du Pratz's narrative of his role in the events that followed, see Sayre, "Natchez Ethnohistory," 421. For discussion of the Natchez Revolt and the Native slave trade in African slaves, see Barbara Krauthamer, *Black Slaves, Indian Masters: Slavery, Emancipation, and Citizenship in the Native American South* (Chapel Hill: University of North Carolina Press, 2013), 21–26; Daniel Usner, *Indians, Settlers, and Slaves in a Frontier Exchange Economy: The Lower Mississippi Valley Before 1783* (Chapel Hill: University of North Carolina Press, 1992), 71; Powell, *Accidental City*, 81. At the time, and in accounts of the war after, both refugees and European observers claimed the Natchez cultivated African slaves as allies only to make it easier to sell them to the British. See d'Artaguette to Maurepas, 20 March 1730, *MPA*, 1:77; Pierre-François-Xavier de Charlevoix, *Histoire et description generale de la Nouvelle France avec le journal d'un voyage fait par ordre du roi dans l'Amérique Septentrionale* (Paris: Chez Rollin Fils, 1744), 4:246; Mathurin le

Petit to d'Avaugour, 12 July 1730, in *The Jesuit Relations and Allied Documents: Travels and Explorations of the Jesuit Missionaries in New France, 1610–1791*, ed. Reuben Gold Thwaites (Lower Canada: Burrows Bros. Company, 1900), 68:189–90.

109. Powell, *Accidental City*, 76. In 1726, almost 130 African slaves resided in New Orleans and surrounding settlements. Recensement, 1726, G1 464, CAOM; Charles R. Maduell, ed., *Census Tables for the French Colony of Louisiana* (Baltimore: Clearfield, 1971), 51–76.

110. *Desseins de Sauvages de Plusieurs Nations, Nue Orleans, 1735*, colored pen and ink by Alexandre de Batz, 1735, held by Peabody Museum, Harvard University, Cambridge, Massachusetts.

111. White Earth may have been named after the nearby Natchez village White Apple (Pomme Blanche). Patricia D. Woods, "The French and the Natchez Indians in Louisiana: 1700–1731," *Louisiana History: The Journal of the Louisiana Historical Association* 19, no. 4 (1978): 424; Sayre, "Natchez Ethnohistory," 410–11. Between 1718 and 1721, a handful of people of African descent arrived on ships from France, including Marie Baude, Jean Baptiste Cesear, Perrin who was a cook, and Isaac Matapan. Jennifer M. Spear, *Race, Sex, and Social Order in Early New Orleans* (Baltimore: Johns Hopkins University Press, 2009), 90.

112. French, *Historical Collections*, 154.

113. Broutin to the Compagnie des Indes, 7 August 1730, *MPA*, 1:128; Usner, *Indians, Settlers, and Slaves*, 70–71.

114. The population of the settlement was 200 French men, 82 French women, 150 French children, and 280 black slaves. Hall, *Africans in Colonial Louisiana*, 100–101.

115. Kathleen DuVal argues that "Native Ground" captures the political and social character of European and Native interaction more accurately than Richard White's "middle ground." "Each people in the Arkansas Valley, no matter how long it had been in the region, portrayed itself as native and thus deserving of a place on the land." While applied to a specific region somewhat to the north of Gulf Coast indigenous territory from Natchez to New Orleans, the term captures the French colonial predicament accurately. The French were outnumbered and, often, outstrategized by indigenous groups surrounding them on all sides except the sea. Kathleen DuVal, *The Native Ground: Indians and Colonists in the Heart of the Continent* (Philadelphia: University of Pennsylvania Press, 2011), 5; Richard White, *The Middle Ground: Indians, Empires, and Republics in the Great Lakes Region, 1650–1815* (Cambridge: Cambridge University Press, 2011). For "shatter zone," another framing that connects the Gulf South to the Caribbean and Spanish America, see Robbie Ethridge and Sheri M. Shuck-Hall, eds., *Mapping the Mississippian Shatter Zone* (Lincoln: University of Nebraska Press, 2009).

116. George Edward Milne, "Picking Up the Pieces: Natchez Coalescence in the Shatter Zone," in Ethridge and Shuck-Hall, *Mapping the Mississippian Shatter Zone*, 404. Anthropologist James Mooney noted the following variations of Natchez: NKTsi-Nache, Nachee, Nach6s, Nahchee, Naktche, Natchee, Nauchee, Notchees, Ani-Na'tst, Anintst, Pine Indians, and Sunset Indians. George Milne, in the most recent English-language history of the Natchez, noted the Natchez referred to themselves as the Théoloëls, or the People of the Sun. For consistency, I use Natchez. James Mooney, "The End of the Natchez," *American Anthropologist* 1, no. 3 (1899): 520; Milne, "Picking Up the Pieces," 387; George Edward Milne, *Natchez Country: Indians, Colonists, and the Landscapes of Race in French Louisiana* (Athens: University of Georgia Press, 2015), 15. For a recent French-language account of the revolt, see Arnaud Balvay, *La révolte des Natchez* (Paris: Félin, 2008).

117. Usner, *Indians, Settlers, and Slaves*, 67.

118. "Punition des Natchez en 1723," Recueil de pièces diverses, la plupart relatives a l'histoire de la première moitié du règne de Louis XV, no. 2550, fols. 3–10, Bibliothèque Nationale de France; Dumont de Montigny, *Mémoires historiques sur la Louisiane* (Paris: J. B. Bauche, 1753), 2:93–98; John Reed Swanton, *Indian Tribes of the Lower Mississippi Valley and Adjacent Coast of the Gulf of Mexico* (Washington, DC: Government Printing Office, 1911), 214–15. Bienville also demanded the heads of the chief, Old Hair, and of nobles from White Apple who had participated in the attacks, including Tchietchiomota, Capine, Ouyou, Nalcoa, Outchital, and Yooua. Milne argues the Great Sun took advantage of the conflict to eliminate Old Hair as a political rival. Milne, *Natchez Country*, 114.

119. Powell, *Accidental City*, 77.

120. Usner, *Indians, Settlers, and Slaves*, 71. Du Pratz suggests the tensions were instigated by the allies of the executed chief, Old Hair.

121. Powell, *Accidental City*, 67–76; Usner, *Indians, Settlers, and Slaves*, 45–47. Frustration with Chépart emanates from a number of sources, including Broutin's letter to the Company in 1730, where he writes "the Indian named Tactal, surnamed Wideawake, who had hunted with Bienville, warned Chépart ahead of time about the attack" and "We wrote to him [Chépart] that a Houma Indian who had been with Dusable in the direction of the Natchez . . . had just informed us that the Indians were coming to attack by land and water." Broutin to the Company, 7 August 1730, *MPA*, 1:127.

122. Powell, *Accidental City*, 84; Hall, *Africans in Colonial Louisiana*, 101.

123. D'Artaguette to Maurepas, 9 February 1730, *MPA*, 1:58: "Several negroes and negresses whom they have with them." Two French men, a tailor and a carter, were also spared, and the tailor was put to work sewing new clothes from the French garments stripped from dead men. The tailor was named Le Beau and the carter named Mayeux. Petit to d'Avaugour, in Thwaites, *Jesuit Relations*, 68:166–67; Marc-Antoine Caillot, *A Company Man: The Remarkable French-Atlantic Voyage of a Clerk for the Company of the Indies: A Memoir* (New Orleans: Historic New Orleans Collection, 2013), 143n332.

124. Petit to d'Avaugour, in Thwaites, *Jesuit Relations*, 68:167–68.

125. Principal accounts of the attack are found in Montigny, *Mémoires historiques*; Du Pratz, *Histoire de La Louisiane*; Charlevoix, *Histoire et general description*; Caillot, *Company Man*. Of these, Du Pratz may have fabricated the most. Sayre, "Natchez Ethnohistory"; Shannon Lee Dawdy, "Enlightenment from the Ground: Le Page du Pratz's *Histoire de la Louisiane*," *French Colonial History* 3 (2003): 17–34.

126. Word reached New Orleans either on 2 or 3 December. Périer to Maurepas, 18 March 1730, *MPA*, 1:76.

127. "While everything was in this state, to cap it all, we were warned that the Negroes of the colony wanted to turn against us too . . . which frightened us a great deal, because they are good fighters, more formidable than ten thousand Indians." Caillot, *Company Man*, 127. On 2 or 3 December, Périer sent word of the Natchez Revolt downriver and told settlers to secure slaves as well as cattle.

128. Périer to the Minister of the Marine, 18 March 1730, *MPA*, 1:64.

129. Périer to Maurepas, 18 March 1730, *MPA*, 1:65, 71. Work on fortifications, levees, digging ditches, and other manual labor used slaves regardless of gender. See Broutin to the Company, 7 August 1730 at New Orleans, *MPA*, 1:127.

130. French, *Historical Collections*, 5:99–102.

131. Burgeoning racial solidarity may also have played a role. By 1725, Natchez described themselves both by their nation and as "red . . . a racial distinction forged in contradistinction to French and African newcomers." George Milne makes this groundbreaking argument, noting, in addition, that the Natchez were the first of the Gulf Coast tribes to refer to themselves as "red men" vis-à-vis Europeans. Milne, *Natchez Country*, 214.

132. *La Diane* arrived in October 1728 with 464 slaves. Voyages, Voyage ID #32902, https://slavevoyages.org/voyage/database#searchId=yNnoZHjI (accessed 14 March 2019).

133. D'Artaguette to Maurepas, 20 March 1730, *MPA*, 1:77.

134. Caillot, *Company Man*, 125–26. In 1730, in response to French attempts to broker peace, Natchez had also demanded a ransom of goods for each woman, child, and black slave to be returned. Their list included guns, gunpowder, hatchets, pickaxes, hats with plumes, coats, wine, and brandy. Petit to d'Avaugour, in Thwaites, *Jesuit Relations*, 68:191. D'Artaguette described their demands as "excessive." D'Artaguette to Maurepas, 20 March 1730, *MPA*, 1:78.

135. Lusser to Maurepas, "Journal of the Journey I made in the Choctaw nation by order of M. Périer, beginning on January 12, 1720 and lasting until March 23 of the same year," *MPA*, 1:88.

136. Périer to Maurepas, 18 March 1730, *MPA*, 1:65.

137. Périer to Maurepas, 18 March 1730, *MPA*, 1:63; Usner, *Indians, Settlers, and Slaves*, 72.

138. Périer to Maurepas, 18 March 1730, *MPA*, 1:63.

139. Caillot, *Company Man*, 133–34; Swanton, *Indian Tribes*, 224.

140. The Natchez wife of a French soldier named Navarre warned him ahead of time and hid him for several days until it was safe. He was later killed on a surveillance expedition along with five other men. Montigny, *Mémoires historiques*, 2:175. Some accounts of saved Frenchmen grew more fanciful in the telling. In John Claiborne's nineteenth-century history of Mississippi, the "traitor princess" Stelona informed on the Natchez to her "white lover" M. de Masse. John Claiborne, *Biographical and Historical Memoirs of Mississippi* (Chicago: Goodspeed Publishing Company, 1891), 1:38. At least one version of the betrayal narrative became part of Natchez oral history "as the cause of their removal from the seat of their nativity" and was captured by Natchez-Creek historian and landowner George Stiggins in the 1830s: "One man escaped because his loving wife, wishing to save him, had prevailed on him to stay with her in the town that night, and after the above catastrophe she effected his escape down the river Mississippi. He carried the news to his countrymen of the disaster to his comrades." George Stiggins, *Creek Indian History: A Historical Narrative of the Genealogy, Traditions and Downfall of the Ispocoga or Creek Indian Tribe of Indians by One of the Tribe* (Tuscaloosa: University of Alabama Press, 2014), 40.

141. Caillot, *Company Man*, 143, on the rape of Madame des Noyers.

142. Montigny, *Mémoires historiques*, 2:203–4; Beauchamp to Maurepas, 5 November 1731, *MPA*, 4:82, 104; mouvements des sauvages de la Louisiane depuis la prise du fort des Natchez par M. de Périer sur la fin de janvier 1731, C13A 13, fol. 87, HNOC; mémoire de Raymond Amyalt, Sieur d'Auseville, conseilleur au Conseil Superieur de la Louisiane, commissaire aux comptes de la Compagnie des Indes, 20 January 1732, C13A 14, fol. 273v., HNOC. For scholarly accounts of the conspiracy, see Hall, *Africans in Colonial Louisiana*, 107; Usner, *Indians, Settlers, and Slaves*, 74.

143. Du Pratz, *Histoire de La Louisiane*, 3:315–17.

144. On "Samba" as a fabrication of Du Pratz, see Peter Caron, "'Of a Nation Which the Others Do Not Understand': Bambara Slaves and African Ethnicity in Colonial Louisiana, 1718–1760," *Slavery & Abolition* 18, no. 1 (1997): 98–98.

145. Caillot, *Company Man*, 130.

146. D'Artaguette to Maurepas, 20 March 1730, *MPA*, 1:78; Petit to d'Avaugour, in Thwaites, *Jesuit Relations*, 68:189; Usner, *Indians, Settlers, and Slaves*, 73; Powell, *Accidental City*, 84–85; Hall, *Africans in Colonial Louisiana*, 102–3.

147. By the end of the war, some five hundred captured Native women and children would be sold into slavery in the Caribbean as well. "Lettre en forme de rançois du Deslayes au sujet du massacre des rançois fair par des sauvages le 28 novembre 1729," 15 March 1730, C13C 4, fols. 179–80, HNOC. See also Hall, *Africans in Colonial Louisiana*, 103.

148. Petit to d'Avaugour, in Thwaites, *Jesuit Relations*, 196–97; Mouvements des sauvages, fol. 87.

149. Charlevoix, *Histoire et description*, 4:279–80. Charlevoix describes Africans "scattered in different boats" for the attack.

150. Montigny, *Mémoires historiques*, 2:202–8; Royal decree, 23 January 1731, *MPA*, 4:57–58; Beauchamp to Maurepas, 5 November 1731, *MPA*, 4:79; Périer to Maurepas, 10 December 1731, *MPA*, 4:102–5; Caillot, *Company Man*, 153–54.

151. Lusser to Maurepas, "Journal of the Journey," *MPA*, 1:103–4; Petit to d'Avaugour, in Thwaites, *Jesuit Relations*, 68:189. It is difficult to identify the Africans scattered among the Choctaw. At least one, Lusser noted, belonged to a Choctaw man named Poulain at the village of Cushtusha. Another was at Bitoulouxy. The difficulty lies in the archive, but may also lie in Choctaw's refusal to relinquish black slaves to French officials.

152. Régis du Roullet to Maurepas, "Abstract of the journal of the journeys made by Sieur Régis du Roullet," *MPA*, 1:180–81; Krauthamer, *Black Slaves, Indian Masters*, 20–23; Usner, *Indians, Settlers, and Slaves*, 45.

153. Lusser to Maurepas, "Journal of the Journey," *MPA*, 1:103–4; Régis du Roullet to Périer, 16 March 1731, *MPA*, 4:68–69.

154. Lusser to Maurepas, "Journal of the Journey," *MPA*, 1:104–6, 109–10; Régis du Roullet to Périer, 16 March 1731, *MPA*, 4:67–68.

155. Stiggins, *Creek Indian History*, 40–41.

156. Périer to the Minister of the Marine, 10 December 1731, C13A 13, fols. 63–64, HNOC.

157. Brad Raymond Lieb, "The Natchez Indian Diaspora: Ethnohistoric Archaeology of the Eighteenth-Century Natchez Refuge Among the Chickasaws" (Ph.D. diss., University of Alabama, 2008), 203–4. The Edisto Natchez-Kusso tribe in present-day South Carolina claims it was founded, in part, by descendants of a Natchez band escaping the French in the eighteenth century. Hannah Alani and Robert Behre Alani, "Just Outside Charleston, a Native American Tribe Seeks to Preserve Its Identity," *Post and Courier*, 28 January 2019, https://www.postandcourier.com/news/just-outside-charleston-a-native-american-tribe-seeks-to-preserve/article_dacocce6-142a-11e9-8471-c726cd1169ff.html (accessed 29 September 2019).

158. Memoire sur la Concession du Senegal, 8 October 1734, C6 11, CAOM.

159. Ira Berlin's emphasis on the importance of time and place, and distinction between "societies with slaves" and "slave societies," provides a useful model for understanding differences in systems of slavery in Africa, the Caribbean, and the United States. According to Berlin, "slave society" is one in which commodity production fueled by slave labor is the central, organizing principle of the society. All social relations stem from the fundamental relationship between slaveowner and slave, master and subordinate. A "society with slaves" is one in which slaves are present but the relationship between slaveowner and slave does not structure all other relations

and the economy is not driven by any single Atlantic product. Atlantic societies transitioned from slave society to society with slaves in nonlinear patterns, becoming one or the other and back again over time. See Ira Berlin, *Many Thousands Gone: The First Two Centuries of Slavery in North America* (Cambridge, MA: Harvard University Press, 1998), 10; Ira Berlin, "Time, Space, and the Evolution of Afro-American Society on British Mainland North America," *American Historical Review* 85, no. 1 (1980): 77–80.

160. During the January 1730 counterattack, the French officials, confident in enslaved men's prowess, even included some of these soldiers in his plans to storm the fort. This plan never went forward. Lusser to Maurepas, "Journal of the Journey," *MPA*, 1:79; Périer to Maurepas, 18 March 1730, *MPA*, 1:70.

161. Doc no. 17300513, 13 May 1730, Records of the Superior Council, LHC; Fleuriau, 13 May 1730, *LHQ*, 4:524; Heloise Cruzat, "Sidelights on Louisiana History," *LHQ* 1, no. 3 (1918): 132–33. The list of slaves freed for their valor is charred and difficult to decipher. I quote these names from Thomas N. Ingersoll, *Mammon and Manon in Early New Orleans: The First Slave Society in the Deep South, 1718–1819* (Knoxville: University of Tennessee Press, 1999), 365n.

162. Grace King, *Creole Families of New Orleans* (New York: MacMillan, 1921), 161–62.

163. Officials may have found a black militia useful, but they continued to fear Native-African insurgency. They avoided using the newly freed black militia to hunt down maroons in the cypress swamp, fearing the result should black freedom of one type encounter black freedom of a different stripe in the woods behind New Orleans. For more on military life in French New Orleans, see Vidal, *Caribbean New Orleans*.

164. Petit to d'Avaugour, in Thwaites, *Jesuit Relations*, 68:198–99.

165. Clark, *Masterless Mistresses*, 76–78; Petit to d'Avaugour, in Thwaites, *Jesuit Relations*, 4:198–99.

166. Kimberlé Crenshaw, "Mapping the Margins: Intersectionality, Identity Politics, and Violence Against Women of Color," *Stanford Law Review* 43, no. 6 (1991): 1241–99.

167. Périer to Ory, 15 November 1730, *MPA*, 4:54.

168. Régis du Roullet to Périer, 16 March 1731, *MPA*, 4:66–67.

Chapter 4

Source of epigraph: Représentation du M. Fleuriau and Decision du Conseil, "Deliberations de Superior Council," 21 November 1725, C13 9, fols. 9–10v, HNOC. "Luy donne sa liberté a ces effet, lui laisse sa femme pour habiter avec luy sans quel Compagnie l'employe a son service."

1. Antoine Simon Le Page du Pratz, *Histoire de la Louisiane* (De Bure, 1758), 3:226–27; Alexandre de Batz, "Plan du camp des nègres avec leur cabannes construites sur l'habitation de la Compagnie de pieux en terre couvertes d'ecorsses levez et dessiné sur les lieux le 9 janvier 1732," CAOM, 04 DFC 91B. Circulating among Africans, free and slave, in the Caribbean and Brazil, the *calinda* appeared in French colonial ordinances and accounts as early as the 1670s. For descriptions of the *calinda* from the Antilles, see the 1678 *kalenda* in Martinique that led to the Superior Council of the colony specifically outlawing such gatherings, Labat's account from his 1696 voyage to Martinique, as well as Jean-Paul Pillet's and Médéric-Louis-Élie Moreau de Saint-Méry's 1790s descriptions of *calenda* in Saint-Domingue. See Adrien Dessalles, *Histoire générale des Antilles* (Paris: Libraire-éditeur, 1847), 3:296–97; Jean-Baptiste Labat, *Nouveau voyage aux isles de*

l'Amérique (La Haye: Chez P. Husson, 1724), 4:154–58; Jeremy D. Popkin, "The Author as Colonial Exile: 'Mon Odyssee,'" *Romanic Review* 103, no. 3/4 (2012): 377; Médéric-Louis-Élie Moreau de Saint-Méry, *Description topographique, physique, civile, politique et historique de la partie francaise de l'isle Saint Domingue* (Philadelphia: Chez l'Auteur, 1797), 1:44–45. Accounts vary but seem to agree the *calinda* was a dance for all ages performed by couplets of men and women. It included drum accompaniment and sometimes a banjo. See Freddi Williams Evans, *Congo Square: African Roots in New Orleans* (New Orleans: University of Louisiana at Lafayette Press, 2011), 99–111; Dena J. Epstein and Rosita M. Sands, "Secular Folk Music," in *African American Music: An Introduction*, ed. Mellonee V. Burnim and Portia K. Maultsby (New York: Routledge, 2014), 38–39; Ned Sublette, *The World That Made New Orleans: From Spanish Silver to Congo Square* (Chicago: Lawrence Hill Books, 2008), 73–74. Du Pratz called the dance event a *Calinda* (also *kalinda* or *calenda*), but there was also an Afro-Atlantic dance style called the *calinda*, as well as a religious ceremony with a similar name. On present-day *kalenda* and *bèlè* in Martinique, see Camee Maddox-Wingfeld, "The Dance Chose Me: Womanist Reflections on Bèlè Performance in Contemporary Martinique," *Meridians* 16, no. 2 (2018): 295–307. For variations in Brazil and Congo/Angola, see Jonathon Grasse, "Calundu's Winds of Divination: Music and Black Religiosity in Eighteenth- and Nineteenth-Century Minas Gerais, Brazil," *Yale Journal of Music and Religion* 3, no. 2 (30 September 2017); James H. Sweet, "Reimagining the African-Atlantic Archive: Method, Concept, Epistemology, Ontology," *Journal of African History* 55, no. 2 (July 2014): 147–59.

2. Du Pratz, *Histoire de la Louisiane*, 3:226–27.

3. Représentation du M. Fleuriau and Decision du Conseil, "Deliberations de Superior Council," fols. 9–10v.

4. Shannon Lee Dawdy, *Building the Devil's Empire: French Colonial New Orleans* (Chicago: University of Chicago Press, 2008), 82.

5. Pierre-François-Xavier de Charlevoix, *Histoire et description générale de la Nouvelle France* (Paris: Chez Rollin fils, 1744); Pierre-François-Xavier de Charlevoix, *Journal d'un voyage fait par ordre du Roi dans L'Amérique Septentrionale* (Paris: Chez Rollin fils, 1744); Marie-Madeleine Hachard, *Relation du voyage des dames religieuses Ursulines de Rouen à La Nouvelle-Orleans* (Paris: Maisonneuve, 1872).

6. "Census enumeration is a means through which a state manages its residents by way of formalized categories that fix individuals within a certain time and a particular space, making the census a technology that renders a population legible in racializing as well as gendered ways." Simone Browne, *Dark Matters: On the Surveillance of Blackness* (Durham, NC: Duke University Press, 2015), 56.

7. For more on Mobile, see Jay Higginbotham, *Old Mobile: Fort Louis de la Louisiane, 1702–1711* (Tuscaloosa: University of Alabama Press, 1991). "Dénombrement de chaque sorte de gens qui composent la colonie de la Louisiane, fait au Fort de la Louisiane le 12 aout 1708," G1 509, CAOM.

8. Governor Antoine de Lamothe Cadillac to the Ministry, Fort Louis, 26 October 1713, C13A 3, fol. 65, CAOM. Hall describes this as the "first documentary evidence of Africans in Louisiana." Gwendolyn Midlo Hall, *Africans in Colonial Louisiana: The Development of Afro-Creole Culture in the Eighteenth Century* (Baton Rouge: Louisiana State University Press, 1995), 57–58.

9. Nancy Surrey, *The Commerce of Louisiana During the French Régime, 1699–1763* (1916; New York: Columbia University, 1968), 231.

10. Merchants from Saint-Domingue found their way to Louisiana at least twice to trade African slaves for Native ones. See Jean-Baptiste Le Moyne, Sieur de Bienville, to the Minister

of the Marine, letter, 12 October 1708, 471–80, C13A 2, fol. 178, HNOC; Jean-Baptiste DuBois Duclos to the Minister of the Marine, 10 July 1713, C13A 3, fol. 120, HNOC.

11. Résumé de diverses demandes d'Iberville, 1699, C13A 1, fol. 91, HNOC; demands diverses, no date, C13A, fol. 93, HNOC; LaSalle to the Ministry of the Marine, 20 August 1709, C13A 2, fols. 400–401, HNOC. See also Hall, *Africans in Colonial Louisiana*, 57.

12. Hall, *Africans in Colonial Louisiana*, 57–95, 130; Lawrence N. Powell, *The Accidental City: Improvising New Orleans* (Cambridge, MA: Harvard University Press, 2013), 70.

13. Daniel H. Usner, *American Indians in the Lower Mississippi Valley: Social and Economic Histories* (Omaha: University of Nebraska Press, 2004), 37; Alan Gallay, *The Indian Slave Trade: The Rise of the English Empire in the American South, 1670–1717* (New Haven, CT: Yale University Press, 2003), 294–95; Patricia K. Galloway, *Choctaw Genesis, 1500–1700* (Omaha: University of Nebraska Press, 1998), 200.

14. The figure of two-thirds of Indian slaves living in eighteenth-century Louisiana being female is derived from Kathleen DuVal, "Indian Intermarriage and Métissage in Colonial Louisiana," *William and Mary Quarterly* 65, no. 2 (2008): 273.

15. Kathleen DuVal notes, "Although censuses show that most slaves lived in households that included a European wife, most of the censuses were based on households, which would have missed any trader or soldier who owned a slave but had no permanent residence." DuVal, "Indian Intermarriage," 275.

16. Kathleen DuVal, *The Native Ground: Indians and Colonists in the Heart of the Continent* (Philadelphia: University of Pennsylvania Press, 2011); Jennifer M. Spear, *Race, Sex, and Social Order in Early New Orleans* (Baltimore: Johns Hopkins University Press, 2009), 23; Usner, *American Indians*; Guillaume Aubert, "'The Blood of France': Race and Purity of Blood in the French Atlantic World," *William and Mary Quarterly* 61, no. 3 (2004): 439–78.

17. Barbara Krauthamer, *Black Slaves, Indian Masters: Slavery, Emancipation, and Citizenship in the Native American South* (Chapel Hill: University of North Carolina Press, 2013); Christina Snyder, *Slavery in Indian Country: The Changing Face of Captivity in Early America* (Cambridge, MA: Harvard University Press, 2010); Tiya Miles, *Ties That Bind: The Story of an Afro-Cherokee Family in Slavery and Freedom* (Berkeley: University of California Press, 2005).

18. For these debates, see Spear, *Race, Sex, and Social Order*; Aubert, "'Blood of France.'" These tensions even appeared in expressive and material exchanges between French and indigenous nations. See Sophie White, *Wild Frenchmen and Frenchified Indians: Material Culture and Race in Colonial Louisiana* (Chapel Hill: University of North Carolina Press, 2012).

19. Cadillac to Pontchartrain, 26 October 1713, in *MPA*, 2:169.

20. Duclos to the Minister of the Marine, 25 December 1715, in *MPA*, 2:207–8.

21. White, *Wild Frenchmen*, 64.

22. White, *Wild Frenchmen*, 195–96.

23. For a Caribbean parallel, see Joan (Colin) Dayan, "Codes of Law and Bodies of Color," *New Literary History* 26, no. 2 (1995): 283–308; Joan Dayan, "Erzulie: A Women's History of Haiti," *Research in African Literatures* 25, no. 2 (1994): 5–31.

24. *Le code noir ou Edit du roy servant de reglement pour le gouvernement & l'administration de justice & la police des isles françoises de l'Amerique, & pour la discipline & le commerce des negres & esclaves dans le dit pays* (Paris: Veuve Saugrain, 1718), 2–12. The discussion of the 1685 Code Noir that follows will be based on the Niort and Richard study of the only extant copy, the 1687 copy registered at Guadeloupe and cited hereafter in the notes as "Le code noir." See Jean-François

Niort and Jérémy Richard, "L'Édit royal de mars 1685 touchant la police des îles de l'Amérique française dit 'code noir': Comparaison des éditions anciennes à partir de la version 'Guadeloupe,'" *Bulletin de la Société d'Histoire de la Guadeloupe* 156 (2010): 73–89. See also Louis Sala-Molins, *Le Code Noir, ou Le Calvaire de Canaan* (Paris: Quadrige, 1987).

25. Articles 2, 22–26, 27, 5–6, 47, 11, *Le code noir*.

26. Articles 11, 15–16, 33, 38, 43, *Le code noir*.

27. Dayan, "Codes of Law," 292.

28. Article 9, *Le code noir*.

29. Joseph Roach, "Body of Law: The Sun King and the Code Noir," in *From the Royal to the Republican Body: Incorporating the Political in Seventeenth- and Eighteenth-Century France*, ed. Sara E. Melzer and Kathryn Norberg (Berkeley: University of California Press, 1998), 130.

30. Article 59, *Le code noir*.

31. Articles 39, 57–58, *Le code noir*.

32. David P. Geggus, "The French Slave Trade: An Overview," *William and Mary Quarterly* 58, no. 1 (2001): 126. See appendix B in the article for slaves landed at Saint-Domingue in the eighteenth century.

33. Laurent Dubois, *Avengers of the New World: The Story of the Haitian Revolution* (Cambridge, MA: Harvard University Press, 2005), 40.

34. Carolyn E. Fick, *The Making of Haiti: The Saint Domingue Revolution from Below* (Knoxville: University of Tennessee Press, 1990), 50–56. See also Jean Fouchard, *The Haitian Maroons: Liberty or Death* (New York: E. W. Blyden Press, 1981).

35. Registered at Cap Français, 22 December 1705, in Médéric-Louis-Élie Moreau de Saint-Méry, *Loix et constitutions des colonies françoises de L'Amerique sous le vent* (Paris: L'Auteur, 1784), 2:36–37.

36. 15 August 1711, in Moreau de Saint-Méry, *Loix et constitutions*, 2:272; Guillaume Aubert, "'To Establish One Law and Definite Rules': Race, Religion, and the Transatlantic Origins of the Louisiana Code Noir," in *Louisiana: Crossroads of the Atlantic World*, ed. Cécile Vidal (Philadelphia: University of Pennsylvania Press, 2013), 39.

37. 7 May 1714, in Moreau de Saint-Méry, *Loix et constitutions*, 2:400.

38. Moreau de Saint-Méry, *Loix et constitutions*, 3:382.

39. Moreau de Saint-Méry, *Description topographique*, 1:99. See also Arlette Gautier, *Les soeurs de Solitude: La condition féminine dans l'esclavage aux Antilles du XVIIe au XIXe siècle* (Paris: Éditions Caribénnes, 1985), 172; Bernard Moitt, "In the Shadow of the Plantation: Women of Color and the *Libres de Fait* of Martinique and Guadeloupe, 1685–1848," in *Beyond Bondage: Free Women of Color in the Americas*, ed. David Barry Gaspar and Darlene Clark Hine (Urbana: University of Illinois Press, 2004), 35–40. A smaller number of slaves, *libres de voyage*, remained free as long as they remained in France. See Sue Peabody, *"There Are No Slaves in France": The Political Culture of Race and Slavery in the Ancien Regime* (Oxford: Oxford University Press, 2002); Jennifer L. Palmer, *Intimate Bonds: Family and Slavery in the French Atlantic* (Philadelphia: University of Pennsylvania Press, 2016).

40. 10 June 1707, in Moreau de Saint-Méry, *Loix et constitutions*, 2:99. The 1571 Freedom Principle, which barred slavery on French soil, had its roots in galley slavery.

41. 24 October 1713, in Moreau de Saint-Méry, *Loix et constitutions*, 2:398. This ordinance needed to be reiterated again on 15 June 1736. Moreau de Saint-Méry, *Loix et constitutions*, 3:453–54. Officials claimed Vaucresson was in a sexual relationship with Babet. Moitt, *Women and Slavery*, 153–57.

42. "Reponses que produit frere Andre mane prefect apostolique et Superieur General des missions de l'ordre des freres prescheurs," F3 252, fols. 543, 577, CAOM, as cited in Aubert, "'Blood of France,'" 466–67. On French Atlantic missionaries' racial ideology, see Sue Peabody, "'A Nation Born to Slavery': Missionaries and Racial Discourse in Seventeenth-Century French Antilles," *Journal of Social History* 38 (2004): 113–26; Sue Peabody, "'A Dangerous Zeal': Catholic Missions to Slaves in the French Antilles, 1635–1800," *French Historical Studies* 25 (2002): 53–90; Cécile Vidal, "Caribbean Louisiana: Church, Métissage, and the Language of Race in the Mississippi Colony During the French Period," in Vidal, *Louisiana*, 125–46; Doris L. Garraway, *The Libertine Colony: Creolization in the Early French Caribbean* (Durham, NC: Duke University Press, 2005), 146–239.

43. Moreau de Saint-Méry, *Loix et constitutions*, 2:327, 399.

44. "Edit concernant les nègres esclaves à la Louisiane," *Publications of the Louisiana Historical Society* 4 (1908): 76–90 (hereafter cited in the notes as "Louisiana *Code Noir*"). The discussion that follows is based on this document. See also notes on "Code Noir B" in Sala-Moulins, *Le Code Noir*; Hans W. Baade, "The Gens de Couleur of Louisiana: Comparative Slave Law in Microcosm," *Cardozo Law Review* 18 (1996): 535–86; Thomas N. Ingersoll, "Free Blacks in a Slave Society: New Orleans, 1718–1812," *William and Mary Quarterly* 48, no. 2 (April 1991): 173–200.

45. Aubert, "'To Establish One Law,'" 23.

46. For background on each of the council members, see Marcel Giraud, *A History of French Louisiana* (Baton Rouge: Louisiana State University Press, 1987), 5:1–26.

47. Article 50-2, Louisiana *Code Noir*. No mention was made of the 1711 edict requiring official permission from the governor and intendant for their manumission to be approved, but that edict may have inspired this change.

48. Article 6, Louisiana *Code Noir*. In the Louisiana code as in the 1685 *Code Noir*, free women of either race gave birth to free children, even if married to enslaved men (i.e., the status continued to follow the mother). However, the additional detail added to the marriage prohibition (Article 6) of the Louisiana *Code Noir* punished concubinage more broadly and irregardless of the race of the man.

49. Article 6, Louisiana *Code Noir*.

50. Article 52, Louisiana *Code Noir*.

51. Compare Article 39, *Le code noir*, to Article 34, Louisiana *Code Noir*.

52. Adrienne Davis, "Don't Let Nobody Bother Yo' Principle: The Sexual Economy of American Slavery," in *Sister Circle: Black Women and Work*, ed. Sharon Harley and Black Women and Work Collective (New Brunswick, NJ: Rutgers University Press, 2002).

53. Dominique Rogers, "Réussir dans une monde d'hommes: Les stratégies des femmes de couleur du Cap-Français," *Journal of Haitian Studies* 9 (Spring 2003): 40–45.

54. "Vente de Canot," 12 February 1768, SDNA 1221, CAOM; John D. Garrigus, *Before Haiti: Race and Citizenship in French Saint-Domingue* (New York: Macmillan, 2006), 74.

55. For an instance of alleged infanticide, see *Jerome Matis v. Marie Jeanne, négresse esclave*, 1749/06/17/01, RSCL LHC. On this case, see M. Scott Heerman, *The Alchemy of Slavery: Human Bondage and Emancipation in the Illinois Country, 1730–1865* (Philadelphia: University of Pennsylvania Press, 2018). On infanticide in the Caribbean, see Karol K. Weaver, "'She Crushed the Child's Fragile Skull': Disease, Infanticide, and Enslaved Women in Eighteenth-Century Saint-Domingue," *French Colonial History* 5, no. 1 (2004): 93–109. On women loving women as resistance during slavery, see Omise'eke Natasha Tinsley, *Thiefing Sugar: Eroticism Between Women in Caribbean Literature* (Durham, NC: Duke University Press, 2010).

56. Dawdy, Building the Devil's Empire, 154.

57. Jacob Gaboury, "Becoming Null: Queer Relations in the Excluded Middle," *Women and Performance: A Journal of Feminist Theory* 28, no. 2 (2018): 11. On null and missing data, see Diane M. Nelson, *Who Counts? The Mathematics of Death and Life After Genocide* (Durham, NC: Duke University Press, 2015); Mimi Onuoha, Library of Missing Datasets, https://github .com/MimiOnuoha/missing-datasets (accessed 4 May 2019). On the importance of accounting for missing information in databases and data sets in histories of slavery, see Gwendolyn Midlo Hall, "Africa and Africans in the African Diaspora: The Uses of Relational Databases," *American Historical Review* 115, no. 1 (1 February 2010): 136–50; Jennifer L. Morgan, "Partus Sequitur Ventrem: Law, Race, and Reproduction in Colonial Slavery," *Small Axe: A Caribbean Journal of Criticism* 22, no. 1 (1 March 2018): 1–17; Jessica Marie Johnson, "Markup Bodies: Black [Life] Studies and Slavery [Death] Studies at the Digital Crossroads," *Social Text* 36, no. 4 (1 December 2018): 57–79.

58. Geggus, "French Slave Trade," 125–26.

59. Moreau de Saint-Méry, *Loix et constitutions*, 2:342.

60. Voyages, Voyage ID #32170, https://slavevoyages.org/voyage/database#searchId=yNno ZHjI (accessed 14 March 2019). The transatlantic slave trade effectively stopped in Louisiana until 1772 and the documented trans-shipment trade was small. Between 1736 and 1748, three ships are recorded as landing along the Gulf Coast (one in "Mississippi" and two at Mobile): the *Monimia* (1736), the *Sarah* (1737), and the *Rattan Packet* (1748). The *Monimia* and *Sarah* landed slaves transshipped from Charleston; the *Rattan Packet* carried captives from Kingston, Jamaica. Voyages, Year Range: 1514 to 1769, Principal Place of Slave Landing: Gulf Coast, https://slavevoyages.org/ voyage/database#searchId=orFbGzsZ (accessed 14 March 2019).

61. Thomas N. Ingersoll, *Mammon and Manon in Early New Orleans: The First Slave Society in the Deep South, 1718–1819* (Knoxville: University of Tennessee Press, 1999), 127–30.

62. On slave societies and societies with slaves, see Ira Berlin, *Many Thousands Gone: The First Two Centuries of Slavery in North America* (Cambridge, MA: Harvard University Press, 1998), 10; Ira Berlin, "Time, Space, and the Evolution of Afro-American Society on British Mainland North America," *American Historical Review* 85, no. 1 (1980): 77–80.

63. Scholars like Shannon Lee Dawdy and Jennifer Spear have recounted the flawed census practices of colonial officials in Louisiana. See Dawdy, *Building the Devil's Empire*, 153–57; Spear, *Race, Sex, and Social Order*, 94–96.

64. Giraud, History of French Louisiana, 5:124–25.

65. Powell, *Accidental City*, 76; recensement, 1731, G1 464, CAOM; Charles R. Maduell, ed., *Census Tables for the French Colony of Louisiana* (Baltimore: Clearfield, 1971), 113–53.

66. Powell, *Accidental City*, 72; Ingersoll, *Mammon and Manon*, 28–30.

67. 1727 Census, G1 464, CAOM. Spear identified this census as the first census to categorize *nègres affranchis*. Before this, those who were free people of color could sometimes be found in the category *engagés*.

68. Marriage register, Sacramental Records, vol. A, Archdiocese of New Orleans, 4 April 1728, SLC. Many thanks to Cécile Vidal for pointing me in the direction of this document.

69. Gwendolyn Midlo Hall, "African Women in French and Spanish Louisiana: Origins, Roles, Family, Work, Treatment," in *The Devil's Lane: Sex and Race in the Early South*, ed. Catherine Clinton and Michele Gillespie (New York: Oxford University Press, 1997), 252.

70. Recensement general des habitations et habitans de la Colonie de la Louisiana ainsi quila se son donnner au premier janvier 1726bis, G1 464, CAOM.

71. Roulhac Toledano and Mary Christovich, *New Orleans Architecture: Faubourg Tremé and the Bayou Road* (New Orleans: Pelican Publishing, 2003), 5–6.

72. The 1726 census listed 1 African and slave in the homes of Company employees St. Quintin and Danville; 1 with the Capuchin priests; 2 in the home of Jean René de Fazende; 2 with Sieur Bru; 1 with Bodson; and 1 with Lazon and his wife. Recensement, 1726bis.

73. Emily Clark, "'By All the Conduct of Their Lives': A Laywomen's Confraternity in New Orleans, 1730–1744," *William and Mary Quarterly* 54, no. 4 (1997): 790.

74. Emily Clark and Virginia Meacham Gould, "The Feminine Face of Afro-Catholicism in New Orleans, 1727–1852," *William and Mary Quarterly* 59, no. 2 (2002): 409. See also *A Celebration of Faith: Henriette Delille and the Sisters of the Holy Family* (New Orleans: New Orleans African American Museum of Art, Culture and History, 2008).

75. Clark and Gould, "Feminine Face," 425; Emily Clark, *Masterless Mistresses: The New Orleans Ursulines and the Development of a New World Society* (Chapel Hill: University of North Carolina Press, 2007), 186.

76. Clark and Gould, "Feminine Face," 436–44.

77. B. F. French, *Historical Collections of Louisiana and Florida* (New York: J. Sabin & Sons, 1869), 3:80–81.

78. Hachard, *Relation du voyage*, 97–98.

79. Clark, *Masterless Mistresses*, 187–89.

80. 1736/06/10/01, RSCL; John E. Salvaggio, *New Orleans' Charity Hospital: A Story of Physicians, Politics, and Poverty* (Baton Rouge: Louisiana State University Press, 1992), 11–12.

81. Douglas W. Owsley et al., "Demography and Pathology of an Urban Slave Population from New Orleans," *American Journal of Physical Anthropology* 74, no. 2 (1 October 1987): 185–97.

82. G1 464, CAOM; Spear, *Race, Sex, and Social Order*, 95.

83. Spear, *Race, Sex, and Social Order*, 94. As Spear notes, in 1727, the category *nègres affranchis* first appeared on a census, but without distinction by race. In contrast: "According to the 1732 census's conceptualization of the social order in this decade-old city, *mulâtres* had emerged as an enumerable category (despite their limited numbers)" (94).

84. "Regulating sex was the principal way in which officials tried to define and maintain discrete racial groups, and therefore the true codification of the tripartite system with which New Orleans would be so closely identified did not happen until 1808 when the Anglo-Louisiana legislature required whites, free people of color, and slaves to find endogamous marriage partners." Spear, *Race, Sex, and Social Order*, 4.

85. "List of Those Persons Whose Death Was Recorded from January 8, 1726 to January 10, 1727," in Glenn R. Conrad, *The First Families of Louisiana* (Baton Rouge: Claitor's Pub. Division, 1970), 2:96.

86. Funeral of Catherine, 13 July 1732, B1, 76, SLC.

87. Baptism of Marie, 6 July 1733, B1, 40, SLC; B2, SLC.

88. Spear, *Race, Sex, and Social Order*, 95.

89. Hall, *Africans in Colonial Louisiana*, 173.

90. Spear, *Race, Sex, and Social Order*, 95.

91. Spear, *Race, Sex, and Social Order*, 96.

92. Drawing from work in the field of Black Code studies, I am suggesting there are "queer, femme, fugitive, insurgent" possibilities even where black diasporic people engage with

surveilling structures and institutions. See Jessica Marie Johnson and Mark Anthony Neal, "Introduction: Wild Seed in the Machine," *Black Scholar* 47, no. 3 (3 July 2017): 1–2.

93. Conviction and sentence of flogging and incarceration, 13 September 1722, RSCSJR LHQ, vol 7, no. 4 (1924), 678.

94. "Robbery Reported," RSCSJR LHQ, vol. 1, no. 1 (1917), 111. See also Bienville demanding the head of a free black man living at White Apple as part of a peace treaty with the Natchez. Dumont de Montigny, *Mémoires historiques sur la Louisiane* (Paris: J. B. Bauche, 1753), 2:93–98; John Reed Swanton, *Indian Tribes of the Lower Mississippi Valley and Adjacent Coast of the Gulf of Mexico* (Washington, DC: Government Printing Office, 1911), 214–15.

95. Marriage of Jean Baptiste Raphael and Marie Gaspart, 4 August 1725, M1, SLC. See also Spear, *Race, Sex, and Social Order*, 79. On John Mingo, see 1727/11/28/01, 1727/11/28/02, 1729/10/21/02, 1730/11/21/01, RSCL.

96. 1736/08/21/01, RSCL; agreement, RSCSJR LHQ, vol. 8, no. 3 (1925), 489.

97. 1728/07/21/02, RSCL; judgment rendered, RSCSJR LHQ, vol. 7, no. 4 (1924), 688.

98. Alice Dunbar-Nelson, "People of Color in Louisiana: Part I," *Journal of Negro History* 1, no. 4 (1916): 361–76.

99. 1729/10/22/01, RSCL; "Petition for Emancipation of Indian Slave, 22 October 1729," RSCSJR LHQ, vol. 4, no. 3 (1922), 355.

100. The Osage woman was likely a victim of raids and warfare between the Osage and the Caddo (and their Comanche and Wichita allies). See Juliana Barr, *Peace Came in the Form of a Woman: Indians and Spaniards in the Texas Borderlands* (Chapel Hill: University of North Carolina Press, 2009), 201–2, 218–20.

101. Dawdy writes, "The rationale behind Congo's selection is unknown, but the power he held to whip or hang Frenchmen seems to symbolize the near equivalence of black slaves and poor whites before absolutist law." Shannon Lee Dawdy, "The Burden of Louis Congo and the Evolution of Savagery in Colonial Louisiana," in *Discipline and the Other Body: Correction, Corporeality, Colonialism*, ed. Steven Pierce and Anupama Rao (Durham, NC: Duke University Press, 2006), 67.

102. Delibérations de Conseil Supérieur de la Louisiane, 24 October 1725, C13A 9, fols. 267–68, HNOC.

103. Dawdy, *Building the Devil's Empire*, 189.

104. Gene E. Ogle, "Slaves of Justice: Saint Domingue's Executioners and the Production of Shame," *Historical Reflections / Réflexions Historiques* 29, no. 2 (2003): 275–93, 286–87.

105. 1727/11/28/01 and 1727/11/28/02 (marriage contracts), 1728/11/03/01 (promissory note), 1730/11/21/01 (petition from Mingo to adjust the accounts detailing the agreement), RSCL.

106. 1727/11/28/03, RSCL; promissory note, 28 November 1727, RSCSJR LHQ, vol. 4, no. 3 (1922), 236.

107. 1729/10/21/02, RSCL.

108. 1730/11/21/01, 1730/11/21/03, 1730/11/25/01 (Darby's response), 1730/11/25/05 (final decision), RSCL.

109. On the gendered differences between *petit maroonage* or truancy and *grand maroonage*, see Stephanie M. H. Camp, *Closer to Freedom: Enslaved Women and Everyday Resistance in the Plantation South* (Chapel Hill: University of North Carolina Press, 2004); Richard Price, *Maroon Societies: Rebel Slave Communities in the Americas* (Baltimore: Johns Hopkins University Press, 1996); John Hope Franklin and Loren Schweninger, *Runaway Slaves: Rebels on the Plantation* (Oxford: Oxford University Press, 2000).

110. Hall, "African Women," 254. In data compiled for lower Louisiana, Hall found 1,483 women of laboring age during the French period; 3.7 percent were skilled in at least one or more ways.

111. Powell, *Accidental City*, 88–89.

112. Daniel H. Usner, "The Frontier Exchange Economy of the Lower Mississippi Valley in the Eighteenth Century," *William and Mary Quarterly* 44, no. 2 (1987): 184–86. Daniel Usner described the frontier-exchange economy as an "interethnic web" of "small-scale, face-to-face marketing." Open marketing by slaves, though prohibited by the 1685 and 1724 versions of the *Code Noir*, "benefitted too many people to be forcibly prohibited" (184).

113. Étienne de Périer, "Mouvements des sauvages de la Louisianne depuis la prise du fort des Natchez," January 1731, 21 and 28 July 1731, C13 A, HNOC. See also Périer to Maurepas, C13A, HNOC, on managing French-Native relations, in *MPA*, 4:352–44.

114. Powell, *Accidental City*, 89.

115. Vidal makes this point about the possible ambiguity around Congo's free status. See also Cécile Vidal, *Caribbean New Orleans: Empire, Race, and the Making of a Slave Society* (Chapel Hill: University of North Carolina Press, 2019).

116. Dawdy, "Burden of Louis Congo," 70–71.

117. Marisa J. Fuentes, *Dispossessed Lives: Enslaved Women, Violence, and the Archive* (Philadelphia: University of Pennsylvania Press, 2016).

Chapter 5

Source of epigraph: 1751/06/15/02, RSCL, LHC. Charlotte's case proceeds over several documents. See the interrogation on the case of "d'Erneville's mulatto," 24 January 1751, Black Books, LHC; 1751/06/15/01, 1751/06/15/02, 1751/06/15/03, 1751/06/2101, 1751/12/02/01, RSCL.

1. Jennifer M. Spear, *Race, Sex, and Social Order in Early New Orleans* (Baltimore: Johns Hopkins University Press, 2009); Stewart R. King, *Blue Coat or Powdered Wig: Free People of Color in Pre-revolutionary Saint Domingue* (Athens: University of Georgia Press, 2001); John D. Garrigus, *Before Haiti: Race and Citizenship in French Saint-Domingue* (New York: Macmillan, 2006); Bernard Moitt, *Women and Slavery in the French Antilles, 1635–1848* (Bloomington: Indiana University Press, 2001); Michele Reid-Vazquez, *The Year of the Lash: Free People of Color in Cuba and the Nineteenth-Century Atlantic World* (Athens: University of Georgia Press, 2011); Alejandro de la Fuente, "Slaves and the Creation of Legal Rights in Cuba: Coartación and Papel," *Hispanic American Historical Review* 87, no. 4 (2007): 339–69.

2. Voyages, Voyage ID# 32908, https://slavevoyages.org/voyages/kX7nG6lI (accessed 29 September 2019); Gwendolyn Midlo Hall, *Africans in Colonial Louisiana: The Development of Afro-Creole Culture in the Eighteenth Century* (Baton Rouge: Louisiana State University Press, 1995), 92.

3. For Suzanne's story, see Chapter 4; for Marie Baude's, see Chapter 3.

4. Deliberations prives en l'assemblé des Directeurs, 29 June 1729, C13A 11, fols. 349–50, CAOM.

5. In November 1737, after Jean's death, Louise was sold by Raguet, the director of the hospital, and repurchased by M. de Belille. Sale, doc no. 17371120, LHC. The sales document details the exchange and names Jean Pinet as her former owner.

6. Recensement des habitations le long du fleuve, January 1731, G1 464.

7. Ignace François Broutin, plan de la ville de la Nouvelle Orleans, 1728, France Guerre Etat Major 7C 217 (2) (PrCt), Newberry Library, lot 168.

8. Bienville et Salmon to Ministre de Marine, 1 May 1735, C13A 20, fol. 80r., CAOM.

9. 1737/07/13/01, 1737/06/28/06, RSCL; contract, RSCSJR LHQ, vol. 3, no. 4 (1920), 551–53; see also vol. 5, no. 3, 401; vol. 4, 366.

10. 1737/06/28/06, fol. 7, RSCL. Another example from farther north at Pointe Coupe: in 1745, Jean Baptiste Marly agreed to serve his wife's owner, Jean Joseph de Pontalba, for three years for his wife's freedom. If Venus died in that time, his daughter would take Venus's place as *affranchie*. 1745/11/09/03, RSCL.

11. 1738/02/15/03, RSCL (includes manumission signed by Périer and Salmon, dated 4 October 1738); petition to manumit slave, 15 February 1738, RSCSJR LHQ, vol. 9, no. 4 (1926), 722.

12. 1737/11/07/01, RSCL.

13. Emancipation paper, 1 October 1733, RSCSJR LHQ, vol. 5, no. 2 (1922), 250.

14. 1743/07/16/01, RSCL; manumission, RSCSJR LHQ, vol. 11, no. 4 (1928), 633.

15. 1736/08/11/03, RSCL; Marcel Giraud, *A History of French Louisiana* (Baton Rouge: Louisiana State University Press, 1974), 5:136; Sophie White, *Wild Frenchmen and Frenchified Indians: Material Culture and Race in Colonial Louisiana* (Philadelphia: University of Pennsylvania Press, 2013), 240n17.

16. 1735/10/09/01, 1737/07/29/02, 1743/11/29/06, 1745/02/06/05, RSCL; manumission, 1735 October 9, RSCSJR LHQ, vol. 8, no. 1 (1925), 143–44; petition to Governor Vaudreuil and Ordonnateur Salmon, 29 November 1743, RSCSJR LHQ, vol. 12, no. 3 (1929), 485; notice served, 29 March 1745, RSCSJR LHQ, vol. 13, no. 3 (1930), 517.

17. 1743/11/29/06, RSCL.

18. Guillaume Aubert, "'The Blood of France': Race and Purity of Blood in the French Atlantic World," *William and Mary Quarterly* 61, no. 3 (2004): 475–76. A 1711 royal edict required slaveowners to secure approval from the governor and intendant. The Louisiana *Code Noir* required Superior Council approval, but it did not mention needing approval from the governor and intendant.

19. 1737/07/29/02, RSCL. In her petition against d'Ausseville, Marie Charlotte argues she was sold to settle the estate debt at a price of 1,500 livres to an S. Barbin.

20. 1743/11/29/06, RSCL.

21. 1745/02/06/05, RSCL; notice served, RSCSJR LHQ, vol. 13, no. 3 (1930), 517. The LHQ transcription and translation states that Marie Charlotte described herself as a "free woman." The original document uses the gender-ambiguous *personne libre*.

22. 1736/08/23/03, 1737/06/29/01, RSCL.

23. 1738/08/26/03, RSCL.

24. 1738/09/07/01, 1739/03/06/02, RSCL; succession of Calixte Descairac, 6 March 1739, RSCSJR LHQ, vol. 6, no. 3 (1923), 304. It is possible Coustilhas also freed Françoise, a *mulâtresse*; her son, Pierrot; and daughter, Petit Marianne, from La Forest in his will. Françoise and her children did not remain in Louisiana. Captain Jean Berry left 2,000 livres to Françoise and each of the children and sent them to France aboard *Le Comte de Maure* "to give them all possible education and every advantage." See "Freed Slaves," in *Afro-Louisiana*.

25. 1738/09/03/01, 1738/09/05/01, RSCL; "Manumission, March 28, 1736," RSCSJR LHQ, vol. 8, no. 2 (1925), 287. My thanks to Vera Gutman for research on this source.

26. 1738/09/03/01, RSCL.

27. 1738/09/05/01, RSCL.

28. 1738/09/03/01, RSCL.

29. 1744/07/14/01, RSCL.

30. Jacques Houdaille, "La fécondité des anciens esclaves à Saint-Domingue (1794–1801)," *Population* 28, no. 6 (1973): 1210; Nicole Vanony-Frisch, "Les esclaves de la Guadeloupe à la fin de l'Ancien Régime d'après les sources notariales (1770–1789)," *Bulletin de la Société d'Histoire de la Guadeloupe*, no. 63–64 (1985): 70. Houdaille used parish registers from Port-au-Prince, Fort Dauphin, Jacmel, and Cayes du Fond from 1780 to 1795 to calculate reproduction rates among enslaved women. Vanony-Frisch used plantation registers from 1770 to 1795 for her calculations. In general, high infant mortality rates combined with low birth rates to prevent natural reproduction of the enslaved population. Moitt, *Women and Slavery in the French Antilles*, 89–92.

31. By 1741, extant data identifies 2,620 creole slaves in Louisiana. Hall, *Africans in Colonial Louisiana*, 175. See also "All Slaves by Gender," in *Afro-Louisiana*, https://www.ibiblio.org/laslave/calculations.php (accessed 14 March 2019).

32. "Ordonnance du Roi, concernant l'Affranchissement des Esclaves des Isles et Ordonnance des Administrateurs en consequences, 15 June 1736," in Médéric-Louis-Élie Moreau de Saint-Méry, ed., *Loix et constitutions des colonies françoises de l'Amerique sous le vent* (Paris: chez l'Auteur, 1784–1790), 3:453–4.

33. Spear, *Race, Sex, and Social Order*, 259n44.

34. 1745/11/14/01, 1745/11/15/01, RSCL.

35. Spear, *Race, Sex, and Social Order*, 264n92.

36. Spear, *Race, Sex, and Social Order*, 264n89.

37. Spear, *Race, Sex, and Social Order*, 259n44.

38. Spear, *Race, Sex, and Social Order*, 89. On the Lemelles, see Virginia Meacham Gould, "Urban Slavery, Urban Freedom: The Manumission of Jacqueline Lemelle," in *More Than Chattel: Black Women and Slavery in the Americas*, ed. David Barry Gaspar and Darlene Clark Hine (Bloomington: Indiana University Press, 1996).

39. 1746/02/01/03, 1767/02/12/01, RSCL.

40. 1745/02/23/01, RSCL.

41. 1765/10/21/02, RSCL.

42. 1769/07/06/02, SJRL.

43. 1740/02/24/01, 1740/08/24/01, 1742/05/24/01, and succession documents (1740/02/24/02, 1740/03/12/01, 1740/03/12/02, 1740/03/19/01, 1740/03/21/01, 1740/03/21/02, 1740/03/24/01, 1740/03/30/01, 1740/04/25/02, 1740/05/11/01, 1740/07/20/01, 1740/07/23/01, 1740/08/02/01, 1740/06/16/01, 1740/06/16/02, 1740/08/20/01), RSCL. Because La Liberté managed a tar pit, a significant enterprise in the eighteenth century, as well as a plantation, the succession documentation generated was extensive. See also the manumission of Jeanneton and Marie Jean, 27 October 1762, RSCSJR LHQ, vol. 24, no. 3 (1941) 557–59.

44. Kathleen M. Brown, *Good Wives, Nasty Wenches, and Anxious Patriarchs: Gender, Race, and Power in Colonial Virginia* (Chapel Hill: University of North Carolina Press, 1996), 227–46.

45. Saidiya Hartman, "The Belly of the World: A Note on Black Women's Labors," *Souls* 18, no. 1 (2016): 166–73, 73.

46. On the rise of French-speaking but Atlantic-born men to local power along the Gulf Coast, see Shannon Lee Dawdy, *Building the Devil's Empire: French Colonial New Orleans* (Chicago: University of Chicago Press, 2008), 135. Work by Vidal sheds further light on this cohort and their

Caribbean connections. Cécile Vidal, *Caribbean New Orleans: Empire, Race, and the Making of a Slave Society* (Chapel Hill: Omohundro Institute and University of North Carolina Press, 2019).

47. 1723/10/01/01, RSCL.

48. 1729/09/27/01, RSCL. M. Trudeau, who brought the complaint before Fleuriau, described Maxama as "always in a fever [fievieux]" and as threatening his life.

49. 1748/02/10/01, RSCL. These are Taca's words, according to testimony given by Flatague in his witness statement against Baraca.

50. 1748/02/09/02, 1748/02/09/03, 1748/02/10/01, 1748/03/09/11, 1748/04/15/01, 1748/04/22/03, 1748/04/25/02, 1748/05/03/02, 1748/05/04/03, 1748/05/04/09, RSCL.

51. On hospitals and enslaved and free black labor in them, see Deirdre Cooper Owens, *Medical Bondage: Race, Gender, and the Origins of American Gynecology* (Athens: University of Georgia Press, 2017). While beyond the scope of this study, for work on slavery, medicine, and the medical profession, see Sasha Turner, *Contested Bodies: Pregnancy, Childrearing, and Slavery in Jamaica* (Philadelphia: University of Pennsylvania Press, 2017); Sharla M. Fett, *Working Cures: Healing, Health, and Power on Southern Slave Plantations* (Chapel Hill: University of North Carolina Press, 2002); Marie Jenkins Schwartz, *Birthing a Slave: Motherhood and Medicine in the Antebellum South* (Cambridge, MA: Harvard University Press, 2006); Jim Downs, *Sick from Freedom: African-American Illness and Suffering During the Civil War and Reconstruction* (New York: Oxford University Press, 2012); Todd L. Savitt, *Medicine and Slavery: The Diseases and Health Care of Blacks in Antebellum Virginia* (Urbana: University of Illinois Press, 1981); Nicole Ivy, "Bodies of Work: A Meditation on Medical Imaginaries and Enslaved Women," *Souls* 18 (2016): 11–31.

52. 1752/06/13/01, 1752/06/13/02, RSCL. The assault on Louison and Babet spans several documents, ending with the decision to hang Pochonet on 26 June 1752: 1752/06/08/01, 1752/06/08/02, 1752/06/12/01, 1752/06/12/02, 1752/06/13/01, 1752/06/13/02, 1752/06/17/01, 1752/06/17/02, 1752/06/19/01, 1752/06/20/01, 1752/06/26/01, 1752/06/26/02, 1752/06/28/01, RSCL.

53. 1752/06/08/01, 1752/06/08/02, RSCL.

54. 1752/06/13/01, 1752/06/13/02, RSCL.

55. 1752/06/13/01, 1752/06/13/02, RSCL.

56. 1752/06/13/01, 1752/06/13/02, RSCL.

57. 1752/06/13/01, 1752/06/13/02, RSCL.

58. 1752/06/13/01, 1752/06/13/02, RSCL.

59. 1752/06/28/01, RSCL.

60. This is a difficult exchange to interpret. Dawdy reads their argument as Le Moine insulting Fanchon with the term *putain*, but notes it is possible that a gender inversion occurred here and that the official was reporting on Fanchon insulting Le Moine. I do not challenge Dawdy's reading of it, but would also like to make the very case she suggests: that Fanchon, having been called, essentially, a whore by Le Moine in the first instance, returns the favor by calling him one in return and sweetens the curse with an insult that tangled the sexual labor of the prostitute with subservience of the indentured servant. See Shannon Lee Dawdy, "La Ville Sauvage: 'Enlightened' Colonialism and Creole Improvisation in New Orleans, 1699–1769" (Ph.D. diss., University of Michigan, 2003), 155n., 301.

61. Charpentier to Commandant at Galam, 12 October 1722, C6 7, CAOM.

62. Marie Thomas Larue, *mulâtresse*, wife of the *ancien capitaine* of the Company, Monsieur Larue, died at Saint-Louis in 1732. Act de Décès, 13 May 1732, acts de naissance, mariage, et décès, *État Civil de Saint-Louis du Sénégal*, 1730–77, CAOM.

63. Dawdy has translated the phrase as "Good evening, mi'lord buggerer," which captures both "the meaning and the intensity of the term." Dawdy, "La Ville Sauvage," 300.

64. 1747/05/05/01, 1747/05/05/02, 1747/05/18/04, 1747/05/19/06, RSCL. See also Heloise Cruzat, "The Documents Covering the Criminal Trial of Etienne La Rue, for Attempt to Murder and Illicit Carrying of Arms," *Louisiana Historical Quarterly* 13, no. 3 (1930): 377–90.

65. Simone Browne, *Dark Matters: On the Surveillance of Blackness* (Durham, NC: Duke University Press, 2015), 69.

66. This mutability is a key characteristic of black, queer, diasporic thought and resistance, just as resisting stable categories is. It is, as Jafari Allen theorizes, a "multiple, luxuriant, and subtle approach." Jafari S. Allen, "Black/Queer/Diaspora at the Current Conjuncture," *GLQ: A Journal of Lesbian and Gay Studies* 18, no. 2–3 (2012): 215. On black femme, see Omise'eke Natasha Tinsley, *Ezili's Mirrors: Imagining Black Queer Genders* (Durham, NC: Duke University Press, 2018); Kaila Adia Story, "Fear of a Black Femme: The Existential Conundrum of Embodying a Black Femme Identity While Being a Professor of Black, Queer, and Feminist Studies," *Journal of Lesbian Studies* 21, no. 4 (2016): 1–13; Kara Keeling, *The Witch's Flight: The Cinematic, the Black Femme, and the Image of Common Sense* (Durham, NC: Duke University Press, 2007).

67. Omise'eke Natasha Tinsley, *Thiefing Sugar: Eroticism Between Women in Caribbean Literature* (Durham, NC: Duke University Press, 2010), 12.

68. Story, "Fear of a Black Femme," 6.

69. Tinsley, *Thiefing Sugar*, 3, 11.

70. There is no evidence that Madame Vaudreuil knew of Charlotte or heard anything about her from Batard before or after she was caught.

71. Stephanie M. H. Camp, *Closer to Freedom: Enslaved Women and Everyday Resistance in the Plantation South* (Chapel Hill: University of North Carolina Press, 2004), xvii.

72. Antoine Simon Le Page du Pratz, *Histoire de la Louisiane* (De Bure, 1758), 3:226–27.

73. Douglas W. Owsley et al., "Demography and Pathology of an Urban Slave Population from New Orleans," *American Journal of Physical Anthropology* 74, no. 2 (1987): 185–97; D. Ryan Gray, "The St. Peter Street Cemetery," *New Orleans Historical*, https://neworleanshistorical.org/items/show/1391 (accessed September 29, 2019).

74. Broutin to the Company, 7 August 1730, in *MPA*, 1:127; Roulhac Toledano and Mary Christovich, *New Orleans Architecture: Faubourg Tremé and the Bayou Road* (New Orleans: Pelican Publishing, 2003), 7; Dumont de Montigny, Plan de la Nouvelle Orleans, ville capitale de la Louissiane (1747), Edward E. Ayer Manuscript Map Collection, Newberry Library, https://collections.leventhalmap.org/search/commonwealth:z603vn56w (accessed 7 May 2019).

75. Article 13, "Edit concernant les negres esclaves à la Louisiane," *Publications of the Louisiana Historical Society* 4 (1908): 76–90.

76. 1746/09/03/05, RSCL.

77. Records from St. Peter's Cemetery, the first internment site in the city, suggest that black females died at the age of twenty to twenty-four years old. Owsley et al., "Demography and Pathology," 49. St. Peter's Cemetery was established at some time between 1721 and 1725, predating St. Louis #1 (founded in 1789). It was not the only internment site in the colonial era: St. Louis Cathedral, the Ursuline convent, and plantations each created their own cemeteries. More research on death rates during the French period is required.

78. 1764/09/04/01, RSCL, for interrogation of Comba and Louison. The full saga begins with enslaved Cezar's arrest and continues through Louis's execution: 1764/07/10/02, 1764/07/10/03,

1764/07/10/06, 1764/09/04/01, 1764/09/04/02, 1764/09/05/01, 1764/09/05/02, 1764/09/10/01, 1764/09/10/02, 1764/09/10/04, 1764/09/10/05, RSCL. See also criminal proceedings, 21 July 1764 and 24 July 1764, Black Books, LHC. Filé is powdered sassafras. It was used by the Choctaw to thicken soups and, into the nineteenth century, was part of the frontier-exchange economy of subsistence items sold by Choctaw women along the Gulf Coast. Daniel H. Usner, *Indian Work: Language and Livelihood in Native American History* (Cambridge, MA: Harvard University Press, 2009), 112; Daniel H. Usner Jr, "Food Marketing and Interethnic Exchange in the 18th-century Lower Mississippi Valley," *Food and Foodways* 1, no. 3 (August 1, 1986): 279–310. It was adopted by Africans as a thickener in what came to be called gumbo, a traditional soup, often with seafood, served over rice. Louisianans hold gumbo in high esteem as a staple of the culture of the Gulf Coast. Thus far, this is the first written reference to gumbo in Louisiana's colonial archive. Charles H. Rowell and Gwendolyn Midlo. Hall, "Gwendolyn Midlo Hall with Charles Henry Rowell," *Callaloo* 29, no. 4 (2006): 1053.

79. Michael A. Gomez, *Exchanging Our Country Marks: The Transformation of African Identities in the Colonial and Antebellum South* (Chapel Hill: University of North Carolina Press, 1998), 74–76.

80. Lolis Eric Elie, *Treme: Stories and Recipes from the Heart of New Orleans* (San Francisco: Chronicle Books, 2013), 156.

81. Cezar reportedly gave Louis 50 sols to purchase the filé. 1764/09/04/01, RSCL.

82. For detailed analysis of this case and the politics of dress among the enslaved, see Sophie White, "'Wearing Three or Four Handkerchiefs Around His Collar, and Elsewhere About Him': Slaves' Constructions of Masculinity and Ethnicity in French Colonial New Orleans," *Gender & History* 15 (2003): 528–49.

83. This was the same Tixerant who broke up the altercation between La Rue and the soldiers.

84. 1748/03/22/01, RSCL.

85. Marie-Madeleine Hachard, *Relation du voyage des dames religieuses Ursulines de Rouen à La Nouvelle-Orleans* (Paris: Maisonneuve, 1872), 98.

86. Marc-Antoine Caillot, *A Company Man: The Remarkable French-Atlantic Voyage of a Clerk for the Company of the Indies: A Memoir* (New Orleans: Historic New Orleans Collection, 2013), 134–41. Caillot's cross-dressing Mardi Gras masquerade included him putting *mouches* on his face. He portrayed a white shepherdess.

87. Emily Clark, *Masterless Mistresses: The New Orleans Ursulines and the Development of a New World Society* (Chapel Hill: University of North Carolina Press, 2007), 177, 188.

88. Emily Clark and Virginia Meacham Gould, "The Feminine Face of Afro-Catholicism in New Orleans, 1727–1852," *William and Mary Quarterly* 59, no. 2 (2002): 409.

89. John E. Salvaggio, *New Orleans' Charity Hospital: A Story of Physicians, Politics, and Poverty* (Baton Rouge: Louisiana State University Press, 1992), 11.

90. Carl A. Brasseaux, "The Administration of Slave Regulations in French Louisiana, 1724–1766," *Louisiana History* 21, no. 2 (1980): 139–58; Gilbert C. Din, *Spaniards, Planters, and Slaves: The Spanish Regulation of Slavery in Louisiana, 1763–1803* (College Station: Texas A&M University Press, 1999), 25–29; Hall, *Africans in Colonial Louisiana*, 117–18, 176–79. Brasseaux described this as the "Panic of 1748," while Hall stresses the African-Choctaw alliances between maroons and indigenous between outposts. Din, however, is more skeptical about the African presence in these raids and their ultimate threat to the colony. However real the threat, German

Coast white slaveowners and settlers formed armed bands and Vaudreuil dispatched soldiers as military support.

91. Charles Gayarre, *History of Louisiana* (New Orleans: F. F. Hanswell & Bros., 1903), 2:361–67. Any "Frenchman" who did the same would be whipped and sent to work for the king's galley for the rest of his days.

92. Dumont de Montigny, *Mémoires historiques sur la Louisiane* (Paris: J. B. Bauche, 1753), 2:242–3. See also Jerah Johnson, "New Orleans's Congo Square: An Urban Setting for Early Afro-American Culture Formation," *Louisiana History* 32, no. 2 (1991): 117–57, 122–23.

93. 1764/09/04/02, RSCL; Johnson, "New Orleans's Congo Square," 126n13.

94. Maryse Condé, "Voyager In, Voyager Out," in *The Journey of a Caribbean Writer* (London: Seagull Books, 2014), 50–62.

Chapter 6

1. 1789/01/29/02, SJRL (hereafter Diligencias). For readability, I have standardized the spelling of each person's name to conform to the most common instance in the trial testimony: María Teresa, Perine Demasillier or Perine Dauphine, and Maurice Dauphine.

2. Diligencias, 4. Antonio Méndez served as María Teresa's *procurador público* (public defender) through most of the case. As described by Gilbert Din, the Spanish *procurador* handled all cases where the Cabildo appointed attorneys or required royal prosecutors, or where the accused could not find their own counsel. For more on the role of the *procurador público* in Spanish Louisiana, see Gilbert C. Din and John E. Harkins, *The New Orleans Cabildo: Colonial Louisiana's First City Government 1769–1803* (Baton Rouge: Louisiana State University Press, 1996), 116–17n35.

3. "Code O'Reilly, New Orleans," Archivo General de Indias (1769); "Ordinances and Instructions of Don Alejandro O'Reilly," in *Historical Memoirs of Louisiana: From the Earliest Settlement of the Colony to the Departure of the Governor O'Reilly in 1770*, ed. B. F. French (New York: Lamport, Blakeman & Law, 1853), 254–91. O'Reilly arrived on 17 August 1769. The first entry in the Actas del Cabildo was 18 August 1769. The Cabildo was not formed until 25 November 1769. Din and Harkins, *New Orleans Cabildo*, 48–50.

4. O'Reilly's proclamation barring Indian slavery was issued on 7 December 1769. Daniel H. Usner, *Indians, Settlers, and Slaves in a Frontier Exchange Economy: The Lower Mississippi Valley Before 1783* (Chapel Hill: University of North Carolina, 1992), 132–33. See also Stephen Webre, "The Problem of Indian Slavery in Spanish Louisiana, 1769–1803," *Louisiana History* 25, no. 2 (1984): 117–35. Both Usner and Webre argue that the policy failed to eliminate Indian slavery in practice and had complicated formal manumission almost from the outset. See also Gilbert C. Din, *Spaniards, Planters, and Slaves: The Spanish Regulation of Slavery in Louisiana, 1763–1803* (College Station: Texas A&M University Press, 1999), 49–50; "Census of Louisiana, 2 Sep 1771," in *Spain in the Mississippi Valley*, ed. Lawrence Kinnaird (Washington, DC: U.S. Government Printing Office, 1949), 2:196.

5. For a detailed study of *coartación* in Cuba, see Alejandro de la Fuente, "Slaves and the Creation of Legal Rights in Cuba: Coartación and Papel," *Hispanic American Historical Review* 87, no. 4 (2007): 659–92.

6. Jennifer M. Spear, *Race, Sex, and Social Order in Early New Orleans* (Baltimore: Johns Hopkins University Press, 2009), 16.

7. Spear, *Race, Sex, and Social Order*, 116, 270n68; Kimberly S. Hanger, *Bounded Lives, Bounded Places: Free Black Society in Colonial New Orleans, 1769–1803* (Durham, NC: Duke University Press, 1997), 25–26.

8. Spear, *Race, Sex, and Social Order*, 101–2, 110. See "Louisiana Free Database, 1719–1820," in *Afro-Louisiana*; Gwendolyn Midlo Hall, "Epilogue: Historical Memory, Consciousness, and Conscience in the New Millennium," in *French Colonial Louisiana and the Atlantic World*, ed. Bradley G. Bond (Baton Rouge: Louisiana State University Press, 2005), 299; Hanger, *Bounded Lives, Bounded Places*, 118, 184n11.

9. For more on *castas* in the Spanish-American empire, see Herman L. Bennett, *Colonial Blackness: A History of Afro-Mexico* (Bloomington: Indiana University Press, 2011); R. Douglas Cope, *The Limits of Racial Domination: Plebeian Society in Colonial Mexico City, 1660–1720* (Madison: University of Wisconsin Press, 1994); Jake Frederick, "Without Impediment: Crossing Racial Boundaries in Colonial Mexico," *Americas* 67, no. 4 (2011): 495–515; Ilona Katzew, *Casta Painting: Images of Race in Eighteenth-Century Mexico* (New Haven, CT: Yale University Press, 2004); Verena Martinez-Alier, *Marriage, Class, and Colour in Nineteenth-Century Cuba: A Study of Racial Attitudes and Sexual Values in a Slave Society* (Ann Arbor: University of Michigan Press, 1989); Maria Elena Martinez, *Genealogical Fictions: Limpieza de Sangre, Religion, and Gender in Colonial Mexico* (Stanford, CA: Stanford University Press, 2008); Stuart B. Schwartz, "Colonial Identities and the Sociedad de Castas," *Colonial Latin American Review* 4 (1995): 185–201; Patricia Seed, "The Social Dimensions of Race: Mexico City, 1753," *Hispanic American Historical Review* 62, no. 4 (1982): 569–606.

10. According to the Voyages database, 9,517 slaves (2,369 from the African continent and 7,148 trans-shipped) disembarked on the Gulf Coast between 1769 and 1803, beginning with the *Amelia* in 1773. See Voyages, Year Range: 1769–1803, Principal Place of Slave Landing: Gulf Coast, https://slavevoyages.org/voyage/database#searchId=orFbGzsZ and https://slavevoyages.org/voyage/database#searchId=orFbGzsZ (both accessed 14 March 2019). See also Jean-Pierre Leglaunec, "Slave Migrations in Spanish and Early American Louisiana: New Sources and New Estimates," *Louisiana History* 46, no. 2 (2005); Jean-Pierre Leglaunec, "A Directory of Ships with Slave Cargoes, Louisiana, 1772–1808," *Louisiana History* 46, no. 2 (2005): 211–30. These figures would be in addition to any illegal (and therefore undocumented) slave trading from North American ports like Baltimore and Charleston.

11. Specific to New Orleans, Spear argues that *casta* did not describe complexion so much as social position. Free people of color were more likely to be perceived and therefore labeled as belonging to a lighter casta because "freedom whitened or at least lightened." Spear, *Race, Sex, and Social Order*, 113. As Jake Frederick has noted for colonial Mexico: "The notion of the *sistema de castas* is in fact shorthand for a variety of inconsistent and often contradictory ideas about how race defined one's status in colonial society. Yet the word *sistema* implies an order and intention that overstates the rigidity of the racial hierarchy of the New World." Frederick, "Without Impediment," 498.

12. Spear, *Race, Sex, and Social Order*, 131.

13. Hanger, *Bounded Lives, Bounded Places*, 27; Spear, *Race, Sex, and Social Order*, 110. According to notarial records for the Spanish period, between 1771 and 1803, 452 slaves were freed by self-purchase; 445 slaves were freed through third-party purchase for a total of 906.

14. Hanger, *Bounded Lives, Bounded Places*, 27. Between 1771 and 1803, 798 slaves were freed *graciosa*; 72 were freed with conditions for a total of 870.

15. Hanger, *Bounded Lives, Bounded Places*, 27. The total New Orleans population in 1788 by status was 2,370 white/free people, 820 free people of color, and 2,131 slaves. Louisiana's official free population of color passed 1,000 at the end of the century.

16. Hanger, *Bounded Lives, Bounded Places*, 22. Sex ratios for free people of color in New Orleans were 47 in 1777, 40 in 1788, 60 in 1791, and 6 in 1805. Types of manumission were *graciosa*, self-purchase, purchase by a third-party, and tribunal.

17. Hanger, *Bounded Lives, Bounded Places*, 27–29.

18. Jane Landers, *Black Society in Spanish Florida* (Urbana: University of Illinois Press, 1999), 183.

19. French rebellion leaders were Nicolas Chauvin de La Frénière, Pierre Hardi de Boisblanc, Balthasar Masan, Joseph Villeré, Pierre Marquis, Pierre Poupet, Joseph Petit, Pierre Caresse, Julien Jérôme Doucet, Jean Milhet, Joseph Milhet, and Jean-Baptiste Noyan. The rebels successfully expelled Ulloa from the colony, but failed to hold it when Spanish Governor Alejandro O'Reilly arrived (with military force) two years later. The leaders were tried and convicted—six were sent to prison, and the rest were executed. For a history of the rebellion, see Carl A. Brasseaux, *Denis-Nicolas Foucault and the New Orleans Rebellion of 1768* (Ruston, LA: McGinty Publications, 1987); John Preston Moore, *Revolt in Louisiana: The Spanish Occupation, 1766–1770* (Baton Rouge: Louisiana State University Press, 1976). For a review of the leaders and assessment of the economic and social status, as well as relationships through marriage and kinship to each other, see Winston de Ville Florence M. Jumonville, "Ties That Bind: The Family, Social, and Business Associations of the Insurrectionists of 1768," *Louisiana History* 47, no. 2 (2006): 183–202.

20. The details of this case are available here 1778/03/28/01, SJRL; "Criminal prosecution of Pedro La Cabanne and the mulâtresse Madelon, belonging to Nicolas Perthuis," vol. 13, no. 3 (1930): 339–43.

21. 1775 September 1, Acts of Almonester y Roxas, fol. 389, NONA.

22. 1782 February 15, Acts of Almonester y Roxas, fol. 97, NONA.

23. In 1786, Bishop Cyrillo denounced "Negroes who at the vespers hour assembled in a green expanse called 'Place Congo' to dance the bamboula and perform the rites imported from Africa by the Yolofs, Foulahs, Bambarras, Mandigoes, and other races." Celestin M. Chambon, *In and Around the Old St. Louis Cathedral of New Orleans* (New Orleans: Philippe's Printery, 1908), 33. Freddi Williams Evans cites this as the earliest documented reference to Congo in relation to Congo Square. Freddi Williams Evans, *Congo Square: African Roots in New Orleans* (Lafayette: University of Louisiana Press, 2011), 6. Ned Sublette and Kimberly Hanger suggest the Place Congo described by Cyrillo was not a designated space in the city (yet) but a gathering or event held by people of African descent that could occur in various contexts—making it a mobile and ephemeral black geography. Ned Sublette, *The World That Made New Orleans: From Spanish Silver to Congo Square* (Chicago: Lawrence Hill Books, 2008), 120–21; Hanger, *Bounded Lives, Bounded Places*, 145.

24. In 1787, Pedro Pizanie collects 81 pesos from "las negras y otros individuos que venden en la Conga del mercado" (black women and other individuals who sell in the Conga of the market). In 1784, the Cabildo authorized construction on a central, permanent market near the levee. It

burned down in the 1788 fire and would not be rebuilt until 1793. Hanger, *Bounded Lives, Bounded Places*, 63–64.

25. Joan Dayan, "Codes of Law and Bodies of Color," *New Literary History* 26, no. 2 (1995): 288.

26. In 1781, free people of color were prohibited from using the honorific "Monsieur" or "Madame" in official documents. Restrictions also applied to work, particularly the professions, with bans on free people of color being employed as clerks of court, notaries, or bailiffs or practicing medicine, surgery, or pharmacy trades in 1764 and 1765. An outright ban on free people of color practicing any trade beyond farming without a pass was instituted in 1788. In 1779, free people of color could not "affect the dress, hairstyles, style, or bearing of whites," ride in carriages, or decorate their homes at will. Léo Elisabeth, "The French Antilles," in *Neither Slave nor Free: The Freedman of African Descent in the Slave Societies of the New World*, ed. David W. Cohen and Jack P. Greene (Baltimore: Johns Hopkins University Press, 1974), 162; Laurent Dubois, *Avengers of the New World: The Story of the Haitian Revolution* (Cambridge, MA: Harvard University Press, 2005), 62.

27. In 1749, colonial administrators banned the *bals* held by free people of color, in particular, "les assemblés qui se tiennent chez les Mulâtresses et Negresses libres" (the assemblies held at the homes of *mulâtresses* and free *négresses*). In 1762, the governor again banned dances held by free people of color unless held with express permission, empowering police to report offenders. In 1765, administrators prohibited free people of color from gathering for feasts at all. This admonition needed to be issued again in 1772, when administrators again forbade *gens de couleur* and *nègres libres* from night dances or *Kalendas*, but allowed dances to be held up to nine in the evening. Médéric-Louis-Élie Moreau de Saint-Méry, ed., *Loix et constitutions des colonies françoises de l'Amerique sous le vent* (Paris: chez l'Auteur, 1784–90), 3:885; 4:466; 4:162; 5:384–86.

28. John D. Garrigus, *Before Haiti: Race and Citizenship in French Saint-Domingue* (New York: Macmillan, 2006), 167, 163.

29. Manuel Lucena Salmoral, "El texto de segundo código negro español, también llamado carolino, existente en el Archivo de Indias," *Estudios de historia social y económica de América* 12 (1995): 267–324. See also Tamara J. Walker, *Exquisite Slaves: Race, Clothing, and Status in Colonial Lima* (Cambridge: Cambridge University Press, 2019).

30. Planters, including those along the Gulf Coast, protested the 1789 *Real cedula*. Din, *Spaniards*, 126–35. On Spanish slave codes, see Javier Malagón Barceló, *Código Negro Carolino (1784)* (Santo Domingo, Dominican Republic: Ediciones Taller, 1974); Manuel Lucena Salmoral, *Los Códigos negros de la América española* (Alcala, Spain: Universidad Alcalea, 1996); Ana Hontanilla, "Sentiment and the Law: Inventing the Category of the Wretched Slave in the *Real Audiencia* of Santo Domingo, 1783–1812," *Eighteenth-Century Studies* 48, no. 2 (2015): 181–200; Ariela Gross and Alejandro de la Fuente, "Slaves, Free Blacks, and Race in the Legal Regimes of Cuba, Louisiana, and Virginia: A Comparison," *North Carolina Law Review* 91 (2012): 1699–756.

31. Dayan, "Codes of Law," 295.

32. Lisa Ze Winters, *The Mulatta Concubine: Terror, Intimacy, Freedom, and Desire in the Black Transatlantic* (Athens: University of Georgia Press, 2016), 78–79.

33. Médéric-Louis-Elie Moreau de Saint Méry, *Description topographique, physique, civile, politique et historique de la partie française de l'isle Saint-Domingue* (Philadelphia: Chez l'Auteur,

1797), 1:97–98, 1:77. See also Omise'eke Natasha Tinsley, *Thiefing Sugar: Eroticism Between Women in Caribbean Literature* (Durham, NC: Duke University Press, 2010), 44.

34. For Charlotte's full story, see Chapter 5.

35. 22 February 1771, Acts of Garic, fol. 78, NONA; October 1773, Acts of Almonester y Roxas, NONA; 9 September 1801, Acts of Pedesclaux, no. 39, fol. 513, NONA.

36. Hanger, *Bounded Lives, Bounded Places*, 99, 63.

37. 25 April 1797, Acts of Pedesclaux, no. 29, fol. 262, NONA.

38. Virginia Meacham Gould, "In Full Enjoyment of Their Liberty: The Free Women of Color of the Gulf Ports of New Orleans, Mobile, and Pensacola, 1769–1860" (Ph.D. diss., Emory University, 1992); Virginia Meacham Gould, "Urban Slavery, Urban Freedom: The Manumission of Jacqueline Lemelle," in *More Than Chattel: Black Women and Slavery in the Americas*, ed. David Barry Gaspar and Darlene Clark Hine (Bloomington: Indiana University Press, 1996), 298–314; Virginia Meacham Gould, ed., *Chained to the Rock of Adversity: To Be Free, Black and Female in the Old South* (Athens: University of Georgia Press, 1998); Gwendolyn Midlo Hall, *Africans in Colonial Louisiana: The Development of Afro-Creole Culture in the Eighteenth Century* (Baton Rouge: Louisiana State University Press, 1995); Hanger, *Bounded Lives, Bounded Places*; Spear, *Race, Sex, and Social Order.*

39. Hanger, *Bounded Lives, Bounded Places*; Paul F. Lachance, "Intermarriage and French Cultural Persistence in Late Spanish and Early American New Orleans," *Histoire sociale/ Social History* 15, no. 29 (1982): 47–81.

40. Dylan Penningroth, Vincent Brown, and Tiya Miles have shown ways bondage, property, and access to resources structured and complicated kinship claims. Using inheritance practices as a lens, the intersection between claims of property and what Dylan Penningroth called the "claims of kinfolk" becomes even clearer. Dylan C. Penningroth, *The Claims of Kinfolk: African American Property and Community in the Nineteenth-Century South* (Chapel Hill: University of North Carolina Press, 2003); Vincent Brown, *The Reaper's Garden: Death and Power in the World of Atlantic Slavery* (Cambridge, MA: Harvard University Press, 2008); Tiya Miles, *Ties That Bind: The Story of an Afro-Cherokee Family in Slavery and Freedom* (Berkeley: University of California Press, 2005). As Vincent Brown has noted for eighteenth-century Jamaica, "The living expected legacies, and the dead, through their bequests, expected to wield continued influence in the society they left behind." Brown, *Reaper's Garden*, 92.

41. Article 56, *Le code noir ou Edit du roy servant de reglement pour le gouvernement & l'administration de justice & la police des isles françoises de l'Amerique, & pour la discipline & le commerce des negres & esclaves dans le dit pays* (Paris: Veuve Saugrain, 1718), 2–12.

42. Moreau de Saint-Méry, *Loix et constitutions*, 1:414; Guillaume Aubert, "'To Establish One Law and Definite Rules': Race, Religion, and the Transatlantic Origins of the Louisiana Code Noir," in *Louisiana: Crossroads of the Atlantic World*, ed. Cécile Vidal (Philadelphia: University of Pennsylvania Press, 2013), 40.

43. 8 February 1726, in Moreau de Saint-Méry, *Loix et constitutions*, 3:159–60; Garrigus, *Before Haiti*, 42. See also Hans W. Baade, "The Gens de Couleur of Louisiana: Comparative Slave Law in Microcosm," *Cardozo Law Review* 18 (1996): 539–42. In New Orleans, officials appeared to have paid some attention to the guidelines restricting inheritance.

44. 831–33 St. Philip St., lot number 22951, 1 January 1722, VCS. See lots 341 and 342.

45. "Census of New Orleans as Reported by M. Périer, Commandant General of Louisiana, July 1, 1727," in *Census Tables for the French Colony of Louisiana*, ed. Charles R. Maduell (New Orleans, 1971), 2:A-27-14.

46. Plan de la Nouvelle Orléans telle qu'elle estoit au mois de dexembre 1731 levé par Gonichon, Décembre 1731, CAOM, 04DFC 89B; "List of Property Owners of New Orleans on the Map Published by Gonichon in 1731," in Maduell, *Census Tables*, 3:A-31.

47. Recensement des habitations le long du fleuve, 1731, G1 464, CAOM.

48. 810 Ursulines St., lot number 22936, 22 March 1749, VCS; 1769/08/02/01, SJRL, LHC. Junon would later own another lot on Ursulines and property on Bourbon. 812-14 Ursulines St., lot number 22937, 27 November 1770, VCS; 1035-37 Bourbon St., lot number 22934, 24 October 1776, VCS; 1770/11/27/01, SJRL.

49. 538 Dauphine St., lot number 18714, 7 February 1786, VCS; 1029 Bourbon St., lot number 22933-C, 20 August 1757, VCS; 929 Dumaine St., lot number 18857, 11 March 1788 and 26 March 1792, VCS, as well as 931 Dumaine St., lot number 18856, VCS.

50. Recensement, 1731.

51. 1727/07/13/01, RSCL. See also "Will of François Deserboy, 13 July 1727," RSCSJR LHQ, vol. 4, no. 2 (1921): 222.

52. 1764/07/07/01, RSCL.

53. 1745/02/23/01, 1747/08/16/01, RSCL.

54. "Testament de la nommée Marie Jemita," 25 March 1777, SDNA 173, CAOM.

55. John D. Garrigus, "'To Establish a Community of Property': Marriage and Race Before and During the Haitian Revolution," *History of the Family* 12, no. 2 (2007): 142–52; Dominique Rogers, "Réussir dans une monde d'hommes: Les stratégies des femmes de couleur du Cap-Français," *Journal of Haitian Studies* 9, no. 1 (2003): 40–51. According to Rodgers, in Cap Français, by the 1770s, much of the property that free women of color owned had been passed on to them by "grandparents, parents, uncles, aunts, brothers, sisters, and godparents," not white men. Rogers, "Réussir dans une monde d'hommes," 42.

56. Under the Spanish, Havana became the seat of imperial government. Appeals on New Orleans court cases went to the higher court at Havana.

57. A final category, *hijo legitimo con gracias al sacar*, meant the Crown had confirmed legitimacy (usually for a price) even if the Church did not. See Karen Y. Morrison, "Slave Mothers and White Fathers: Defining Family and Status in Late Colonial Cuba," *Slavery and Abolition* 31, no. 1 (2010): 34n25–26. See also Ann Twinam, *Purchasing Whiteness: Pardos, Mulattos, and the Quest for Social Mobility in the Spanish Indies* (Stanford, CA: Stanford University Press, 2015).

58. Morrison, "Slave Mothers and White Fathers," 34.

59. See the discussion in Martinez-Alier, *Marriage, Class, and Colour*, 11–19. As Martinez-Alier notes, although free people of color or *libres* in Cuba enjoyed inheritance rights, Spanish officials made decisions that impacted succession, like giving heads of households the option of preventing "unequal marriages."

60. 24 November 1801, Acts of Narciso Broutin, no. 3, fols. 367, 370, NONA. Maria Juana was born in Louisiana, the legitimate daughter of Janeton La Liberté and Gran Jacot. She was legitimately married to Pedro Thomas, *negro libre*. Their children were Mariana (44), Maria (43), Luis Pedro (39), Felipe (32), Certene [*sic*] (31), and Pedro (25). Her goods consisted of land inherited from her mother. Maria Juana named her children her equal and universal heirs, and noted a debt owed Felipe of 200 pesos. Felipe also had all of her furniture.

61. María may have arrived during the French period, but the French slave trade all but stalled after 1743. It is more likely she arrived as a slave while the Spanish were in power.

62. In Spanish colonial wills, universal heirs (*heredero universal*) needed to be named. Universal heirs inherited all undistributed property. In practice, universal heirs were often the forced

heirs or the legitimate and legitimated children of the deceased. However, this was not always the case. Karen Graubert, *With Our Labor and Sweat: Indigenous Women and the Formation of Colonial Society in Peru, 1550–1700* (Stanford, CA: Stanford University Press, 2007), 103–5.

63. The following discussion is based on a survey of fifty-two testaments registered by free people of color between 1771 and 1803 and found at the NONA. A special thank you to my research assistant, Vera Gutman, who compiled and translated these records and helped me draw larger conclusions across the data set. The data set includes the majority of testaments registered by free people of color but not all. In her study, Kimberly Hanger found sixty-nine total testaments registered by free people of color during the Spanish period. Hanger's summary centered on slaveownership by free people of color and included the following statistics: thirty-one wills listed other free people of color as part of their estates; free people of color owned a total of 102.3 slaves with some sharing ownership. Slaveownership ranged from individuals (or co-owners) owning 1 to 13 slaves each with an average of 3.3 slaves per testator. Three-fifths of slaves claimed by free people of color were female. Almost two-thirds of slaveowners were female and female owners owned just over two-thirds of the slaves. Hanger, *Bounded Lives, Bounded Places*, 75. The trends presented here are useful and instructive, but not comprehensive; they offer a framework for understanding the relationship between kinship, property, and inheritance practices in the city during the Spanish period. Although this analysis focuses on willed inheritance, testaments were not the only opportunity that free people of color took to imagine their legacies. Marriage contracts, for example, sometimes specified where property entering the marriage would go or return to once either the husband or wife passed.

64. The gender imbalance likely reflects a gender imbalance in New Orleans' free population of color.

65. Ana Marta was the daughter of Marie or "Mariana" Genoveva Bienville, also born in New Orleans. In 1791, Ana Marta's estate included land inside and outside of the city, three slaves, and a lot on Bourbon left her by her deceased husband, Simon Calfa. 2 May 1791, Acts of Pedesclaux, no. 12, fol. 275. A year later, in his will, her brother, Jean-Baptiste Hugon and also the son of Marie Bienville, enumerated a slave and furniture, as well as a house and land in the city neighboring his sister Catalina Destrehan. 29 July 1792, Acts of Pedesclaux, no. 15, fol. 414. Catalina Destrehan stated she was the daughter of Genoveva Bienville, *negra libre*. Other free testators of color "born in this province" during the French period included Luisa, who claimed land on the corner of St. Ursula and Bourbon, furniture, and clothes in her 1784 will; and Angélica, *negra libre*, who claimed a "lot with a house" on Delphine Street in her testament. Actas de Rafael Perdomo, 13 January 1784, no. 3, fol. 18; Actas de Leonardo Mazange, 5 November 1781, no. 4, fol. 891, NONA.

66. Hanger, *Bounded Lives, Bounded Places*, 73.

67. Bellehumeur owed only a peso each to two gentlemen, one a Catalan named Francisco, the second a man named Carlos Poncal. Actas de Ximenes, 9 March 1799, no. 16, fol. 35, NONA. Other examples include Naneta Collet who owed her daughter, enslaved to Mr. Collet of Attakapas, 80 pesos; Catarina Dorville who owed Gabriel, a slave of the Ursulines and Carlota Gronon some 10 pesos; and Catarina Astier, *negra libre*, who owed 4 or 5 pesos to Ynez Mathieux and 40 pesos to the well-propertied free woman of color Louison Vivant. Actas de Ximenes, 1 January 1795, no. 9, fol. 1; Actas de Pedesclaux, 14 October 1797, no. 30, fol. 595; Actas de Perdomo, 27 August 1787, no. 10, fol. 440; Actas de Narciso Broutin, 21 August 1801, no. 3, fol. 250, NONA. Some free people of color owed several hundred pesos at the time they registered their wills. Ana Marta owed nearly

400 pesos in all to Miguel Fortier, Francisco Cheval, and Carlota Grenoble, *negra libre*. Luison Duran Brouner dit Luisa, *india libre*, owed Jose de la Pena 400 pesos he had lent her without interest.

68. Actas de Perdomo, 10 December 1786, no. 8, fol. 638, NONA. Like Isabel, Ana Marta endeavored to collect money from a wide range of individuals. She declared that Mr. Boulin, a ship captain named Mr. Lamarre, a man named Robinet, Domingo dit Balize, a pilot, and her son Francisco all owed her money. Actas de Pedesclaux, 2 May 1791, no. 12, fol. 275, NONA. See also Magdalena Naneta, who declared a free black man named Lavioleta owed her 250 pesos; Carlota Derneville, who claimed 100 pesos from Pedro Bacandaz, "the tanner on Bayou Road"; Augustín Malet, who declared that "various persons owe him money" but did not provide names; Mariana Meuillon, who claimed one white woman and five free people of color—four women and one man—owed her money; African-born Catarina Vilemon, who claimed about 150 pesos from Enrieta, *negra libre*, Antonio Bouligny, *negro libre*, and the aforementioned Augustín Mallet; Elena, also born in Africa, who claimed 20 pesos each from a *negra* named Margarita Toutain and from Carlos Marcason. Actas de Mazange, 29 May 1782, no. 6, fol. 833; Actas de Pedesclaux, 9 September 1801, no. 39, fol. 513; Actas de Narciso Broutin, 23 June 1800, no. 2, fol. 165, NONA; Hanger, *Bounded Lives, Bounded Places*, 73; Actas de Pedesclaux, 11 March 1794, no. 20, fol. 220; Actas de Carlos Ximenes, 25 August 1795, no. 9, fol. 337, NONA.

69. Primogeniture does not appear to have dominated among free people of color in late eighteenth-century New Orleans. For a contrast in the British Caribbean, see Brown, *Reaper's Garden*, 93–94. Although testators of color did not consistently describe their relationship to their heirs, in over half (twenty-five) of the wills surveyed for this chapter, free people of color named multiple legitimate or natural children their universal heirs and did so across race, gender, and sometimes status.

70. Hanger, *Bounded Lives, Bounded Places*, 85.

71. Hanger, *Bounded Lives, Bounded Places*, 75.

72. Hanger, *Bounded Lives, Bounded Places*, 76. Sambas also requested freedom for his brother, Francisco, still enslaved.

73. Actas de Pedesclaux, 16 June 1802, no. 41, fol. 445, NONA.

74. Actas Juan Bautista Garic, 27 August 1779, no. 12, fol. 461, NONA.

75. Hanger, *Bounded Lives, Bounded Places*, 62.

76. Actas de Pedesclaux, 29 July 1792, no. 15, fol. 414, NONA.

77. Actas de Broutin, 24 March 1800, no. 2, fol. 78, NONA.

78. Actas de Broutin, 13 January 1801, no. 3, fol. 14; and 24 March 1800, no. 2, fol. 78, NONA.

79. Hanger, *Bounded Lives, Bounded Places*, 82; Actas de Broutin, 8 April 1801, no. 3, fol. 108; and 23 April 1803, no. 5, fol. 192, NONA.

80. Actas de Mazange, 5 November 1781, no. 4, fol. 891, NONA.

81. Actas de Ximenes, 9 March 1799, no. 16, fol. 35, NONA.

82. Actas de Pedesclaux, 6 January 1794, no. 20, fol. 6, NONA. María Teresa's relationship to Yzurra, while unclear, extended well beyond the debt she owed. Although María Teresa claimed she was not involved in "the trade he conducts on the coast," she did authorize her estate to pay "whatever he owes the *contador*" (accounting official). She left him "all the money that remains in her house upon her death" and the house itself.

83. Hanger, *Bounded Lives, Bounded Places*, 73–74.

84. Hanger, *Bounded Lives, Bounded Places*, 83–84.

85. Perine Dauphine's parentage (and by extension her siblings') is difficult to determine. In her 1814 will, Perine described herself as the daughter of "Marie Daupaine," *négresse libre*, and "M. Daupaine," and stated the two never married. "Pelagie Dauphaine ditte Perine Demasillier, f. m. l.," 19 April 1814, Recorder of Wills, Will Books, vol. 1, NOPL.

86. Actas de Ximenes, 20 July 1797, no. 12, fol. 203, NONA.

87. 1786/09/02/02, SJRL.

88. In the 1770s, three white Dauphine brothers, Joseph, Juan Pedro, and Santiago, manumitted multiple enslaved women they had formed liaisons with, along with their mixed-race children. Joseph lived with a free consort of color who may have been the thirty-five-year-old creole slave María Teresa, whom he freed in 1779 for "much love and affection and many services." The *parda* María produced five children with Santiago. In 1779, Santiago freed her and three daughters, María Teresa, Margarita, and María. The manumission was *graciosa* "for good service of the Mother and particular love." Between 1775 and 1799, Martona gave birth to eleven children by white slaveowner Juan Pedro Dauphin. "Louisiana Freed Slaves, 1720–1820," in *Afro-Louisiana*; Roulhac Toledano and Mary Christovich, *New Orleans Architecture: Faubourg Tremé and the Bayou Road* (New Orleans: Pelican Publishing, 2003), 93; Hanger, *Bounded Lives, Bounded Places*, 99–100.

89. Actas de Rodriguez, no. 13, fols. 1143–52, 6 December 1787. The moneda corriente was a version of the peso.

90. Maurice left behind a house at the corner of Dauphine and Conti, land about four leagues north of the city, furniture and other material items, and a *grifo* slave, Silvestre, "something of a carpenter." Diligencias, 317, 320, 337, 339. It would make sense for Maurice, who appears to have worked in construction, to own a slave with carpentry skills.

91. Though not in wide usage, *grifo/a* could indicate either *negro/a* and *mulato/a* descent or African-Native descent. See Spear, *Race, Sex, and Social Order*, 160–62. If of Native descent, María Teresa may have gained her freedom through one of the thirteen successful Indian-slavery related lawsuits filed before the New Orleans Cabildo. Spear, *Race, Sex, and Social Order*, 163–72; Hall, *Africans in Colonial Louisiana*, 336; Webre, "Problem of Indian Slavery," 125–26.

92. For a similar Gulf Coast example, see David Wheat, "My Friend Nicolas Mongoula: Africans, Indians, and Cultural Exchange in Eighteenth-Century Mobile," in *Coastal Encounters: The Transformation of the Gulf South in the Eighteenth Century*, ed. Richmond F. Brown (Lincoln: University of Nebraska Press, 2007), 117–31. Wheat writes, "While the term 'mulato,' for example, often is associated with people of both African and European ancestry, French and Spanish officials in colonial Mobile applied this term frequently to people of mixed Amerindian and African or Amerindian and European ancestry" (130).

93. Charles E. Nolan and Dorenda Dupont, eds., *Sacramental Records of the Roman Catholic Church of the Archdiocese of New Orleans: 1804–1806* (New Orleans: Archdiocese of New Orleans, 2002), 3:89; Diligencias, 180; 1788/03/14/01, SJRL. Nicolas and Francisco Rixner, both free men of color, asked for satisfaction of debts incurred on the house ordered by "Mauricio Dauphine." After Maurice's death, Demasillier continued construction. Perine ordered the executor, Dusseaux, to pay the debt.

94. Diligencias, 9–10.

95. Diligencias, 9.

96. Diligencias, 22–24.

97. Diligencias, 70.

98. Diligencias, 135, 73–74.

99. Din and Harkins, *New Orleans Cabildo*, 75–78.

100. Diligencias, 65–67, 135.

101. Diligencias, 135, 87, 53–55.

102. Glenn R. Conrad, *A Dictionary of Louisiana Biography* (Lafayette: Center for Louisiana Studies), 529–30; Kimberly S. Hanger, "Coping in a Complex World: Free Black Women in Colonial New Orleans," in *The Devil's Lane: Sex and Race in the Early South*, ed. Catherine Clinton and Michele Gillespie (New York: Oxford University Press, 1996), 224. Macarty would become the mayor of New Orleans in 1815.

103. Diligencias, 31–32, 44–45, 43–44, 42–43.

104. Diligencias, 75–76.

105. Diligencias, 67–80.

106. "Thus it is seen that of the three bastards, Pedro and Sesamie are different in color and in hair [texture], and the first for having the color and hair of a *mulato* and the second the ... color of a *negra*, in this I can definitely say they are the children of their mother" (Diligencias, 79–80).

107. Diligencias, 78–80.

108. "Whereupon I can conclude that the difference is that Margarita is the daughter of a *mulato*, Pedro [the son of] a white, and Sesamie is that of a *negro* and [with] knowledge also [of] the declarations that they have of their legitimacy, believe that it is true that the *Negra Grifa* is the mother of all three but none can say for certain the identity of the father" (Diligencias, 78–80).

109. Diligencias, 60–62.

110. Diligencias, 58–59.

111. Diligencias, 125.

112. Diligencias, 132–33.

113. Diligencias, 177–78.

114. Eugenio may have been the son named Pedro. As with the father, whose full name was "Pedro Maurice" but who went by Maurice, Eugenio could have been Pedro's middle name or vice versa. However, there is no clear evidence of any such connection. "Eugenio, Mauricio's son," could as well be another child of Maurice's by the same or another woman.

115. "Pelagie Dauphaine ditte Perine Demasillier, f. m. l." 19 April 1814, Recorder of Wills, Will Books, vol. 1, NOPL.

116. There is a strong likelihood, given naming patterns and Perine's previous will, that Marie Maurice Thomas was "María *grifa libre*," the daughter of Maurice Dauphine. This remains unconfirmed.

117. "Petitions de Fergus Duplantier de cette paroisse," 16 February 1816, Recorder of Wills, Will Books, vol. 1, NOPL.

Conclusion

1. On the Haitian Revolution, see Laurent Dubois, *Avengers of the New World: The Story of the Haitian Revolution* (Cambridge, MA: Harvard University Press, 2005); C. L. R. James, *The Black Jacobins: Toussaint L'Ouverture and the San Domingo Revolution* (New York: Penguin, 2001); Carolyn E. Fick, *The Making of Haiti: The Saint Domingue Revolution from Below* (Knoxville: University of Tennessee Press, 1990). On the impact of the Haitian Revolution on the Atlantic seaboard and Gulf Coast, see Emily Clark, *The Strange History of the American Quadroon: Free*

Women of Color in the Revolutionary Atlantic World (Chapel Hill: University of North Carolina Press, 2013); Rebecca J. Scott and Jean M. Hébrard, *Freedom Papers: An Atlantic Odyssey in the Age of Emancipation* (Cambridge, MA: Harvard University Press, 2012); Nathalie Dessens, *From Saint-Domingue to New Orleans: Migration and Influences* (Gainesville: University Press of Florida, 2010); Alfred N. Hunt, *Haiti's Influence on Antebellum America: Slumbering Volcano in the Caribbean* (Baton Rouge: Louisiana State University Press, 2006).

2. In 1804, members of the free men of color militia sent a petition to the territorial government defending their rights. It read, in part, "We are duly sensible that our personal and political freedom is thereby assured to us for ever . . . and we are also impressed with the fullest confidence in the Justice and Liberality of the Government towards every Class of Citizens which they have here taken under their protection." Ira Berlin, *Slaves Without Masters: The Free Negro in the Antebellum South* (New York: Oxford University Press, 1981), 118. See also John W. Blassingame, *Black New Orleans, 1860–1880* (Chicago: University of Chicago Press, 2008); Caryn Cossé Bell, *Revolution, Romanticism, and the Afro-Creole Protest Tradition in Louisiana, 1718–1868* (Baton Rouge: Louisiana State University Press, 2004).

3. Robert L. Paquette, "'A Horde of Brigands?' The Great Louisiana Slave Revolt of 1811 Reconsidered," *Historical Reflections / Réflexions Historiques* 35, no. 1 (2009): 81; Adam Rothman, *Slave Country: American Expansion and the Origins of the Deep South* (Cambridge, MA: Harvard University Press, 2005), 111–16.

4. Charles Gayarre, *History of Louisiana* (New Orleans: F. F. Hanswell & Bros., 1903), 204–5; Luis M. Perez, "French Refugees to New Orleans in 1809," *Publications of the Southern Historical Association* 9, no. 5 (1905): 293–321; Paul F. Lachance, "The 1809 Immigration of Saint-Domingue Refugees to New Orleans: Reception, Integration and Impact," *Louisiana History* 29 (1988): 109–41. On the 1809 migration, see Dessens, *From Saint-Domingue to New Orleans*; Thomas Fiehrer, "Saint-Domingue/Haiti: Louisiana's Caribbean Connection," *Louisiana History* 30, no. 4 (1989): 419–37.

5. Mayor's Office, "An Extract from the Lists of Passengers Reported at the Said Office by the Captains of Vessels Who Have Come to This Port from the Island of Cuba, July 18–August 7, 1809," in *Official Letter Books of W. C. C. Claiborne, 1801–1816*, ed. Dunbar Rowland (Jackson, MS: State Department of Archives and History, 1917), 4:381–82.

6. Mayor's Office, "Extract," in Rowland, *Official Letter Books*, 4:381–82. Only one ship arrived from Havana.

7. Lachance, "1809 Immigration," 111.

8. The number of adult white men reported was 729; white women was 376; white children, 362. Mayor's Office, "Extract," in Rowland, *Official Letter Books*, 4:381–82.

9. James Mather to William C. C. Claiborne, Extract of a Letter from the Mayor of the City of New Orleans, Dated March 28, 1810," in Rowland, *Official Letter Books*, 5:30-1. After seven or eight months in the city, over a dozen free men of color left New Orleans on the schooner *Lenora*, bound for St. Bartholomew, in search of work.

10. On the rival geographies created in and through New Orleans by people of African descent in the nineteenth century, see Rashauna Johnson, *Slavery's Metropolis: Unfree Labor in New Orleans During the Age of Revolutions* (New York: Cambridge University Press, 2016).

11. Section 40, "Black Code," in Médéric-Louis-Élie Moreau de St. Méry, *A General Digest of the Acts of the Legislature of Louisiana* (New Orleans: Benjamin Levy, 1828), 1:112. See also Judith K. Schafer, "Roman Roots of the Louisiana Law of Slavery: Emancipation in American Louisiana, 1803–1857," *Louisiana Law Review* 56 (1996): 409–22, 410; Judith Kelleher Schafer,

Slavery, the Civil Law, and the Supreme Court of Louisiana (Baton Rouge: Louisiana State University Press, 1997).

12. Bell, *Revolution, Romanticism*, 76.

13. See the discussion of *Adele v. Beauregard* and related Supreme Court cases in Schafer, *Slavery, the Civil Law, and the Supreme Court of Louisiana*. For a close study of a (possibly) white woman presumed to be a slave, see Walter Johnson, "The Slave Trader, the White Slave, and the Politics of Racial Determination in the 1850s," *Journal of American History* 87, no. 1 (1 June 2000): 13–38.

14. Peter J. Kastor, *The Nation's Crucible: The Louisiana Purchase and the Creation of America* (New Haven, CT: Yale University Press, 2008).

15. Emily A. Owens, "Promises: Sexual Labor in the Space Between Slavery and Freedom," *Louisiana History* 58, no. 2 (2017): 179–216; Owens, "Fantasies of Consent: Black Women's Sexual Labor in 19th Century New Orleans" (Ph.D. diss., Harvard University, 2015); Judith Kelleher Schafer, *Brothels, Depravity, and Abandoned Women: Illegal Sex in Antebellum New Orleans* (New Orleans: Louisiana State University Press, 2009); Clark, *Strange History of the American Quadroon;* Paul F. Lachance, "Intermarriage and French Cultural Persistence in Late Spanish and Early American New Orleans," *Histoire sociale/Social History* 15, no. 29 (1982): 47–81; Paul F. Lachance, "The Formation of a Three-Caste Society: Evidence From Wills in Antebellum New Orleans," *Social Science History* 18, no. 2 (1994): 211–42.

16. Emily Clark argues *plaçage* was less a reality and more of a *"plaçage* complex" of myths and fantasies about free women of color. See Clark, *Strange History of the American Quadroon,* 148-59.

17. Benjamin Henry Latrobe, *The Journal of Latrobe: Being the Notes and Sketches of an Architect, Naturalist and Traveler in the United States from 1796 to 1820* (New York: D. Appleton and Company, 1905), 179–80.

18. Roulhac Toledano and Mary Christovich, *New Orleans Architecture: Faubourg Tremé and the Bayou Road* (New Orleans: Pelican Publishing, 2003), 15–16.

19. "Petitions de Fergus Duplantier de cette paroisse," 16 February 1816, Recorder of Wills, Will Books, vol. 1, NOPL.

20. Bell, *Revolution, Romanticism.*

21. In 1758, the British captured Saint-Louis and Gorée. The end of the war in 1763 restored Gorée to France, but the British held Saint-Louis and created the Province of Senegambia. When the American Revolution sparked a new war between Britain and France, the French recaptured Saint-Louis and reunited the two *comptoirs* until the British recaptured Gorée later that year. France did not secure both Saint-Louis and Gorée again until late 1783. The Napoleonic Wars began a new round of imperial shuffling: The British captured Gorée in 1800 and held it until the French recaptured the town in 1804. The British took it back later that year. In 1809, Saint-Louis surrendered to the British.

22. Michael David Marcson, "European-African Interaction in the Precolonial Period: Saint Louis, Senegal, 1758–1854" (Ph.D. diss., Princeton University, 1976), 57–58.

23. George E. Brooks, "The Signares of Saint-Louis and Goree: Women Entrepreneurs in Eighteenth-Century Senegal," in *Women in Africa: Studies in Social and Economic Change,* ed. Nancy J. Hafkin and Edna G. Bay (Stanford, CA: Stanford University Press, 1976), 42; Marcson, "European-African Interaction," 27; James F. Searing, *West African Slavery and Atlantic Commerce* (Cambridge: Cambridge University Press, 1993), 106, 108–12.

24. Brooks, "Signares," 40–41.

25. European and African traders based at Saint-Louis participated in the gum trade as early as the 1720s, but it was not until the 1790s that trade in gum arabic became a priority for Europeans over trade in slaves. James L. A. Webb Jr., "The Trade in Gum Arabic: Prelude to French Conquest in Senegal," *Journal of African History* 26, no. 2 (1985): 152–53. By the 1850s, peanuts were outpacing gum.

26. Annette Mbaye d'Erneville is a Senegalese poet and a foremother of African women's publishing and activism. She began publishing in the 1950s; founded *Awa*, the first magazine by and for francophone African women, in 1963; and in 1964 was one of the founders of the Association des Écrivains du Sénégal. Work on the museum began in the 1980s. On the Derneville/d'Erneville genealogy in Senegal, see Hilary Jones, *The Métis of Senegal: Urban Life and Politics in French West Africa* (Bloomington: Indiana University Press, 2013), 19–20.

27. Ronnie W. Clayton, *Mother Wit: The Ex-Slave Narratives of the Louisiana Writers' Project* (New York: Peter Lang, 1990), 33-6.

28. Emily Clark and Virginia Meacham Gould, "The Feminine Face of Afro-Catholicism in New Orleans, 1727–1852," *William and Mary Quarterly* 59, no. 2 (2002): 434.

29. Ina J. Fandrich, *The Mysterious Voodoo Queen, Marie Laveaux: A Study of Powerful Female Leadership in Nineteenth-Century New Orleans* (New York: Routledge, 2005); Carolyn Morrow Long, *A New Orleans Voudou Priestess: The Legend and Reality of Marie Laveau* (Gainesville: University Press of Florida, 2007); Omise'eke Natasha Tinsley, *Ezili's Mirrors: Imagining Black Queer Genders* (Durham, NC: Duke University Press, 2018). In the 1930s, Lyle Saxon and Marcus Christian organized interviews of formerly enslaved and free people of color as part of the Federal Writers Project. Several informants offered vivid descriptions of Marie Laveau. They described her practices (Marie "would take vinegar and egg and write the name of the person she wished to be voodooed, put [it] in a bottle or jar, seal it with wax, and bury [it] around the house"), her community ("Marie employed men to go around—principally at night—to fill the orders of people she wanted victimized"; another described almost being recruited by Marie), and her lifestyle (she was a gambler to one informant, she went to court and represented people to another, she was humble and "unconcerned as any washerwoman" to another). In nearly all of these portrayals, whether positive or negative, Marie Laveau was a figure with power—financial or spiritual power—and a figure of note. See Clayton, *Mother Wit*, 121, 113, 35.

30. Mike Scott, "The Former Slave Who Opened the First French Market Coffee Stand," *The Times-Picayune* 15 November 2018, https://www.nola.com/300/article_868c404b-68ca-5683-81f0-cfe01ebb1806.html (accessed 10 September 2019)

31. *The Bamboula*, 1886, sketch by Edward Kemble, held by the Historic New Orleans Collection, New Orleans, Louisiana.

32. David Scott, "That Event, This Memory: Notes on the Anthropology of African Diasporas in the New World," *Diaspora: A Journal of Transnational Studies* 1, no. 3 (1991): 261–84.

33. On the Mothers of New Orleans, see Brenda Marie Osbey, "Why We Can't Talk to You About Voodoo," *Southern Literary Journal* 43, no. 2 (26 May 2011): 1–11.

Index

The letters *t* and *f* following a page number denote table and figure, respectively.

Acknowledgments

Like this book, I am obsessed with kinship. This project does not exist without a long list of interlocutors, friends, and family. Thank you to my mentor, the late Ira Berlin and to Elsa Barkley Brown, Hilary Jones, A. Lynn Bolles, and Psyche Williams-Forson for pushing and critiquing me when I needed it most. Thank you to Bob Lockhart and Kathy Brown for understanding where I wanted the project to go from the outset, and for your patience, prodding, and confidence in my ability to get to the end. Thank you to Erica Ginsburg and everyone at Penn Press; and to the anonymous peer reviewers for your labor—this is a better book for your insight and feedback. All mistakes are mine alone.

Fellowships from the Consortium for Faculty Diversity (Bowdoin College), the Woodrow Wilson Center, and the Mellon-Mays Undergraduate and Professional Initiatives Fellowship Program; the Richards Civil War Era and Africana Research Center at the Pennsylvania State University; and a Mellon Postdoctoral Fellowship at the Library Company of Philadelphia allowed me to complete research needed for this book, including necessary time in the archives in Senegal. Thank you to the many archivists who held my hand as I struggled to navigate an array of classification systems across multiple empires. A special thank you to Krystal Appiah at the Library Company of Philadelphia; Susan Tucker, Erin Kinchen, and the archivists at the Louisiana Historical Center; Siva M. Blake (who pointed me to the Vieux Carré Survey) at the Historic New Orleans Center; Irene Wainwright and Greg Osborn at the New Orleans Public Library; and Mamadou Ndiaye at the Archives Nationales du Sénégal. Thank you to the research assistants who made this book possible: Vera Gutman, Tranise Foster, Gayle Perry-Johnson, Sarah M. Reynolds, Malaurie Pilatte, and Brooke Lansing.

This book benefited from critique and feedback offered in presentation spaces and workshops around the world. A special thank you to Elsa, Hilary, Jennifer Morgan, and Emily Clark, who read the entire manuscript in one form or another and played a significant role in reframing the project to make it more accountable to African women and women of African descent. A special thank you to the presenters at the École des hautes études en sciences sociales workshops in Senegal (Université de Cheikh Anta Diop) and New Orleans (Tulane University), organized by Emily Clark, Ibrahima Thioub, and Cécile Vidal; the "Slave Resistance in the Atlantic World in the Age of Revolution (1750–1850)" workshop at McGill University in Montreal; the symposium "Closer to Freedom: Honoring the Work and Legacy of Stephanie Camp" at the University of Pennsylvania; "Lose Your Mother: A Symposium in Honor of Saidiya Hartman," held at Northwestern University; the Women and Gender History "Geminar" at Johns Hopkins University; and the students in the Black Womanhood course (and my co-teacher Martha Jones), the Sex and Slavery Lab, and the Black World Seminar at Johns Hopkins University. This book is better for the critical engagement I received from dear colleagues in these spaces.

Thank you to my colleagues who read sections of the manuscript at critical junctures, including Guillaume Aubert, Bill Blair, Tess Chakkalakal, Hanétha Vété-Congolo, Jessie Dunbar, Sylvia Frey, Lindsey Gish, Gwendolyn Midlo Hall, Jean Hébrard, Matt Klingle, Elizabeth Neidenbach, Brian Purnell, Patrick Rael, Jen Scanlon, Rebecca Scott, Ibrahima Seck, Christina Sharpe, C. Riley Snorton, Will Sturkey, Ibrahima Thioub, Olufemi Vaughan, Cécile Vidal, and Nan Woodruff. Sophie White, thank you for your grace and advice (and, yes, I will always buy the jacket). Erica Armstrong Dunbar, Gabrielle Foreman, and Tiffany Gill created space for writing and fellowship when I needed it. Nathan Connolly, Martha Jones, François Furstenburg, Todd Shepherd, Liz Thornberry, Katie Hindmarch-Watson, Yumi Kim, Tamer el-Leithy, Casey Lurtz, and Christy Thornton at Johns Hopkins University read sections, offered feedback, or poured rum as necessary. They are model colleagues and I am so grateful for their generosity and friendship. Thank you to the friends in my mind with whom this book has incubated over the years: Mark Anthony Neal, Kevin Browne, Keguro Macharia, Marisa Fuentes, and Joan Morgan. Our conversations and camaraderie made all of the difference.

Material in Chapter 6 previously appeared in the following publication and is reprinted by permission: Jessica Marie Johnson, "Death Rites as Birthrights in Atlantic New Orleans: Kinship and Race in the Case of María Teresa V. Perine Dauphine," *Slavery & Abolition* 36, no. 2 (2015): 233–56. Material in Chapters 2 and 3 previously appeared in the following publication and is also reprinted by permission: Jessica Marie Johnson, "Wives, Soldiers, and Slaves:

The Atlantic World of Marie Baude, La Femme Pinet," in *New Orleans, Louisiana, and Saint-Louis, Senegal: Mirror Cities in the Atlantic World, 1659–2000s*, ed. Emily Clark, Cécile Vidal, and Ibrahima Thioub (Baton Rouge: Louisiana State University Press, 2019). Thank you to the editors at *Slavery & Abolition* and Louisiana State University Press for allowing that work to appear here.

Thank you to Dean Mary Laurita, Gerald Early, Robert Vinson, Rafia Zafar, Tim Parsons, and Raye Mahaney for making African and African American Studies at Washington University in St. Louis a safe space; thank you to Walter Hawthorne, Dean Rehberger, Helen Veit, Emily Conroy-Krutz, Leslie Moch, Pero Dagbovie, LaShawn Harris, Glenn Chambers, and Terah Chambers for doing the same at Michigan State University. Thank you to mentors and cheerleaders at the University of Maryland: Leslie Rowland, Sharon Harley, Francille Rusan Wilson, Barbara Weinstein, Daryle Williams, and Clare Lyons. Thank you always to Clyde Woods. Thank you to my cohort, Dennis Doster, Eliza Mbughuni, Tina Ligon, Thanayi Jackson, Herbert Brewer, Jessica Brown, Rob Bland, Laticia Willis, and Sonia Prescott.

Thank you to my kin folk: Judith Casselberry (maroon!), Rosanne Adderley (alpha), Rae Paris (big sis), Django Paris, Delia Fernandez, Tamara Butler, Tacuma Peters, Vanessa Holden (co-friendspirator), Derrais Carter and members of the Queering Slavery Working Group; Aisha Finch, Tamara Walker, Tanji Gilliam, and Johonna McCants of the Writing Violence and Resistance Group; Uri McMillan, Elizabeth Todd Breland, and the Mellon Mafia. To my ratchets Brittney Cooper and Tanisha Ford; the "alchemists" Moya Bailey, Bianca Laureano, Sydette Harry, Danielle Cole, Meagan Ortiz, I'Nasah Crockett, and Trudy; the black feminist metaphysicians Alexis Pauline Gumbs and Julia Sangodare Wallace; the sorceress Savannah Shange; Baltimore belles Jessica Solomon, Shani Mott, Tara Bynum, Hosana Asfaw-Means, Mia Beauttah, Schaun Champion, Sharayna Christmas, and the Bennus; and my support network beyond academia—Ladies of Brunch, BBG, D2B, and Flava—you have saved my life. Thank you to the Wifey Treva B. Lindsey and the boyfriend Yomaira S. Figueroa. These are your black femme labors as much as mine.

I have spent the last twenty years going back and forth to New Orleans. Thank you to the family created from those visits: Kristin Pulley, Adrian and Jennifer Baudy, Catherine "Mama" Baudy, Deb Kharson, Daniella Santoro, Jordan Shannon, Tania Dall, Tia Vice, Lupe Garcia, Shana M. Griffin (#always ClydeWoods), Soraya Jean-Louis McElroy, Spirit McIntyre, Mwende Katwiwa, Desiree Evans, Rosana Cruz, Rebecca Mwase, Ron Ragin, and Michael Quess?

Moore. I'm also grateful for the artscapes created by Gia Hamilton, Lydia Nichols, and Kristina Kay Robinson for being inspirations and models for how to love black New Orleans.

Thank you to my land of women: Mae Frances Johnson, Mary Nuñez née Matos, and Aliette "Cuqui" Medina. Kristin, Tina, and Aly: "I knew you before I met you / I've known you my whole life." Sandra Nuñez, I am yours, always.

Thank you Thomas Felton Cuffie II and Crescent Aliette Johnson-Cuffie: one day I will have eloquent words for this happiness. Until then: I love you.

Thank you, New Orleans.